Astrology, Psychology, and Transformation:
Discovering Your Sacred Sky

Astrology, Psychology, and Transformation: *Discovering Your Sacred Sky*

Bernie Ashman

Copyright©2022 by Bernie Ashman

All rights reserved. No part of this book may be reproduced or used in any form or by any means—graphic, electronic or mechanical, including photocopying, mimeographing, recording, taping or information storage and retrieval systems—without written permission from the publisher. A reviewer may quote brief passages.

ISBN: 9781944662-77-6

Printed in the United States of America

Published by Realization Press

Author photo by Keith Papke

Cover Design by Diana Henderson, CreativeType.biz

Cover Art by Jozef Klopacka

Dedication

To the creative minds and dreamers who have inspired me to stay on a path filled with being open to new learning and to see that life is overflowing with a magical spirit of synchronicity.

Acknowledgments

I have to thank my wife, Beth for her continuing support for many years of my writing, lecturing and work with my many clients. Many thanks to Diana Henderson and Drew Becker for helping me get this book published through their wonderful company, Realization Press. I thank the readers of my books who inspire me to keep writing and to continue doing astrology consulting for people around the world!

NOTE TO READERS:

Many of the tables in this book may be challenging, and you may have to turn the book sideways to view them.

To help the reader, a PDF file including many of these charts, which can be printed out for reference while reading the book is provided on Bernie's website.

Go to *bernieashman.com/AstroPsycho.pdf* to download and print or view the graphics in that file.

Table of Contents

Introduction 3

PART I

CHAPTER ONE ASTROLOGY: A LANGUAGE OF CYCLES
AND SYMBOLS 5

    Map and Mirror of the Sky: The Birth Chart 5

    The Foundation 6

    Order out of Chaos 7

    Planets: One Tone of Each Chord 8

    Signs: Another Tone of Each Chord 8

    Houses: Last Tone of Each Chord 8

    Subtones 9

    Synthesis, Harmony and Discord 10

    Games 13

    Elements 15

PART II

Fire Element 18

CHAPTER TWO FIRST CHORD: SELF-EXPRESSIVE EMBODIMENT 19

    Mars 20

    Aries 21

    1st House 21

    Counseling Issues 24

    Games 26

    Summary of Issues with 1st Chord Games 37

    Subtones 38

CHAPTER THREE FIFTH CHORD: SELF-EXPRESSIVE PROCREATION 41

- The Sun 43
- Leo 44
- 5th House 46
- Counseling Issues 47
- Games 49
- Summary of Issues with 5th Chord Games 56
- Subtones 56

CHAPTER FOUR NINTH CHORD: SELF-EXPRESSIVE DISCOVERY 60

- Jupiter 62
- Sagittarius 63
- 9th House 64
- Counseling Issues 65
- Games 66
- Summary of Issues with 9th Chord Games 73
- Subtones 74

PART III

EARTH ELEMENT 78

CHAPTER FIVE SECOND CHORD: DESIRE FOR PHYSICAL COMFORT 80

- Venus 82
- Taurus 83
- 2nd House 84
- Counseling Issues 85
- Games 86
- Summary of Issues with 2nd Chord Games 91
- Subtones 92

CHAPTER SIX SIXTH CHORD: DESIRE TO CREATE ORDER 94

    Mercury 95

    Virgo 97

    6th House 98

    Counseling Issues 100

    Games 101

    Summary of Issues with 6th Chord Games 109

    Subtones 110

CHAPTER SEVEN TENTH CHORD: DESIRE FOR SUCCESS 112

    Saturn 114

    Capricorn 117

    10th House 118

    Counseling Issues 120

    Games 121

    Summary of Issues with 10th Chord Games 135

    Subtones 136

PART IV

AIR ELEMENT 140

CHAPTER EIGHT THIRD CHORD: CONCEPTUALIZATION
OF PERCEPTION 142

    Mercury 144

    Gemini 145

    3rd House 147

    Counseling Issues 149

    Games 150

    Summary of Issues with 3rd Chord Games 158

    Subtones 159

CHAPTER NINE SEVENTH CHORD: CONCEPTUALIZATION OF RELATIONSHIP 161

    Venus 162

    Libra 165

    7th House 167

    Counseling Issues 169

    Games 170

    Summary of Issues with 7th Chord Games 183

    Subtones 183

CHAPTER TEN ELEVENTH CHORD: CONCEPTUALIZATION OF DIRECTION 186

    Uranus 188

    Aquarius 191

    11th House 194

    Counseling Issues 196

    Games 197

    Summary of Issues with 11th Chord Games 206

    Subtones 207

PART V

WATER ELEMENT 211

CHAPTER ELEVEN FOURTH CHORD: SECURITY INSTINCTS 212

    Moon 213

    Cancer 218

    4th House 220

    Counseling Issues 222

    Games 223

    Summary of Issues with 4th Chord Games 229

    Subtones 231

CHAPTER TWELVE EIGHTH CHORD: POWER INSTINCTS 234

    Pluto 236

    Scorpio 244

    8th House 248

    Counseling Issues 250

    Games 252

    Summary of Issues with 8th Chord Games 260

    Subtones 261

CHAPTER THIRTEEN TWELFTH CHORD: MERGING INSTINCTS 265

    Neptune 267

    Pisces 270

    12th House 273

    Counseling Issues 276

    Games 277

    Summary of Issues with 12th Chord Games 289

    Subtones 290

PART VI

CHAPTER FOURTEEN ASTROLOGICAL SYNTHEISIS: THE ART OF
INTERPRETING THE BIRTH CHART 294

    Section One: Primary Ingredients 294

        Repeating Themes 295

        Cycles 296

        Solar System: Birth of the Planets 296

        The Ecliptic: Birth of the Signs 298

        Horizon and Meridian: Birth of the Astrological Houses 300

        Celestial Combinations: Planets in Signs and Houses 307

        Planetary Aspects 312

        Complex Aspects: Gestalt Aspect Configurations 316

Section Two: Spices 326

    Stellia..327

    Planets in Angular Houses...328

    Singletons 331

    Hemispheres 340

    Retrograde Motion of the Planets...346

    Asteroids..348

Section Three: Character Sketches 351

CHAPTER FIFTEEN AN ASTROLOGICAL RENAISSANCE:
THE ART OF COMMUNICATING THE BIRTH CHART 386

    Responsibility 387

    The Counselor's Responsibilities..388

    Client Responsibilities...391

    Building Rapport..392

    Counseling Strategies and Skills...393

    Conclusion 400

PART I

Introduction

Welcome to my first book that was originally published by ACS Publications in 1987 with the title *Astrological Games People Play*. I decided in this second edition to give the book a new title, *Astrology, Psychology and Transformation* that I feel more accurately captures the true essence of the book. My book offers you creative insights and perhaps will open your mind to new exciting life paths. Astrology is an art and a science. The art speaks to our intuition and not to be afraid to embrace it. The science of astrology shows how the magic of the universe is constantly offering us new growth opportunities. If you are trying to learn astrology the symbols can appear complicated to understand. The material in this book is designed to give you an easier ride into understanding astrology as a beautiful empowering language.

Within us is a vast universe of consciousness. Astrology can open our mind to our unique wonderful ecosystem of self-expression. This book is organized to give you a fast glimpse of the planets, signs and what are known as the twelve astrological houses. The planets, signs and houses have symbolic meaning that can be interpreted to give you a clear view of your present and future.

If you are watching a play the planets are similar to actors on the stage. The signs further define the characters in the performance by showing their personality and emotions and communication tendencies. The houses are where the play is taking place. They give a focus to the planets and signs. The

Bernie Ashman

houses have their own symbolism that is as psychological as the planets and the signs.

Each of us has freedom of choice. There are no good or bad planets or signs. When you get your astrology chart created based on your own birthday, birthtime and city/state/country of birth it represents a blueprint showing your inner world and how you might go about walking your talk. There is a strong relationship formed by astrology and psychology. Also, an astrology chart can show your past life patterns you came here to integrate positively linked to your current incarnation. Your astrology chart can reveal new creative options and help you have a clear picture of your current and future goals.

I discovered astrology in 1973. I have now been the author of seven astrology books and several astrology software programs. It is likely a synchronicity type of experience which Carl Jung described as a "meaningful coincidence" has guided you to read my book. It is my hope that the knowledge I am sharing in this book will inspire you to keep learning and evolving in your own life journey!

Bernie Ashman, April 2022

CHAPTER ONE

ASTROLOGY: A LANGUAGE OF CYCLES AND SYMBOLS

> Symbols do not flow from the unconscious to tell us what we already know but to show us what we have yet to learn.
> Robert Johnson in *We* (p. 56)

The word astrology is from the Greek astron or "star," and from *logos* or "discourse." Astrology has been referred to as "the science of the stars." Its beginnings date back to civilizations that precede recorded history. This ancient wisdom of the skies has been acknowledged by some people as an art or language filled with meaningful symbolic messages.

Map and Mirror of the Sky: The Birth Chart

I consider astrology to operate much as a mirror does. When a person looks into a mirror, he or she is looking at a reflection of himself but takes her reflected image quite seriously. If one sees an unwanted gray hair or an unexpected pimple in a mirrored image, one does not grow concerned about the appearance of the mirror! The mirror is obviously a device used to get a clearer view of oneself.

Astrology's symbolism mirrors consciousness. The birth chart or horoscope is a kind of looking glass that reflects back to us the emerging and changing psychological processes that come, go and remain in our lives. The birth chart can no more dictate the correct responsible choices we should make than a glass mirror can tell us how to change our appearance that is being reflected back to us. The birth chart can offer a clarification of possible choices or psychological issues. Like a glass mirror, perhaps this mirror of the sky can get us to take another look at our psychological processes and reconsider our options. Also, perhaps this mirror of the sky can act as a catalyst for a person to take a deeper look within, a look that goes beyond outer appearance and gazes straight into the depths of consciousness and penetrates our deepest urges for transformative growth!

The Foundation

The astrology that I practice is based on counseling experiences with my clients. I have found that traditional astrological theories and the concepts associated with the astrological symbols are often too antiquated and limiting in describing our modern psyches as they do not provide enough flexibility in describing the dynamics of human potential.

Traditional astrology is typified by a language suggesting that the future is predestined and that our ability to make choices cannot really alter our destiny. A counseling approach affirms personal responsibility and power. While traditional astrology labors to view an individual's potential through a rigid one-dimensional lens, a modern counseling-oriented astrology sees the individual's potential through a multidimensional focus. Whereas traditional astrology is a closed system relying on its own narrow concepts, a counseling astrology operates from an eclectic approach enriching itself as an open system by borrowing from the various branches of psychology and related disciplines which further enhance a counseling perspective.

Order out of Chaos

Astrology offers much useful information to help us understand the complexity of our identities, but it can be a chaotic process if not properly interpreted by the astrologer and assimilated by the client. There are many diverse factors to consider in the horoscope: ten planets, twelve signs and twelve houses, as well as numerous other components which can be found in countless combinations.

Therefore, astrology requires an organized foundation to help understand its inherent synchronicity and spontaneity. My concept of twelve astrological **chords** offers a system for organizing the vast amounts of information available in astrology.

An astrological chord is similar to a musical chord in that both are composed of **tones** that identify the chord as a distinct sound. An astrological chord is composed of three tones—a planet, sign and house that correspond to the chord name, or vibrational frequency. These tones indicate psychological patterns that correspond to essential images and impressions within our consciousness. C. G. Jung in *Memories, Dreams, Reflections* (pages 392-3) describes these essential images and impressions as archetypes or themes in human behavior. Each chord provides a structure for understanding the essential similarity of the astrological tones (a planet, sign and house) and the themes they represent. For example, Mars/Aries/1st house tones of Chord 1 all share a theme of assertion. Although Mars, Aries and the 1st house each denote a unique focus on assertion, all three share that issue as a focus.

The planet, sign and house tones are the arms and legs of a chord, carrying out a particular expression of the same principle and symbolizing archetypal themes in relation to the chord. Learning the major themes of 12 fundamental chords in astrology is much simpler than trying to master 10 planets, 12 signs and 12 houses (plus other factors).

Planets: One Tone of Each Chord

The planet is the most visible of the tones in a chord. Each planet is a cosmic indicator of a particular psychological expression in motion within an individual. I think of a planet as a cosmic delegate, personifying its chord nature within an individual's consciousness and often acted out by an individual's self-expression. This does not imply that an individual is controlled by planetary energy, but simply that an individual has at her disposal potentially active energies on conscious and subconscious levels.

Signs: Another Tone of Each Chord

A sign differs from a planet in that a planet represents a catalyst for bringing the chord functions into individual conscious action, while a sign symbolizes an individual's awareness of a particular kind of energy in a more subtle manner. A sign shows shadings and coloration of the themes represented by a planet and house. A sign as a tone indicates an individual's particular method of weaving the energies shown by planets and houses into a singular expression resulting in the selection and pursuit of life goals.

Houses: Last Tone of Each Chord

A house provides a frame of reference for the planet and sign themes. The twelve houses symbolize an individual's basic attitudes in making life choices. Traditional astrology often describes the houses as "where" life circumstances occur. The houses are explained more in terms of external events. However, the houses indicate an individual's basic psychological attitudes as much as the planets and signs.

Subtones

In addition to the three major tones of a chord (planet, sign and house), there are also certain **subtones** that refine and affect the quality of the meanings associated with the combination of the three major tones. The subtone associated with a planet is the **planetary aspect,** the subtone corresponding to a sign is known as a **quality,** and the subtone associated with a house is known as a **house classification.**

Planetary aspects are discussed in more detail in Chapter 15. The specific aspect subtone associated with each chord is discussed in the chapter describing that chord.

The sign **subtone,** known as a **quality,** is the energy focus of a sign. The quality of a sign describes the particular way the characteristics of a sign are directed when combined with, or coloring the themes of, a particular planet or house. The qualities are: cardinal, fixed and mutable.

Each of the **cardinal** signs (Aries, Cancer, Libra and Capricorn) initiates a season of the year. They typify an active energy movement encouraging the initiation of experiences in a direct and immediate manner with a **spontaneous outpouring of energy.** The **fixed** signs (Taurus, Leo, Scorpio and Aquarius) typify a **stationary energy** movement, encouraging the maintaining and securing of experiences in a stabilizing, sometimes stubborn, manner. The **mutable** signs (Gemini, Virgo, Sagittarius and Pisces) represent an **excitable energy movement,** encouraging the seeking of stimulation through multiple outlets in life experiences. Each specific chord chapter includes a further description of the qualities as they are associated with each sign in a chord.

The house **subtone,** the **house classification,** characterizes an individual's energy level in dealing with different environmental factors. The house classifications are known as: angular, succedent and cadent. Each of the **angular houses** (1, 4, 7 and 10) focuses an individual's energy on the **initiating**

of circumstances contained within each house. If a planet is located in one of these houses, an individual is likely to utilize the planetary themes in a direct manner in dealing with the particular life circumstances associated with each house. The **succedent houses** (2, 5, 8 and 11) represent a focus on **securing and maintaining life circumstances.** If a planet is located in one of these houses, an individual is likely to express the planetary themes to **create stability** within the scope of the circumstances governed by these houses. The **cadent houses** (3, 6, 9 and 12) denote a focus on **seeking new learning and growth-promoting experiences** associated with each house. The themes represented by planets located in these houses help develop the discrimination to express the circumstances of these houses to their fullest potential. The subtones of sign quality and house classification are discussed in more detail after each individual chord is described.

Synthesis, Harmony and Discord

Since the tones and subtones of the twelve chords can be found in countless combinations with each other, it is essential that one have a clear understanding of each chord before embarking upon interpreting them in combination. Astrology is similar to music in that the notes and chords really support and depend upon each other, and together they produce a recognizable melody. And, just as in music, certain astrological chords are naturally more harmonious when combined, while others contain notes inclined to clash. As with music, we have to "play" our lives sensibly to maximize harmony and minimize discord.

The organization of the astrological symbols into chords displays the shared threads between the planet, sign and house. Traditional astrology often makes associations between planets and signs while only awkwardly exploring their interrelatedness, and describes the house as only superficially related to the planets and signs. A chord shows that its tones spring from the same origin, each with its own variation in theme and with its own contribution to a created harmony.

The planets, signs and houses manifest in a horoscope in many combinations. This potentially vast and complex mixture of astrological symbols is beyond the scope of a traditional textbook approach to chart interpretation, which merely assigns definitions to each symbol in an oversimplified manner. Using that approach is rather like trying to cook with a recipe that lists the ingredients without showing how to combine them, or like creating a book by merely using words from a dictionary without addressing the difficult task of combining them into meaningful sentences. Many traditional astrology books would have us believe that memorizing a list of planet, sign or house meanings will give us the information needed to understand our own charts as well as interpret the charts of others. It is not always understood that the practice of astrology is an art, synthesizing very diverse information of metaphysical and psychological character into a common unity and mirroring an individual's inner identity.

1ST CHORD: SELF-EXPRESSIVE EMBODIMENT

Tone	Archetypal Themes	Functions	Positive Expressions	Negative Expressions	Potential Counseling Issues
Planet: Mars Symbol: ♂	The directing of physical energy to embody and assert the self.	1. To embody the self-image concept. 2. To take immediate action toward accomplishing desired aims. 3. To embody personal strength, physical energy and force. 4. To assert the self. 5. To confront obstacles and to direct anger. 6. To initiate experiences.	1. Self-confidence through acting out the impulses of the self. 2. The ability to initiate experiences and accomplish desired aims. 3. The ability to lead and inspire others through action. 4. The ability to be assertive. 5. Courage. 6. To initiate experiences.	1. A tendency to be too self-centered. 2. An inclination toward aggressiveness. 3. A proclivity for impulsivity. 4. A tendency to be extremely competitive. 5. An inclination toward losing interest in people and projects quickly, with a lack of follow-through 6. A lack of sensitivity for the feelings of others. 7. Abrasiveness due to the misuse of anger. 8. Impatience with self and others.	**Key Phrase:** Asserting The Self **Games:** 1. Battering Ram. 2. Bully. 3. Cracked Mirror. 4. Dump Truck. 5. Fools Rush In Where Angels Fear to Tread. 6. Frozen Mirror. 7. Hidden Hormone. 8. Hiding Behind the Persona. 9. Hit and Run. 10. Macho-Facho. 11. Me First. 12. Missing the Boat. 13. Need for Constant Action 14. Perfect Look.
Sign: Aries Symbol: ♈	The manner through which immediate action is initiated and embodied to assert self.				
House: 1st	One's identification with a self-concept or image and physical body.				

Figure 1: First Chord
See the Note to Readers after Acknowledgments

Each of the chord descriptions in the chapters that follow is accompanied by a table that should be read from left to right. The name of the chord is at the top, followed by a key phrase summarizing the basic theme of that chord. The first column lists the corresponding planet, sign and house tones of that chord. Each tone (planet, sign or house) is accompanied by a brief statement indicating how this tone will function in an individual's life. That description will hereafter be referred to as the tone's **archetypal theme**.

The **functions** of the chords are listed in the second column. The archetypal themes produce the functions, which are the underlying psychological motivations through which an individual might express the chord tones. The functions are potential issues that have a bearing on a person's life.

The next two columns in the chord tables illustrate the positive (or harmonious) and negative (or discordant) qualities associated with an individual's expression of the functions of each related chord. The positive and negative qualities listed represent a spectrum of **possible choices** through which a person could express these basic issues, but is by no means an exclusive list. Once again, a counseling-oriented astrologer would not attempt to limit the scope of a client's life with a narrow list of possibilities since each individual's life is unique. The tables for each chord serve as a guide in moving from the functions to an individual's own choice of possible behaviors.

Games

The final column lists potential counseling issues, called games, which may occur if a certain tone is expressed as a highly accentuated theme. The games arise, not just by the negative expression of a certain chord tone, but by the continuous expression of problematic patterns that become psychological issues in a person's life. A game represents an imbalance of energies within a person's psychological nature. Modern psychology emphasizes the necessity for balancing the different conscious and unconscious forces within a personality. Likewise, astrology attempts to explain a person as a mixture of drives which are represented in the individual horoscope.

Typically, when we have an imbalance in our psyches, we are overdoing one theme and underdoing another. Astrology demonstrates that certain themes are more likely to compete with one another for our attention and expression. For example, it takes energy and discipline to make room in life for our need for freedom along with our need for emotional attachments. Each astrological chord has certain other chords which are likely to be competitive with it. These are shown by certain astrological aspects—the square, opposition and quincunx—which are discussed more fully in Chapter 14. When counseling issues are discussed and imbalance is a problem, other chords which are relevant may be mentioned. Once the individual understands the different needs she is trying to meet, it is easier to find a compromise position which allows one to enjoy all the sides of life shown by the 12 chords.

Each chord contains a significant phrase that emanates from the central focus of the chord itself (listed at the top of each table). The key phrase captures the main theme of the counseling issues (games) within each chord as these issues relate back to the archetypal themes stated within each chord. The counseling issues or games represent the struggles that a person may be undergoing in trying to enact the main thrust of a particular chord tone.

I plan to make the strongest statement possible about each archetypal theme and how it is related to counseling issues. Because of the inherent chord synthesis, each game can be related to two or more of the tones and the archetypal themes contained within that particular chord. Other counseling issues not listed could also be related to more than one tone in each particular chord, but in the interest of clarity, I have focused on the central counseling issues and themes that illustrate the main thrust of each tone.

Some **games could be related to more than one astrological chord.** I will discuss some chord combinations, although it is not possible to cover all of them. The major focus here, however, is on the pure forms of each chord. Once readers get a sense of the core essence of each of the 12 chords, they can logically mix and match on their own.

Elements

The four "elements" of nature were defined by the ancients. Fire, earth, air and water have been valued as equally important to human life dating back to the fifth century BC. It was then that the Greek philosopher Empedocles stated that no one element was greater than another in importance, each having a sacred purpose. Likewise, the elements have symbolic importance in astrology. **Fire** represents the spontaneous outpouring of energy into action, inspiration and visionary faith; **air** symbolizes mental processes as related to perception and logic; **water** denotes one's intuitive and emotional natures; **earth** represents the physical senses and basic survival instincts.

Each of us is a complex mixture of these energies. The astrological language is a great vehicle through which to explore the elements as they symbolically combine to mirror our personalities, needs, instincts, likes and dislikes and most cherished forms of self-expression.

Unfortunately, astrology is often taught without stressing the importance of the elements. Stephen Arroyo, a noted counselor and astrologer, and author of *Astrology, Psychology and the Four Elements,* says, "The element of any particular sign shows the specific type of consciousness and method of most immediate perception to which the individual is attuned." (Planets and houses have elements just as much as signs do.) It is essential that a counseling-oriented astrologer have a firm grasp of the elements to know how to tune into the vibrational frequency levels of an individual and to communicate in the language that she can comprehend. Even more important is that an individual tune into her own elemental motivations to achieve a sense of harmony in life.

The chords have been organized in each chapter according to their elemental families to illustrate the relationship and compatibility of the three chords within each element. The three chords within an element build on and relate to each other, and describe energy expressions that are similar, but with a variation in theme.

The chapters that follow describe the chords in this order: fire, earth, air and water. Part II covers the fire element. Part III discusses the earth element chords. Part IV explains the chords of the air element, while water chords are depicted in Part V. Part VI shows how the chords and their respective tones and subtones can be combined into a meaningful language for chart interpretation. This can be useful for students and practicing astrologers, as well as for everyone interested in expanding their knowledge of themselves and the world around them.

PART II

FIRE ELEMENT

Fire indicates an active expression of the self. The fire element represents intensity, initiative, enthusiasm, faith, courage, humor and an independent spirit. This element shows an accelerated rhythm for acting out and manifesting the self in life experiences.

A person with fire as a dominant element by having the fire signs (Aries, Leo and Sagittarius), or the fire houses (1,5 and 9), well emphasized often exudes a self-perpetuating confidence and a faith in life that sometimes appears colored by naivete and unrealistic ideals. Tight aspects formed by fire planets (Mars, Sun and Jupiter), especially to each other, can also point to a fire focus. It is the ideals and visions of the fire-chord consciousness that are the very fuel an individual requires to act out the impulses to enter new and risk-taking adventures.

The three fire chords point to an individual inspired to act upon impulses. An individual may have a highly accentuated emphasis on this element in the horoscope in any of the following ways: the Sun, Moon, Ascendant, four or more personal planets (Sun, Moon, Mercury, Venus, Mars, Jupiter and Saturn) in fire signs, key planets in fire houses or strong aspects formed by fire planets. Such people often see a great need for dramatic action in order to maintain a clear sense of self. Their basic chemistry and natural inclination is to initiate, activity without immediate concern for the consequences on self or others

The planets, signs and houses that comprise the fire chords manifest through an individual in the forms of physical (**1st Chord**), procreative (**5th Chord**) or expansive (**9th Chord**) action. The common ingredient of Chords 1, 5 and 9 is a self-focus or identification of the self through action.

CHAPTER TWO

FIRST CHORD: SELF-EXPRESSIVE EMBODIMENT

> If you go ahead, if you keep running, wherever you run you will meet danger and evil, for it drives you, it chooses the way you go. You must choose. You must seek what seeks you. You must hunt the hunter.
>
> Wizard of Earthsea by Ursula K. LeGuin (page 148)

The 1st Chord is an expression of the fire element in its most basic form of direct action. The 1st Chord is composed of three tones: the planet Mars, the sign Aries, and the 1st house. These tones symbolize an individual's need to recognize identity through action. Normally, there will be self-confidence, self-assertion, energy, risk-taking, spontaneity and need for variety. The archetypal themes stemming from the three 1st Chord tones reflect three different, but interrelated, forms of this recognition of the identity through action:

1. **Mars**—the directing of physical energy to embody and assert the self.
2. **Aries**—the manner through which immediate action is initiated and embodied to assert the self.
3. **Ascendant** or **1st house**—one's identification with a self-concept or image and physical body.

Mars

The planetary tone (Mars) of the 1st Chord represents an individual's main energy thrust to assert the self. Mars symbolizes an individual's primary level of striving for identity. Because certain psychological factors, such as anger, sexual behavior, physical energy and competition are extensions of the self-assertion principle, they are largely pictured by the particular placement of Mars in a person's chart.

A person's assertive use of the energy shown by Mars embodies one's identity through action. Mars has been referred to as the angry red planet due to its red surface. In Greek and Roman mythology, Mars is the god of war. In astrology, it symbolizes our capacity to enact our warrior-like selves. The drive denoted by Mars ignites a person's anger and fuels the raw energy that is required to break through obstacles, set new goals, excite himself and others to take new and sometimes impulsive risks.

The positive expressions of Martian themes include direct assertion of the self with courage and spontaneity. The fact that Mars springs forth from the 1st Chord typifies its meaning: the reinforcement of an individual's physical force to incorporate new experiences. An individual's leadership abilities and ability to energize others to act upon their assertive impulses is inherent in the archetypal theme of Mars: the embodying and directing of actions that assert and identify the self.

The forceful energy symbolized by Mars can be expressed negatively as well. A person's misuse of the warrior-like self can be expressed as over-aggressiveness, impatience, excessive or brutalizing anger, and a general lack of sensitivity toward the needs of others. Counseling issues related to these negative expressions are discussed with such games as **Me First, Need for Constant Action,** and the **Hit and Run.**

Aries

Aries is the sign which makes up one of the tones of Chord 1, and fiery Aries complements the planetary tone, Mars. Aries represents the coloring of an individual's assertion which inspires an individual to act on impulses. When the Ascendant, Sun, Moon or several other planets are located in Aries, an individual is probably permeated with sudden bursts of energy. A sense of immediacy prompts him to initiate action. Aries, like Mars, reflects a person's warrior identity. The Aries impulse is to act first and think about the consequences later. Aries indicates a competitive uprising from within a person that encourages one's deepest assertive impulses.

The positive expressions of Aries stem from the archetypal theme, the manner through which immediate action is embodied and initiated to assert the self. An individual embodies the forcefulness of Aries positively by initiating experiences and accomplishing desired aims. Self-confidence follows successful acting out of the impulses of the self.

The negative manner of expressing Aries results from an individual's over-assertion with Aries force. An individual's impatience with self and others, misuse of anger and a selfish preoccupation with personal needs are characteristic negative expressions of Aries themes.

1st House

The house tone of the 1st Chord is of special significance as it contains the sign that is rising (on the eastern horizon) at the time of birth, known as the rising sign or Ascendant. The Ascendant has a special emphasis. It is an integral part of understanding one's identity. This central point in the horoscope indicates actions that embody a true sense of the self. The Ascendant also represents an image that a person naturally projects, with which he feels comfortable, and it is through this image that he can perform actions embodying a true sense of self.

An individual can embody the Ascendant as if it were a persona (mask). This occurs when a person overidentifies with an Ascendant and hides behind the energy. This can lead to a limiting behavior as will be seen in the **Hiding behind the Persona** game. The Ascendant and 1st house planets indicate an individual's unique and personal identification with a self-concept or image, which is one's way of behaving naturally and responding instinctively to surrounding circumstances. The Ascendant essentially serves to support an individual's core identity and represents the particular way of energizing one's own vitality that is true to one's self-image.

It is often a person's 1st house aura that is initially projected to others and is perceived as a characteristic expression of the individual. The widely divergent ways in which an individual can embody a self-image through the Ascendent are clearly illustrated in the following example. An individual with Capricorn (10th Chord sign tone) on the Ascendant could project a mature and sophisticated image to others and might appear emotionally reserved, cautious and even businesslike in demeanor. An individual with Pisces (12th Chord sign tone) on the Ascendant would be more likely to project a childlike and idealistic image to others and might appear emotionally sensitive, open and vague in demeanor.

Since the Ascendant also symbolizes an individual's particular manner of initiating experiences from a self-image, that which would propel a Capricorn Ascendant individual into new situations is going to be different than for an individual with Pisces as the Ascendant. The Capricorn-rising individual would be more inclined to seek out new experiences that are practical in nature as well as functional, giving a grounded or solid sense of self. The Pisces individual would be more inclined to seek out new experiences that are romantic and fluid in nature, giving an emotional sense of self. The Capricorn-Ascendant individual is more apt to be energized by practical experiences that lead to stability and strengthen his status in the world, while the Pisces-rising individual is more likely to be energized by emotionally fulfilling experiences that lead to transcending or romanticizing his participation in the world.

If a planet is located in the 1st house, an individual is likely to incorporate the planetary motifs into the expression of the ascending sign. Let's consider an individual with Pisces on the Ascendant and with the planet Venus located in Aries also in the 1st house. The Pisces Ascendant, as stated earlier, might be projected as idealistic, vague or shy, while the Venus in Aries will show this individual as direct and confident in the expression of social urges and affection. The Venus-in-Aries confidence and warmth in relating to others might suddenly shift into a feeling of disorientation and a desire for withdrawal due to the drives shown by the Pisces Ascendant. The individual with these contrasting themes in the 1st house will need to seek a balanced life that provides for both expressions. This conflict produced by two contrasting inner needs could prove to be problematic. This person may have difficulty in understanding his own nature, and he could project an unstable or inconsistent image to others.

I would like to emphasize that the Ascendant is not just symbolic of one's self-image. It can represent a tremendous expression of one's creative energy. The clearer one's self-image and ability to be assertive, the clearer are one's actions in the world. Since the Ascendant is symbolic of instincts a person inherits from childhood, it is important that he does not sacrifice adulthood in favor of the Ascendant energy. This is often a key as to whether one's assertion instincts will lead to success or frustration, aggression rather than assertion, or reckless impatience rather than a clear sense of purpose.

Counseling Issues

The functions (listed in the table following) are the underlying psychological motivations of a chord. They are the basic human drives symbolized by each chord. The archetypal themes of the three basic tones (Mars, Aries, 1st house) of Chord 1 create the functions as listed in the table. The positive and negative qualities are essentially the harmonious and discordant expressions of the planet, sign and house tones. If these themes are not expressed in a balanced way, there could be a need for counseling concerning the pertinent assertion issues.

The counseling issues typified by Chord 1 tones are representative of an individual's ability, or lack thereof, to successfully express the basic nature of this chord, **self-expressive embodiment.** My key word phrase for these counseling issues, **asserting the self,** is from the synthesis of the tones—Mars, Aries, and the Ascendant (including 1st house planets). The 1st Chord tones represent the projection of one's self-image, indicated by the Ascendant, and the embodying of individuality through assertive action, indicated by all three 1st Chord tones (Mars, Aries, 1st house). The archetypal themes of the 1st Chord capture both of these principles.

Each 1st Chord tone mirrors the ability to project or assert the self in a direct manner. An individual can give a true representation of self and focus energy into worthwhile activities. The counseling issues of this chord are twofold: (1) an overidentification with the needs of one's self-image, or, stated another way, emphatic and repetitive actions that serve only to gratify one's self-centered identity; (2) a tremendous lack of assertion due to a weak self-image.

Astrology, Psychology, and Transformation

1ST CHORD: SELF-EXPRESSIVE EMBODIMENT

Tone	Archetypal Themes	Functions	Positive Expressions	Negative Expressions	Potential Counseling Issues
Planet: Mars Symbol ♂	The directing of physical energy to embody and assert the self.	1. To embody the self-image concept. 2. To take immediate action toward accomplishing desired aims. 3. To embody personal strength, physical energy and force. 4. To assert the self. 5. To confront obstacles and to direct anger. 6. To initiate experiences.	1. Self-confidence through acting out the impulses of the self. 2. The ability to initiate experiences and accomplish desired aims. 3. The ability to lead and inspire others through action. 4. The ability to be assertive. 5. Courage. 6. To initiate experiences.	1. A tendency to be too self-centered. 2. An inclination toward aggressiveness. 3. A proclivity for impulsivity. 4. A tendency to be extremely competitive. 5. An inclination toward losing interest in people and projects quickly, with a lack of follow-through. 6. A lack of sensitivity for the feelings of others. 7. Abrasiveness due to the misuse of anger. 8. Impatience with self and others.	**Key Phrase:** Asserting The Self **Games:** 1. Battering Ram. 2. Bully. 3. Cracked Mirror. 4. Dump Truck. 5. Fools Rush In Where Angels Fear to Tread. 6. Frozen Mirror. 7. Hidden Hormone. 8. Hiding Behind the Persona. 9. Hit and Run. 10. Macho-Facho. 11. Me First. 12. Missing the Boat. 13. Need for Constant Action 14. Perfect Look.
Sign: Aries Symbol ♈	The manner through which immediate action is initiated and embodied to assert self.				
House: 1st	One's identification with a self-concept or image and physical body.				

Figure 1: First Chord
See the Note to Readers after Acknowledgments

Games

An individual's overidentification with a self-image is sometimes an overidentification with the Ascendant. Instead of using this energy to simply initiate experiences, an individual may have what I call the **Hiding behind the Persona** game, where he becomes too involved in hiding behind this self-image. The sign and element of the Ascendant will indicate the particular manner in which the individual might conceal himself. An individual could become so fixated on compulsively enacting this self-concept that he neglects to define himself through his Sun sign, or core identity. He may go so far as to sacrifice many basic emotional and creative expressions to preserve this self-image.

The Ascendant's element is important to consider. The key to finding one's way beyond this game may reside in the opposing element. Oppositions (discussed in more detail in Chapter 14) signify a need for balance between two sides. For example, a person with a water Ascendant (or water planets in the 1st house) might need to assume more responsibility for life as found in the earth element. (Earth signs are opposite water signs and vice versa.) He may exhibit a dependent and helpless nature that encourages others to take care of him. Also, the earth element can ground the emotional and dreamy water disposition.

An individual with an air Ascendant might be hiding behind an extremely intellectual nature. Perhaps he needs to become more directly involved in life activities as in the fire element. (Air signs oppose fire signs and vice versa.) Thinking last and acting first might bring more of the real person forward. He could be hiding a very fiery and energetic personality under an "air" of calmness.

A person with a fire Ascendant could be hiding behind a front of false self-confidence. The opposite air element points to the need to better communicate with others. The self-centeredness of fire sometimes requires the more objective and tactful air element to balance the self-focused energy.

The individual with an earth Ascendant can become too attached to practicality, repressing the opposite water element. The person may need to allow the more intuitive and emotional (water) sides of the nature to surface.

Another 1st Chord counseling issue is what I call the **Me First** game, which is a compulsive drive for attention or to occupy center stage in life circumstances. There can be a tremendous competitiveness to be number one when an individual is confused by the electricity of heightened 1st Chord tones. When using Mars, Aries or 1st house energy, one must be careful not to become entrapped by the self-focusing emphasis of these tones.

The key to getting beyond this game is sometimes restructuring one's aggressive tendencies. Individuals with many planets in the 1st house, key Mars placements, or planets in Aries, are naturally competitive and full of physical energy. They usually need regular exercise, competitive sports or physical jobs to release this energy. These individuals make great leaders and lovers if they can channel this energy.

This can also be an angry person. He is hungering for the attention that may have been denied by peers or lovers as indicated by the 1st Chord's opposition to the 7th Chord. Also, the 7th Chord points to the need to develop a more objective attitude concerning the needs of others and perhaps learning the arts of cooperation and diplomacy.

Another area not addressed very significantly by traditional astrology is a compulsive attraction to enter relationships, which I see as connected to 1st Chord tones. Taking the path of least resistance is a contradiction to the inherent strength and independence of the 1st Chord. Looking to others to complete the self-image undermines an individual's ability to embody the self-assertion principle. Over a period of time he could begin to lose a sense of who that "self" really is. As a matter of fact, an respect, or even self-hate, if he denies himself the responsibility of completing his own self-concept. The "self-focus" of Chord 1 opposes the "other-focus" of Chord 7. Some individuals with a focus on Chord 1 have "sold out" to the opposing Chord 7, and deny their strength and assertion, believing other people have the power. Rather than expressing their own needs, they seek to find themselves through relationships.

If an individual does have an unclear self-concept, Mars and Aries can further support this behavior, because both are vehicles for the directing of energy and the initiation of experiences, quickly and even unconsciously. This can produce what I call the **Fools Rush In Where Angels Fear to Tread** game.

This game is a combination of two 1st Chord themes. The first theme is rashness and impulsiveness in moving very quickly into new situations. The second theme is usually the underlying issue of rushing into new relationships to avoid facing the self.

The individual in this game needs to learn to tune into his more reflective water or stabilizing earth sides. There is often a lot of undiscovered strength within the person, and he may be very accomplished in other areas of life. Any inner restlessness is not resolved until he stops long enough to do some soul-searching.

On the other hand, an individual with a weak and underdeveloped self-image may have tremendous difficulty in asserting the self as the strength to project a self-image is blocked. Self-expression is paralyzed by the lack of a clear self-image in what I call the **Frozen Mirror** game. This individual can miss out on many productive life experiences and relationships. A fear of assertion keeps him from initiating action.

This game can be thawed a bit if a person can warm up to his self-image. For instance, I have noticed people with Virgo, Pisces or Capricorn rising (and Saturn or Pluto in the 1st house) at times express a negative self-image. Some of these individuals have been the most creative and productive people I have met. However, the tendency for putting themselves down was equally strong.

The key here is learning to be satisfied with the "real" self. Also, not being afraid to change one's self-image is important. There are people involved in this game who have suffered greatly due to being negatively programmed during childhood by parents (1st Chord squares 4th and 10th) or peers (1st Chord opposes 7th). It is important for the individual to develop a new and refreshing set of internal programming that frees him from too much negativity.

An individual's inability to accept the self-image, especially one's physical appearance, can result in the **Cracked Mirror** game. The enacting of self-hating behavior, whether it be conscious or unconscious, could be indicative of a denial of one's self-image and could produce injuries to the body in an attempt to punish or hurt oneself. Illnesses to the part of the body corresponding to the sign on the Ascendant (or planets located in the 1st house), or constant displeasure with one's body and physical appearance, could also be symptoms of this form of self-hatred.

This game calls for more self-acceptance. The individual may be expecting too much from the self. There may be emotional repression (quincunx to 8th Chord) and self-criticism due to strong drives to improve and perfect one's life (quincunx to 6th Chord).

A person's overidentification with a self-concept could also take the form of worshipping one's own physical appearance in the **Perfect Look** game. This person's fascination with beauty is compulsive and can lead him to expect others to constantly compliment his appearance. Desirability to attract a relationship is not what matters to him; he needs others merely to reassure him that he is desirable in the eyes of everyone, because his self-image is so connected to the appearance of his physical body.

The Ascendant is a very powerful self-focusing energy in the horoscope. The individual can use the Ascendant as a symbolic key to unlock energy. Assertion is strengthened through experiences that reflect the Ascendant's sign and perhaps better channel the excess of energy being directed into the physical appearance. For example, an individual with Sagittarius rising can further assertion strength through encountering new expansive learning situations. Expression through travel, educating oneself and teaching can inspire self-confidence. On the other hand, an individual with Virgo rising might gain strength and confidence by developing a successful routine regarding health and work habits. Mastering new skills might also be energizing.

Just as the Ascendant is a key to experiences supporting one's strength, so is it a key to how an individual might spontaneously enter new experiences. The planet tone, Mars, and the sign tone, Aries, also have particular meanings that indicate how an individual might initiate new experiences.

The counseling issues related to initiating experiences reflective of all three tones (Mars, Aries, 1st house) include the **Hit and Run** game, where an individual might initiate new experiences and then quickly lose interest. For instance, he might begin a relationship and suddenly move on to another one, without fully exploring the depths of the first one; or he might begin a project with other people and simply not finish it, due to boredom or the promise of something more exciting looming on the horizon. This behavior alienates the person from others and from himself, causing him to seem undependable and fickle, and preventing him from establishing a healthy sense of continuity of the self.

It is important to remember that 1st Chord tones can be symbolic of an individual with a capacity to accomplish difficult tasks requiring courage and much energy. However, the chords that naturally square the 1st Chord must be incorporated into the life, to balance the impulsiveness of this 1st Chord game.

The earthy 10th Chord slows down and disciplines the impatient, driving force of the 1st Chord, while the watery 4th Chord sensitizes one to exploring possible inner motives for not completing projects. The key here is for a person to pour energy into the completing phase of a cycle as well as into the beginning phase.

Another counseling issue due to the initiation-of-experiences principle is the **Need for Constant Action** game, where an individual does not feel alive unless constantly busy. This is once again the 1st Chord manner of running away from oneself by not stopping long enough to face one's problems. The **Hit and Run** and **Need for Constant Action** games are especially true of the impulsive and impatient energies represented by both Mars and Aries in their call for immediate action. An individual with many planets in the 1st house sometimes needs to balance tendencies toward impatience as well.

A person may play the latter game to escape responsibility as the 1st Chord does square the 10th Chord. The individual can use the desire for constant stimulation as an excuse to escape present responsibilities. The key in this case is learning to follow through on commitments which strengthen the individual. The person may need to tap into his stabilizing earth side.

Another 1st Chord game is the **Battering Ram**. The mythological symbolism of Aries as the ram has an impatient streak that can be typical of each 1st Chord tone. The **Battering Ram** type of individual acts before thinking and often causes a lot of unnecessary problems for himself and others due to lack of foresight. This individual's behavior is like an ancient battering ram used by an army to break through enemy walls. He tries to force issues when a little patience and diplomacy would be the wiser path to follow. This individual may have a headstrong attitude and often it is best to simply get out of the path when he rams his way by you—often headfirst and on a direct collision course!

The individual in this game needs to develop the tact of the opposite 7th Chord as he is being direct a bit too literally. Some of these individuals resent authority figures (square to 10th Chord). The opposite airy 7th Chord suggests a need to balance the 1st Chord temperament. The objectivity of air can be helpful in choosing more options. The water element might also cool down angry 1st Chord people (or indicate extreme moodiness). Water is reflective and can point people in the right direction in understanding aggressive behavior.

Counseling issues related to the initiating principle can be caused by an individual's inability to assert one's needs or actions in a direct manner. The **Missing the Boat** game concerns an individual who probably has a weak self-image and is not able to make important decisions quickly. This game may cause other people to become irritated and impatient due to his constant hesitation to take needed risks. He may become even more dissatisfied as a lack of direct action leads to missing new friendships, relationships, opportunities, etc.

There is a bit of procrastination in this game sometimes. One of the keys is for a person to change his concept of losing and not see "failure" as a loss, but rather as a lesson learned. He needs to learn to take risks. People with air signs on the Ascendant can miss the boat due to thinking too much and not taking action. People with water signs rising can be afraid of risking emotional hurt. People with earth signs rising may be reluctant to risk their material security or simply prefer status quo. Fire signs are most likely to act, but may also miss the boat due to lack of enthusiasm, especially if the fire side of the nature is blocked by an overemphasis on other needs (physical safety, emotional security, etc.). Once the fire is lit, there is no end to what these people are capable of doing!

Perhaps one of the biggest counseling issues related to the 1st Chord is the expression of anger. Most traditional astrology books do not consider the Ascendant as related to the expression of one's anger. These books speak of the Ascendant mainly in connection with one's personality traits and physical appearance. However, the Ascendant is a primary entity in the chart indicating the projection of the self-image, hence the assertion of oneself. All three tones of **Chord 1** are important vehicles for the expression of anger and assertion drives. The house that contains Aries in a person's chart will show in which circumstances a person will especially need to assert in order to experience emotional balance, and the house that contains Mars will give important clues as to which life circumstances will provide assertion challenges. The sign coloring Mars will indicate the particular manner in which anger and assertion will likely be expressed. A person with Mars in a fire sign tends to project anger more directly and immediately, though sometimes haphazardly, while Mars in an air sign tends to indicate a verbal and highly rational expression of anger. A person with Mars in a water sign often has difficulty with anger. He may experience anger with tremendous emotional intensity, but a natural emotional reserve may dilute the anger before it is expressed. The resulting emotional turmoil can make the individual wonder if it was even worth getting angry. A person with Mars in an earth sign generally finds the expression of anger beneficial if it will help preserve or stabilize a situation.

The house position of Mars must also be carefully considered and in many cases is more important than the sign containing Mars. The water houses (4th, 8th and 12th) are especially testy for fiery Mars. The assertion energy of this planet may be drowned out by the repressing and subjective nature of these houses unless a person is very tuned into his emotions. One tends to turn the anger inward or let it out awkwardly if out of touch with emotions.

Theodore Isaac Rubin begins the introduction to *The Angry Book* by stating: "This book is about a basic human emotion—anger." He goes on to say: "Too often, anger is not seen as basic or human." Anger is perhaps the most difficult emotion for an individual to balance. Dr. Rubin states that repressed anger is stored in a slush fund if not expressed. It appears that this slush fund is responsible for many inappropriate outbursts of anger.

A person with a healthy self-image, who is in touch with his anger and assertive needs, understands that genuine anger is not only a natural feeling, but is essential for a healthy self. He does not allow a large slush fund of unexpressed anger to develop. Some individuals, however, will hold onto their anger in many transactions in their lives, especially situations where they feel they have little power, causing a great deal of anger to collect inside of them. Unexpressed anger seems to be related to an unclear self-image and to a tremendous repression of one's assertive drives.

A person who does have a large slush fund of anger may exhibit the **Dump Truck** game. This occurs when a person who has a very large amount of unexpressed anger dumps this anger upon safe and convenient targets, especially mates and children. An individual playing this game has a very repressed emotional nature. The combination of fire and water in a horoscope can be very symbolic of this game. (The fire/water mixtures can come through planets, as in a Mars/Pluto conjunction; through planets in houses as in Mars, the Sun and Jupiter falling in the 4th, 8th or 12th houses, or Moon, Pluto and Neptune falling in the 1st, 5th and 9th houses; through planets in signs as in Mars/Jupiter/Sun in water signs, or Moon, Pluto and Neptune in fire signs; or through sign/house combinations as in all the water signs occupying fire houses or all the fire signs occupying water houses.) The water contains the fire for a time, until the person suddenly erupts with explosive anger. The slush fund fills and fills until a circumstance bursts the bubble.

The individual needs to more consistently express emotions. Moods may be the first indication that he is repressing too many feelings, keeping things inside instead of draining emotions. Regular watery reflection can help prevent intense emotions from building up to an explosive point. The individual needs to learn how to direct forceful energy into more productive activities.

A person with very dominant 1st Chord tones could exhibit the **Bully** game. This person enjoys the experience of having power over other people that a forceful nature provides. He probably has unexpressed anger on some more basic level than surface situations would indicate. Like the **Dump Truck** individual, he has repressed this anger in a slush fund which, because of an already powerful nature, he is able to take out on anyone with whom he comes into contact.

Many of the bullies are carrying around painful past experiences with parents, spouses, bosses, etc. This game shows a desperate person with a lot of misdirected emotional strength. The individual may need to face the fact that he fears being rejected by others (1st Chord opposing 7th). An inner lack of security leads him to threaten others.

People who know their own strength do not have to "prove" it. If the dynamic intensity of the individual can be converted into a clear self-expression, the person is capable of forming strong relationships and reaching difficult goals.

It was interesting for me to do a volunteer internship with a counseling program designed to help deal with the anger of men who batter women. Many of these men did not realize that they were angry until they actually hit their mate. Most of these men needed to be taught to concentrate on their bodies, to identify such physical symptoms as rapid breathing, dry ness in the mouth, the clenching of teeth and tightness of the chest, that often accompany feelings of anger. In other words, to get in touch with their feelings, they were taught how to get in touch with their bodies.

The combined keys of the Ascendant, 1st house planets, the sign and house containing Mars and any emphasis on the sign, Aries, especially significant personal planets in Aries, should be given careful consideration in counseling issues involving expressions of anger. Since the Sun is of such tremendous significance in a person's overall energy expression, the Sun's sign, element and house placement also need to be considered when evaluating the assertion drive of an individual.

If Mars or Aries is emphasized in an individual's horoscope and is expressed negatively, I have seen many cases where repressed anger produced headaches and jaw problems. Both tones are associated with the head and jaw areas of the body, and repressed anger creates bodily tension that can result in headaches or a chronically clenched jaw. I sometimes advise a client who has problems with appropriate anger expression to keep an anger journal, noting the situations that produce angry feelings and his responses to those situations and feelings. I ask him to note what body signals are produced by feelings of anger because it is important for people who unconsciously block their anger to determine if they are even angry at all, by noticing what their body signals are telling them.

There are sexual implications to 1st Chord counseling issues as well. This unconscious use of Mars or Aries energy can result in a person's overprojection of sexual energy in an overwhelming manner that I call the **Macho-Facho** game. Even when this makes others uncomfortable, the individual may be so self-focused that he is quite unaware of invading the space of others through a strong projective nature.

The **Macho-Facho** individual is quite insecure about his identity and overcompensates by trying to impress others with a superhuman sexual image. This is a warrior type image intended to conceal an inner sense of emotional confusion. Some of the people playing this game exhaust themselves trying to impress others. They are often very passionate lovers but do not really give themselves the opportunity to experience healthy, honest relationships because they are afraid to reveal their true self. This game usually has roots in self-hate. If the person is able to drop the **Macho-Facho** image, he often enjoys the satisfaction of someone accepting him at face value!

An individual's overidentification with a weak self-concept or a repressed Mars or Aries energy could lead to difficulties in establishing a clear expression of sexual behavior. He might be too self-conscious and, due to this shyness and fear of showing the self, may have difficulty embodying sexual energy in the **Hidden Hormone** game.

This game may be typical of a person who has been involved in unbalanced relationships. Some of these individuals have chosen partners who have been overcritical of their sexual performance. The person in this game often needs to become less fearful of taking risks in relationships. Also, the person may be extremely self-critical, which inhibits tapping into sexual energy.

Summary of Issues with 1st Chord Games

The 1st Chord games may indicate an underemphasis of the assertion principle such as in the **Missing the Boat, Frozen Mirror** and **Hidden Hormone**. These individuals need to focus more on strengthening their assertion instincts.

The 1st Chord games may also involve an overemphasis upon the assertion principle as in the **Me First, Battering Ram** and **Macho-Facho**. It could be that developing the chords that square the 1st Chord (4th and 10th) are a key to balancing a 1st Chord game. The 4th Chord relates to compassion and sensitivity, while the 10th Chord relates to a proper structuring of one's self-expression within societal limits. The opposing 7th Chord is important to consider as it symbolizes the concept of cooperation which is needed to balance an overdevelopment of assertion.

Since the expression of anger is such an integral part of the 1st Chord, it is important that an individual be in touch with his anger. Emotional outburst can be alleviated by not building up a slush fund of anger.

The assertion strength of the 1st Chord suggests people with an emphasis on the 1st Chord possess great amounts of physical strength and psychological fortitude. These are often the natural leaders who are not afraid of risking failure. Their very presence can inspire others to go beyond their own limits. It is only when

1st Chord energies become hijacked by selfish desires or a fear of expressing the true self that 1st Chord games become the identity.

Subtones

The 1st Chord represents a lot of ego-focus. The fire element shows a self-centering type of energy with a lot of intensity in the major fire tones of Chords 1, 5 and 9. Likewise, the three subtones associated with Chord 1 have a strong energy-promoting basis. The three subtones of Chord 1 are: the planetary aspect known as the conjunction, the energy focus of Aries known as cardinal, and the house classification known as angular.

The **conjunction,** as a **subtone** of the 1st Chord planetary tone (Mars), is similar in its archetypal theme. The planets involved in a conjunction combine their themes, requiring an individual to find expressions that blend both themes. The conjunction often emphasizes an individual's need to satisfy a self-oriented desire.

For instance, an individual with the fiery Sun, the 5th Chord planet, conjunct watery Neptune, the 12th Chord planet, may feel a dramatic and immediate need to express the core identity (Sun) through an aesthetic vehicle that embodies ideals (Neptune). The individual may cherish and protect aesthetic ambitions above all other considerations. This individual may even retreat into a secluded lifestyle to further enhance aesthetic endeavors. Due to astrology's inherent capacity for multidimensional interpretation, the preceding explanation of the Sun conjunct Neptune represents only one possibility among many others of this specific aspect.

I would like to **emphasize** that the nature of the planets involved in an aspect must be considered, even in the dynamically powerful conjunction. Certain planets, especially water planets, do not suggest assertion or action. In the above example, the fiery Sun portion of the conjunction implies action and initiative. On the other hand, watery Neptune highlights a meditative and dreamy type of energy. Also, 10th Chord Saturn can denote restraint or caution in a conjunction. The watery Moon implies reflection in a conjunction, and watery Pluto suggests secrecy. However, even in these conjunctions, the natural self-expression (Chord 1) of the two planets must be combined if the person is to find a harmonious expression. This is not always easy, especially if the planets are from very different chords as in the Sun (fire) and Neptune (water) example. In this case, the contrasting nature of the planets by element as well as by aspect (5th Chord naturally quincunxes 12th Chord) indicates that this particular conjunction is challenging to blend into a harmonious expression.

Therefore, as a 1st Chord subtone, the conjunction identifies behavior that is an active part of an individual's self-expression, but it may not always be extremely obvious! Planets forming a conjunction can represent an individual's most direct form of asserting the self. If Mars is involved in a conjunction, the conjunction will be that much more significant because the self-focused, fiery theme of Mars naturally reinforces the hard-hitting impact shown by a conjunction.

A **second subtone** of the 1st Chord is the energy movement of the sign Aries known as **cardinal.** The key-word phrase for cardinal is the **spontaneous outpouring of energy.** There is one cardinal sign belonging to each element and Aries is the cardinal **fire** sign. The combustible outpouring of spontaneity and the tremendous release of energy that Aries indicates bring attention and focus to the self.

The initiating manner shown by the sign Aries inspires an individual to enter new experiences. This is an example of the archetypal theme of a major tone, Aries, corresponding to its cardinal subtone. The archetypal fiery theme of Aries (the manner in which immediate action can be embodied and initiated) is fanned even stronger by its subtone counterpart, cardinal energy movement. Cardinal energy represents the catalyst for a radiating outpouring of the self and is well expressed by the sign of Aries. When Aries is highly emphasized in an individual's horoscope, he is often greatly challenged to perform as a leader in new or unpredictable situations. He can, however, be so gratified by immediate action in working toward desired aims that he may feel no need to complete them.

The nature of the 1st house is yet a third example of the archetypal theme of a major tone supported by its subtone. The **angular subtone** of the 1st house corresponds to initiating experiences from one's self-concept. As stated earlier, there is one angular house belonging to each element, so the 1st house is the angular **fire** house. The key word for angular is **action,** and the angular subtone of the 1st house points to an individual likely to act upon his self-concept in a very physical and noticeable way. The issues of a planet located in an individual's 1st house serve as extra fuel which combines with the drives shown by the Ascendant to help project and color the individual's self-image (especially if the planet is located within 5° of the Ascendant). The angular subtone of the fiery 1st house indicates an individual acting upon a self-concept with the help of any themes mirrored by planets in the 1st house. The angular nature of the 1st house demonstrates what an individual is actively seeking to manifest in a visible way.

The remaining fire chords will further illustrate the unity of the astrological tones and subtones that characterize each chord. Just as the tones and subtones show variations on a chord theme, the three chords that belong to the fire element are variations of the fire-chord themes, expressing a self-focus or identification of the self through action.

CHAPTER THREE

FIFTH CHORD: SELF-EXPRESSIVE PROCREATION

> "Goodbye," said the fox. "And now here is my secret, a very simple secret: it is only with the heart that one can see rightly; what is essential is invisible to the eye."
>
> "What is essential is invisible to the eye," the Little Prince repeated, so that he would be sure to remember.
>
> *The Little Prince* by Antoine de Saint Exupery (page 87)

The 5th Chord is an expression of the fire element in the form of procreation. The planet (Sun), sign (Leo), and house (5th) tones of this chord symbolize an individual's need to define identity through creative action. The self-concept and assertion emphasis of the 1st Chord is given a further focus in the 5th Chord through the development of an ego or creative identity. There is an interesting distinction between letter one and letter five in that chord one simply wants be left alone to do what he or she pleases, chord five wants to do something bigger and to be noticed for it. Chord one is our instinctive identity. Chord five is our ego.

5TH CHORD: SELF-EXPRESSIVE PROCREATION					
Tone	Archetypal Themes	Functions	Positive Expressions	Negative Expressions	Potential Counseling Issues
Planet: Sun **Symbol** ☉	The directing of actions to define and express the Power of will and create the core identity of the self.	1. To establish a core identity and sense of direction.	1. A strong sense of purpose and creative identity through action.	1. A tendency to take excessive pride in self or be an exhibitionist.	**Key Phrase:** Defining The Self
Sign: Leo **Symbol** ♌	The manner through which creative action expresses and embodies a sense of self.	2. To establish a purpose for the self.	2. Self-confidence producing an ability to utilize the creative self in career and other dimensions of life.	2. A proclivity toward extravagance and excessive indulgence in pleasure.	**Games:** 1. Clown. 2. Compulsive Gambler. 3. Creator of All.
House: 5th	Attitudes related to one's creative expression of self and pleasurable activities.	3. To establish self-respect. 4. To develop a creative identity and sense of vitality. 5. To have an expressive love nature.	3. A strong sense of creative humor and pleasure. 4. A drive to be a leader. 5. An ability to care for children and others in a benevolent way.	3. An inclination toward dictatorial attitudes. 4. A tendency to gamble life away recklessly due to a misguided sense of self-confidence and purposeful action. 5. A tendency to react to situations childishly due to egocentric behavior.	4. Cute Child. 5. Dictator. 6. Exhibitionist. 7. Extravaganza. 8. Head in the Sand. 9. I Plead the Fifth. 10. I Rule by Divine Right. 11. Sexual Promiscuity. 12. Spoiled Child. 13. Stress-Aholic.

Figure 2: Fifth Chord
See the Note to Readers after Acknowledgments

The self-focus of the fire element is symbolized in this chord. Each tone reflects an individual's need to extend the self—the creative core self (Sun), manner of creative action (Leo), and procreative life circumstances (5th house).

The drives represented by these tones motivate an individual to define the self through the functions listed in the table for Chord 5. The positive expressions of each 5th Chord tone have their origins in the pride-and-pleasure principles that are typical of the 5th Chord synthesis of the tones and subtones. The negative expressions of each tone are related to an internal imbalance of these principles.

The Sun

It is very important to realize that the 5th Chord is the home of the Sun. Though the Sun is the closest star to the Earth, it is commonly referred to as a planet. The Sun defines and is the center of our solar system, with the other planets, including the Earth, revolving around it. The apparent movement of the Sun through a different part of the sky each month, coinciding with an individual's birthday, creates the Sun sign. Just as the Sun in the sky defines the very solar system in which we live and gives its light and heat to sustain life on the Earth, likewise the Sun in the horoscope and the particular sign in which it is placed denotes an individual's central life force and ability to energize and define a procreative self. Therefore, the Sun in the horoscope represents an individual's core identity and symbolizes a need to exhibit the power of will to embody a true sense of self. It is one's need to create a core identity which causes an individual to define the self in a particular way. This core identity is represented by the particular Sun sign that an individual is associated with at birth. Most astrological texts do not substantiate Sun sign descriptions with the depth required to see that a person is seeking to **expand** the core self through the Sun sign, rather than aimlessly listing a set of characteristics associated with a particular sign.

In astrology the Sun rules the heart of the human body, and it is also the heart of the horoscope. The sign coloring the Sun at an individual's birth shows the particular path or direction that an individual must recognize to manifest a true expression of self. It could be said that the Sun sign indicates the colorful manner through which an individual will make the choices to define and expand the self in an internal world, as well as in the external world. I would go so far as to say that everything else in the horoscope is secondary to the Sun, only in that the Ascendant, Moon and other planets and the signs, houses, and aspects point to the support system for the individual to get the most effective use of the potentials shown by the Sun. It is important for an individual to make use of the Sun sign capacity in order to properly energize one's psyche. Because the Sun sign indicates the major energy thrust for an individual, it is the greatest key to expressing a creative identity. Second in importance to the sign placement of the Sun is the house placement as it indicates circumstances that could best lead to fulfilling experiences on the most profound levels of self-satisfaction.

The Sun sign is the primary creative tool for the expression of one's core identity. It is the most encompassing astrological energy through which an individual can accomplish life goals, and it is the most sustaining force in one's creation of self as a whole entity.

Leo

The sign tone (Leo) of Chord 5 complements the planetary tone by coloring an individual's creative identity. Leo is a fire sign that offers enthusiasm, warmth, self-confidence and dramatic display. The archetypal theme of Leo, the manner through which creative action expresses and embodies a sense of self, encourages an individual to act out creative impulses. A planet or the Ascendant located in this sign indicates the individual is endowed with self-expressive flows of energy that can act out different forms of behavior with tremendous force. She can express any roles which require a strong, intense projection of the self.

The 5th Chord archetypal themes have a common origin. A quality that is central to Leo and each 5th Chord tone is willful strength. Traditional qualities, such as dramatic display of force, warmth and creative action reinforce this strength of will.

The positive expressions of Leo stem from a healthy sense of pride and a true sense of oneself within the creative process. It is an individual's natural extension of self through the will of Leo that roars with the ferociousness and power of the lion image traditionally associated with Leo. She forcefully seeks a true creative reflection of the self. A person who is in touch with Leo energy can dramatically embody roles that project warmth in personal interactions, as well as allow one to assume leadership positions without alienating others in authority. As a lion cares for its cubs, Leo energy can inspire an individual to care not only for the development and direction of offspring, but also to help and guide others from a place of genuine empathy.

The negative expressions of Leo operate through an individual's fascination with ego-oriented tendencies. When operating from this perspective, she wants to possess her creations and can become overidentified with the pride that results from procreative activities.

It is in these circumstances that an individual uses the ferociousness of the lion to impel others to relate to or accept her rather than compel with a true expression of genuine love and sincerity. Rather than caring for her cubs, the lion now wishes to own and rule them. Rather than helping and guiding others, the lion wishes to exercise authority, to show off power, and to exhibit a false sense of pride.

For instance, if an individual has Mars in Leo, the combination of the archetypal themes of these two tones could result in the directing of actions to assert the self with dramatic enthusiasm, confidence and strength. Due to the coloration of this planet's motifs by Leo, this individual could assert herself purposefully and creatively. On the other hand, this individual could express these Mars themes more negatively by taking excessive pride in self with an inclination toward dictatorial attitudes. Once again, it is important to note that a person can choose to use these planetary energies in many ways. This limitless power of choice is the keystone to a counseling-oriented astrology.

5th House

The third tone of this chord, the fiery 5th house, is best defined by its archetypal theme: one's attitudes related to creative expression of self and pleasurable activities such as recreation, sex, child-rearing and other things that involve the giving and receiving of love. It is an environment in which one can find fulfillment in the expression of love through different roles in life, whether it be channeled through romantic liaisons, sexual activity or relationships with children. The 5th house is also a key to an individual's capacity to give and receive love.

The positive manifestations of the 5th house include growth through the creative expressions and procreative activities. An individual can develop a healthy attitude toward love, sex and romantic expressions of 5th house themes, and enjoy learning and growth-promoting activities through sharing love with others. The drive for leisure and relaxation associated with this house in traditional astrology has a special meaning in modern astrology. Opportunities for the expression of love in 5th house activities can lead one to a sense of relaxation and peace within oneself, and help to experience the true humor, joy, love and meaning reflected in creative life circumstances.

The negative expressions of the 5th house often manifest when the individual simply cannot separate the true identity from thecircumstances through which she chooses to express. Rather than expressing through creations, she often becomes the expression of them. In other words, she tries too hard to be liked by others through an overdramatized display, such as promiscuous sexual behavior, or trying to show she is the best at whatever she does. In being out of touch with true self-expression, creative force erupts like a volcano in attempts to express love for self or others. The ability to relax is limited, as she is constantly in search of applause, like a smiling clown who is suffering underneath a mask to just be loved for her true and natural self.

If a person has Jupiter in the 5th house, for example, she may like to be generous to loved ones because it provides a feeling of self-importance in the expression of love. Due to the combination of the archetypal themes of Jupiter and the 5th house, this individual could enjoy acting out different roles such as the traveler, the student or the teacher, as a way to define and expand a sense of self. I have also noticed another interesting facet of the 5th house that relates to a person's basic expression. Even though career ambitions are usually associated with the 10th house, planets located in the 5th house often play an important role in a person's career choice because a career is a statement of what one takes seriously, and an individual often desires to make the career a creative extension of the self. Also, Chord 5 is strongly connected to where one wants to "shine," and many find opportunities for significance through careers.

Counseling Issues

The counseling issues characteristic of 5th Chord tones are representative of an individual's inability to successfully meet the challenge of the basic nature of this chord, **self-expressive procreation**. Since the synthesis of these three tones is a creation of self through action, my key word phrase for the counseling issues of the 5th Chord is **defining the self**. The planet, sign and house tones have this emphasis on self-definition inherent in their archetypal themes, which, once again, are:

1. **Sun**—the directing of actions to define and express the power of will and create the core identity of the self.
2. **Leo**—the manner through which creative action expresses and embodies a sense of self.
3. **5th house**—one's attitudes related to creative expression of self and pleasurable activities.

The counseling issues of this chord concern self-definition in relation to the pride principle. Each 5th Chord tone can be used by an individual to bring greater self-expression that strengthens self-definition.

In the struggle for self-definition, these games of negative behavior can lead one to overindulge in pride or can lead one to feel a lack of pride, both resulting in an unclear self-definition. The issues of excess pride or lack of pride in self, are strongly related to an individual's inability to nourish and love the self in a balanced way. Though each of the 5th Chord tones relates to an individual's need to actively express love, it is essential that a person make use of the particular Sun placement to express this love for the self. This is particularly true since the Sun is the single most dynamic tone within the horoscope and is the central energy which a person uses to create a core identity.

Without a clear sense of one's core identity, a person can experience a great deal of fear, and might compulsively seek a substitute for a core identity in life circumstances. Since the core identity is largely based on an individual's self-love, a substitute identity is a denial of this love for oneself. This individual is not properly developing the core self in the ways that are appropriate, especially related to the Sun sign and element, or through the circumstances associated with the house placement of that Sun. An individual in this situation often lives life by assuming roles that do not nourish a core identity and that starve the basic nature.

Games

A lack of pride in one's core identity sometimes causes an individual to fear powerlessness, and, therefore, she might reach outside of the self to demonstrate power in another way. She might become entrapped in what I call the **Dictator** game. The pride and love needed for the self is blocked by a fixed identity that leads to misusing her power of will by controlling others. This individual is seeking to substantiate this false identity at the expense of her real self.

The natural aspects formed by the 5th Chord to other chords indicate options to conquering this game. For instance, since the 5th Chord quincunxes the 12th Chord, hidden emotional issues could be a key. The 5th Chord opposes the airy 11th Chord which relates to satisfying personal goals and becoming an individual. A strong 5th Chord person playing the **Dictator** game may need to concentrate more on individual aims (11th Chord) and less on trying to control others (quincunx from 5th to 10th Chord). The squares formed to the 2nd and 8th Chords could point to issues around inner feelings of powerlessness.

There are cases where someone's core identity is so splintered that she cannot project the power of will outside of herself. A person can gradually become so locked inside that she becomes entrapped by the Head in the Sand game. A person exhibiting this extreme lack of pride often isolates from others trying to hide any vulnerability and low self-esteem. The 2nd Chord is usually involved with this game as the 2nd Chord deals with valuing the self.

This individual needs to learn the art of thinking positively, which comes naturally if the fire is balanced. This person is sometimes quite blocked emotionally and creatively. Tapping into one's emotional nature is important and taking a creative risk once in a while helps to build personal power.

Another related counseling issue that can appear when an individual lacks pride in the core self is an egocentric compulsion to see that everything in the world bears her own image. This is what I call the **Creator of All** game. To feel secure in her identity, she wants to see everything that means something to her, whether it is significant others or material accomplishments, as an extension of herself. This tremendous external orientation causes a great deal of fear for the individual. By starving her basic nature, this person is depending upon externals for satisfaction.

This individual can be very driven to produce external expression to prove she is lovable and successful. She would do herself a favor by including the messages of the 2nd Chord into her repertoire. The 2nd Chord's emphasis upon peace and love as well as enjoying life's simple pleasures helps balance this individual's compulsive drive to feel comfortable only when in control. The opposition to Chord 11 also points out that an overdevelopment of one's need to be significant—Chord 5—can be assisted by focusing on the essential equality of all people through Chord 11.

A lack of pride can also result in an individual's being trapped in the **Exhibitionist** game. This individual is so starved for a true center that she hungrily seeks to exhibit herself through all sorts of behaviors to attract attention. The individual is trying to prove that she is a healthy, sustaining individual, but in reality is only seeking reassurance for an undernourished, core self.

A self-honesty is called for to begin the healing process. Strong 5th Chord types often possess great creative skills. They love to be directly involved in the drama of life. It is when the person acts for show only that she gets into problems. A genuine emotional expression will release even more energy to be happy in love-filled relationships and to fulfill goals. The desire for attention and applause is a natural part of life—Chord 5. How we act to gain that attention and admiration will garner either rewarding or frustrating results. The horoscope shows the issues. We choose the details of expression.

The other two 5th Chord tones can embody the games previously mentioned and may also have other related games concerning the issue of lack of pride. The sign tone Leo, rather than being expressed with warmth and self-love, can be expressed by an individual in a distorted and self-destructive manner. Activities and circumstances associated with an individual's 5th house could become filled with egocentric tendencies, rather than being expressed by an individual in ways that are love- and growth-promoting.

Leo and the 5th house can point to an individual displaying a false humor that I call the **Clown** game. This individual uses humor to portray to others that she is alive and well and does not need anything. This is not the humor that naturally comes from a healthy sense of loving the self, but results from a tremendous denial of self-love.

The **Clown** is often a person trying too hard to please others in order to be loved. It is important for this person to become more concerned with an inward expression rather than trying to "win" at this game with a false, outward behavior. Admiration based on the false perceptions of others inevitably tastes sour. We all want to be loved for ourselves.

The **Cute Child** game can also manifest through Leo or the 5th house. This individual hopes to draw others to herself by adopting a childlike demeanor to appear adorable in order to be liked. The individual does not believe in her own natural ability to relate to others, so she adopts this substitute role as either the helpless or cute child.

This person will sooner or later realize the limitations of this game. Overindulgence in worn-out or childish roles stunts her growth. The individual must learn to accept her true identity and stop projecting false images. One key is tapping into her water element in order to face blocked emotions. The natural square to Chord 8 can indicate the need to face inner, psychological depths, to probe her own psyche, separating false images from true ones, transforming facades into reality.

An individual can also exhibit the **Compulsive Gambler** game when locked into behavior that detracts from loving oneself. This game is another reflection of a person starving the basic nature by seeking importance and attention through "making it big." However, the individual is usually only gambling herself away and abandoning the self to a form of self-hating behavior. Some people do allow the risk-taking impulses of the 5th Chord to get out of control.

The 5th Chord naturally trines the fiery 1st and 9th Chords. I feel it is particularly true that fire trines, if negatively manifested, can point to a person who disregards universal laws. Such people may mistakenly think that their way of doing things has no limitation. Instead of the faith in life which fire can represent, the result is an outward show. These individuals may need to understand their earth energies to balance and stabilize reckless fire energies. Some people playing this game need to learn forgiveness of self and others, symbolized by water (natural square to 8th Chord and natural quincunx to 12th Chord).

The 5th Chord, as stated earlier, also relates to counseling issues that stem from an excess of pride in oneself. An individual can exhibit an exaggerated sense of self-importance if misusing the power that is inherent in the 5th Chord tones. A showing-off type of behavior to get attention, or an egocentric display, is a typical misuse of this power that can lead one away from a clear self-definition.

The games mentioned earlier—the **Dictator,** the **Creator of All,** and the **Exhibitionist,** can certainly manifest due to excessive pride, as well as lack of pride. The only difference is that excessive pride is not from feelings of powerlessness, but from an addiction to power that comes from an exaggerated belief in one's self-importance. However, each of these games still involves self-hate and deep insecurities. The individual feels driven to prove over and over again that she is okay by convincing others that she is great. It is an exhausting game!

When a 5th Chord tone manifests through an individual with tremendous force, she can fall prey to the **I Plead the 5th** game, where she does not wish to explain any actions to others. She believes so much in her own power that others are supposed to follow her authority in an unquestioning manner. This is often found in combination with another 5th Chord game, **I Rule by Divine Right,** where an individual is too attached to pride and self-importance to explain any offensive actions to others.

These games are related to the fixity of the 5th Chord. Fixity symbolizes doing things on one's own terms. The individual will not change until she decides to do so. Power drives can be the downfall of the 5th Chord—when they are a false show of power to hide an insecurity. Fire can manifest as a person's inability to show vulnerability. In these games, the individual closes off any sensitivity to the needs of others and holds onto stubborn, old behavior patterns. The individual may need to open up to new ways of relating to others. She may need to surrender some of the fire element's drive to always be "right" or the center of attention. The king or queen role expressed by the individual in either of these games is an outward show of power that may only be covering emotional insecurity. A more authentic self-expression is needed.

An individual can surround herself with grandiose material things to hide a weak self-definition in what I call the **Extravaganza** game. This individual is trying to make others believe that she is happy and living a self "fulfilled existence, but in reality she is not having a grand experience in defining herself.

This game can be indicative of a person's lack of self-worth and sometimes is a game adopted by those who receive little support for their goals in life. The **Extravaganza** individual is trying to win acceptance much like the **Exhibitionist.** The individual must learn to explore an extravagant inner world before the outer world will reflect a true sense of pleasure and happiness. The person may need to become more self-accepting.

The **Exhibitionist** game is more likely to become a **Sexual Promiscuity** game when an individual is using the sign tone Leo, or the 5th house tone, in an egocentric way to show off a sexual image. When this sexual promiscuity reaches compulsive proportions, the individual is letting use of power lead away from the true self by substituting sexual appeal for an ill-defined self. The fire desire for excitement may be channeled solely into the sexual arena.

The 5th Chord can denote very creative and passionate energy. However, it does require sensitivity and discipline to get fruitful results. It is not always easy for the self-centered and impulsive fire element to accept discipline or limits. The individual needs to find healthy, creative outlets for dynamic fire energy to express a sense of power—whether physically or psychologically.

An ego-centered behavior similar to the **Cute Child** game associated earlier with lack of pride can also manifest in connection with an excessive amount of pride, I call this 5th Chord issue the **Spoiled Child** game. This individual ignores the needs of others, and willfully and forcefully seeks to get her own way at all costs.

The individual needs to understand her own water or emotional nature. Manipulation of others is ultimately self-destructive as she stops herself from developing her own strengths and abilities by channeling energy into getting other people to do things for her. Once she recognizes the value of building personal competence, she can give up manipulation in favor of encouraging her own talents and abilities.

Once again, the **Compulsive Gambler** game and other compulsive, risk-taking forms of behavior can result from an overindulgence in the pleasure principle, as well as from pride issues. An individual simply gets lost in the thrill of a compulsive risk situation and loses perspective of the self.

The fire trine nature of this element can manifest as recklessness. It is as though the inward harmony of the fire element strengthens the individual's compulsive drive to defy universal laws. She feels she cannot lose when taking dangerous risks. She may, in fact, be losing an identity or creative talents by abandoning the inner nature with this insatiable thirst for more stimulation and excitement.

The **Stress-Aholic** game can also manifest for an individual who denies the luxury of relaxation through recreation connected with the pleasure principle. (The 2nd Chord is also connected with the pleasure principle, as we will see in the next chapter.) Since the Sun and Leo are associated with the heart and blood, symptoms such as high blood pressure, high or low blood sugar and heart problems can result for those who are stress-aholics. People who misuse 5th house themes can also suffer tremendous stress problems by denying the need for relaxation through recreation. Type A personalities overdo the ambition of Chord 5 (and Chord 1) and overdo the impatience of fire.

The 5th Chord quincunx to the 10th Chord cautions that too much work and excessive responsibilities become a problem. The will to power of the 5th Chord must be balanced with the practicality and patience of Chord 10. The quincunx to the 12th Chord shows that some restful moments may help balance the hecttic pace of modern life. Some meditative or reflective time is relaxing. The square to the 2nd Chord reminds us that laid-back pleasures are just as important as stimulating ones, while the square to Chord 8 emphasizes the importance of self-control within our seeking of fiery excitement. The 2nd and 8th Chords also indicate the need to find a balance in life's pace between extremes, especially where physical appetites and emotional intensity are concerned.

The **Sexual Promiscuity** game mentioned earlier in connection with pride issues can also be found in relation to the pleasure principle. The issue here is on sex for pleasure, which is a 5th house emphasis in traditional astrology books. However, rather than sex for a sense of pleasure, this is more exhibitionist in nature. The individual's relationships often lack depth and definition due to such an extreme emphasis on the sexual content and/or sexual performance within the relationship.

The extravagance and lavishness referred to earlier as the **Extravaganza** game can also occur in relation to the pleasure principle. Problems associated with this game encompass more than merely having fun through recreation and pleasurable activities. This game describes a compulsive drive to substitute an external show of wealth for a rich, true inner expression.

Summary of Issues with 5th Chord Games

The 5th Chord games are an extension of the pride principle. They are the result of an extreme excess of pride in one's self-expression or too little pride in oneself. A person can use the energy shown in the 5th Chord for warmth and sharing love with others. There is a tremendous amount of creative potential in this chord, and a natural passion for life.

It is only when a person forgets that the creative identity is separate from one's creations that she goes beyond the boundaries of 5th Chord balance. The end result is no longer based on a healthy sense of love or an inner creative identity. On the contrary, children, lovers and creations are then expressions of the 5th Chord games.

Subtones

The tones and subtones of the 5th Chord represent an expression of the self through creative action. The three subtones help secure, maintain, and expand the basic thrust of self-expression. The subtones are the planetary aspect known as the **trine,** the energy focus of Leo known as **fixed,** and the house classification known as **succedent.**

The **trine** as a 5th Chord **subtone** has a related archetypal theme. The forms of behavior represented by a trine aspect relate to the archetypal theme of the Sun in encouraging expression of the creative identity. The themes of planets involved in a trine combine to manifest with a flowing ease. The individual can express the self in a relaxing or pleasurable manner. The trine sometimes symbolizes an individual's vision of a creative or expansive idea that is a combination of the planetary motifs involved. Due to the soft nature of the trine, it can be a pleasing and harmonious extension of the self which does not always manifest itself as action.

However, since the trine aspect indicates an inner agreement, the planetary themes can reinforce each other quite forcefully, especially fire trines! There is often an excess of action symbolized by the trine as it is an aspect encouraging self-expression. It becomes a negative expression mainly when a person has little regard for the opinions and rights of others. Charles Manson is a classic example as he has Pluto in Cancer trining his Venus and Sun in Scorpio. He used his charismatic image to manipulate his followers and to control his cult. Manson felt that he had the right to do anything—even murder.

The trine reinforces the active fire nature of the 5th Chord. It is consistent with the optimism that is inherent in the enthusiastic nature of the fire chords because of the emotional electricity generated by such visions and expansiveness.

Let us go back to the example of Sun conjunct Neptune, where the individual felt an immediate and self-oriented need to act upon aesthetic impulses. With the Sun trine Neptune, there is a similar attunement toward aesthetics, but instead of this aesthetic affinity materializing in the form of direct participation, the individual may only show an appreciation or enjoyment of aesthetic activities. The trine sometimes suggests an individual will follow the path of least resistance (especially when the planets, houses and signs involved represent passive principles). Activation of a potential inspiration may be shown when the planets forming a trine aspect have "harder" aspects from other planets. It is interesting to note that when the Sun is involved in a trine, the natural reinforcing themes of the Sun and the trine can represent an intense and natural expression of the planetary motifs in question. On the other hand, the expanding nature shown by the trine aspect can diffuse and relax the intensely focused energies which the planets represent, leading to a comfortable, complacent, but not very productive use of these energies. It very much depends on the planets involved in the trine and the conscious awareness of the individual. Also, it is important to consider whether or not the aspect is a central theme in the chart.

The maintaining feature of Leo is further defined by its **subtone** known as **fixed.** There is one fixed sign belonging to each element, and the key word phrase for fixed is **focused energy.** Since Leo is the fixed fire sign, and the overriding focus of the fire element is the self, the fixed energy of Leo is very focused on solidifying and stabilizing the self.

Procreative action, such as childbearing, is a reflection on the self that helps an individual maintain her identity. It enables one to take pride in being an active part in the creative process and emphasizes one's self-importance. The emphasis on the maintenance of the self, inspiring an individual to establish and secure her identity through creative action, is an example in Chord 5 of the archetypal theme of Leo corresponding to its fixed subtone.

A **third subtone** of the 5th Chord is the energy field of the 5th house known as **succedent.** There is one succedent house associated with each element. The key word phrase for succedent is **securing.** The nature of the 5th house, to secure one's identity through a creative expression of the self, is supported by the succedent subtone of the house. If a planet is located in the 5th house, an individual is likely to use that planetary energy to help secure her identity. When a person performs a creative action and is able to see the self reflected in the creation, it enlarges one's definition of who she is and thus helps to secure the identity.

Although each chord has a major significance of its own, the 5th Chord is especially important, as it contains the central force of each horoscope, the planetary energy of the Sun. It is the search for a core identity, a self-definition, and the individual's striving to create a meaningful and purposeful existence that makes the 5th Chord the key to **self-expressive procreation.**

CHAPTER FOUR

NINTH CHORD: SELF-EXPRESSIVE DISCOVERY

> Feeling important makes one heavy, clumsy, and vain. To be a man of knowledge one needs to be light and fluid.
>
> *A Separate Reality by Carlos Castaneda* (pages 5-6)

The 9th Chord is an expression of the fire element in the form of discovering the self. The planet (Jupiter), sign (Sagittarius) and house (9th) tones of this chord symbolize an individual's need to discover identity through expansive action based on visions of ideal truths and faith. Chord nine includes Jupiter, Sagittarius and the 9th house of the chart, the goal here is nothing less than the truth with a capital "T."

Both the tones and subtones of the 9th Chord symbolize an individual's self-discovery through action. The three subtones support the tone themes of self-discovery through excitable, expansive and curious drives for learning. The three subtones are: the planetary aspect known as the trine, the energy focus of Sagittarius known as mutable, and the house classification known as cadent.

The themes shown by these tones motivate an individual to understand the self through the functions listed in the table for Chord 9. The positive expressions of each 9th Chord tone have their origin in the expansion principle that is typified by the 9th Chord tones and subtones. The negative expressions of each tone are related to either a misuse or denial of the expansion principle.

Astrology, Psychology, and Transformation

9TH CHORD: SELF-EXPRESSIVE DISCOVERY

Tone	Archetypal Themes	Functions	Positive Expressions	Negative Expressions	Potential Counseling Issues
Planet: Jupiter Symbol ♃	The directing of actions for the inspiration to expand and grow through the processes of eclectic learning	1. To experience growth and expansion through new experiences.	1. A drive to share knowledge and personal philosophy through counseling, teaching and writing.	1. A tendency to be too rigid in one's opinions and personal perspective. 2. The potential to act upon blind faith.	**Key Phrase:** Understanding The Self
Sign: Sagittarius Symbol ✗	The manner through which traveling on the mental and physical planes can be integrated into the process of adventurous self-discovery.	2. To penetrate and communicate the realm of abstract thought.	2. Self-confidence due to a sense of optimism and faith in life.	3. Excessive confidence. 4. A proclivity for jumping to conclusions.	**Games:** 1. All Roads Lead to Rome, Don't They? 2. Arrogant Individualist. 3. Do Tomorrow What I Can Do Today.
House: 9th	One's attitudes related to broadening life's perspective and fostering long-range growth.	3. To learn and teach others.	3. A broad perspective and eclectic reasoning power.	5. A tendency to expand in too many directions, causing one to be undependable and to neglect commitments.	4. Everything Is Okay. 5. Everything Will Get Better. 6. Fixation on Limitation. 7. Grass Is Greener.
		4. To think and act with faith and inspiration.	4. Wisdom based on assimilated knowledge and the ability to use this knowledge to envision the future.	6. An exaggerated sense of self-importance.	8. Here Come's the Judge. 9. I Can't Possibly Lose
		5. To act directly—honestly.	5. The ability to inspire others with the power of positive thought.	7. Laziness due to expecting things to come too easily.	10. My Way Is the Only Way. 11. Not Now, Not Now.
		6. To travel on the mental and physical levels.	6. Humor as a function of the expansive spirit.		12. Not Seeing the Trees for the Forest. 13. Proselytizer.
		7. To create the challenge of adventure.	7. Generosity and benevolence.		14. Rolling Stone. 15. Serve Me on a Silver Platter.
			8. Gregariousness.		

Figure 3: Ninth Chord
See the Note to Readers after Acknowledgments

Jupiter

The planetary tone of the 9th Chord, Jupiter, represents an individual's capacity to embrace growth through exposure to different experiences such as travel, abstract thinking, philosophy and other forms of expansive experiences. A person's Jupiter is indicative of an ability to discover oneself and broaden understanding through expansive actions.

Jupiter is the biggest planet in the sky and weighs more than twice as much as all the other planets put together, even though Jupiter spins on its axis faster than any other planet. Jupiter's astronomical description matches its astrological meanings as it is an expansive and potentially exciting symbol in the horoscope. Jupiter's archetypal theme is the directing of actions for the inspiration to expand and grow through the process of eclectic learning. A person can enlarge perspective through activities that promote growth and through such roles as the traveler, student, teacher, philosopher or counselor.

An individual's positive expressions of Jupiter motifs stem from the expansion principle that can manifest as optimism and faith. The material wealth that Jupiter sometimes indicates is a reflection of an individual's enthusiasm, inner faith and a positive mental outlook that attracts good luck. An individual who is experiencing the winds of Jupiter blowing and beckoning toward learning and growth in consciousness can naturally share knowledge through counseling and teaching, inspiring others with the strength of his convictions. There is a broad perspective and wisdom inherent in Jupiter's symbolism that encourages an individual to seek a greater knowledge.

The negative expression of Jupiter themes is mainly related to the expansion principle manifesting in the forms of overconfidence and exaggeration. There may be a blind faith that life situations will become something greater and change for the best, though a more objective common sense would indicate otherwise. An individual could also have a tendency to expand into too many directions, spreading too thin and neglecting commitments. There is a laziness that can be shown by Jupiter, as one may overindulge and expect life to provide without any personal effort. Perhaps the most noticeable negative quality that Jupiter could point to is a narrow or dogmatic life philosophy, as this is a strong antithesis of Jupiterian themes.

Sagittarius

The 9th Chord sign tone, Sagittarius, captures the essence of the fire element's love of adventure, self-confidence, opinionatedness, restlessness and independence. Traveling on the mental and physical planes is the trademark of this sign, as well as the seeking and conveying of truths or principles. The expansion instincts of an individual are emphasized by the coloring of Sagittarius.

The heartfelt quest for knowledge, one positive Sagittarian expression, lights a restless fire within an individual to find principles, knowledge or truth. It often leads one to develop a broad perspective and eclectic reasoning power from which to share a personal philosophy through teaching or writing. The self-confidence and faith denoted by this sign can also be inspirational to others and stimulate them to develop a more positive attitude toward their own lives.

As with Jupiter, the negative expressions of Sagittarian motifs include excessive self-confidence and blind faith without sound reality testing. Also, a laziness in attitude may be shown by Sagittarius as a dominating theme in the horoscope. One can expect a life of comfort without putting forth any effort. There is sometimes a fickleness that leads an individual to adopt a "grass is greener" theory when faced with difficult life circumstances. Some of these negative expressions will be discussed in more detail in the counseling issues.

Sagittarius can also point to an individual with a tremendous propensity toward an independent arrogance coupled with a highly opinionated and insensitive nature that can offend others. A rigidity in one's opinions can become a self-righteous form of behavior, a possibility with Sagittarius as well as Jupiter.

9th House

The house tone of Chord 9, the 9th house, encompasses the expansion principle in the form of circumstances that foster long-range growth, which is the archetypal theme of the 9th house. The planetary tone, Jupiter, personifies actively through an individual, as the student, traveler, philosopher or as a risk-taking individual. The sign tone, Sagittarius, can indicate an individual who clothes himself in such roles. The 9th house offers broad types of stimulating circumstances and learning experiences that encourage an individual to expand knowledge and personal philosophy. The common theme of Jupiter, Sagittarius and the 9th house is the striving for expansive experiences.

Traditional astrology chiefly associates the 9th house with long journeys, philosophy and higher education. Even though the roots of traditional astrology are embedded within a focus on predictive events, they form the basis for a new perspective. Rather than using the astrological symbols to focus on events, the chords focus on the actual psychological processes related to the traditional meanings of the symbols. This more modern perspective describes 9th house circumstances as those which induce an individual to creatively envision new horizons. It is this expansive vision and urge for the discovery of one's identity through 9th house circumstances that gives birth to long journeys, principles, faith in self, counseling and teaching skills, and the development of a philosophy and system of beliefs.

The positive expressions of the 9th house include educating oneself, whether it be through a formal or a more unorthodox type of education to take responsibility for one's direction in life. The faith and courage shown by the fire element of the

9th house encourage an individual to enjoy creating a sense of freedom. First house planets are part of an individual's self-image and tools for projection. Fifth house planets help support or maintain one's creative expression and urge for self-definition. Ninth house planets urge one to master long-range perceptions and pursue growth by enlarging philosophy through eclectic learning, traveling, faith in self and taking risks that accentuate the developing of an expansive life perspective.

An individual's negative expressions of this tone can result from a misuse of 9th house freedom, by developing an independent nature filled with arrogance that neglects commitments to life situations and is insensitive to the needs of others. An individual's drive to develop a personal 9th house philosophy through a dedication to finding an ultimate truth can turn into a ruthlessly opinionated and self-righteous behavior that brings explosive and unstable life circumstances. The expanding principle becomes confined to a narrow, fixed belief system. Also, a disorientation can result from expanding into too many directions or commitments. The 9th house points to the future, emphasizing one's need to make responsible future plans and to develop a sound personal philosophy and decision-making process in the present.

Counseling Issues

The counseling issues related to the 9th Chord tones are indicative of an individual's struggle with the spirit of this chord, **self-expressive discovery.** My key word phrase for these counseling issues, **understanding the self,** is from the synthesis of the tones—Jupiter, Sagittarius and 9th house. The 9th Chord tones represent a particular energizing quality that encourages an individual to seek outlets which foster growth through expanding the capacity for self-understanding. The archetypal themes are:

1. **Jupiter**—the directing of actions for the inspiration to expand and grow through the processes of eclectic learning.
2. **Sagittarius**—the manner through which traveling on the mental and physical planes can be integrated into the process of adventurous self-discovery.
3. **9th house**—one's attitudes related to broadening life's perspective and fostering long-range growth.

The counseling issues of this chord concern self-understanding in relation to the expansion principle. Each 9th Chord tone can indicate greater understanding and enrichment through growth-promoting experiences and a broadening of one's life perspective. Counseling issues that relate to understanding the self arise, not just by manifesting a negative expression of a 9th Chord tone, but more so by adopting a pattern of behavior that leads one to overinflate or indulge in self-discoveries. Underexpansive behavior patterns that deny the fulfillment of self-understanding are also possible.

Games

The major counseling issues for an individual related to over-expansion include the **All Roads Lead to Rome, Don't They?** game. This is the scattering of energies into many different directions that causes one to feel disoriented. Each 9th Chord tone, whether it be Jupiter, Sagittarius or the 9th house, can denote a compulsive habit of excessive or overindulgent behavior. The 9th Chord tones require much self-discipline as they can indicate wasteful actions under the guise of productive behavior.

Someone involved in this game usually needs to focus his expansive energy. He would be wise to develop the earth element which teaches how to stabilize a sense of direction. The individual may be running away from responsibility. A balanced sense of growth occurs by combining adventurous energy with commitments and discipline. The square from Chord 9 to Chord

6 shows the need for both expansion (Chord 9) and discipline (Chord 6) in reaping optimum results.

Another counseling issue for a strong 9th Chord individual could be the **Serve Me on a Silver Platter** game. This individual's understanding is that the good things of life will come without any effort, and this is the laziness that is inherent in the expansion principle. The fire element calls on a person to take initiative in life experiences. This can be a person who has never been that successful in reaching goals. He needs to better define his life rather than try to manipulate others to get his own way. The self-centered indulgence of Chord 9, if overdone, can be balanced by compassion for others (Chord 12) and a willingness to work hard and serve humbly (Chord 6).

The adventurousness and tremendous impulsiveness of the fiery 9th Chord can also show an individual missing many details, as the **Not Seeing the Trees for the Forest** game can demonstrate. The stimulation caused by the 9th Chord expansion principle can sometimes cause an individual to envision an end product or result so quickly that he may miss certain key steps in the development of a process or action. The excitement produced by such rapid motion often produces an equally intense impatience that causes the individual to resist seeing what was missed.

The natural square formed to the 6th Chord indicates that attention to detail is easily overlooked, especially if one is forcefully projecting opinions or philosophy. Perhaps incorporating more sensitivity and even compassion (12th Chord is a natural square) into one's self-expression will bring the individual into a more eclectic life approach. The air element (opposition to Chord 3) can also help one to think more objectively.

Another 9th Chord counseling issue is the game called **Do Tomorrow What I Can Do Today.** This is an interesting combination of two different aspects of the expansion principle: (1) laziness or not wanting to be bothered by demands regarded as inconvenient or unimportant; (2) a desire not to be limited by expectations or responsibilities because this could involve not feeling free to take advantage of new and expansive opportunities as they might come along. Both aspects can contribute to an overriding desire in a person to procrastinate in fulfilling obligations, leading to a reputation for being too freewheeling and irresponsible.

The earth element is often vital for strong fire-type people to develop. Earth is important here because it represents the commitment to the present that is often lacking with fire. Also, the water element indicates a sensitivity to the needs of others. Other people's demands can be viewed as an opportunity to share one's energy rather than as an imposition on one's time. Chord 9 squares the committed earth of Chord 6 and the sensitive, intuitive water of Chord 12. Chord 9 quincunxes the patient, dedicated earth of Chord 2 and the nurturing water of Chord 4.

These two attributes of the expansion principle (laziness and a desire to escape limitations) can also produce another game, known as **Not Now, Not Now**. This is a very specific form of procrastination that can surface as an avoidance of conflict with others. Though the 9th Chord contains tones that symbolize a lot of positive force, there can be tendencies within that force that lead an individual away from dealing directly with dissension. There is the sense that any positive force should be directed toward other expansion opportunities and that the current discord will dissolve with little effort expended by the individual. This is often a rationalization for blatant escapism and for a distaste for the prospect of being limited by the considerations of others.

The individual in this situation sometimes needs to have the faith that confronting unpleasant situations directly will be in his best interest. He is usually exhibiting too much faith in happy endings that "just happen"and not enough faith in an ability to make those happy endings come to pass. He usually will encounter the same type of situations repeatedly until he changes certain behaviors. The natural square formed by the 9th

Chord to the 12th Chord indicates that transcending escapist behavior can promote spiritual growth for the individual. The square to Chord 6 shows the importance of being practical. Quincunxes to Chords 2 and 4 show the importance of a solid, realistic, material base (Chord 2) as well as a secure, psychological foundation (Chord 4).

The overexpansion principle is also evident in another form of behavior—the denial of limitations. The positive thinking and idealism shown by Jupiter, Sagittarius and the 9th house, with an attraction for abstract principles, often causes an individual to negate sensible reality testing. It is as though an individual will deny the truth or reality of present situations by rationalizing it with positive thoughts about the future. I call this the Everything Will Get Better game. It is often typical of someone staying in committed relationships (or other situations) long beyond the point of being a good, healthy experience. Strong 9th Chord individuals can exhibit an enduring faith when many others would have long since given up hope. It can be that individuals with a strong 9th Chord emphasis in their charts have an undying belief in themselves or others. It is when a person fails to acknowledge reason (air) and the limits of common sense (earth) and feelings (water) that he often gets into trouble.

In the **Everything Is Okay** game, feelings of pain or discomfort are ignored. This is another escape-oriented game. It is easy for a 9th Chord person to hide negative experiences under a false positivism. I do not want to belittle the capacity of those individuals who can express 9th Chord energy in the form of rising above limiting circumstances, or who can use creative thinking to help themselves or others. It is the individual who cannot face reality that gets lost in this game.

The other side of the coin can be a problem as well if the expansive tendencies of 9th Chord drives make it difficult to establish committed relationships or situations. **The Grass Is Greener** game is emphasized here as the individual believes there is always a better situation waiting. This is often rationalization for not working hard enough to develop present circumstances. It can also result in the avoidance of conflict or unpleasant circumstances, and is, in reality, an avoidance of commitments because of the fear of being limited by the present.

The key to winning this 9th Chord game is finding the green in present circumstances. When a person does take the risk of following through on commitments, 9th Chord energy can take him into great creative depths. A person with heavy emphasis on this chord will always be looking into new visionary horizons. However, with feet planted on the soil of the present, one's visions gain power and become part of one's reality. Without stability, dreams are evaporating illusions.

An offshoot of **The Grass Is Greener** game is the **Rolling Stone** game. This is the gypsy instinct of the 9th Chord, full steam ahead. The **Rolling Stone** individual is a restless soul who never remains in one locale for a very long time. He may be a very intelligent and creative individual but fears being tied down to any form of commitment. He is mistrustful of the present, forgetful of the past and excited by the future. Later in life he often wishes he had been more settled as he grows weary of constant traveling from one home to another with no true home of his own.

The 9th Chord naturally quincunxes the 4th Chord which indicates that a perspective of one's roots can be out of balance here. It is important that the person tap into his more reflective water and stabilizing earth energy (quincunx to 2nd Chord and square to 6th Chord). There seems to be some of the gypsy in many strong 9th Chord individuals. However, facing one's past and present helps provide even more adventures in one's future.

If an individual is not satisfying the need to discover the self, the overexpansion principle of the 9th Chord can throw self-understanding off balance in the form of taking compulsive risks. In traditional astrology, gambling has often been associated with either Sagittarius or Jupiter in the horoscope, mainly due to the fact that each has been known as funloving and adventurous symbols (also, see the 5th Chord). A modern perspective realizes that Sagittarius, Jupiter and the 9th house represent adventurousness, and definitely funlovingness. But it is from an innate drive for self-expressive discovery that an individual will take risks. Compulsive gambling and other forms of risk-taking that are self-destructive forms of behavior are a substitute for the real understanding that an individual is seeking. An individual's drive for these substitute expressions of self-discovery reaches epic proportions when he forgets the limits and falls into the **I Can't Possibly Lose** game. A compulsive gambler will sacrifice family, health and future happiness to satisfy this addiction, and often loses awareness of personal limits.

The person may need to reexamine his value systems. Also, he may be indulging in compulsive risk-taking to hide from emotional confusion (square to 12th Chord and quincunx to 4th Chord). The fire element is not exactly the most reflective of elements but does indicate a person capable of changing his life direction. Sometimes it really takes a new faith in oneself and in a Higher Power to bring the needed changes (square to 12th Chord).

The expansion principle can also inflate an individual's ego to the point of insensitivity to the needs of others. This is what I call the **Arrogant Individualist** game. This is an individual who demands that everyone agree with his own expansive lifestyle and principles. This person often is not really a true individual and able to stand alone. He fears vulnerability and hides behind an arrogant self-centered nature. He may demand that others care for him, even when he is unwilling to care for the needs of others.

The self-centeredness of fire is too dominant here. The opposite 3rd Chord points to the need for listening to the ideas and needs of others. The individual is sometimes surprised to learn that his own opinions and sense of importance do not need to be forced upon others. However, it is vital that he truly allow for two-way communications. Also, the water element can help one balance dependency needs.

If either Sagittarius, Jupiter or the 9th house are highlighted in an individual's horoscope, the heart of many 9th Chord counseling issues could be the underexpansion principle in the form of a lack of faith or self-confidence. This can produce a stagnation in one's life and result in what I call the **Fixation on Limitation** game. When experiencing stagnation, an individual feels poisoned by life. In a strong 9th Chord type of person, such as Sun, Moon, Jupiter, or Ascendant in Sagittarius and/or many planets in the 9th house, feeling stymied can disorient the mental chemistry because it is often a fascination with future life developments that turns him on.

This person may fear taking risks. Sometimes he needs to get in touch with the flow of positive energy. His mind has become negatively programmed. It is important for a person in this game to begin reprogramming his mind with thoughts and experiences that lift him out of negativity. It can be that simply initiating some energy to break any stagnation is the first step in the process. Also, the individual may be too much of a perfectionist, finding it difficult to live up to his own expectations (square to flaw-finding Chord 6 and opposite idealistic Chord 12).

Another 9th Chord poison related to the underexpansion principle is dogmatism. This is what I call the **My Way Is the Only Way** game. This is an individual with a highly opinionated nature that must be proven right at all times. This is substantiated by a self-righteous indignation when the individual's opinions are confronted by others.

He needs to be more sensitive to the needs of others (shown by the square to Chord 12 and the quincunx to Chord 4). It is important for this person to not always feel he has to be in control of situations.

A 9th Chord game closely related to the **My Way Is the Only Way** game is the **Proselytizer.** This individual feels compelled to convert others to his way of thinking. He often alienates others with a "I am holier than thou" attitude. He may be so zealously involved in a cause, group or personal belief that he has a very limited awareness of the rights of others to think for themselves.

I remember many years ago, while traveling through California, being approached by a very zealous "true believer" of a certain religion. After listening to her explanation of why I needed to accept her doctrines, I tactfully told her I was not seeking to change my own spiritual beliefs. She angrily told me that I was surely going to Hell and walked away. She clearly had no interest in my point of view! The **Proselytizer** needs to adopt some 12th Chord compassion and universal perspective. The "high" he is experiencing from his own beliefs and causes needs a broader perspective which will respect the beliefs of others.

The wisdom of 9th Chord energy can be used to counsel others and to make impartial and fair judgments. In another 9th Chord game **Here Comes the Judge!**, a person is extremely judgmental of others. People are guilty until proven innocent and must live up to the value system of the "judge." The solution to this game is similar to some of the other 9th Chord games. The individual must learn to be more open to the value systems of others. People seem to respond more to the encouragement and inspiration themes expressed by the 9th Chord than to coldhearted judgments.

Summary of Issues with 9th Chord Games

The 9th Chord games are a product of principles related to expansion and escape from confining responsibilities. Faith, learning experiences, communicating openly and eclectic adventures are possible forms of 9th Chord energy. The tremendous faith in life and resilient strength of 9th Chord individuals to bounce back from adverse circumstances should never be underestimated. It is only when a person allows adventurous and expansive instincts to always steal center stage, or when he blocks confidence and growth potentials, that he acts out the drama of the 9th Chord games.

Subtones

The **trine** as a **subtone** of the 9th Chord planetary tone supports the expansive and optimistic nature of Jupiter, much in the same way that it related to the expansive, pleasure-seeking nature of the Sun. The trine further illustrates Jupiter's expansive and visionary qualities. As stated earlier, the planets forming a trine can symbolize a creative vision or idea, and this is very consistent with the enthusiasm and self-confidence inspired by a Jupiterian faith in the future. Jupiter is similar to the Sun in that when it is involved in a trine, it suggests a natural tendency to expand and to adopt a broader perspective, though tendencies toward exaggeration, unfounded idealism, laziness and overexpansion could also be heightened. Jupiter's characteristics are greatly accentuated when it is directly involved with another planet in a trine aspect.

The changeable and expansive meaning of Sagittarius is supported by its **subtone** known as **mutable.** There is one mutable sign for each element and the key word phrase for mutable is **adaptable energy.** Since Sagittarius is the mutable fire sign, the prominent focus here is an adaptation of the self to new adventurous experiences.

The archetypal theme of Sagittarius, developing a broad perspective and futuristic vision through traveling on the mental and physical planes, often results from an impatience with the finiteness of the present. The archetypal theme of Sagittarius corresponds to its subtone in that the adaptability of its mutable energy encourages an individual to seek change to promote growth for the future. However, an individual must be careful in seeking this change, as he may only be responding to boredom with the present, neglecting responsibilities and going off into many different directions in an aimless manner. The mutable nature of Sagittarius can denote an individual attempting to juggle many different life experiences simultaneously in a search for the right path or life direction.

The 9th house is supported by its **subtone** house classification, **cadent.** There is one cadent house belonging to each element. The key word phrase for cadent is **eagerness to learn.** The self-discovery and expansion urges through the acquisition of knowledge associated with the 9th house, whether it be through developing the abstract thought process or risk-taking adventures, is well supported by its cadent subtone. The fire theme of the 9th house brings its cadent subtone into an eagerness to learn about one's self.

The 9th Chord is a natural extension of the 1st and 5th Chord themes of asserting and defining the self, and completes the thrust of the fire chords—an active and enthusiastic expression of the self through the processes of self-discovery and understanding. It is through the 9th Chord principles of expansion and growth, that one is inspired and stimulated to broaden perspectives and learn the lessons that life has to offer.

The archetypal themes of each fire chord personify through human behavior that is dramatic, expressive and ultimately self-focused. The fire element in a horoscope shows intensification and acceleration of the life through the processes of initiation, creation or expansion of experiences. It is the fire chord tones in every person's horoscope that represent our faith in ourselves, which gives us the courage and strength to face life's changing circumstances.

PART III

EARTH ELEMENT

Earth indicates a pragmatic expression of the self. The earth element points to a consciousness of practicality, work ethics, determination, cautiousness, common sense and an avid concern for understanding material matters. The three earth chords indicate a slowing-down rhythm in dealing with life circumstances. The characteristics represented by the earth element can sometimes act as a sedative for someone suffering from fire element burnout. Earth principles can have a calming affect upon the nervous system or an exhausted psyche.

An individual with earth as a dominant element (by having the earth signs Taurus, Virgo and Capricorn or houses 2, 6 and 10 well emphasized or strong aspects formed by the earth planets) often portrays a conservative demeanor colored by a "grounded" philosophical life perspective. It is usually the solid foundation supported by the earth chord consciousness that provides the framework for an individual to sustain the effort needed to achieve desired goals.

An individual may have a highly accentuated emphasis on this element in any of the following ways: the Sun, Moon, Ascendant, four or more personal planets in earth signs or simply key planets in earth houses or earth planets strongly aspected. Such people feel more secure through developing carefully thought-out plans than by acting on sudden impulses. The basic chemistry and natural inclination represented by the earth element is to first "buckle up for safety" by considering the consequences of actions rather than risk the loss of resources or the embarrassment of personal failure due to unstable or disorderly situations.

The planets, signs, and houses that comprise the earth chords symbolize the themes of possessing (2nd Chord), analyzing (6th Chord) and achieving (10th Chord) material aims. The common ingredient of Chords 2, 6 and 10 is the preservation of the self through practical and well-organized behavior.

CHAPTER FIVE

SECOND CHORD: DESIRE FOR PHYSICAL COMFORT

> For eons, the Earth was Mother, sacred and revered, the source and symbol of life. We were her sons, and women were her daughters. The Great Mother lived before us, and after. Omnipotent, her fertility represented life; her barrenness, death. We worshipped her and feared her at the same time: she giveth and she taketh away.
>
> *A Choice of Heroes* by Mark Gerzon (page 16)

The 2nd Chord is an expression of the earth element in the form of comforting the self through ownership and establishing material values. Chord two symbolizes our desire for pleasure in the physical sense world." The planet (Venus), sign (Taurus) and house (2nd) tones of this chord symbolize an individual's drive to preserve physical comfort through the accumulation of material resources as well as to develop a psychological wealth reflected in self-esteem. The archetypal themes of the 2nd Chord tones reflect three manifestations of establishing a sense of comfort.

The earth element's predilection for stability, conserving energy and collecting resources is symbolized in this chord in the major tones as well as the subtones.

Astrology, Psychology, and Transformation

2ND CHORD: DESIRE FOR PHYSICAL COMFORT

Tone	Archetypal Themes	Functions	Positive Expressions	Negative Expressions	Potential Counseling Issues
Planet: Venus Symbol ♀	The directing of actions to satisfy social, aesthetic and epicurean urges and to establish a sense of comfort through ownership, material values and relating.	1. To build material values. 2. To understand and use the desire nature.	1. The ability to use values toward self-fulfillment. 2. The ability to efficiently use material resources.	1. A tendency to establish fixed value systems. 2. An inclination toward fixed desires.	**Key Phrase:** Valuing The Self
Sign: Taurus Symbol ♉	The manner in which physical needs can be solidified and the desire to maintain a sense of security through ownership.	3. To build self-esteem and a sense of personal stability and serenity.	3. The desire to love and to express affection.	3. The potential to be limited by material consciousness.	**Games:** 1. All Dollars and No Sense. 2. Aphrodisiac. 3. Borrower.
House: 2nd	One's attitudes concerning ownership and acquisition as related to maintaining and securing oneself in the world and developing material values as related to one's sense of self worth.	4. To establish ownership concepts. 5. To develop an awareness of aesthetics, sensuality and affection.	4. The capacity to share. 5. The ability to give support to others. 6. The determination to finish what is started. 7. Physical stamina. 8. An aesthetic sense. 9. The ability to enjoy serenity.	4. A predisposition toward self-indulgence due to enslavement to the desire nature. 5. A tendency toward stubbornness. 6. A tendency toward greediness. 7. An inclination toward laziness and lethargy. 8. Vanity. 9. Mismanagement of resources.	4. Bullheaded. 5. Desert. 6. Earthworm. 7. Give Me, Give Me! 8. Hole in My Pocket. 9. I Want to Own You. 10. Poverty Consciousness. 11. Scrooge. 12. Sweet Tooth. 13. Tortoise That Didn't Win.

Figure 4: Second Chord
See the Note to Readers after Acknowledgments

Venus

The 2nd Chord planetary tone, Venus, represents an individual's affinity for surrounding the self with beauty or appreciating comfort and simplicity in life experiences. Venus is a very attractive heavenly body. It is the brightest planet in our solar system being the planet closest in proximity to the Earth. In Roman and Greek mythology, Venus was the goddess of love and beauty, known to the Greeks as *Aphrodite*.

Just as the brightness of Venus in the sky charms us into admiring her beauty, Venus in the horoscope can signify how an individual might direct charm or social urges to attract the affections of others. Venus represents a person's degree of ease in establishing emotional closeness and expressing affections. For instance, an individual with Venus in a fire sign or house might enter relationships very quickly as self-confidence inspires the affections to bubble forward enthusiastically and idealistically. An individual with Venus in an earth sign or house might exhibit a reserved emotional nature until "warming-up" to others and feeling at ease with exhibiting affections openly.

Venus in relation to the 2nd Chord (Venus will also be discussed in the 7th Chord) denotes an individual's desire to own luxury items and to adorn the self with jewelry, cosmetics, and attractive apparel. The placement of Venus by sign and house also indicates an individual's drive to satisfy the physical senses through food, drink and sensual experiences, including the creation and appreciation of beauty.

A key symbolism for Venus in regard to the 2nd Chord is an individual's capacity to create a sense of balance, stability and calm. For instance, a person with Venus in the 9th Chord sign tone of Sagittarius might find traveling or beginning a new subject of study centering and comforting experiences, while an individual with Venus in the 4th Chord sign of Cancer might find that buying items to improve the home is relaxing. In other words, Venus indicates ways in which a person might choose to establish peace and balance for the psyche.

The positive expressions of 2nd Chord Venus include a capacity to warmly express affections and develop an emotional closeness. People who possess a balanced Venus expression know how to interact with lovers, friends and strangers without feeling the need to steal center stage. Another positive expression of Venus for an individual is an ability to center the self when life circumstances are in turmoil. She has aesthetic or creative outlets of expression and knows how to approach others with whom she has established emotional closeness. Other positive Venus expressions include a desire to share resources, give support to others and to enjoy serenity.

The negative expressions of 2nd Chord Venus include manipulating or possessing others rather than honestly expressing affections. The ownership theme of the 2nd Chord becomes owning significant others and not letting them live their lives freely. Another negative manifestation of Venus is denying one's sensuality or love of beauty. This is a person who rather than letting a natural attracting power (shown by Venus) express itself, keeps a lid clamped on it. Affections and emotions are repressed often due to low self-esteem. The individual may even be afraid to wear apparel that attracts attention. Another negative expression of Venus is enslavement to one's desires for excessive amounts of food, drink or sex. This individual's life is often in a state of imbalance and emotional confusion.

Taurus

The sign tone, Taurus, further expresses the desire for physical comfort found in the 2nd Chord. Taurus indicates an individual's drive to secure the self through ownership and possessions. The acquisition emphasis of Taurus is captured by its archetypal theme, the manner in which physical needs can be solidified and the desire to maintain a sense of security through ownership. When an individual has the Sun, Moon, Ascendant or several other planets in Taurus, she often feels the need to collect and invest resources and to improve buying power in the world.

The sign Taurus has traditionally been referred to as slow-moving, and an individual with Taurus strongly accentuated is often rather steady and deliberate in movement. She may even give the appearance of seeking leisure and comfort in the midst of busy actions. Traditionally Taurus is known as "the bull."

Taurus reflects an individual's need for self-nurturing and comforting. It is no surprise that one of the classic images of Taurus is our Mother Earth or nature. The sign Taurus symbolizes an individual's capacity and need to promote activities that calm the nervous system. Taurus, in my opinion, represents the ultimate calming potion of the earth element.

Positive expressions of Taurus include an individual's ability not to waste material resources and to have a green thumb, both in the garden and in managing "green energy" or money. An individual may also have a natural inclination to share resources for the benefit of others. The giving of support to others may be not only monetary but also offering a distressed friend a shoulder to lean upon. Perhaps the strongest expression of "the bull" is a determination to finish what is started and an ability to appreciate the serenity of the present.

Negative expressions of Taurus include a tendency to be limited by material consciousness, and a surrender to fixed material and physical values that enslave one's creative capacity. Other pitfalls for Taurus include a stubbornness and determination to resist change even if it would be beneficial and growth promoting. The bull is at its worst when greedily guarding and selfishly cherishing territory, succumbing to states of laziness and self-indulgence that dull one's senses and put the creative spirit to sleep.

2nd House

The third tone of this chord, the 2nd house, symbolizes choices that an individual will need to make concerning ownership and managing resources to maintain and sustain the self in the world. Traditional astrology often limits the 2nd house to one's possessions and money, avoiding any psychological link to this area of the horoscope. A counseling approach does not attempt to deny the relevance of an individual's material needs, but perceives the 2nd house as a means for an individual to develop attitudes and values concerning ownership and earning money that reflect awareness of personal self-worth. Therefore, the 2nd house symbolizes an individual's attitudes toward earning power and values that relate to self-esteem.

A positive expression of the 2nd house includes an ability to manage resources efficiently, not being ruled by the approach that money is everything. There is a natural give-and-take for the individual concerning sharing of resources. Another positive expression is to value self-esteem and not confuse self-worth with possessions. Such an individual feels valuable to herself and others regardless of any present bank balance. Also, a positive 2nd house expression includes taking a risk when required to grow and establish broader values. The challenge here is to keep the spiritual and physical worlds in balance.

Negative expressions of the 2nd house include a tendency to develop fixed values and to be limited by an inflexible material consciousness. A stubborn resistance to change and an overcautious nature could hinder self-enrichment and block fresh, new, and stimulating ideas. Another possible negative manifestation of the 2nd house is either the extreme of greed in possessively hoarding material wealth, or an inability to manage resources.

Counseling Issues

The counseling issues related to the 2nd Chord originate from an individual's inability to balance expression of the basic nature of this chord, **desire for physical comfort**. My key word phrase for these counseling issues, **valuing the self**, is from the synthesis of the 2nd Chord tones. Venus, Taurus and the

2nd house have an emphasis on material values inherent in their archetypal themes, which are:

1. **Venus**—the directing of actions to satisfy social, aesthetic and epicurean urges and to establish a sense of comfort through owner ship, material values and relating.
2. **Taurus**—the manner in which physical needs can be solidified and the desire to maintain a sense of security through ownership.
3. **2nd house**—one's attitudes concerning ownership and acquisition as related to maintaining and securing oneself in the world and developing material values related to one's sense of self-worth.

The counseling issues associated with the 2nd Chord are related to an individual's values in regard to the self-esteem principle. The 2nd Chord tones can be expressed in a positive manner by an individual who bolsters self-esteem and a degree of comfort through establishing a value system that expresses balanced physical and material drives. However, counseling issues often arise when an individual's self-worth dipstick registers several quarts low. The counseling issues of this chord are twofold: (a) an individual's tendency to overcompensate for low self-esteem through the defense mechanism of establishing fixed or rigid values; (2) an individual's immobilization due to low self-esteem and a lack of the vitality and determination to establish a clear value system.

Games

When an individual succumbs to rigid or fixed values to hide low self-esteem, compulsive materialistic drives and possessive actions can dominate the behavior. Material accomplishments often become a source of frustration as she lacks self-love and does not find refuge in wealth. Fixed or rigid values may lead an individual into what I call the **Scrooge** game. This is a person who is attempting to squeeze all the love and affection that she denies in herself out of possessions. She greedily collects possessions to preserve a misguided image of self-worth. It is important for this person to honestly assess her value system. She is tenaciously attempting to hold on to a sense of personal power. The key to this game can reside in the opposite 8th Chord which symbolizes an emotional sharing of oneself and self-mastery as opposed to the natural self-indulgence of Chord 2.

The **Scrooge** game is closely related to another game, **All Dollars and No Sense.** This individual worships money as God because true belief in her own value is bankrupt. The comfort that she is trying to provide for herself is always just out of reach. Dollars in the pocket do not satisfy a void in the psyche for love and meaning in life.

The individual displaying this game needs to concentrate on creative self-expression. The key to this game can be developing a more transcendent type of value system, as typified by the 12th Chord. Also, since the 2nd Chord quincunxes the 9th Chord, it could be that a more expansive vision in terms of raising one's consciousness or learning new life directions is important.

The **Scrooge** and **All Dollars and No Sense** games often lead an individual into the **Desert** game. This is an individual who accumulates all the riches that she desires and finally realizes that something is missing. Her life has become a puzzle with missing parts. It is as though the wealth and sacred possessions have lost their magic and become like grains of sand that escape through her fingers. She is frightened by the emptiness in life and feels as if she has lost a precious oasis. Riches have suddenly become mirages with no lasting value, containing a false reality and not providing the fertility of love, peace and joy that they promised to bring.

This person often needs to focus more on humanitarian goals and sharpen the sense of individuality (11th Chord squares the 2nd). The earth element can lead one to get lost in materialism. The fire element (square to Chord 5) can help one find new enthusiasm for life and fresh joy. The water element (opposition to Chord 8) offers new emotional life to a very dry existence.

An individual's behavior can involve a manipulative use of the 2nd Chord tones in the **I Want to Own You** game. This is an individual who aspires to possess lovers, mates, children or friends. She fears her own lack of self-worth and does not believe others will accept her at face value. Therefore, she attempts to manipulate others by buying them gifts and doing other financial favors. She tries to get people dependent so that she can control their actions.

The fixed chords (including Chord 2) deal with issues of power. Balancing personal control of money and resources with the control of others is one issue in the opposition between Chords 2 and 8. Very often there is a need to become more trustful when relating to others, and to not always think in terms of control or power. Finding ways to enhance inner serenity and security will enable one to be more relaxed and trusting of others. The less we trust our own inner strength, the more of a threat we perceive in other people.

Another manipulative 2nd Chord game includes the **Give Me, Give Me!** This individual feels the world owes her a free ticket in life. She does her best to con others into feeling guilty if they refuse to make a donation to her whining demands. This individual has a difficult time in trusting others. The 2nd Chord quincunxes the 7th Chord, indicating that one's personal value system and self-esteem are crucial in relationships to peers and lovers. An overemphasis on material gain can steal away time and energy better devoted to improving one's associations with others.

A related game is the **Borrower.** This individual is always borrowing money or items from others but with no intention of repaying the debt. This can be a person who is out of touch with earth energy. She angers others by abusing their property or simply not sharing emotional or physical energy. She may need to develop a more bonding attitude, typical of the opposite 8th Chord, and respect the ownership of others.

The fixity that is symbolized by the 2nd Chord can sometimes motivate an individual's tendency toward stubbornness. This is typified by the sign Taurus in the **Bullheaded** game. The stubbornness can reach tremendous proportions when an individual resists change and is determined that her values remain unchallenged. She refuses to acknowledge another person's point of view and will not compromise. The objectivity and wide perspective of the airy Chord 11 can be helpful here. Also helpful is the fiery imagination of Chord 5 (a square) which joyfully plunges into new enthusiasms and involvements.

Another 2nd Chord game, the **Earthworm,** occurs when an individual becomes so preoccupied with material concerns that the consciousness becomes enslaved to the gravity of a limited vision. Nothing motivates her unless it has dollar signs in front of it. This individual retreats deeper and deeper into the soil of rigid values and becomes blinded by fixed material desires.

This person often needs to find new spiritual horizons in life. The individual exhibiting this game in many instances has a tenacious spirit which is simply in need of new direction. The challenge is to generate enough enthusiasm and vision to change. Focusing on the fiery optimism and aspirations of the 9th Chord (a quincunx) is often helpful.

An individual's determination to hide from feelings of low self-worth can lead to the **Aphrodisiac** game. This game is symbolized by a misuse of 2nd Chord energies. This individual becomes desensitized to personal self-worth and sacrifices a sense of beauty and sensuality to lustful appetites in the form of excess food, drink or sex. However, the appetites do not subside until the hunger to form loving relationships is satisfied. The first step is for the individual to begin loving herself. The 8th Chord is opposite, indicating the person may need to stop hating herself and begin transforming and redirecting emotional energy.

When an individual becomes disoriented due to an unclear value system, she may exhibit the **Poverty Consciousness** game. This individual does not believe that she is entitled to creature comforts and deprives herself of opportunities to improve her standard of living. This is often a self-punishment type of behavior reflecting an individual's low self-worth. Such a person belittles her importance at every opportunity, denying herself of physical necessities or anything that even hints of an abundant life.

The individual's outward denial is a direct reflection of an inward denial. The person may need to tap into a true 2nd Chord expression and allow herself to comprehend that she is entitled to some beauty, peace and simple joy. She may wish to put to use the themes of the chords making squares to Chord 2. Chord 11 emphasizes uniqueness and individuality; Chord 5 emphasizes a healthy pride in the self and the ability to love oneself. Also, the person may need to develop a clearer sense of personal power which can be strengthened through a focus on the opposite chord 8.

An individual with a vague value system or unclear sense of self-worth may exhibit the **Hole in My Pocket** game. This is an individual who is always plain broke. She may earn a large salary and have relatively few living expenses but still has nothing to show for it at the end of the month. She is terrible at managing resources and is as irresponsible as the individual described in the **Borrower** game. This person may be responding more to the fire and air elements and living a life of extremes. The slowing-down rhythms of earth and water may need to be cultivated.

The **Sweet Tooth** game is an overeating disorder that an individual manifests when substituting food desires for the sweetness and love that she craves. She is trying to satisfy a hunger for love and becomes victimized by low self-esteem. A search for pleasure is human and natural but, misdirected, can lead to problems. Physical sweetness can never satiate a hunger for emotional sweetness. There is often negativity at the root of this game. The fire element can help this individual tap into a more positive outlook in life: the confident faith in life of Chord 9 and Chord 5's willingness to risk in order to gain love and applause.

The 2nd Chord qualities of calmness, patience, determination and stamina become inertia and laziness if an individual falls prey to the **Tortoise That Didn't Win** game. In the famous fairy tale, the tortoise defeats the much swifter hare through persistence and a tremendous determination to finish the race. However, in this game, a strong 2nd Chord type of individual loses the steady tenacity to accomplish life goals while a confused sense of self-worth interferes with the sense of direction in life. She becomes too fearful of failure and is easily distracted, forgetting her purpose. I have often seen heavy dominance of earth and water elements for people in this game. Such individuals need to learn to be a bit more adventurous and free-spirited. They can benefit from the natural optimism of Chord 9 (a quincunx) and courageous risk-taking of Chord 5 (a square). Since earth can be too "solid" and reluctant to move, such people might also want to consider the wider perspective and openness to the new shown by Chord 11 (a square).

Summary of Issues with 2nd Chord Games

The 2nd Chord games are a result of fixed material value systems with underlying issues involving comfort and ease. The energies of the 2nd Chord can be expressed as beauty and love in an articulate manner and as enjoyment of a balanced life. It is when a person attempts to conceal low self-worth behind rigid material values and loses a sense of direction in establishing a clear value system that she falls prey to 2nd Chord games.

Subtones

The three subtones of Chord 2 are: the planetary aspect known as the **semisextile**, the energy focus of Taurus known as **fixed** and the house classification known as **succedent**.

The **semisextile** has a definite 2nd Chord ring. Though this aspect is largely ignored by astrologers and considered to be an insignificant aspect due to its lack of intensity, the planets forming the semisextile can indicate a valuable resource for an individual. The major challenge is that the semisextile lacks the driving force symbolized by the more intense aspects such as the conjunction, square, quincunx or opposition. The semisextile usually points to themes below the threshold of an individual's conscious awareness unlike the trine or sextile which usually symbolize motifs of which the individual has knowledge.

Consider a semisextile aspect formed between the 5th Chord planetary tone, the Sun, and the 12th Chord planetary tone, Neptune. This semisextile could indicate a capacity to define oneself (Sun) through learning an artistic expression (Neptune) or enjoying a rejuvenated and calmed vitality (Sun) through a meditative experience (Neptune). The possibilities shown by the semisextile will be activated only with the stamina and patience that are needed to cultivate the potential energy and bring it into conscious reality. If Venus is involved in the semisextile aspect with another planet, the 2nd Chord theme (the desire for physical comfort) will resonate that much more strongly, symbolizing an individual's attempt to beautify and balance inner and outer worlds.

The maintaining quality of Taurus is further exemplified by the nature of its **fixed** subtone. As stated in the 5th Chord, the key word phrase for fixed is **focused energy.** Since Taurus is the fixed earth sign and the focus of the earth element is on preserving the self, the fixed energy of Taurus is very focused on solidifying and stabilizing security orientations.

The ownership of material things and the satisfying enjoyment of a comfortable life help an individual maintain a feeling of security and stability. Maintaining one's physical needs by earning money and enhancing one's sense of comfort by owning possessions are examples in the 2nd Chord of the archetypal theme of Taurus corresponding to its fixed subtone.

A **third subtone** of the 2nd Chord is the energy field of the 2nd house which is **succedent**. The key word phrase for succedent is **securing**. The symbolism of the 2nd house as an individual's attitudes concerning 2nd house choices to secure the physical and psychological worlds is supported by its succedent subtones. A planet located in an individual's 2nd house represents an individual's attitudes toward securing material values and wealth and preserving self-esteem.

The 2nd Chord largely concerns an individual's balance in the physical world and the ability and determination to create an inner and outer sense of comfort. The 2nd Chord symbolizes an individual's potential to develop material values that strengthen self-worth which is the key to fulfilling the desire for physical comfort. The remaining earth chords will further illustrate the sustaining of the self through practical and security-oriented behavior.

CHAPTER SIX

SIXTH CHORD: DESIRE TO CREATE ORDER

> Obviously, the real work revolution won't come until all productive work is rewarded—including child-rearing and other jobs done in the home—and men are integrated into so-called women's work as well as vice versa.
>
> Outrageous Acts and Everyday Rebellions by Gloria Steinem (page 167)

The 6th Chord is an expression of the earth element in the form of organizing the self through analysis and refinement. The planet (Mercury), sign (Virgo) and house (6th) tones of this chord symbolize an individual's drive to learn skills, organizational abilities and self-discipline to preserve order in life circumstances. With chord six, we learn to work, to handle the small details of a job, including all the virtues. We can describe the essence of chord six as efficient functioning including our ability to handle a job well and our ability to be healthy, to function effectively in our bodies.

The earth element denotes preoccupation with transforming the unseen into visibility. Molding idealistic visions into practical reality reaches its zenith with the symbolism of the 6th Chord. The 6th Chord is the earth element's most basic attempt to prescribe a healthy regimen for the body, mind and soul. The tones and subtones of this chord can symbolize the nagging and persistence of an individual's psyche for perfection, purity and clarity.

Mercury

The 6th Chord planetary tone, Mercury, represents an individual's fluidity of thought, ability to communicate and power of mental concentration and discrimination. Mercury moves quickly through the sky as though in a hurry to circle the Sun in 80 days rather than the 88 days it requires to complete the journey. Mercury is the Sun's closest planetary neighbor. The brilliance of the light emanating from the Sun makes it difficult to observe Mercury's planetary appearance, unlike Venus whose adornment of white clouds reflects sunlight to show off her beauty.

In mythology, Mercury was the winged messenger of the gods, associated with commerce, manual skill, cleverness and travel. The astronomical and mythological significance of Mercury corresponds to its astrological symbolism. Just as Mercury in the sky moves swiftly and restlessly, Mercury in the horoscope can signify an individual's restless and even nervous drive to communicate, analyze or digest information. Mercury denotes an individual's mental alertness and ability to formulate and articulate concepts as well as to perceive his inner and outer worlds. The "Messenger of the Gods" is the messenger and interpreter of the conscious mind. In the 6th Chord, Mercury represents a special emphasis on directing mental energy into organizing and analyzing one's life due to the quest for order. (Mercury will also be discussed in the 3rd Chord.)

The positive expressions of the 6th Chord Mercury include an ability to analyze and give order to complex problems and situations. People who are very much in touch with their Mercury-associated skills are great problem solvers and have a natural capacity to develop expertise in learning new skills. Other positive qualities include a talent for keeping track of details, a thorough grasp of communicating information, and the offering of constructive criticism when solicited.

6TH CHORD: DESIRE TO CREATE ORDER

Tone	Archetypal Themes	Functions	Positive Expressions	Negative Expressions	Potential Counseling Issues
Planet: Mercury Symbol ☿	The directing of mental activity for the conscious mind to process, analyze and communicate information and to perceive the environment.	1. To clarify and order information and to perfect the environment.	1. An ability to provide constructive criticism and analytical insight for self and others.	1. A tendency to be too critical and narrow.	Key Phrase: Analyzing The Self
Sign: Virgo Symbol ♍	The manner through which the process of analysis can be assimilated as related to organization, attention to detail, service and health.	2. To develop analytical abilities.	2. An ability to organize.	2. The potential of thinking negatively due to an overuse of analytical skills.	Games: 1. Abused Body. 2. Dead End Job.
House: 6th	One's attitudes concerning organization and analysis in regard to work habits, service to others, learning skills and caring for physical and mental health needs.	3. To learn and develop skills especially those practical in nature.	3. An ability to develop expertise.	3. A predisposition to get too caught up in details.	3. Grass Is Cleaner. 4. Hypochondriac. 5. I Can't I Can't!
		4. To learn and develop a sense of humility.	4. An ability to work hard and tirelessly.	4. A tendency to be too limited by routine.	6. Litterbug. 7. Martyr. 8. 9 to 5.
		5. To develop consciousness of diet and health.	5. An affinity for detail.	5. The potential of ignoring proper diet and health.	9. Not Seeing the Forest for the Trees. 10. Picky Picky.
		6. To serve others.	6. An innate ability to offer skills and services to others due to feelings of responsibility.	6. A proclivity for unrealistic standards of perfection.	11. Somebody Please Kick Me. 12. Too Finely Sifted. 13. White Tornado.
			7. A capacity to comprehend the nature of healing energy and to make use of it in the healing arts.	7. An inclination toward subservience.	14. Workaholic. 15. WorryWart.

Figure 5: Sixth Chord
See the Note to Readers after Acknowledgments

Negative expressions of Mercury include an individual's tendency to think in a narrow manner and to be too picky and critical of others. Another negative manifestation includes developing a life so centralized around routines and schedules that spontaneous behavior seems impossible. Also, Mercury can be symbolic of a nagging kind of behavior and an excessive indulgence in negativity which alienates significant others.

Virgo

The archetypal theme of the 6th Chord sign tone, Virgo, focuses on the concept of creating order through the process of analysis in regard to organization, attention to detail and health matters. Virgo has traditionally been associated with purity as reflected by the mythological symbol of the virgin. The sign Virgo represents tendencies toward refinement in thought and action and an attempt to remove the impure and coarse from the fine and pure particles. An individual with the Sun, Moon, Ascendant or several other planets in Virgo often feels compelled to dispel impurities from the mind and body and to perfect skills whether in the service of self or others.

Virgo symbolizes an individual's determination and sometimes compelling drive to learn new skills. Virgo is a restless sign and indicates an individual's need to find meaningful outlets. Virgo like its earth sign counterparts, Taurus and Capricorn, seeks practical results. Virgo is the workhorse of the earth element. Perhaps even more than Taurus or Capricorn, Virgo is willing to pay the price of sowing the fruits of its own labor to fulfill the promise of a rewarding and bountiful seasonal crop. A strong Virgo type may be a complicated individual to understand with an elaborate and self-conscious nature that can vacillate between a humble and well diversified nature to a tendency to overcriticize the self and others.

The positive expressions of Virgo include the ability to organize oneself and to assist others in establishing order in their lives. Also, an individual can inspire others through working hard and taking a positive and service-oriented attitude. Other positive qualities include developing and perfecting skills as well as utilizing healing energy in the service of others. There are few who can work as diligently with details as people with a strong emphasis on Virgo. Their ability to systemize the most disorganized circumstances or situations can astound others.

Negative expressions of Virgo include a compulsive preoccupation with finding fault in the actions of self or others and ruthlessly criticizing those who do not live up to unrealistic standards of perfection. An overanalytical nature can lead one to become too cautious, to develop a rigidly routinized life with narrow and uneventful boundaries. There may be a tendency to be too entrapped by details that will be illustrated in the **Not Seeing the Forest for the Trees** game. Also, a needless concern with too many details can cause an individual excessive worry. Another negative quality is ignoring proper diet and health by carrying the work ethic to extremes or by denying oneself proper nutrition. (This will be seen in the **Abused Body** game.) Perhaps the biggest Achilles' heel for Virgo is negativity. It is often the root cause for the dis-ease that strong Virgo types sometimes suffer when they cannot live up to their own high standards of perfection.

6th House

The house tone of the 6th Chord, the 6th house, symbolizes an individual's attitudes concerning the desire to create an orderly life especially regarding mental and physical health, establishing work habits and learning new skills. Traditional astrology explains the 6th house mainly in terms of one's work environment and as a potential indicator of physical health problems. My own experience is that the 6th house symbolizes one's attitudes concerning physical health and keeping a mental balance. I have consulted with many clients who have done much abuse to their mind and body through a compulsive and self-hating type of behavior symbolized by a dysfunctioning 6th house. The forms of negative behavior ranged from starvation and overeating, to simply lacking a conscious awareness of a tremendous mental imbalance.

The 6th house indicates the type of yoga that can stimulate an individual to achieve a balanced approach in exercising the body and mind. This particular house symbolizes the forms of behavior that an individual might need to cultivate with discipline and patience. The nagging worry and frustration that people sometimes experience may be indicated by a dysfunctioning 6th house. Problems are often due to an undisciplined use of 6th house themes, and overindulgence in negative thinking.

The 6th house also has an interesting relation to service. There is a devotional aspect of the 6th Chord that has its roots in the 6th house as much as in the sign tone, Virgo. Humility and the willingness to serve others are part of the 6th house symbolism. People with planets in the 6th house are often seeking outlets to channel this service-oriented energy whether it be into relationships or causes. The healing energy that is sometimes symbolized by the 6th house seems to have its origin in an individual's inner need to act as a channel to help others.

The positive manifestations of 6th house themes include properly caring for the maintenance of body and mind through a balanced diet, exercise and an orderly life. Other positive attributes are working with details and acquiring practical or useful skills as well as a capacity to offer skills and service to others. Another positive expression is understanding healing energy and making use of it in the healing arts.

Negative qualities include a lack of confidence in perfecting skills or expertise. Also, an individual expressing 6th house motifs discordantly may exhibit a spaced-out consciousness concerning proper hygiene. He could ignore the physical body by eating a poor diet and overindulging in substance abuses such as drugs and alcohol. An individual may also live a very disorderly life reflecting a disorganized mind. Another negative potential of the 6th house is involvement in humiliating relationships due to a low opinion of the self. It is as though the individual is purposely creating a situation to punish himself. The individual's humility is expressed by a slavish devotion to someone who has no respect for him.

Counseling Issues

The counseling issues of the 6th Chord are representative of an individual's inability to express the basic nature of this chord, **desire to create order**. My key word phrase for these counseling issues **analyzing the self** is from the synthesis of the tones Mercury, Virgo and the 6th house. The 6th Chord tones have an emphasis upon analysis inherent in their archetypal themes, which are:

1. **Mercury**—the directing of mental activity for the conscious mind to analyze, process and communicate information and to perceive the environment.
2. **Virgo**—the manner through which the processes of analysis can be assimilated as related to organization, attention to detail, service and health.
3. **6th house**—one's attitudes concerning organization and analysis in regard to work habits, service to others, learning skills and caring for physical and mental health needs.

The counseling issues of this chord concern an individual's lack of balance in utilizing the faculties of analysis and discrimination. Each 6th Chord tone can be used by an individual to make the right choices that will bring growth and to establish a sense of order and meaning in the life. The counseling issues of this chord are twofold: (1) a compulsive tendency to criticize self and others coupled with an extreme desire for order and perfection; (2) an underdeveloped or confused analytical nature that leads one into self-denying behaviors and an overindulgence in negativity.

When an individual grows too fond of the power to analyze, he can become entrapped by the very perfection and order that he is seeking much like a spider that gets caught in the web he is spinning. The art of perfecting is strong in the 6th Chord. (Perfection will also be discussed in the 12th Chord.) My favorite image of an individual's yearning for perfection is symbolized in the sculpture, the Pietà, created by the famous artist, Michelangelo. Supposedly he created this depiction of the crucifixion by carving away what did not belong in his vision of the sculpture. In other words, he removed piece by piece and in painstaking detail the superfluous qualities until all that remained was a magnificent, breathtaking masterpiece. This is the optimum message of the 6th Chord tones, especially Virgo and the 6th house, to remove imperfection through the power of analysis. However, not everybody is as intuitive as a Michelangelo in that some individuals do not know when to stop perfecting.

Games

The **Grass Is Greener** game of the 9th Chord becomes the **Grass Is Cleaner** game in the 6th Chord. This is an individual who becomes too critical of present circumstances, whether it concerns job, relationships, etc., as he is seeking perfect situations. The individual sets standards for happiness and satisfaction so high that nobody can reach them including himself. This can lead from one frustrating experience to another with no real sense of purpose or direction chasing an illusion of a perfect life, much like a cat frantically running in circles chasing its own tail. It is not that this individual must completely disregard his standards. However, in order to sidestep this game, an individual may wish to tap into his air energy and gain a more objective perspective on life. Chord 6 can take life too seriously, while the square to Chord 3 reflects the needed balance of a flippant attitude, knowing when to laugh. The humor indicated by Chord 9 (another square) can also assist a heavy Chord 6 type in "lightening up."

An individual's misuse of 6th Chord tones in the form of over-utilization of analytical ability can show someone enacting the **Picky, Picky** game. This individual is very difficult to please as he has had years of practice in scrutinizing the imperfections of the world. He believes himself to be the world's greatest critic and is an expert in pointing out the faults of others. If you have cooked his favorite dish from your most cherished recipe, he will tell you the missing ingredients. If you play an album by your favorite vocalist, your **Picky, Picky** friend will find something wrong with the lyrics. The **Picky, Picky** person is often at war with himself and has surrendered any peace of mind to a sarcastic attempt to make life miserable for others. This individual can achieve balance by incorporating more compassion (shown by the Chord 12 opposition). The water element helps sensitize one to intuitive and emotional energies, freeing him from making life miserable for the self and others. The natural square formed by the 6th Chord to the 9th Chord indicates that developing a more positive life attitude can be helpful in this game. The squares to both the 3rd and 9th Chords point to a need to be more open in communication and to broaden one's perspective.

The **Picky, Picky** game may be accompanied by the **White Tornado** game. This is a person who tries to keep everything in life clean, prim and proper. This behavior is often annoying to others because as in the previous game, the individual judges others by his own specialized standards of perfection. Sometimes the key to solving the limitations of 6th Chord games calls for a person to reeducate the mind (natural square to the 3rd Chord) and expand moral systems, exploring new horizons (natural square to 9th Chord). In each of the 6th Chord games thus far discussed, the person is often quite intelligent but trapped into one life perspective. The opposite 12th Chord points to a more transcendent direction. Perhaps the key to these games lies not so much in conscious mind logic, but in true inner vision. Chords 9 and 12 emphasize not losing sight of the overall picture.

In the expansive 9th Chord it was stated that 9th Chord tones can be so stimulating that an individual gets into a lazy habit of avoiding details as in the **Not Seeing the Trees for the Forest** game. In the 6th Chord variation of this game an individual is so busy investigating the steps within a process or life development that he loses sight of the overall situation. He keeps attempting to chip away imperfections but has no real vision as to what he is trying to create.

Once again the individual is far too dominated by left-brain logic. He may need to nourish a starved right brain through meditation or other intuitive, wholistic approaches (opposition to Chord 12). An excessive focus on details can be augmented by broad overview associated with Chord 9 (a square).

Another game related to an overdeveloped analytical nature is the **Worry Wart.** This individual is so concerned that life be in perfect order that he is always looking over one shoulder to make sure everything is the way it "should" be. If even the slightest bit of surprise ruffles the order of events in life, he begins to feel nervous. This individual is often suffering from excessive worry and a fear of failure due to a compulsive need for perfection.

Remembering the symbolism of the opposite 12th Chord can be helpful. The person may be too preoccupied with an external orientation and ignoring the inner being which is calling for a deeper, spiritual search (Chord 12). The person may need to develop fiery faith (square to Chord 9) which allows one to trust in the best and believe everything will work out even if it does not fit into neat categories.

The 6th Chord house and sign tones are sometimes symbolic of an individual's compulsive concern for the physical body. This can lead to the **Hypochondriac** game: the individual so preoccupied with analyzing health that he begins to believe he is sick. Eventually this person may become so mesmerized by health concerns that he develops psychosomatic illnesses.

In many instances, the person needs to direct the focus away from the self. This behavior can be a means of seeking attention. Finding new alternatives for individuality and life goals (quincunx to Chord 11) can bring something different for the individual to focus on. The opposing 12th Chord points to a possible need to reevaluate one's emotional body and to develop faith in a Higher Power.

When an individual becomes too fond of collecting details, he can engage in the **Too Finely Sifted** game. This person keeps sifting the same information, reviewing it needlessly in a repetitive manner until nothing worth knowing about the situation remains. He not only bores himself but irritates others with this meticulous behavior, analyzing the spontaneity out of life.

The opposite watery 12th Chord points to the need for allowing one's intuitive energy to flow and be accessed consciously. There is much exciting creativity in the mutable chords. It requires that a person trust the self enough to allow these creative thought processes to begin. It is a lack of faith in one's creative mind that bring people into this and many other 6th Chord games. (The square formed to Chord 9 and the opposition to Chord 12 indicate that many 6th Chord games have their root causes in a lack of faith.)

A strong 6th Chord type may exhibit the **9 to 5** game. This individual believes that life is meant to fit into rigid routines and be lived by the clock. He often misses out on new experiences because he is too attached to punctuality and a schedule. He lacks the imagination to broaden life perspectives. An overdevelopment of the earthy need for exactness in the 6th Chord needs to be balanced with relying on intuition.

One of the more difficult games related to the 6th Chord tones is an individual's surrender to negative and self-denying behaviors in the **I Can't, I Can't!** game. This individual creates failing situations. He has analyzed himself as a hopeless failure and desires to negate or sabotage the essence of his existence.

This game can be typical of an individual who is too compulsively trying to create a perfect world as well as an individual who believes himself to be incapable of accomplishment. The former sets goals too high and the latter sets goals too low. In this game the individual hits the rock bottom of negativity and cannot see any purpose in making the effort to get afloat again. He is too exhausted by doubts and feelings of inferiority to change the course of his life.

This individual may need to explore the enthusiasm of the fire chords to generate the momentum to move ahead. Chord 9 (the square) points to faith and eagerness to explore journeys into new, uncharted territories. Chord 1 (the quincunx) offers a willingness to assert one's own rights and to change one's identity—to a more positive sense of self.

Another 6th Chord game related to negativity is the **Litterbug**. This individual litters his mind with the harmful debris of self-criticism. He has a tendency to pollute his mind with negative thoughts and may even try to convince others to think negatively about themselves. This individual is desperately seeking love but doesn't know how to say the magic healing word, "Help!"

This is a person who often needs to lighten-up. Most of all he needs to find the origins of this negativity. There is often a confused sense of identity (quincunx to 1st Chord) and individuality (quincunx to 11th Chord). Strengthening one's sense of self and uniqueness can enable one to get beyond negative programming. The opposite watery 12th Chord points to a need for examining one's underlying emotional motives and developing more faith, as does the square to the 9th Chord.

The **I Can't, I Can't!** and **Litterbug** games are often accompanied by another 6th Chord game, the **Martyr**. This is an individual who puts on an air of self-sacrifice to arouse pity or guilt in others. He often is a manipulative person who is trying to get his own way or to escape responsibility.

An individual's water energy may be related to this game. The person often possesses a powerful, intuitive nature that is working overtime. Unfortunately, this beautiful energy is being misdirected toward emotional manipulation of others. Directing the energy inward to better understand the self could prove highly rewarding (opposition to 12th Chord).

There is a tendency to escape from personal problems associated with the 6th Chord. This may take the form of the **Workaholic** game. This game is more likely found in connection with Virgo or the 6th house (than with Mercury) as these tones are associated with perfecting skills, hard work and serving others. The **Workaholic** is not just directing the mind away from problems for a brief period of time to gain a more objective view of the situation. The **Workaholic** would rather drown himself in work than face problems. This is an avoidance type of behavior. He is always too busy to deal directly with conflict or uneasy situations.

This person would find more energy when he stops running away from situations. Clearly facing emotional problems frees blocked, creative material and makes problem-solving more effective. Sometimes the **Workaholic** is an individual who simply carries a "good thing" too far. Such people know that they are efficient and productive workers, so they put all their emphasis into work because they fear they would "fail" at other life activities. They turn what is a major talent into a liability by doing it **all** the time. If they allow themselves to face other areas, they will discover they can also be effective in arenas other than work.

The square to the 9th Chord and opposition to the 12th Chord indicate that this 6th Chord game can be the result of not defining one's limits. Both of these chords (9 and 12) highlight going beyond one's limitations. However, some 6th Chord earthy common sense is needed to have a balanced expression.

Another form of self-denial or negative behavior is found in the **Dead End Job** game. Once again this game is more associated with Virgo or the 6th house than with Mercury. This is an individual who continuously moves from one job to another or remains in a job far below his intelligence while not improving job skills. He feels his intelligence and talents are inferior to others and lacks the initiative to develop skills that would bring a higher income and lead to a more suitable employment situation.

This individual needs to find a new faith (square to Chord 9) in himself (quincunx to Chord 1). Outside observers may be feeding self-doubts. He needs to strengthen a sense of self (Chord 1) and realize that he really has a right to expect more from life (Chord 9).

The **Somebody Please Kick Me** game is another form of overindulgence in self-denial. The humility and service orientations of the 6th Chord are twisted by this individual into a slavish devotion to other people. He may be completely devoted to a lover who has no respect for him or surrender individuality to a religious leader or a cult-like group. This individual is seeking humiliating situations that support a desire for self-denial.

The polarity of Chords 6 and 12 addresses the issue of "savior" and "victim" mentalities. The strong need to serve of Chord 6 when combined with the devotional instincts of Chord 12 can unconsciously lead some people into bizarre relationships. Such individuals need to use the discriminating talents and common sense shown by the 6th Chord while seeking the transcendence and inspiration desired by the 12th Chord. They must not enslave their individuality (quincunx to 11th Chord).

The **Abused Body** game is related to the perfectionistic and self-denial tendencies of compulsive 6th Chord individuals, especially those with key planets in Virgo or having difficulty in expressing planetary themes in association with 6th house motifs. Denying oneself a proper diet in this game can be an individual's form of self-punishment for not living up to Mount Everest elevation levels of perfection. This is the case for women who deny themselves food in the starvation diet known as anorexia. I have seen clients who exhibit another eating disorder, bulimia, also known as bulimia nervosa. Bulimia is an eating disorder consisting of large food binges followed by a purging of the body through induced vomiting or a heavy use of laxatives. Dr. Susan Wooley, Co-director of the University of Cincinnati Medical Center's Clinic for Eating Disorders, has stated that "Bulimics are often perfectionists, seeing everything in black and white in terms of success and failure." (From an article in *Harper's Bazaar,* March 1982, p. 148.) Bulimia causes many harmful side effects to one's body.

The **Abused Body** game is also found among individuals who gain tremendous amounts of weight that can be damaging to the health. These individuals are often disappointed that they are not more successful in life and may be punishing themselves for not meeting their own perfection standards. This is an attempt to make themselves as undesirable to others as they are to themselves by gaining tremendous amounts of weight.

The self-punishment tendencies can be ameliorated by focusing more on free, spontaneous self-expression (quincunx to Chord 1) rather than careful reasoning and disciplined action. A focus on one's need for independence from rules and unrestricted individuality (quincunx to Chord 11) can also break up the narrow focus of too much Chord 6 emphasis.

The **Abused Body** game may also be found in individuals who are substance abusers such as those addicted to drugs or alcohol. This is another form of self-hatred or self-denial where an individual is attempting to negate existence by dulling conscious awareness of one's self and destroying one's health. (The **Abused Body** game will also be discussed in the 12th Chord.)

Summary of Issues with 6th Chord Games

The 6th Chord games have their origin in too much self-analysis and criticism of others as well as self. There can be an overabundance of negativity. Sixth Chord talents can be used to excel at discipline, hard work, detail and helping others to better organize their lives. The flaw-finding lens of the 6th Chord can be a valuable asset if properly applied. It is when the attraction to detailed perfection is allowed to overshadow other parts of life (such as a positive sense of self or healthy relationships) that 6th Chord games arise.

Subtones

The three **subtones of the 6th Chord** are: the planetary aspect known as the **quincunx,** the energy focus of Virgo known as **mutable,** and the house classification known as **cadent.**

The **quincunx,** as a subtone of the 6th Chord planetary tone supports the archetypal theme of Mercury. The planets forming a quincunx aspect indicate that an individual needs to create a sense of order through exercising powers of discrimination in relation to the particular symbolisms of the planets involved. An individual can suffer physical health problems or severe mental stress through not facing the issues symbolized by the particular planets forming this aspect. Also, the quincunx can indicate a compulsive type of behavior that an individual may be required to conquer—or at least control through discipline or by developing a healthier attitude concerning the issues involved. Stephen Arroyo offers an excellent description of the quincunx in his book, *Astrology, Karma and Transformation* (p. 114). He states that the quincunx may be experienced by an individual as "compulsive or consistently annoying" and goes on to say that discrimination and discipline will be needed to make the best personal adjustment to the issues involved.

Consider the planets discussed in our previous aspect examples, the 5th Chord planetary tone (the Sun) and the 12th Chord planetary tone (Neptune) forming a quincunx in a person's chart. This could denote an individual's compulsive drive to perfect artistic talents, and he may need to exercise caution so that he does not ignore his health in the process. The vitality and energy needed to sustain the core self (Sun) could be sacrificed to ideals and hypnotic fancy to perfect artistic talents (Neptune). He may overwork, forget to rest and eat a poor diet. However, the same individual could accomplish an important and transcending passage in life by incorporating this energy with common sense and self-discipline concerning work habits and health.

The quincunx often represents an energy that is experienced by an individual as unsettling. Illnesses are sometimes symbolized by this aspect, as the body is giving signals to the individual that something is not in order in the life. When Mercury is involved in the quincunx aspect, the discrimination and discipline qualities of the 6th Chord will be that much more needed and emphasized as the archetypal theme of Mercury in the 6th Chord context is especially related to a person's ability to organize life in such a way that physical and psychological health are purified. When a person expresses a quincunx in a balanced manner, it can indicate a form of self-mastery and a well-disciplined creativity.

The refining and perfecting features of Virgo are well supported by its subtone, a **mutable** energy movement. As stated in the 9th Chord, the key word phrase for mutable is **adaptable energy.** Since Virgo is the mutable earth sign, the focus here is adapting oneself to practical needs by learning new skills as well as perfecting and refining the mind and body to adjust to changing situations.

The 6th house is supported by its subtone house classification, **cadent.** As stated in the 9th Chord, the key word phrase for cadent is **eagerness to learn.** The urge to learn new skills and to develop efficient work habits, associated with the 6th house, is supported by its cadent subtone. The earth theme of the 6th house combines with the cadent subtone to suggest an eagerness to learn how to become more efficient in work skills and taking care of one's health.

The 6th Chord symbolizes an individual's common sense and capacity to create an orderly, efficient and healthy life. It is through a proper self-analysis and discrimination concerning life challenges that an individual can achieve balanced expectations of self and others as well as developing a clear perspective concerning perfection and a sense of order in life.

CHAPTER SEVEN

TENTH CHORD: DESIRE FOR SUCCESS

> Only a relative and fortunate few continue until the moment of death exploring the mystery of reality, ever enlarging and refining and redefining their understanding of the world and what is true.
>
> *The Road Less Traveled* by M. Scott Peck, M.D. (page 45)

The 10th Chord is an expression of the earth element in the most basic form of solidifying the self through determination and taking responsibility for one's actions. The planet (Saturn), sign (Capricorn) and house (10th) tones of this chord symbolize an individual's need to make concrete a niche in the world through achievements and a sustained effort to fulfill ambitious success drives. Saturn, Capricorn and the 10th house represent all forms of the law: natural cultural regulations such as stopping for red lights and going through green lights; authority figures who carry out the law, usually including fathers, boss, policemen, teachers; and our conscience—our internalized law, which punishes us with guilt if we go astray.

The archetypal themes of the 10th Chord tones reflect three forms of establishing one's sense of accomplishment within the laws and boundaries of the world.

The earth element's concern for initiating material accomplishments and responsible actions is symbolized in the 10th Chord tones and subtones.

10TH CHORD: DESIRE FOR SUCCESS

Tone	Archetypal Themes	Functions	Positive Expressions	Negative Expressions	Potential Counseling Issues
Planet: Saturn **Symbol ♄**	The directing of actions to solidify one's inner strength, manage one's life structures, make the appropriate adjustments in focused responsibilities and develop a realistic assessment of life circumstances, ambitions and understanding of authority.	1. To secure the self by structuring, controlling and managing one's life. 2. To be a grounding force for self and others. 3. To apply wisdom gained through experience in a concrete manner. 4. To embody practical values. 5. To accept responsibility. 6. To establish and accomplish career goals. 7. To respond to the demands of time and the maturation process.	1. An ability to discipline oneself and focus energies to achieve goals. 2. The capacity to manage others and to help structure their lives. 3. Ambition. 4. Conscientiousness and commitment. 5. An ability to face reality. 6. Dependability. 7. Patience. 8. An ability to provide parental stability. 9. Enjoyment of solitude. 10. Maturity.	1. Excessive ambition and status seeking. 2. Lack of imagination due to overstructuring. 3. A tendency to be too impersonal in relating to others due to a lack of trust. 4. Career confusion. 5. Rigidity and lack of spontaneity. 6. Overly authoritarian demeanor. 7. Repressed emotional nature. 8. Easily depressed. 9. Too focused on external solutions. 10. Unreliable.	**Key Phrase:** Structuring The Self **Games:** 1. Austerity Trip. 2. Career Blahs. 3. Climbing the Ladder of Success. 4. Conditional Love. 5. Father Time. 6. I Am the President. 7. I Give up. 8. I Shall Not Be Ruled. 9. I'm OK, You're Not OK 10. I'm Not OK, You're OK 11. Internalized Parent. 12. On My Guard. 13. Retirement Blues. 14. Sad Sack. 15. Scapegoat. 16. Tree That Won't Bend.
Sign: Capricorn **Symbol ♑**	The manner through which one's ambition, structures and practicality can be initiated and managed to ensure success and stability.				
House: 10th	One's attitudes concerning authority, public reputation, destiny, responsibility and the management of professional aspirations.				

Figure 6: Tenth Chord
See the Note to Readers after Acknowledgments

Saturn

The 10th Chord planetary tone, Saturn, symbolizes an individual's striving to build life structures that are sound and practical, serving to secure a station in life. In mythology, Saturn was associated with Chronos, the god of time. Saturn denotes the strength to face the challenges and dilemmas presented by the maturation process. Also, Saturn represents the willingness to grow through assimilating past experiences and to develop a realistic assessment of our present life circumstances.

Years ago Saturn was sometimes referred to as the Lord of Karma or the evil taskmaster. Many astrologers believed its position foretold fated events that would bring burden, loss or other disastrous circumstances into the individual's life.

A modern astrology views Saturn's symbolism more in relation to how an individual can free the self from limitation through responsible actions and establishing meaningful commitments. Saturn's position is seen as indicating a grounding force for the psyche to concentrate energy, rather than as frustration, torment and limitation.

In the sky, Saturn is encircled by beautiful shining rings composed of millions of small particles of ice. Only Jupiter is bigger in size and only Jupiter has a more rapid speed of rotation, symbolizing an individual's potential to move swiftly when integrity or social position is challenged.

The rings that encompass Saturn in the cosmos give the appearance of a buffer or protection from outside influences. Likewise, Saturn's astrological significance by sign and especially house, indicates an individual's most characteristic mode of putting safe distance between oneself and the world by building stable foundations whether it be in the form of establishing a family, career or reputation. Individuals sometimes feel a sense of heaviness in manifesting their Saturn energy, forgetting to "lighten up." Astronomers say that Saturn is light enough to float in the ocean. There is a lightness or ease that an individual can attain through Saturn motifs, if she can stay away from becoming overserious or burdened in life responsibilities and maybe even learn to laugh at life's paradoxes.

The planets closest to the Earth (i.e., Saturn and the planets within its orbit) symbolize an individual's personal and evolving actions. The planets extending beyond Saturn's orbit symbolize generational, collective and more unconscious images and impulses. Until the discovery of Uranus in 1781, Saturn was the furthermost planet known to us.

Saturn's symbolism in astrology indicates the kind of experiences that can promote the inner strength and commitment to break into new levels of consciousness beyond mere conscious boundaries as typified by the more recently discovered planets Uranus, Neptune and Pluto. It seems that Saturn's house position is of extreme importance in counseling situations. Since Saturn remains in one sign for as much as 2½ years, its sign position is bordering on the generational significance symbolized by the sign placements of Uranus, Neptune and Pluto. However, Saturn's house location indicates attitudes concerning the taking of responsibility for decisions and the ability to move forward in life with a sense of purpose. I have found that a blocked or frozen Saturn energy has been the root cause of many personal problems in adjusting to the demands of one's life.

Individuals who overidentify with their external achievements often scorn Saturn as an evil taskmaster when their lives seem filled with frustration, pain and lack of success. However, if these individuals were honest with themselves, they might see that their lives have become too rigid, enslaved to outer success. Rings of ice have formed around their hearts. Their resistance to bend before the tests of time has hardened with their dismay at the rigorous obligations imposed by life. These individuals often do see Saturn as a devil. Liz Greene in her book, *Saturn: A New Look at an Old Devil* (p. 11), says of Saturn, "Anyone who enjoys her pain is considered to be a masochist; however, it is not enjoyment of pain which Saturn fosters but rather the exhilaration of psychological freedom. This is not often recognized because not many people have experienced it."

Perhaps the rings of Saturn symbolize the parasitic illusions which can develop in our consciousness over the years, and feed off our irrational fears and insecurities, keeping us separate from our true selves. Saturn can symbolize experiences that might challenge our deepest insecurities and vulnerabilities but at the same time can lead us to tremendous stability and growth when these fears are confronted.

The positive expressions of Saturn include an individual's ability to discipline the self and focus energies to achieve goals. The staying power of someone in tune with her Saturn side can be awesome. Individuals can also display a strong management ability and help others to structure their own lives, especially evident in the role of providing parental guidance for a child. Other positive expressions include dependability, patience, ambition and following through on commitments. Perhaps one of the most positive expressions symbolized by Saturn is facing reality within the test of difficult circumstances, and maintaining a balanced perspective about life without becoming overcautious or rigid.

The negative expressions of Saturn include an individual's becoming too ambitious. She views life as a daily struggle to rise to power as is seen in the **Climbing the Ladder of Success** game. Individuals sometimes fall prey to the rigidity that Saturn can symbolize in not trusting others and developing an overbearing authoritarian demeanor (illustrated in the **I am the President** and **Yes Sir!** games).

Other negative expressions of Saturn include an individual's insensitivity to the feelings of others due to a repressed emotional nature and a tendency to resent all authority figures. Perhaps the Achilles' heel indicated by a blocked expression of Saturn energy is resisting change. Due to insecurities and fears, individuals can become too attached to certain phases of their lives. An adult may continue to behave like a child and resist the transition that is now required. This resisting of change can result in feelings of loneliness, depression, and projecting one's problems onto others as in the **Scapegoat** game.

Capricorn

The 10th Chord sign tone, Capricorn, complements the archetypal theme of the planetary tone by symbolizing an individual's initiation of responsible actions to manage and structure energy into ambitious and practical enterprises. Capricorn symbolizes an individual's self-respect and represents the signature of her integrity much like Saturn. Most traditional astrology books emphasize Capricorn as the sign that reflects one's external awareness or drives for success. Although I do not necessarily disagree with this description, it is also apparent that traditional astrology often does not acknowledge the tremendous inner strength that can be indicated by a strong emphasis on this sign such as the Sun, Moon, Ascendant or several other planets in Capricorn. The power that Capricorn can denote is a power that comes from a strong conviction that once the journey has begun, it must be seen to the finish. The traditional symbol of Capricorn, the goat, is a rare goat indeed! She is more like a mountain goat that thrives on work and gets stronger as she ascends higher and higher up the mountain.

While the 6th Chord stresses order, the 10th Chord symbolizes the backbone and foundation behind order. Capricorn is the master of controlling and planning—delegating work assignments to others and surveilling the surroundings. Capricorn symbolizes authority figures such as the boss, police, provider, parent, president, etc. There is a mystical loneliness symbolized by Capricorn. It is the sign that must stand alone, sometimes at the top, policing the borders of the inner and outer worlds, to make sure the contents are well guarded, functioning soundly and, most of all, under control.

The positive expressions of Capricorn include expertise in managing large and complicated operations, knowing how to make them work smoothly. An individual in tune with Capricorn energy knows how to treat others with dignity and respect. Conscientiousness, dependability and patience can be Capricorn virtues along with a balanced self-discipline that helps an individual focus energies to achieve goals. Another positive expression is dealing realistically with life circumstances and handling crisis situations.

The negative expressions of Capricorn include a fixation on ambition. All one's time is devoted to schemes for becoming successful and powerful; the individual often forgets to rest while climbing the mountain. Perhaps Capricorn's biggest potential downfall is lack of trust. A strong Capricorn type who is negatively manifesting these themes often fears trusting others, lest it make her feel too vulnerable to the whims of others. Another negative expression is rigidity. Usually the emotions are repressed and the individual exhibits a moody, overserious disposition that alienates people. Another negative expression is establishing relationships around conditional love. The affections are structured in order to keep in control of the situation. Unfortunately, an individual often cheats herself of receiving love from others if she is too protective of herself. Other negative expressions include an unreliable nature and a tendency to become easily depressed due to an overserious life attitude.

10th House

The third tone of this chord, the 10th house, is located at the top of the horoscope, symbolizing an individual's public status and attitudes toward attaining great heights or success in life. The 10th house, like the other 10th Chord tones, represents the ability to manage life and build a solid and dependable existence. It could even be said that the 10th house is the destiny that an individual creates for herself.

The 10th house symbolizes an individual's attitudes concerning a place in the community or the level of ambition to find a meaningful role in society. An appropriate career or role is one that truly expresses herself whether it be feminist, banker or musician. In traditional astrology, the 10th house is often regarded as the career house. Modern astrology views the 10th house as one's attitudes concerning career aspirations as well as the initiative to assume responsibility for oneself. The 10th house is an indicator of one's ability to manage life and shows one's style as an authority figure whether it be parent, citizen or executive. One's respect or lack of it for authority figures is also symbolized.

The positive expressions of the 10th house include taking the initiative to develop a meaningful career or a place in society that is a true reflection of one's ability. Another positive expression is being able to manage one's life and to help others manage their own lives. An individual with a highly accentuated 10th house may be well respected for the ability to use a powerful and prestigious position in a benevolent manner. Her opinion might be highly valued to mediate local affairs in the community. A strong 10th house individual might inspire others through an ability to set a good example of dependability and success in a public role. Another possible 10th house expression is an individual who must assume responsibility for the family due to an ill or irresponsible mate.

The negative expressions of the 10th house include too much emphasis on public status or obtaining a powerful position within society. This individual makes the sole aim in life to "get to the top." She is typified by an overly authoritarian and sometimes ruthless behavior. A lack of trust is another negative expression as the individual refuses to delegate responsibility to others. This can be a domineering husband or wife who must make all the important decisions or an authoritarian supervisor who has no trust for workers. A rigid attitude leads to a defensive approach that alienates others. Another negative expression is an individual's refusal to take responsibility in life. Mistakes are always the fault of others. She may also display an undependable nature.

The sign on an individual's 10th house as well as planets situated in this house symbolize the types of expressions that energize one's career ambitions. These factors indicate one's attitude toward managing life successfully, accepting responsibility, and one's opinions concerning authority figures. (Saturn's placement in the horoscope should, of course, be given careful consideration as well.)

Counseling Issues

The counseling issues of the 10th Chord are indicative of an individual's inability to express the spirit of this chord, **desire for success.** My key word phrase for these counseling issues, **structuring the self,** is from the synthesis of the tones—Saturn, Capricorn and the 10th house. The 10th Chord tones have an emphasis upon structure embedded in their archetypal themes, which are:

1. **Saturn**—the directing of actions to solidify one's inner strength, manage one's life structures, make the appropriate adjustments in focused responsibilities, and develop a realistic assessment of life circumstances, ambitions and authority.
2. **Capricorn**—the manner through which one's ambition, structures and practicality can be initiated and managed to ensure success and stability.
3. **10th house**—one's attitudes concerning authority, public reputation, destiny, responsibility and the management of professional aspirations.

The counseling issues of this chord concern an individual's lack of balance in achieving ambitions and accepting responsibility for life. The 10th Chord tones can be used by an individual to develop a dependable and reliable character. The counseling issues of the 10th Chord are twofold: (1) a compulsive tendency to exert too much self-control coupled with a forceful control of others and extreme success drives; (2) an individual's lack of control or inability to structure and assume responsibility for life due to either a fear of failure or confusion concerning one's appropriate role in the world.

Games

When an individual displays too much self-control in the manifestation of 10th Chord tones, she may exhibit the **On My Guard** game. This individual often suffers from a severe emotional restriction and will not allow herself to spontaneously interact with others. A need for control dominates the life. She usually does not trust herself or others. Her personality may be as cold as the rings of ice encircling Saturn. The **On My Guard** game can be emotionally suffocating like a medieval knight wearing a helmet with a visor that will not open and has no openings through which to breathe. When dysfunctioning, 10th Chord tones can indicate rigid and outworn forms of behavior much like the character armor defense mechanism described by the psychologist Wilhelm Reich. The structuring of the self has become a rusty set of armor due to an individual's compulsive desire for control.

I have observed this game to be especially prevalent for individuals having the 4th Chord planet, the Moon, or the Ascendant in Capricorn. These individuals sometimes display an extreme caution in expressing emotions due to difficulty in trusting others. Saturn located in an individual's 1st house or strongly aspecting personal planets may symbolize an individual a bit more susceptible to this game.

Since the Moon is a water planet, its placement in the 10th house or in Capricorn can denote a focus on both physical (earthy) and emotional (watery) security. The individual with a sense of **inner** security will identify with such configurations through being a "mother of the world" type. She feels compelled to take care of everyone. The individual not yet in touch with inner emotional power (4th Chord) or competence (10th Chord) may project this onto the world. The world can be perceived as a threat to her safety, and the individual retreats into caution and repression.

I have observed individuals with the Moon in the 10th house or in Capricorn who are quite capable of balancing emotional expression and external accomplishments. With a clear sense of emotional power, they do not fear taking responsibility for themselves and others.

Similarly, the individual with Saturn in the 1st or Capricorn rising can symbolize a person who attracts responsibility at an early age, but has risen above feelings of "heaviness" or blocked emotional expression. The assertion of Chord 1 (1st house or Ascendant) has been optimally blended with the responsible accomplishments of Chord 10. However, since the planets are the **most emphatic** of the three major tones in a chord, Saturn in the 1st house is more likely to go initially into self-blocking—with Saturnian fears and inhibitions interfering with self-assertion and initiative—until the individual gains a sense of her own power. By contrast, Mars in Capricorn or Mars in the 10th house is more likely to go initially into overdrive—the individual pushing too hard, feeling her energy and self-expressive drive (Chord 1) can conquer the world and overcome any blocks (Chord 10). Either extreme shows the need for balance and integration. Each placement can lend itself to creative self-expression that makes an impact in the world if the individual has a balanced sense of reality, responsibility and personal power.

Although many popular astrology books describe Capricorns as cold and cautious, I have not observed this to be so true. Perhaps due to the strength and vitality of the Sun, Capricorn Sun individuals are initially reserved but can "warm up" after the "ice is broken." The fiery Sun shines through with an inner vitality energizing success and achievement drives. By contrast, there is more of a danger with Saturn in Leo or in the 5th house that the individual might block creativity and the ability to shine through critical, inhibiting, restrictive standards and demands. Of course, all combinations of Chords 5 and 10 can denote power, leadership and the potential of creative competence when integrated.

Another game related to too much control is **Conditional Love.** This individual is very fearful of becoming vulnerable and therefore must in no uncertain terms prescribe the way that someone is to love her. This is a very unrealistic method of relating to others. The individual is often very sensitive to how a lover or mate behaves and sometimes has an explicit set of rules to follow, such as no display of affections in public. An individual exhibiting this game is often very afraid of being rejected by others and will only give love or affection "after" the partner follows guidelines to prove that he really cares about her.

This game and the previous 10th Chord game require that a person stop attempting to control the creative self-expression of others. The individual caught in this game may feel trapped in a frozen identity with emotional blockage. The person may need to gain the courage to tap into her emotional strength and not fear being rejected by others. There may be impatience with self and others while rules interfere with self-expression and relationships. Some nurturance of self and others can soften the icy structure of Chord 10. Also, 10th Chord games can involve difficulties in one's early childhood and may require looking again at one's roots.

Another 10th Chord game symbolic of an individual's developing a rigid control pattern of behavior is the **Tree That Won't Bend.** This is the stubbornness expressed by an individual who refuses to surrender the reins of control even though circumstances are indicating this is what she must do to ensure balance and success. However, she becomes the tree that refuses to bend, failing to heed the advanced warnings that a great storm is coming. Even though the other neighboring trees bend to save themselves before the mighty winds, she alone stands in defiance. Unfortunately, she is not able to withstand the force of the winds and is shattered into many fragments. This game often symbolizes someone who fears powerlessness and must prove to others that she is a powerful individual, always able to stay in control. The price paid in denying oneself love and affection often outweighs the small amount of respect sometimes received from others for feigned strength.

The key to this game is tapping into one's water energy and not fearing vulnerability. This person often demands a lot of herself and is emotionally frustrated. Great healing of emotional pain will occur if the person takes the risk of expressing this emotional intensity more constructively and directing it inwardly as well as outwardly. Individuals who put off seeing a doctor because they want to "be strong" and handle it "on my own" end up spending more time under the doctor's care or in the hospital than people who check out the first serious sign of a problem. Sensible acceptance of one's vulnerability leads to **more** strength and accomplishment in the end.

The previous game is related to another 10th Chord game, the **Sad Sack.** This individual becomes bogged down with the weight of responsibility she puts upon her own shoulders. Her drive to be in control of situations makes her sack heavier and heavier, filled with experiences of loneliness, emptiness and a sense of isolation as nobody really understands her. Perhaps the most ironic thing about many of these individuals is that there really are people in their lives practically dying to get to know them whether it be a friend, child or mate. However, the individual is often so severed from feelings due to an overserious disposition that she creates a wall between herself and others. The emotional body has become very barren as she cannot bear the thought of someone communicating with her innermost feelings or facing the fact that she really might need someone. (Counseling issues related to intimacy will be discussed in the 4th Chord and are often related to 10th Chord games.)

People experiencing this game feel the burden of caring for the world and deny too many of their own emotional needs. They must stop running from their own fears and fears of trusting others. They may be adopting warlike attitudes (squares to 1st and 7th Chords) that keep others at a distance. They may give responsibility such a priority that they deny their own personal needs and self-expression (square to Chord 1) as well as their need for balanced relationships (square to Chord 7). Their overacceptance of responsibility blocks them from their vulnerable side (opposition to Chord 4). The **Sad Sack** must gain a true understanding of her inner world in order to become successful in the world of form.

The 10th Chord could just as well have been named the desire for reality or a true destiny. The essential success symbolized by this chord is developing a balanced inner reality that naturally leads to a successful outer world. When an individual follows a path that departs from inner reality through a negative manifestation of 10th Chord tones, she may become victimized by another control-oriented game, **Climbing the Ladder of Success.** This is an individual with a compulsive drive to achieve status and position at any cost—whether it means betraying the trust of friends, peers or loved ones. An excessively ambitious nature has blurred clarity. In real life situations an individual may appear like a winner as she climbs higher up the ladder. However, very often within herself she is a continual loser. Finally, there comes a day when a rung of the ladder fails, and her life comes to a startling halt, often in the form of a major life setback such as a career flop, physical illness or a faithful mate tiring of these selfish success drives and leaving her. The individual may experience a desperate helplessness and perhaps long for those she so easily sacrificed to selfish ambitions.

There is a tendency in the 10th Chord to get too engrossed in trying to impress others with external achievements. The individual must not forget dependency needs. The 10th Chord is a very work-oriented chord, and it is easy to forget to have some fun and relaxation with loved ones. Responsibility must be balanced with free self-expression. It is important to remember that there is a place for peers and partnerships as well. The 10th Chord can point to a self-reliant individual. It may be necessary to show other people that she really does need them. Establishing emotional closeness allows the people to take turns caring for one another's needs.

Another 10th Chord game related to control is the **Yes Sir!** To assure them of their importance, these individuals compulsively demand proper respect from family members or employees. In the home they are usually addressed by children as "Yes Ma'am" or "Yes Sir." The individual is often in a position of authority such as a supervisor and purposely creates tension in others to remind them that she is in command. Some individuals who enact this game are repeating the model of a powerful parent who ruled the family with an iron hand. I have observed more than one client with strong aspects to Saturn in the natal chart, especially conjunctions, squares, quincunxes or oppositions, who was exposed to a very dominating parent. Saturn can symbolize the atmosphere of parental guidance during an individual's early growing-up years.

Difficulty in relating to one's father may be symbolized by strong aspects to Saturn in the horoscope. I have had clients experience difficulty in exchanging love with the father whose Saturn formed any of the previously mentioned aspects. It was as though a barrier needed to be broken between father and child.

I have had several clients with the Moon located in Capricorn experience difficulty in communicating emotions and relate this problem to a dominating mother. The Moon denotes our nurturing instincts as will be seen in the 4th Chord. A strongly aspected Saturn or Moon in Capricorn is a potential indicator of emotional blockage, and often this can be traced to the client's roots.

This is not to say that either Saturn or the Moon in Capricorn always symbolize problems with a dominating parent. A person with 4th/10th Chord combinations such as the Moon in the 10th house or Saturn in the 4th house will face issues around the integration of conditional and unconditional love.

Children require unconditional love ("I love you because you are; you do not have to do anything"), especially when very young and experiencing their first impressions of dependency (4th Chord). However, the child must eventually meet conditional love ("I love you when you behave properly") as they grow older, in order to learn limits and to live within the boundaries of society (10th Chord).

If a person has strong mixtures of the 4th and 10th Chords in the horoscope, she may have experienced an overdose of conditional or unconditional love—or a balanced integration—with her parents. It is important to remember that a person has choices. Even if her experiences with her own parents were not positive, she need not repeat those negative patterns in being a parent or authority herself. A person does **not** have to overidentify with a parent or overreact by adopting the opposite extreme in behavior. She can choose to express a give-and-take of affections in adult life. Responsibility and nurturing can be shared in a balanced fashion.

The **Yes Sir!** game alienates others and is similar to the **On My Guard** game in keeping people at an emotional distance. A person exhibiting the **Yes Sir!** game often has a strong external orientation and relies on the discipline of external circumstances, such as a fondness for rank, to provide a sense of balance. She may command a domestic life much like that of the highly structured home in which she was raised or as though she was still in the armed forces where she once served.

The **I'm OK, You're Not OK** game is typified by an individual who is desperately seeking to protect insecure feelings concerning career goals and position within the family or community. She makes every attempt to prove others are either too unsophisticated in intelligence or simply too inadequate to question her opinions or ambitions. This is another mask for an individual's lack of trust and feelings of powerlessness. She wants to be loved and cared for affectionately but instead chooses to control others by making them feel incompetent or inferior. This game also typifies an individual strongly attached to an external orientation. She chooses to surround herself only with people that will not question her authority.

This person needs to trust her capacity to receive love from others so she can stop overstructuring the environment and relationships with others. This pattern of behavior is a projection of fear learned early in life and inhibits emotional growth. A person can get beyond the lack of trust and look for authentic strokes that help free and develop the emotional being. This calls for self-examination and a restructuring of one's inner identity. Useful in the process will be courage to change the self (square to Chord 1), nurturing support and willingness to be vulnerable (opposition to Chord 4) and desire to share openly with others (square to Chord 7).

The **Scapegoat** game is another 10th Chord counseling issue having its origin in the **I'm OK, You're Not OK** game. This is an individual who refuses to take responsibility for personal actions. It is always the fault of someone else or a "fated" situation that causes all her problems. She is always looking for an excuse to prove why unsuccessful endeavors are not her fault.

She is sometimes continuing a pattern from childhood where the parents never defined clear limits. This can also be an individual who refuses to examine the emotional scars from growing-up years or past relationships. The individual needs to drop some defenses. When she stops hiding behind this blaming behavior, she can tap into a true sense of strength (square to Chord 1).

The **I am the President** game is related to an individual's infatuation with prestige and social status. This game is named after President Nixon (a Capricorn Sun individual) who popularized this statement by reminding all of us, on numerous occasions in his speeches, that he was indeed the president. This game is true of an individual who feels she must overwhelm others with important titles or great external accomplishments. This individual often does not believe she will be loved or given attention unless she can win us with title or fame.

The 10th Chord naturally forms a quincunx to the 5th Chord. The 5th Chord can be expressed as an individual's attempt to impress others by doing things in a "big way." The drive to satisfy one's external accomplishments can become the most important thing in life. This person needs to tune into her self-image in a clear manner and express the true essence of the 5th Chord, which is defining oneself honestly. Once again, the opposite 4th Chord offers another solution: establishing a close friendship with one's emotional nature and not fearing dependency in exchanges with others.

Anger can be related to 10th Chord games, especially in regard to dislike of authority figures. In the **I Shall Not Be Ruled** game a person detests authority figures from all walks of life. A balanced manner of asserting oneself is needed. The person does not need to overly compromise her life to those "superior" in position or power. However, a tactful approach is more appropriate than always adopting a warlike style when negotiating with these people. The squares formed by the 10th Chord to the 1st and 7th Chords indicate that one must balance assertion and cooperation in relating to others.

Strong 10th Chord individuals by sign, planet or house sometimes get over their heads in controlling their actions and become entrapped by the **Austerity Trip** game. These individuals are much tougher on themselves than in the 6th Chord, 9 **to** 5 game, which is being caught in a routine-oriented life. This 10th Chord game goes one step further and is an individual's manner of punishment for being a "failure" by imposing a rigid and disciplined schedule upon herself. She denies herself forms of recreation or leisure and imposes a serious life attitude upon herself at all times. Humor and fun are seen as a waste of time, and life is lived as though it is a guard duty. Needless to say, these individuals usually suffer a lonely and loveless life. As the **Sad Sack** described earlier, they need to "lighten up" their loads.

Once again, it is important to remember that the 10th Chord quincunxes the 5th Chord, indicating that learning to enjoy oneself through hobbies, recreation, sexuality and spending time with children may need to be scheduled into the life. The fire element encourages a zest for life with many varied expressions. Fire combines well with serious earth. The individual can balance seasons of work and pleasure, learning to alternate between the two.

An individual's loss of control or inability to structure life due to a misuse of 10th Chord tones can result in an individual not taking responsibility for her actions. The **I'm Not OK, You're OK** game is typified by an individual who is irresponsible and not dependable though she hungers for positive regard. She is afraid of taking risks as she does not want to be seen as a failure, having a similar theme to the **I Can't, I Can't!** 6th Chord game. This game may find an individual believing that she is too incompetent to form meaningful commitments or undeserving of successful and enduring love relationships.

This game calls for a person to stop trying to prove self-worth to others. The peers (square to 7th Chord) a person chooses are very important. In many instances this person has received a lot of negative feedback concerning the self-image. She needs to develop a healthy sense of pride in herself (quincunx to Chord 5). She needs encouragement to accept herself just the way she is (square to Chord 1) and give up the relentless and endless climb up the imaginary mountain.

Unfortunately, for some individuals the **I'm Not OK, You're OK** game leads into the **I Give Up** game. This is an individual who becomes so depressed by life that she does not know what to do next. She is consumed by a tendency to withdraw from society or sees herself as nothing more than a failure. The optimism of the fire chords may be an underdeveloped ingredient here. The self-expectations of this individual are usually very high, and this is a self-hating behavior. It can sometimes be cured by a person forgiving herself and loving herself unconditionally.

Another 10th Chord game related to a lack of control or structure in one's life is **Career Blahs.** This has some of the overtones of the 6th Chord game, **Dead End Jobs.** This individual is not sure how to change the course of current career direction. She is usually bored and frustrated with the job situation and does not know which profession to choose or how to get into a career she desires. The individual often lacks the initiative and inner clarity to change circumstances. She complains incessantly about a supervisor, fellow employees, the work itself but never really makes a serious attempt to take the necessary steps to change her situation. She may remain in the same frustrating position blaming life for her predicament.

The square formed to the 1st Chord focuses upon the key issues here: assertion and risk-taking. There is a bit of the 1st Chord **Missing the Boat** game in this 10th Chord game. The individual must learn to follow her own assertion instincts. Perhaps she looks too much to others for direction. She can learn to see a little risk-taking as exciting, rather than as a fearful experience.

The **Retirement Blues** is another 10th Chord game related more to Saturn or Capricorn. This is an individual who cannot accept that she can no longer work at the same profession because she has reached retirement age. She has not developed any other hobbies or skills to occupy time and is now bored and sad, nostalgically longing for the "good old days." She feels useless and unproductive. She devoted her entire life to a profession and perhaps neglected developing other interests. She cannot find any means of relaxation as she will not forget the past. This individual must realistically face the present and find a new direction to provide the momentum to establish meaning once again in life.

This game confronts many individuals at the time of Saturn's second "return" to its birth position in a person chart, around age 58 to 60. An individual is carefully reevaluating a career or professional life that is coming to an end in the not-too-distant future. Aging can be a difficult process in Western societies. In many cases, people are not really prepared for life after retirement. A new kind of success must be created, whether the individual continues to work at a job, does volunteer work, travels, or finds a new hobby or creative outlet. The quincunx formed to the 3rd Chord calls on a person to find new life directions and interests. The quincunx to the 5th Chord shows the need for new creative self-expressions to better define oneself in the present. The person must realize that life still means something during this challenging passage.

Other games previously mentioned due to exercising too much control or structure in situations may also be attributed to a lack of control such as the **Scapegoat** as the individual is still trying to find external causes for problems. The **Sad Sack** and **Austerity Trip** games related to an overserious disposition are even more likely to be caused by an individual's tremendous frustration with the self for not taking responsibility for life.

Another 10th Chord game greatly symbolized by a dysfunctioning Saturn energy is the **Internalized Parent.** This can be a nagging type of internal voice that makes comments to an individual that she is a born failure and should not bother trying to accomplish a meaningful life. This is often the imprint of an authoritarian parent or other dominating people in the individual's life who gave a lot of negative feedback to her as a child. The **Internalized Parent** game can take the form of not trusting others as perhaps the individual was taught as a child that trust and emotional expressions only lead to heartache, or perhaps the child was punished if she cried or tried to show an emotional self.

The key to this game is relating to the opposite watery 4th Chord and making peace with one's emotional roots. This game shows the potential of the 10th Chord to be very psychological in nature. It is not simply a chord of outer success concerns. The person playing this game must learn not to sit in judgment of herself. Taking the risk of trusting others and opening up emotionally are often healing antidotes for this 10th Chord game.

Perhaps the most significant game of the 10th Chord is what I call **Father Time.** This game is mostly related to the symbolism of the planetary tone, the mythological god of time, Chronos or Saturn. The ability of an individual to handle transitions or major crises in adult life has been well discussed by Gail Sheehy in her excellent books, *Passages* and *Pathfinders.* Saturn's position in the horoscope and its current movement through an individual's horoscope (known as a transit) are symbolic of an individual's need to develop the strength and wisdom to structure a meaningful and growth-filled life. The 10th Chord greatly challenges an individual to avoid making past mistakes and to ask important questions such as: Who am I at this point in my life? Do I need a change of life direction to induce greater self-growth? How could I better use my valuable time? Do I need to redefine my commitments or establish new ones?

Saturn in the horoscope indicates how an individual will risk making a major change and react to the consequences that a transition can bring such as anxiety or fear. Gail Sheehy in *Pathfinders* describes four phases or steps to a successful passage or transition into a significant life change in the chapter entitled "Anatomy of a Passage." She refers to a person approaching a major life transition as a pathfinder.

Sheehy describes the first phase of a pathfinder as "anticipation." Sheehy explains that in this first stage a person must be ready to handle transitions and not get lost in everyday details or other procrastinations. Sheehy states that loss comes with change in the next phase of the transition process: "separation and incubation." This second stage is colored by anxiety and fear. One sheds an old identity within a state of constant change. Sheehy calls the third phase "expansion." This phase involves risk as one enters new unchartered territory. Sheehy states "time itself expands." A person experiences numerous possibilities for personal growth and toward settling conflicts such as compromising one's own goals versus satisfying one's own aspirations. Sheehy calls the fourth phase of the pathfinder "incorporation." This final phase includes solidifying the new self and is a reflective stage. This is also a time to play and relax to balance stress created by change.

In the **Father Time** game an individual is often caught somewhere in between the above phases. Sometimes she is so stuck in life situations and weighted down by the heaviness of it she cannot even get to phase one. Anticipation is quite remote from her mind. Her life script is stuffed away in a back pocket and full of too many frustrating and painful creases that have become wrinkles of worry in her brow.

Some individuals make it from phase one to phase two, separation and incubation but eventually backslide into past behavior patterns with old, worn-out roles, refusing to move ahead. Perhaps they reenter harmful relationships or marriages due to strong unbalanced dependency needs or return to careers that bring no sense of inner fulfillment.

Saturn in the birth chart symbolizes our determination to risk failure or temporary difficulty to make a significant life change. Saturn also represents the wisdom and common sense to have a good sense of timing changes and possessing the flexibility to follow through when opportunity is at hand. Gail Sheehy in *Pathfinders* explains that one is not limited because one direction is chosen rather than another or life circumstances have dictated a particular path. Sheehy describes a pathfinder as an individual who never loses sight of future possibilities. When the time arises the pathfinder has the flexibility to risk a change.

The **Father Time** game is essentially based on the ancient proverb: "We reap what we sow." It is the challenge of adult life that an individual keep structuring and restructuring a life script to make sure it does not just become a repetitive, rigid and worn-out part in an outdated play. Gail Sheehy emphasizes that no significant outer change for a pathfinder was really possible without there first being an inner change. Saturn also symbolizes our degree of reality in assessing our life circumstances and adjusting our life script to fulfill our innermost needs even if this involves some insecurity and anxiety.

The greatest message of the 10th Chord is to strengthen our ability to capture the reality of life without destroying our spontaneous instincts (square to Chord 1); to give ourselves the freedom to grow in new directions and not to inhibit the growth of significant others in our lives as well (square to Chord 7). The 10th Chord symbolizes the test of our reality and our courage to live within it! Perhaps Saturn symbolizes the key to the ultimate passages and is the pathfinder's true compass to embark upon a path of enlightenment.

Summary of Issues with 10th Chord Games

The 10th Chord games are given birth by an individual's handling of the need for structure, predictability and control in life. Some individuals structure the emotional spontaneity out of their lives, try to control others and engage in compulsive success drives. Other individuals defy basic structures, resenting authority figures and ignoring life's realistic limits. Some people limit their own accomplishments through inner fear, insecurity and self-criticism; they become afraid to take the risks necessary to accomplish life goals.

The 10th Chord denotes energies which are difficult to rival when it comes to reaching for goals and achieving them. The 10th Chord is filled with rugged determination and seeks self-sufficiency. It is only when a person looks to the outer world for complete fulfillment, denying the emotional nature and other needs, that the 10th Chord games take up too much time and become the only reality.

Subtones

The **three subtones** of this chord are: the planetary aspect known as the **square,** the energy focus of Capricorn known as **cardinal** and the house classification known as **angular.**

The square as a subtone of the 10th Chord planetary tone further emphasizes the archetypal theme of Saturn. The planets forming a square indicate a potential that can be problematic if an individual lacks focusing power. The square aspect represents a challenge to the individual. She must build the psychological strength as well as external structures that are able to contain and express dynamic energy and at the same time allow adequate flexibility to adapt to new situations.

Traditionally the square has been considered a malefic aspect. It is said to encourage an individual to exhibit disruptive or careless behavior. Modern astrology acknowledges that the square can be symbolic of problematic behavior as well as quite productive energy. As a matter of fact, individuals without squares in their charts may lack the drive needed to achieve their goals as they are often fearful of conflict and only gravitate to easy-flowing situations. Squares can indicate problematic behavior in that an individual can get carried away with the energy symbolized by the planets involved, becoming very willful and inflexible. The square calls for integration of the themes of the planets involved. Ignoring the themes of either planet to focus only on the themes of the other will create problems. Balance means making room for both.

Consider an individual with the 10th Chord planetary tone, Saturn, in square aspect to the 1st Chord planetary tone, Mars. This particular aspect could indicate that the individual is a good self-starter (Mars) in expressing career drives (Saturn). She may enjoy challenges and inspire others with tremendous energy. She may win the admiration of others with a competitive spirit and the courage to deal with crisis situations. However, this same aspect could indicate an individual who tries to bully others or force them to follow her lead. This could also denote an individual who is overly competitive and extremely selfish. The drive for success (Saturn) could have a compulsive **Me First** (Mars) focus.

This is a good example of one chord which "naturally" squares another. In other words, the tendencies and impulses of two chords that naturally square each other (such as the 1st and the 10th) require that a person integrate the natural tension symbolized. The 10th Chord requires restraint, practicality and working patiently for the future. The fiery and impulsive 1st Chord is very concerned with immediate conditions and will usually work hard if the results can be realized quickly. Integration requires that the person not repress the themes of either chord. She needs to balance the two expressions.

The square aspect requires an individual to exercise a conscious awareness of her actions. Squares are often more difficult to manifest constructively for individuals who have strong external orientations coupled with inflexible natures and lacking common sense. If Saturn is involved in a square aspect, an individual will need to cultivate even more patience and discipline, as well as listening to her "Inner Voice." The driving force symbolized by the square requires dependable outlets to structure and focus this energy.

Capricorn's archetypal theme is supported by its **cardinal sub-tone.** Cardinal energy is an **initiating spark that can inspire an individual to embark on new and challenging experiences.** The cardinal subtone of Capricorn is the fuel for an individual to reach back for the extra effort and the inner strength to accomplish life aims that require self-discipline and commitment.

The subtone of the 10th house is **angular**. The key word phrase for angular is action. The angular subtone of the 10th house symbolizes an individual's initiating **actions** to develop career aspirations, manage life and to assume responsibility. The angular subtone of the earthy 10th house inspires an individual to demonstrate goals publicly and to become a responsible member of a community as a citizen, parent, leader, etc.

Human behavior personifies the archetypal themes of each earth chord with pragmatic, focused, structured and security-oriented approaches. The earth element represents the raw materials of our personal history, the stability of the present, and the groundwork of the future—which solidify and strengthen a person's life. The energy to change what can be changed and to sometimes transcend what cannot be changed is mirrored by the inspiring fire chords. The patience, stamina and wisdom to time a change, and to accept what we cannot change, are shown by the earth chords.

PART IV

AIR ELEMENT

Air indicates a mental expression of the self. The air element shows curiosity, inventiveness, sociability, perceptive ingenuity and a propensity to developing a persuasive and convincing spirit. This element, like fire, points to an accelerated rhythm for acting out life experiences. However, air symbolizes a tendency to contemplate action rather than a spontaneous movement as in the fire element. Both air and fire symbolize an urge to seek exciting and energy-promoting experiences.

A person with air as a dominant element by having the air signs (Gemini, Libra and Aquarius) or air houses (3rd, 7th and 11th) well emphasized, or with the air planets strongly aspected, often displays an intellectual urge to share perceptions and knowledge with others. There is an inner restlessness denoted by the air element sometimes manifesting as nervousness, absent-mindedness or lack of concentration.

The three air chords denote creative imagination and mental sparks. Air can symbolize an individual's drive to enter new situations for the thrill of stimulating experiences that promise surprises and mentally exhilarating responses. An individual can have a highly accentuated emphasis on this element in any of the following ways: the Sun, Moon, Ascendant, four or more personal planets in air signs, key planets in air houses or the air planets strongly aspected. Such people often rely heavily on their thought processes and social instincts to establish a clear sense of self. The natural tendency symbolized by the air element is to first make sure the mental defroster has melted away any confusing thoughts and then to proceed quickly on to the highway of life with curious and investigative eyes—full speed ahead!

The planets, signs and houses comprising the air chords indicate mental faculties in the forms of perceiving (3rd Chord), relating (7th Chord) and planning (11th Chord).

Astrology, Psychology, and Transformation

The common ingredient of Chords 3, 7 and 11 is a strong drive to find appropriate channels through which to broadcast or communicate the self as well as to maintain a mental balance and clarity to integrate one's concepts into a meaningful life.

CHAPTER EIGHT

THIRD CHORD: CONCEPTUALIZATION OF PERCEPTION

> You teach best what you most need to learn.
> *Illusions* by Richard Bach (page 60)

The 3rd Chord is an expression of the air element in its most direct form of communication. The planet (Mercury), sign (Gemini) and house (3rd) tones of this chord symbolize an individual's primary urge to explain and communicate perceptions to others. With chord three we begin the process of socialization. Mercury, Gemini and the 3rd house of the chart give us our first air letter, so here we move into the conscious mind." She also says: "Individuals with a strong emphasis on letter three are often marked by an insatiable curiosity about everything plus an enthusiastic eagerness to talk about it all."

The 3rd Chord is symbolic of the air element's potential for fast mental reflexes analogous to the narrowing of a riverbed where the water moves more swiftly. The tones and subtones of the 3rd Chord symbolize a quickening of the thought processes and communication tendencies.

Astrology, Psychology, and Transformation

3RD CHORD: CONCEPTUALIZATION OF PERCEPTION					
Tone	Archetypal Themes	Functions	Positive Expressions	Negative Expressions	Potential Counseling Issues
Planet: Mercury Symbol ☿	The directing of mental activity for the conscious mind to process, analyze and communicate information and to perceive the environment.	1. To develop the conscious mind. 2. To direct intelligence and mental acuity. 3. To communicate effectively. 4. To experience excitement in response to mental stimulation. 5. To be adaptable. 6. To impart information.	1. Mental dexterity and adroitness. 2. The ability to interpret information and to communicate concepts. 3. The capacity to adapt to changing situations. 4. The ability to embody paradoxes due to an awareness of the dual nature. 5. Skill in counseling people and clarifying problems. 6. An eagerness to communicate and an ability to teach others.	1. An excessive use of the dual nature to evade responsibility. 2. A tendency toward superficial consciousness due to a desire to impress others with factual knowledge. 3. A lack of logic when drawing conclusions or establishing procedures due to an affinity for paradoxes. 4. A tendency to want to appear clever through the misuse of mental abilities. 5. Imitation. 6. Gullibility. 7. Nervous exhaustion. 8. Indulging in malicious gossip.	Key Phrase: Communicating The Self Games: 1. Anxiety Prone. 2. Chameleon. 3. Communication Breakdown. 4. Dim Wit. 5. Double Messages. 6. Dual-Exhaustion Burnout. 7. Forked Tongue. 8. Intellectualizer. 9. Interpreter. 10. Juggler. 11. Roadrunner. 12. Sarcastic Mouth. 13. Scatterbrain.
Sign: Gemini Symbol ♊	The manner through which perceptions related to communication and the thought process can be stimulated and articulated.				
House: 3rd	One's attitudes and perceptions related to the process of communication and the processing of information within the conscious mind in response to stimulation from the immediate environment.				

Figure 7: Third Chord
See the Note to Readers after Acknowledgments

Mercury

The 3rd Chord planetary tone, Mercury, is very much the "Winged Messenger" in this chord perhaps even more so than the Mercury that was discussed in relation to the 6th Chord. In the 3rd Chord, Mercury can really flap its restless wings and symbolize enhancing one's intellect through accumulation of new facts or data, whereas the primary focus of 6th Chord Mercury is directing mental energy into organizing and analyzing one's life to achieve order and perfection. The 3rd Chord Mercurial focus is the exchange of ideas with others for cultural enrichment and for exhilarating mental stimulation.

Mercury has a wide wingspan in the 3rd Chord and is freer to roam than in the practical-minded atmosphere of the 6th Chord. It is as though somebody has pulled the switch to change the tracks when Mercury is considered in its air home rather than its earth chord domain. Both chords typify Mercury's symbolism related to intellectual pursuits and potential discriminating powers. However, the air element of the 3rd Chord shows Mercury to have a special significance in regard to perception and communication. A strongly accentuated 3rd Chord points to an individual inclined to wear a traveling cloak and to be a bit more of an intellectual wanderer.

The positive expressions of the 3rd Chord Mercury include a mental dexterity as well as a speedy sense to interpret or understand information in a spontaneous manner. Other positive qualities include a capacity to adapt to changing situations and an ability to deal with paradoxes due to an acute awareness of the principle of duality. Individuals with pronounced Mercury emphasis often make good counselors as they can illustrate to a client the pros and cons of situations with their animated and colorful personalities.

The negative expressions of the 3rd Chord Mercury include an individual's excessive use of the cloak of a dual nature to evade responsibility and to purposely confuse others. Another negative tendency is a superficial consciousness that is the result of careless and restless scattering of energy. A related negative tendency is a lack of logic when drawing conclusions and an inclination to want to appear clever through the misuse of mental ability.

The element that contains Mercury in an individual's horoscope indicates the type of activities that engulf the conscious mind. For instance, an individual with Mercury in a fire sign or house is probably stimulated by action. He may not have all of the facts in the midst of verbal enthusiasm. His body language repertoire might include a dramatic facial expression with restless hand movements. A person with Mercury in an earth sign or house might have thoughts stimulated by practical situations and be a bit more reserved in body language. He might display a deliberate or logical delivery in communicating concepts due to a strong factual orientation. Someone with Mercury in an air sign or house might be mentally stimulated by social and learning situations and enjoy an articulate ability to communicate concepts as well as a nervous mental disposition. A water type of Mercury by house or sign might point to an individual who is mentally stimulated by emotional situations. Perhaps his greatest moments of moral inspiration come during times of quiet introspection. The Sun sign and house of the individual must be considered to ascertain the overall energy temperament. If Mercury and the Sun are situated in the same sign or house (this is not so unique since Mercury never travels more than 24° from the Sun), the individual is likely to exhibit a mental nature that is quite reflective of the element(s) involved.

Gemini

The 3rd Chord sign tone, Gemini, symbolizes the ears, arms, hands and legs of the conscious mind, indicating one's perceptions related to communication and the thought processes. Both Gemini and Mercury can symbolize the reporter or excited carrier of news. Gemini has a close association with excitation of the nervous system indicating an individual's quick reaction time and speedy thought processes especially if the Sun, Moon, Ascendant or key personal planets are located in this sign.

Gemini can symbolize a restless and communicative mental nature colored with adaptability and versatility. An individual with an accentuated Gemini nature may personify a writer, teacher, broadcaster, salesperson and other communication-oriented expressions. Gemini points to people who hunger for mental food in their social wanderings, thriving on intellectual exchanges with others.

Gemini's glyph, written as ♊, is similar in appearance to a Roman numeral two and fits the sign's association with the principle of duality. Strong Gemini people are accused sometimes of possessing a dual nature and often do attempt to juggle simultaneously two or more careers, lovers, homes, etc. The curiosity and desire to learn shown by this air sign leads Gemini types on mental pilgrimages with many divergent paths.

The Gemini fondness for worshipping paradoxes may easily tire or confuse the more practical earth types and leave them behind in its fleet-footed tracks! Individuals with an emphasis on fire may be able to keep pace with Gemini types, but could grow impatient or bored with all the stops and starts along the way. People with a focus on the other air chords may become nervous wrecks dealing with the apparent inconsistencies and changes of direction which Gemini can indicate. Gemini represents an intellectual approach that is not generally as concerned with the end results, as much as with the interesting mental imagery and other sites of learning that can offer mental stimulation.

The positive expressions of Gemini include a sharp mental ability to explain difficult concepts articulately. Other positive expressions include an ability to adapt to changing situations and a capability to accomplish multiple tasks without losing one's focus. Like Mercury, positive Gemini expressions include an ability to counsel others and help clarify their problems.

An individual very much in tune with Gemini themes is difficult to match in speaking and writing skills. The capacity to change a life direction spontaneously without becoming mentally disoriented is another Gemini virtue.

The negative expressions of Gemini include becoming too attached to wit or cleverness in showing off one's intelligence. This can produce a superficial consciousness which tries to impress others with a lot of facts that lack real depth. Another related negative expression is imitating someone else's personality and incorporating it as though it was one's own in order to hide oneself from others as is seen in the **Chameleon** game. Other negative expressions include an inability to form clear concepts or to communicate effectively due to numerous changes of direction and flooding one's mind with too many inconsistencies. Nervous exhaustion or anxiety due to a scattering of energies and jamming one's mind too full of useless information are also negative expressions.

3rd House

The 3rd Chord house tone is yet another heartbeat of the 3rd Chord emphasis on perceptions. Traditional astrology usually refers to the 3rd house as the house of communication. Each air tone has its roots in a communicative spirit and the 3rd house has a particular link to conscious mind perceptions. I think of the 3rd house as symbolizing one's capacity and drive to develop the "eyes to see and the ears to hear."

The 3rd house also indicates an individual's ability to process information as related to the conscious mind's response to contact with the immediate environment. This house symbolizes an individual's attitudes about communicating the self to others, such as openly versus secretively, fluidly versus slowly or adaptably versus rigidly. The sign associated with the 3rd house as well as any planets located in this house indicate an individual's most precious thought patterns or types of experiences that energize the thought processes. Aspects to

Mercury need to be considered also. These factors represent his most natural tendencies in dealing with the input and output of information and stimuli from the environment. Since the 3rd house is traditionally associated with one's earliest perceptions and peer group formations, it is believed to have a link to one's growing-up years, especially interactions with brothers and sisters.

Consider an individual having the Sun (5th Chord planet tone) located in the 3rd house. He can be really "juiced up" when talking about creative expression. Close communication encounters with others accelerate his mental circuitry. He may be attracted to people who let him dominate or lead a conversation or who feed his ego by complimenting his intellectual pursuits. An individual with a 3rd house Sun might display a strong ego drive (Sun) to sell personal ideas (3rd house). Perhaps he feels compelled to impress others with knowledge and self-assurance. Social perceptions and the communication sense could be extraordinary with a strong desire to broaden the intellectual sphere through self-education. This individual might feel as at ease when speaking to large audiences as when relaxing at home alone watching "Monday Night Football." He may have numerous methods of exercising the mind from conquering difficult mental problems to reading books to being a journalist or educator.

Positive expressions of the 3rd house include an acute perception. People expressing this theme can read between the lines of situations and anticipate when it is time for a change of life direction that will promote growth and fulfillment. An alert mind not clouded by biased opinions, mental confusion or self-deception is another positive expression. A strong teaching ability and a talent for communicating oneself clearly are other positive qualities.

Negative expressions of the 3rd house include indulging in mental deception in the form of lying to oneself or others. There may be a confused mind with thoughts having roots that extend deep into uncontrollable subconscious urges to manipulate others. Another negative expression is a tremendous anxiety or nervous mental disposition caused by a compulsive need for change and a lack of clarity in perceptions. Like the other 3rd Chord tones, the 3rd house when negatively expressed can symbolize a tendency to fritter away energies whether it is through overindulgence in meaningless gossip or a dual nature burnout due to a nonintegrated personality.

Counseling Issues

The counseling issues of the 3rd Chord are indicative of an individual's inability to achieve a clear and balanced expression of this chord's theme: **conceptualization of perception.** My key word phrase for these counseling issues, **communicating the self,** is from the synthesis of the 3rd Chord tones: Mercury, Gemini and the 3rd house. Although each air chord in a sense is related to communication, the 3rd Chord has a special emphasis upon communicating the self as embedded in the archetypal themes of each of the three tones:

1. **Mercury**—the directing of mental activity for the conscious mind to process, analyze and communicate information and to perceive the environment.
2. **Gemini**—the manner through which perceptions related to communication and the thought processes can be stimulated and articulated.
3. **3rd house**—one's attitudes and perceptions related to the process of communication and the processing of information within the conscious mind in response to stimulation from the immediate environment.

The counseling issues of this chord are related to an individual's developing confused or inconsistent communication and thought patterns based on unclear perceptions. The 3rd Chord tones point to an individual's desire to keenly perceive life and to communicate perceptions clearly and directly. The counseling issues of this chord are twofold: (1) an individual's improper use of intellectual and communicative skills due to either a lazy and dull mind or a nervous and overstimulated mental nature; (2) a compulsive and manipulative misuse of a well-developed dual nature that leads one astray from the true self.

Games

When an individual stops developing mental aptitude, as is sometimes symbolized by a dysfunctional 3rd Chord tone, he may exhibit the **Dim Wit** game. Mental perceptions lack clarity and he may suffer from a mental inertia. There is often a laziness or stubborn resistance to change in this game as the individual lacks the ambition to sharpen and deepen the mental faculties. Real problems begin when he grows suspicious of others who are more intellectually oriented. He may fear their ability to expose his mental numbness. This game can also typify an individual who overindulges in malicious gossip about others and perhaps is susceptible to a gullible mentality that is easily flattered by others.

This individual needs to tap into the flexibility and mental eagerness of the 3rd Chord. Some individuals playing this game fear their inferiority when matching wits with others. Developing confidence (opposition to Chord 9), perhaps through educating oneself or being taught new skills (square to Chord 6), is a good idea. Spending less time discussing others and more time focusing on self-growth is also important.

The 3rd Chord tones can be symbolic of extreme nervous expressions as planet, sign and house denote a quick response to stimuli. Very powerful 3rd Chord type of individuals can fall victim to the **Anxiety Prone** game. This is similar to the **Worry Wart** game of the 6th Chord. Whereas the nervous irritability of the 6th Chord is largely associated with one's drive to create perfection and order, the nervousness within the confines of the 3rd Chord is more often than not a result of an overstimulated or hyperactive mind. I have seen this game especially prevalent in individuals who have difficulty in expressing an active mental nature as symbolized by either a Gemini Sun, Moon, Ascendant and/or a strongly aspected Mercury and/or a 3rd house containing key planets. Sometimes the mental currents indicated by 3rd Chord tones are extremely active to the point that an individual has difficulty in calming down. The anxiety that ensues is often due to an individual's inability to channel thoughts into creative outlets. The **Anxiety Prone** game is typical of individuals who repress their thoughts and spend too much time thinking rather than doing.

This individual may need to jump into some of the action themes of the opposing fiery 9th Chord. A lot of nervousness and anxiety can be released if the individual decides to act on thoughts. He may need to learn to use his earthy side (square to Chord 6) in order to discipline the mind and focus his energy.

Another 3rd Chord game related to an overstimulated mental nature is the **Scatterbrain.** This is indicative of an individual who has trouble focusing or concentrating as he is easily distracted. He may forget in the middle of a sentence or thought what he had intended to say. His mind is so active it quickly leaps to and fro in an aimless manner. This individual often irritates others as his listening ability is not much to brag about either! He may look as though a million miles away, thinking about a galaxy far, far away, when you attempt to communicate something important.

The dreaminess of this individual can illustrate the natural square of the 3rd Chord to the highly imaginative 12th Chord. When someone is trying to understand the entire cosmos, it can be a bit overwhelming and confusing. Trying to take in everything results in understanding little. The **Scatterbrain** is, in many cases, a highly intelligent and intuitive person, but has difficulty in consciously directing mental energy. The natural square formed by the 3rd Chord to the 6th Chord points to the need for discipline and order in the life (especially in the mind).

A related 3rd Chord game to the **Scatterbrain** is what I refer to as the **Roadrunner.** This is an individual who chases one goal after another in a haphazard manner and never really reaches a destination. He has a confused logic and an extremely short attention span. He may appear to others like the coyote in the cartoon that relentlessly chased the roadrunner and tried to run him into a trap. However, the coyote often could not slam on the brakes fast enough and became the victim of his own traps. This individual may lack dependability, chasing after fathoms of imagination with no tangible results.

The mutability of 3rd Chord themes can denote individuals who are impressionable and changeable. It is important for people with a strong emphasis on the 3rd Chord to develop continuity in life processes. The focused discipline of the natural square to Chord 6 can be helpful. The opposition to Chord 9 points to the importance of a value hierarchy and having clear goals which allow one to establish priorities rather than scattering forces. It is often concentration that converts 3rd Chord mental confusion into alertness and brilliance. The tenacious earth element could be a factor needed to ground this person's visions into reality.

Another 3rd Chord game is **Communication Breakdown.** This is an individual who has difficulty translating what others are trying to communicate. He may also have a strong resistance to communication that does not fit into his mode or style of thought. He may not want to hear what is being transmitted or may have difficulty understanding due to poor communication skills and fixed opinions. The opposite 9th Chord symbolizes eclectic or broad perspectives in communicating. This person may need to widen his vision and truly listen to others. He may even need to reeducate his communication skills.

A dual nature is related to other games in the 3rd Chord. Strong 3rd Chord individuals with an accentuated emphasis on either Gemini, Mercury or the 3rd house are often thinking about situations from many different angles and searching for different alternatives just for the experience. Third chord games occur when an individual is not capable of balancing or understanding the paradoxes that arise due to an overindulgence in dual expressions. Paradox and duality seem to be close allies. Unfortunately, too many unresolved paradoxes sometimes leave a bad taste in your mind.

There is a type of self-denial when an individual hides behind the camouflage of dual expression as an attempt to disguise the true identity. Thoughts and words may conceal true feelings and purposely lead himself and others away from his real self. His mind pumps thoughts at a fast and steady pace though not necessarily always with clarity or the logic to substantiate any reasoning. His intellect may be sharper than a two-edged sword ready to strike in any direction with wit and sarcasm without a split second's notice.

An individual who bounces around from one paradox to another sometimes forgets what is truly his own identity. A lack of self-awareness and indulgence in nonintegrated personalities can lead to what I call the **Chameleon** game. Each of us has subpersonalities to express different sides of ourselves. As we mature and expand our intellect in adulthood, we need to find creative outlets for these subpersonalities. However, in the **Chameleon** game an individual is not really expressing through subpersonalities. In actuality there is not enough unity and clarity in mind to coherently manifest different natures. Unfortunately, he has devoted too much time copying or imitating the actions and thoughts of others to win social approval. This game is typical of a fickle individual who changes personality and life direction much like a lizard that can change its skin color rapidly to blend with the surroundings. The chameleon-like person is often living in a state of chaos and never quite sure who to be next.

It is important for a person heavily indulging in the **Chameleon** game to allow others to see him in reality. This game is typified by an individual who has self-hate and is not satisfied with his true self. Chord 6 reminds us that physical reality and order must be included in the life. One must not give all the power over to other people and their opinions. Important to avoid themes related to selff-delusion and emotional confusion. It is important for the person to stop using mental ingenuity as a shield. When he drops defenses, the natural process of unifying the inner being has a chance to begin.

The **Chameleon** game is often accompanied by another game, **Dual-Exhaustion Burnout.** This is an individual who literally burns out the nervous system trying to portray the different false personalities he has constructed. He is sometimes so busy playing a role that he forgets what he has told certain people about himself. Another side of this game is an individual who simply cannot rest the mind. As in the **Anxiety Prone** game mentioned earlier, this individual has become too stimulated and does not know how to relax mentally except by resorting to extra strong Valium.

The individual needs to reexamine value systems (opposition to Chord 9) and get in better touch with emotional needs. The **Chameleon** and **Dual-Exhaustion Burnout** have escapist tendencies in them. The square to Chord 12 can indicate a desire to hide from issues, but the creative imagination and intuition can be valuable tools if put to use. The quincunx to Chord 8 can point to the issue of giving others too much power and the need to stay in touch with one's own psychological depths. The relaxed flow of water can soften the hyper tendencies of Chord 3.

The **Juggler** game is also an extension of the duality principle. This is an individual who has difficulty enjoying simplicity in life experiences. He has a sharp intellect and a drive to master the challenge of juggling many life experiences. He may overwhelm himself trying to do it all, even when it might be better to settle for one focus. Though the ambitions and goals may be sincere, he over-extends himself and frustrates others who feel he is irresponsible.

This is an overexpansion instinct in the 3rd Chord much like in its opposite, the 9th Chord. The overexpansiveness sometimes symbolized by the 3rd Chord is related to an individual's unceasing drive for mental stimulation. The **Juggler** is not satisfied with one of anything. He wants two or more lovers, mates, careers, destinies, right now! The **Juggler** seeks several outlets to satisfy an insatiable curiosity. A problem arises when he tries to juggle one too many situations and begins to drop one after the other, alienating those who love him as well as bringing tremendous mental confusion into the life. He is often seen as an untrustworthy individual because nobody is ever sure what exciting thrill might lure him away next. Concentrating more on the moment and learning to provide a stable focus can help this individual be more grounded. Others will perceive him more positively, and life is less likely to be confusing.

An individual's misuse of 3rd Chord tones may lead to the **Forked Tongue** game. This is an individual who seldom speaks the truth. Often he is an intelligent person but misuses the intellect to confuse others and especially to distort the truth. This is yet another means of hiding one's real self; the person does not wish to establish meaningful communication that might reveal personal vulnerabilities.

This game is often played by an individual suffering emotional pain that has never healed. It is a person's way of hiding inner pain and mistrust of others. There are people who indulge in this game to keep intimacy at a distance. The quincunx to Chord 8 and square to Chord 12 shows the importance of digging into festering wounds, transforming hurts and completing emotional transactions. What is unpleasant must be confronted, and forgiveness (of self as well as other people) may be necessary to create more positive interactions with others.

The **Sarcastic Mouth** game is typical of an individual who attacks others with a ferocious onslaught of words. This individual is often suffering from an emotional confusion and is bitter toward others due to an inward frustration. He has a biting tongue that lashes out with criticism and seeks to purposely hurt others. Often this individual resorts to guerilla warfare tactics by launching a surprise attack at inopportune moments such as while sitting down for dinner or entering a movie theater. He will bring up past unrelated events or invent material to put you down. He might indulge in gossip to spread bad propaganda about others to damage their reputations.

It is not that this person is wicked or vengeful, as much as he is desperately wanting to be understood. There is often an emotional blockage that needs to be released rather than used to verbally attack others. This is commonly a person who has been extremely disappointed by unfilled ideals and expectations (opposition to Chord 9 and square to Chord 12). Power may be an issue in relationships (quincunxes to Chords 8 and 10) and he protects his vulnerability by attacking before someone else can. He may need to forgive himself and/or a lover to allow the healing process to begin. Communicating the pain to a trusted friend or helper may speed up the cure.

Related to the **Sarcastic Mouth** game is another game based on trickery and cunning, **Double Messages.** This is someone who has mastered the art of paradox so well that he knows just how to con you by mixing verbal communication with inappropriate body language. He may be extremely angry but is smiling while telling you what a rotten person you are. Better yet, he might be saying nice things about you in an ugly tone and with glaring eyes. He may insist everything between you is okay but continue to hint by body language that something is very much wrong.

The **Double Messages** game is typical of people who want to manipulate and produce guilt in others. The **Double Messenger** usually does not realize how badly he is poisoning himself through this manipulative behavior. He is not really expressing a creative identity but instead is responding to his own negative energy. The key to this game is tapping into the underlying emotional confusion and dealing with it. Adopting some of the positive attitudes of the opposite fiery 9th Chord could be helpful. The water element can add a sensitivity for self and others that is lacking in this game.

Another 3rd Chord game is the **Interpreter.** This is a person who can drive you crazy by interrupting your flow of conversation to explain a better way of saying what you mean. He is so fond of his own choice of words that he second guesses or edits what you are communicating. He may also interpret your language to others so you can be better understood. This annoying kind of behavior does not always win the **Interpreter** a lot of friends. An increased sensitivity to others needs to be incorporated (square to Chord 12 and quincunx to Chord 8). Also, putting the more deliberate and slow-moving energy of earth (quincunx to Chord 10 and square to Chord 6) to use is likely to minimize interruptions.

The **Intellectualizer** game is an individual who intellectualizes emotional expressions. This game can be quite problematic for all three air chords as the mental acuteness of strong air-type individuals often leads them to search for intellectual rationalizations. It is difficult for the **Intellectualizer** to say in a direct manner how he is feeling. He often digresses into complicated details of situations to mentally entertain us and may not even realize that he is not expressing any emotion. This game can be troublesome and frustrating in intimate relationships when one person is not willing to express feelings. There is too often an emptiness in the relationship as issues are discussed with a careful diplomacy and intellectualized to death. The reality and substance that an emotional exchange could bring into the relationship is never realized.

The **Intellectualizer** has to learn to value feelings as much as the mind. An emotional blockage could be part of the problem, leading to a fear of trusting. The individual must learn to establish true emotional and intimate exchanges in relationships.

Summary of Issues with 3rd Chord Games

The 3rd Chord games stem from one's manipulative use of mental energy or lack of trust in mental capacities. Also, when a person allows perceptions to become nervously scattered due to too much stimulation, he can succumb to 3rd Chord games.

3rd Chord themes can be used to express mental creativity and excellent communication skills. Individuals very much in touch with 3rd Chord themes can exhibit an unusual ability to adapt to new situations. They make good problem solvers and counselors. It is only when one allows perceptions to run wild and distract from a real perception of the self and others that he indulges too much in 3rd Chord games.

Subtones

The three **subtones** of this chord are: the planetary aspect known as the **sextile**, the energy focus of Gemini known as **mutable** and the house classification known as **cadent**.

The **sextile** as a subtone of the 3rd Chord planetary tone supports the archetypal theme of Mercury. The sextile aspect symbolizes a mental type of energy. Planets forming a sextile indicate the potential for an individual to develop an objective nature and to create new mental direction. An individual with key planets or even the Ascendant involved in a sextile aspect can potentially use the themes symbolized to enjoy new social contacts, inventive ideas and satisfying mental interests. However, due to the instability symbolized by the sextile aspect, the motifs of the two planets forming this aspect may require a lot of discipline to bring concrete results. Charles Carter describes the sextile as related to intellectual energy in his book *The Astrological Aspects*. He mentions that the sextile can be expressed in some instances as laziness and lack of ambition, the sextile can be symbolic of brainpower and can be quite emphasized in the charts of those with active mental energies.

Consider once again the 5th Chord planet, the Sun, forming a sextile aspect to the 12th Chord planet, Neptune, in an individual's horoscope. The individual might enjoy meeting people who have similar aesthetic tastes and might find personal creative expression greatly stimulated by such social contacts. The individual might have an inner sense about how best to establish a clear inner attunement. He might possess a spiritual and compassionate nature that enhances the basic character and core identity. However, due to the openness and potential restlessness sometimes indicated by the sextile, this same individual could exhibit a mental laziness or even spaciness. He may fantasize about the future or have a foggy perspective about the present. Although more likely to occur in an extreme manner with the conjunction, square, quincunx or opposition, this sextile could indicate that basic self-expression (Sun) may be easily indulged and led astray by colorful illusions or unfounded dreams (Neptune). If an individual has Mercury involved in a sextile aspect, the mental processes are sharper or more acutely attuned. The symbolism of the "Winged Messenger" is fanned even faster by the excitation and mental stimulation shown by the sextile.

The curiosity, learning and desire for mental stimulation inherent in Gemini's symbolism are well supported by the adaptability of **mutable** energy, the **subtone** of Gemini. Since Gemini is the mutable air sign, the focus here is adjusting one's perceptions to different life situations by acquiring new communication skills or learning new ways of perceiving life with clarity.

The 3rd house is supported by a **cadent** house classification. The cadent subtone represents mental stimulation which enriches the urge to communicate one's intelligence or perceptions clearly (indicated by the 3rd house). It is not accidental that both Mercury-related houses, the 3rd and 6th, have a cadent backdrop. The mental curiosity and restlessness associated with each of these cadent houses is true to the Mercurial form of seeking out, refining and investigating new mentally exhilarating situations.

The 3rd Chord is symbolic of our need to develop real and accurate perceptions of ourselves and others as well as our need to communicate clearly. Perhaps it could be said that the 3rd Chord indicates our ability to listen to our thoughts. The 3rd Chord challenge is being able to differentiate when it is time to act rather than to think only. The 3rd Chord is greatly symbolic of our conscious mental reasoning power. The 7th and 11th Chords will further illustrate the drive for mental expression that resonates within the metaphoric winds of the air chords as they blow against the sails of our minds to stimulate us to engage in the socialization process and to plan and execute future goals.

CHAPTER NINE

SEVENTH CHORD: CONCEPTUALIZATION OF RELATIONSHIP

> Love one another but make not a bond of love: let it rather be a moving sea between the shores of your souls.
>
> *The Prophet* by Kahlil Gibran (page 16)

The 7th Chord indicates an attraction to displaying social graces and a fondness for companionship. The planet (Venus), sign (Libra) and house (7th) tones of this chord represent one's need to form significant relationships. Chord seven moves us into a new stage of our developing adulthood. With chord seven we are learning to establish lasting peer relationships. The first step in this process involves air, the capacity to see others objectively to understand them and to accept them as they are without trying to change them." The archetypal themes of the 7th Chord tones have an emphasis upon relating the self to others.

Whereas the 1st Chord, **self-expressive embodiment** is chiefly a concentrated self-focus, its opposite chord, the 7th Chord, is a person's search for balance through close encounters with others and a grasp of social consciousness. The tones and subtones of the 7th Chord point to participation in the arena of relationships.

Venus

The 7th Chord planetary tone version of Venus has somewhat of a different theme than in the 2nd Chord. The Venus experience in relation to the 2nd Chord is greatly associated with satisfying the senses and indulging in worldly pleasures. The 7th Chord Venus represents a social personality and a strong inclination for interaction with others. The 2nd Chord Venus harmonies, slow and cautious in tempo, suddenly become allegro when conducting in the 7th Chord. Venus literally cannot sit still in this air chord atmosphere. The love goddess avidly seeks her lovers, mates and absolutely thrives on social gatherings of all kinds.

It was stated earlier that a key function for the Venusian roots embedded in the earthy 2nd Chord was its symbolism of an individual creating a sense of balance and calmness. In the 7th Chord, Venus energy also symbolizes a quest for balance but in the context of relating to others. The true comfort for 7th Chord Venus is not just relating to those who satisfy and resemble romantic images, but also to initiate and develop relationships with those who can fulfill our deepest needs for friendship, affection, meaningful feedback and most of all, love.

Generally an individual having Venus located in the fire or air signs and even more so if also located in a fire or air house tends toward a gregarious type of social spirit. The individual often seeks a social gratification and may find it essential to feed the psyche with stimulating social contacts to feel alive and fulfilled. There is a natural outward and forward projection shown by the fire and air elements. Such individuals also motivate others to take action in their own lives.

I have observed that when an individual has Venus in a planetary aspect to one or more of the planets beyond Saturn's orbit (Uranus, Neptune or Pluto), especially the opposition, square, quincunx or conjunction, she often forms relationships

7TH CHORD: CONCEPTUALIZATION OF RELATIONSHIP

Tone	Archetypal Themes	Functions	Positive Expressions	Negative Expressions	Potential Counseling Issues
Planet: Venus **Symbol ♀**	The directing of actions to satisfy social, aesthetic and epicurean urges and to establish a sense of comfort through ownership values and relating.	1. To establish meaningful relationships and associations.	1. An ability to have shared experiences.	1. A tendency to look for a sense of self in others.	**Key Phrase:** Relating The Self
Sign: Libra **Symbol ♎**	The manner through which the cultivation of relationships, social interactions and one's concept of beauty can be initiated and balanced.	2. To act upon social urges.	2. An ability to realistically perceive others.	2. A tendency to lack depth in relationships due to wearing social masks.	**Games:** 1. Aphrodisiac. 2. Broken Scales. 3. Close Encounters of the Worst Kind.
House: 7th	One's attitudes and objective awareness concerning social interaction, cooperation with others and the initiation of intimate relationships; the principle of attraction and repulsion in relating to others. One's competitive spirit and the desire to take the risk of confronting others.	3. To create a sense of artistry, beauty and romance in life practices. 4. To create a sense of balance in one's life. 5. To exhibit the power of attraction.	3. An ability to maintain balance in relationships. 4. A sense of comfort in union. 5. A strong appreciation of aesthetics, possibly manifested as creative expression. 6. An ability to be a mediator in disputes. 7. A sense of social grace.	3. A tendency to be too compromising and indecisive. 4. A tendency to be overly sensitive to criticism from others due to a fear of rejection. 5. A tendency to be too self-centered. 6. A tendency to overindulge in epicurean tastes. 7. A tendency to not perceive others realistically and to project one's fears and insecurities on to others, especially in intimate relating.	4. Compulsive Strategist. 5. Flattery Will Get You Everywhere. 6. Glitter Bug. 7. I Am Addicted to You. 8. Masquerade. 9. On Stage. 10. One-upmanship. 11. Please Fulfill Me. 12. Romantic. 13. Sitting on the Fence. 14. Style Versus Substance. 15. Super Compromiser. 16. Warmonger.

Figure 8: Seventh Chord
See the Note to Readers after Acknowledgments

with many different types of individuals ranging from young to old, conservative to radical, calm to neurotic, heterosexual to gay, etc. In other words she is seeking to express an adept social awareness and social versatility that thrives on stimulation and input from varying personalities in this culture or even abroad. Aspects of Venus (and any personal planet) to the outer planets can symbolize accelerated or transformative growth potential of magnificent proportions. Stephen Arroyo in his book *Astrology, Karma and Transformation* has some wonderful descriptions of the power of transformation that can be symbolized when an individual has the personal planets aspecting outer planets. Other astrologers have also emphasized the impact and possibility for growth symbolized by the outer planets aspecting personal planets.

Venus in the earth or water signs and especially if also located in an earth or water house does not necessarily indicate that an individual is inhibited or is socially backward. Venus indicates the vibes or social signals an individual transmits to others, so a person with Venus in an earth or water sign (or house) may be a bit reticent or not project a direct introduction of self with the fervor of the fire and air types. This can be especially true if the Ascendent or Mars is also in a water or earth sign (see 1st Chord). Once again it must be remembered that the art of interpreting an individual's horoscope depends greatly on considering the interaction of its parts.

The positive expressions of 7th Chord Venus include the ability to form close personal relationships without losing or sacrificing one's entire identity to a partner (or expecting a partner to sacrifice her entire identity). Maintaining a balanced perspective in relationships is the goal. Another positive expression is experiencing a sense of emotional closeness in relationships and an ability to enjoy shared experiences. We do not feel our individuality or uniqueness is lost due to sharing a life with others. A strong application of aesthetics and a sense of social grace are also positive attributes of a smoothly functioning 7th Chord Venus.

Negative expressions of 7th Chord Venus include a tendency to look to others for a sense of self or to define oneself by the standards of other people. There can also be a tendency to lack depth in relationships due to a desire to wear a social mask (as in the **Masquerade** game). A tendency to be too self-centered and an overindulgence in epicurean tastes are also negative expressions. Perhaps the biggest Achilles' heel for an individual with a dysfunctioning 7th Chord Venus is a fear of rejection that drives one to be liked at all costs.

Libra

The 7th Chord sign tone, Libra, has mythologically been associated with a set of scales. These are not ordinary scales as they are quite sensitive to the powers of the mind and the weight of mental reasoning as in decision making. Libran symbolism bears a resemblance to the plight of a jury. The individual minds of the jurors must reach one consensus of verdict. In the midst of much discussion and debate there may be a vacillation of the jury from guilty to not guilty until the pendulum of justice finds its mark as the jury collectively decides upon a verdict.

It is often the contemplation period before a decision is reached that makes or breaks the Libran ability to be objective. Libra indicates the ancient strategist and diplomat, awaiting the results of personal decisions. Being a social animal, the person with a Libran emphasis is very sensitive to the reactions and echoes of public opinion. Comparisons infiltrate the lives of people dealing with Libra issues—pretty versus ugly, single versus married, etc. Whereas Gemini types are fascinated with their own ability to enjoy contrasts in situations, Libra types are too busy feeling responsible to solve life's apparent paradoxes. People with a focus on Libra take care not to disrupt the symmetry displayed by opposites. They also desperately seek to maintain a balanced perspective due to the tremendous respect they have for the pull of opposing viewpoints or forces.

An individual with a Libra emphasis (Sun, Moon, Ascendant or several planets clustered in the sign) is seeking a balanced life position as conflicting circumstances present difficult choices. The responsibility of decision making has been cursed as: why me? The loneliness of Libra is felt within the hesitation of wondering which way to turn and whom to ask for counsel.

The spotlight for Libra is on relating. This is not limited to people only but includes beauty and form as well. Libra symbolizes the appreciation of beauty and the arts in all their magical forms—dance, music, sunrises, etc. Beauty and the aroma of sensuality entice action and capture the spontaneity of thoughts channeled into harmonious, creative, aesthetic expression. Engaging in such Libran activities may excite the nervous system until it tires from exhaustion.

The Libran quest for companionship is often a yearning to steady an off-balanced self. The individual may restlessly and hungrily seek a suitable match. Libra denotes a need for feedback from others to reassure that life is being lived to its potential.

Perhaps most of all Libra indicates the desire for an audience to admire one's expression and relationship with beauty. Libra can denote a state of calmness when beauty is an ally. However, when individuals with an emphasis on Libra grow too bold and try to prove they have mastered beauty, the result is an endless, bottomless cup of insatiable desire for love. A battle to conquer rather than truly express beauty leads to a compulsive and bitter lifestyle that seeks admirers. This does not fulfill the deepest desire indicated by Libra, to be loved for just being oneself. Libra can point to a desperate desire for love, affection and friendship, needing companionship and wanting to join forces with love-filled souls!

The positive expressions of Libra include an ability to share one's life with others and to enjoy a balanced sense of comfort in unions such as marriage or other forms of partnership. An ability to maintain a balanced and objective life perspective (that can mediate disputes or counsel others) is also a positive expression. A sense of social grace may be evident. Individuals very much in tune with Libra energy might display a strong appreciation of aesthetics possibly manifested as creative expression.

The negative expressions of Libra include a tendency to look for a sense of self in others. Relationships lacking depth may be established, due to a strong desire to win social approval (which can also be shown by Venus). Other negative expressions include a tendency to be too compromising or indecisive as well as an inclination to be overly sensitive to criticism from others. A romanticized social image and unclear relationship values can lead to disastrous relationship experiences. There can also be a tendency to overindulge in epicurean tastes and laziness.

7th House

The 7th Chord house tone reflects the fast pulsating rhythm of the air element to seek social stimulation. The 7th house symbolizes an individual's developing awareness of relationships and especially contractual types of agreements with others. The 7th house symbolism is not limited to only legal partnerships such as marriage or business but also includes one's entire awareness of forming a cooperative effort with others.

Planets located in the 7th house and the sign associated with an individual's 7th house indicate one's openness to forming relationships and the tendency to attract or repel others. There is perhaps more of a temptation to project what we do not like or cannot accept about ourselves onto other people related to the 7th and even 8th Chords than the other chords. When we deny the potential of the planets, signs or houses involved with the 7th or 8th Chords, we often unconsciously attract those same potentials in other people

The 7th and 8th houses are sometimes representative of the blind spot areas for an individual. It is as though the lights went out and every once in a while someone comes along who has a way or manner which penetrates the blind area as though shining a flashlight upon the darkest recesses of our mind. This penetrating person may be a therapist, friend, astrologer, lover or even enemy! Concerning projection, Maritha Pottenger in her book Healing With the Horoscope says: "The most common area of projection is in the 7th and 8th houses. Long associated with 'other people,' it is quite easy for the individual to deny that side of his or her character and live it out through others. This can be encouraged by culture, family, sex roles and unwary astrologers. I feel very sad when I hear astrologers talk of placements in the 7th and 8th houses as if they had only to do with partners and other people. Everything in our charts is us. Those houses show parts of our own nature which we tend to meet through our close peer relationships. To talk of the planets there as only applying to partners is to encourage people to give away much of their talent and abilities."

Recently a client came to me for an astrological consultation. She had the 8th Chord planet, Pluto, located in her 7th house. She was depressed about the type of men she attracted, stating that men often took advantage of her generosity. She felt used sexually and materially. The client said that she so badly wanted a relationship, she often lost her sense of power. As it turned out, the client has a strong drive to project onto others the personal power symbolized by Pluto (see 8th Chord) that she denies within herself. Unfortunately. she usually attracted men blocked emotionally or who deliberately manipulated her to get what they desired. In other words, her own sense of personal power (Pluto) was not being used by her in a balanced manner, and she attracted individuals who misused that power. This emphasizes the importance of developing a clarity in regard to the 7th house as it symbolizes the types of people we sometimes might attract and more importantly our own romantic images and potential to develop meaningful relationships.

Positive expressions of the 7th house include an ability to perceive others realistically. The 7th house mirrors a capacity to accept the basic nature of loved ones rather than trying to change them to fit into our own standards. An ability to enjoy a sense of comfort in close unions and an ability to encourage others to be at ease with themselves are also positive 7th house expressions.

Negative expressions of the 7th house include a tendency to ask too much from a partner in order to create a sense of self. This can also take the form of projecting onto others one's own shortcomings or sense of power and individuality. A compulsive need for attention and an overpowering drive for love at any cost can also be debilitating tendencies. One's desire for relationships can also be problematic, when 7th house themes are unbalanced. The person may dread being alone or fear others.

Counseling Issues

The counseling issues of the 7th Chord reflect the need to develop a balanced perspective concerning the basic nature of this chord, **conceptualization of relationship**. My key word phrase for these counseling issues, **relating the self**, is from the synthesis of the tones: Venus, Libra and the 7th house. The 7th Chord focus upon relating the self is emphasized by the archetypal themes of each tone, which are:

1. **Venus**—the directing of actions to satisfy social, aesthetic and epicurean urges and to establish a sense of comfort through owner
ship, material values and relating.
2. **Libra**—the manner through which the cultivation of relationships, social interactions and one's concept of beauty can be initiated and balanced.
3. **7th house**—one's attitudes and objective awareness concerning social interaction, cooperation with others and the initiation of intimate relationships; the principle of attraction and repulsion in relating to others; one's competitive spirit and the desire to take the risk of confronting others.

The counseling issues of this chord demonstrate an individual's confusion or loss of perspective in personal relationships. There may be a lack of sound reasoning in important choices concerning life circumstances. The 7th Chord tones can be expressed with a mental alertness and clarity that attracts harmonious relations with others and a balanced decision-making process. The counseling issues of this chord revolve around the principle of balancing opposing forces. There are two main themes to these counseling issue: (1) an individual's off-balanced perspective within personal relationships often due to unclear relationship values and needs; (2) an inability to judge or weigh the outcome of decisions when confronted with obstacles or challenges.

Games

When an individual lacks clear relationship values, confusion may surface in the **Style versus Substance** game of the 7th Chord. This is an individual who chooses relationships based solely on the outer appearance of others. She does not really understand her needs in a relationship and therefore forms relationships based on nice looks only. There is not anything wrong with an attraction to pretty or beautiful people. However, a lack of depth in understanding the self within the dynamics of relationships often leads to a lack of discrimination in selecting lovers, friends or mates. A primary concern for style can result in very artificial substance, leading to disastrous consequences. This is an individual whose unclear relationship values make for very unstable relationships. Often either she or her partners have never really learned how to cooperate for smooth functioning in a relationship. This individual's relationships often fall apart at the first sign of conflict as she is not really prepared to deal with the emotional intensity of the relationship.

The key to this game is often related to the opposite 1st Chord. The individual needs to have a closer understanding of her self-image. The quincunx to the 2nd Chord suggests she may need to reexamine or better define values and what provides pleasure. The natural square to the 4th Chord suggests that examining emotional foundations, and where emotional security is sought, could prove fruitful.

The **Romantic** game picks up on ancient, mythological 7th Chord symbolism. Each 7th Chord tone symbolizes love, romance, beauty, heroines and heroes. An individual in this game lives in a fantasy world, wearing rose-colored glasses and lacking objectivity when interacting with others. Many 7th Chord games are the result of both an individual's poor reality testing (natural square from 7th Chord to the 10th Chord) concerning relationships and failure to understand underlying emotional motivations (square to 4th Chord). The **Romantic** is often more interested in falling in love than in establishing a committed relationship. Romanticized images of the perfect lover often lead to bizarre relationships. The **Romantic** is commonly disappointed that lofty first impressions of idealized others are not accurate.

This game requires some patience as the **Romantic** has been captured by idealized images of love for several years. The fact that the 7th Chord naturally quincunxes the watery 12th Chord is important as this game is often a combination of both chords. (The **Romantic** is also discussed in the 12th Chord.) The **Romantic** needs to understand her inner motivations for forming relationships. She needs to learn to see others as they really are, rather than as projections of ideals, fantasies, movie stars or novels.

The **Please Fulfill Me** game occurs with an individual who does not believe she can be complete without a relationship. She is not sure of her own creative talents and believes life can be fulfilled only by a relationship. She is often "used" by others, and the price she pays for a relationship often leaves her in the "red" and feeling quite unfulfilled.

This is usually a person who denies many of her own potentials and attracts the same qualities in others. She probably needs to clarify assertion instincts (opposition to Chord 1) in order to achieve balanced relationships. She may be lacking in self-confidence. Nurturing herself (square to Chord 4) and proving her competence in the outer world (square to Chord 10) may help her gain the strength to give herself equal time in relationships.

The 7th Chord can symbolize an individual who tries to please everybody as in the **Super Compromiser** game. This individual is extremely sensitive to the opinions of others and goes beyond the call of duty to not create any waves in relating to others. She will do anything to be liked and to avoid conflict. However, in the process she often compromises away too many personal needs. She may neglect taking proper care of inner emotional needs as she is so busy pleasing other people.

Once again, the individual may need to tap into the fiery 1st Chord energy and find assertion strength. A fear or confusion concerning anger and a confusing self-image can contribute to a person's entrapment in this game. Learning to put herself first is a challenge.

The 7th Chord tones can also indicate an individual who is so in need of recognition or assurance that she exhibits the **Flattery Will Get You Everywhere** game. This individual is easily manipulated by others who perceive her vulnerability to be adored and appreciated. Often she is so unsure of how others perceive her that a little flattery can make her the target of people who do not have her best interests as a top priority.

She may need to tune into water energy in order to learn the inner motivations behind her behavior. An unclear self-image (opposition to Chord 1) can encourage the seeking of attention from others. By creating her own emotional security (square to Chord 4) and sense of achievement (square to Chord

10), she will not be so vulnerable to the approval of other people.

Individuals with difficulty in expressing 7th Chord tones can demonstrate poor reality testing in choosing partners. One possibility is the **Close Encounters of the Worst Kind** game. This game is played by an individual who may remain quite ignorant of the harm done by faulty selection of lovers, friends or even business associates. Friends and family may try to talk some sense into her, but she refuses to listen until some blatant form of mistreatment occurs in the relationship. Sometimes it can take years for an individual to "see the light" within a relationship or to discover a habitual pattern of choosing harmful relationships.

The natural square formed to the 4th Chord hints that the person may be disoriented by emotional confusion. The origin of many 7th Chord games is past relationships with parents (squares from Chord 7 to Chords 4 and 10), lovers, spouses or peers. A cleaning-up of the past by changing one's patterns in relating to others is often the first step to winning this game.

The most potent and potentially destructive of all 7th Chord games is the **I Am Addicted to You.** The previously mentioned 7th Chord games describe people who lack the experience, perception or common sense to make clear relationship choices, but at least they might display some freedom of choice in a relationship. This is not so in the addicted personality. In the **I Am Addicted to You** game an individual is at the mercy of her own overpowering and extremely compulsive nature. She seeks to glue herself to someone who can satisfy an incessant addiction drive.

In his excellent book , *How to Break your Addiction to a Person*, Dr. Howard M. Halpern describes the compulsively addicted relationship and its limiting choices for freedom. He states that addictive relationships contain love and commitment but lack freedom of choice due to the compulsive drive of the individual.

Dr. Halpern goes on to state the indicators of an addictive relationship. He notes parallels to other addictions such as alcohol or drugs. Dr. Halpern states that an addiction includes compulsiveness and the panic that results when one fears the absence of the substance. He states that addiction is also composed of withdrawal symptoms. The break-up is experienced as devastating. Dr. Halpern notes that there is a mourning period after the breakup of an addictive relationship. He points to a sense of exhilarating freedom and triumph which follows the mourning period. This sense of liberation is the fourth hallmark of an addiction. Dr. Halpern explains that a non-addictive loss features a much slower healing process with an eventual sad acceptance.

Dr. Halpern describes the similarity of all addictions. He says emptiness, despair and sense of incompleteness characterize a person addicted to a substance or a person. The individual believes the only way to satisfy this addiction resides in something or someone outside the self. The individual will do anything to maintain this reliance upon a substance or a person that has become the main focus of life.

The addicted person often has a poor sense of life direction. It is as though the relationship is a strong magnet that keeps all attention fixated upon it. Dr. Halpern states that there are "levels of linkage" that can cause one to stay in unhealthy relationships. These levels consist of "practical considerations" for staying in the relationship and "beliefs" one has concerning oneself, relationships, and about a specific relationship. (A "practical consideration" might be: "I need someone to help pay the rent while I'm in school." A "belief" might be: "Most desirable partners are already married.") Dr. Halpern goes on to say that the deepest layer or stage of addiction to a person has an emotional intensity greater than either practical considerations or beliefs. He calls this deepest level one's "attachment hunger." This powerful root of addictive behavior can cause one to disregard practical considerations and beliefs.

Dr. Halpern states that attachment hunger can drive a person to seek out a certain type of person who attracts and excites this hunger. Dr. Halpern explains that a person who becomes the object of this hunger is one's "Attachment Fetish Person." The Attachment Fetish person may not only be sexually attractive. Other categories of the attachment fetish person may include physical qualities, a particular type of personality or simply the way the individual acts toward someone. A woman might, for example, find cold, aloof men arouse her Attachment Hunger (as she seeks to break down their barriers and elicit warmth). An emotionally distant man could become an Attachment Fetish Person for such a woman.

In some cases planets placed in an individual's 7th house can indicate an individual prone to relationship addiction. The particular planet could symbolize the type of person that is the object of these addictive qualities. I have found this to be especially true of Saturn and the planets beyond its orbit—Uranus, Neptune and Pluto. Perhaps the themes related to these planets are difficult for a person to individualize or integrate into self-expression due to their generational significance. The potential creative energy symbolized by these planets is projected onto another person, and suddenly they become the possessor of qualities that we have denied in ourselves. Usually horoscope factors beyond the 7th house placement of one of the planets will support this behavior. Stressful or tension aspects may be involved from personal planets, especially the opposition, square, conjunction or quincunx. However, I have observed that trines from personal planets (especially Venus) to outer planets can point to unpredictable behavior in relationships that could have an addictive nature. I am saying only that this can help in understanding an individual who has strong addictive tendencies based on a tremendous Attachment Hunger.

For instance, an individual with Saturn (see 10th Chord) in the 7th house or powerfully aspected (especially by opposition or quincunx) who has a potent Attachment Hunger could be addicted to someone older who appears full of wisdom and will take responsibility for all decisions, this Attachment Fetish Person might be a substitute parent or authority figure missing in earlier years. The addicted person might feel she is not deserving of warmth in a relationship and therefore attaches to someone manifesting the "Dark Side" of Saturn, coldness, lack of emotional closeness or absolute control.

It is important that the individual take slow and constructive steps to conquer a fear of responsibility. The more capable she can become and the more inner security she can develop, the less likely she is to project too much responsibility (and control) on others. Balanced relationships incorporate her strength as well as her partner's strength.

An addicted type of person with Uranus (see 11th Chord) in the 7th house or powerfully aspected (especially by opposition or quincunx) might satisfy an Attachment Hunger by attaching to irresponsibly independent and erratic individuals that come and go as they please. The addicted person fears questioning the romantic exploits or wanderings of her Attachment Fetish Person as she might not return if asked to account for her rash actions.

The individual needs to develop a balanced sense of her own unique qualities. If she denies individual self-expression, her relationships remain quite unstable with a tendency to attract extremely aloof people. A balanced sense of give-and-take in relationships, an equal sharing of responsibility and an appreciation of one another's uniqueness is needed.

An addicted type of person with Neptune (see 12th Chord) in the 7th house or powerfully aspected (especially by opposition or quincunx) might satisfy an Attachment Hunger by forming relationships with individuals who are drug-and-alcohol oriented or who are escape artists and never make reliable commitments. The addicted person is attracted to individuals who cannot deal with reality. The addiction can run so deep that she fails to acknowledge the lack of love offered by the Attachment Fetish Person.

This person is often yearning to "save" those in need. Unfortunately, idealism and the quest for a beautiful dream can express as a confused emotional nature, which she often projects onto those people she attracts. Her partners may fear commitments. She needs to stop denying her own emotional needs in order to form relationships. A balanced sense of dependency is essential. Also, the addicted person may need to do a better job in reality-testing romantic ideals. Neptune's symbolism can indicate falling in love with romantic images and myths rather than seeing the "real" person.

An addicted type of person with Pluto (see 8th Chord; addictive relationships are also discussed in the 8th Chord) in the 7th house or powerfully aspected (especially by opposition or quincunx) might satisfy an Attachment Hunger by forming relationships with individuals who are manipulative and secretive. Since Pluto's symbolism is greatly linked to the sexual bonding of a relationship, the addiction here could center around an extreme sexual attraction to the Attachment Fetish Person and the addicted individual may become easily manipulated due to a physical infatuation. Pluto is also related to an individual's awareness of personal power, and the addicted person in this situation is transferring her personal power to the Attachment Fetish Person. The addicted individual projects a tremendous amount of her own qualities upon others. What she adores and feels she cannot live without from another person are often valuable attributes of her own that she needs to develop.

The individual must begin to appreciate her own sense of power. The more she looks to others to empower her with their strength, the less likely she is to maintain balanced relationships. The addicted person sometimes fears her own emotional intensity and self-expression. Perhaps she has been through painful rejections. Again, the opposition and the squares indicate potential assistance: self-assertion with opposing Chord 1, competence with squaring Chord 10 and emotional security with squaring Chord 4.

It is not uncommon for addicted individuals to need to do some cleaning-up of the past. Pluto can especially point to one's need to forgive or let go of the past. The key to releasing the hold of the past is changing one's perceptions—as the actual circumstances of the past cannot be changed. For instance, perhaps a person had a dominating parent who was extremely unloving and unfeeling. The parent's behavior may have been perceived by the addicted person as a reflection of her (low) self-worth. ("If Mommy/Daddy does not love me, I guess I am unlovable.") Reassessing the past allows the person to see the parent's behavior as a reflection of her/his inability to express warmth and caring. When the individual can change her perception of the past, she can change her present and her future. The personal script can shift from: "Mommy/Daddy never loved me therefore I am unlovable and can never expect warmth from others" (hence unconsciously attracting rejection) to "Mommy/Daddy never loved me because s/he was unable to express caring. I am a lovable person and have a right to share my love with others."

An individual's misuse of 7th Chord tones can manifest as the developing of too many social identities in what I call the **Masquerade** game. This person has become so many different selves that she is like a kaleidoscope presenting our eyes with many changing visual effects but no stable focus. These different social masks or false pretenses are really not true extensions of herself. She presents so many images to others that she loses a sense of self.

The individual needs to develop a truer self-image (opposition to Chord 1). This game can be characteristic of a very talented and artistic person. It is important that the individual realize who resides behind all social masks. She probably needs to tap into her watery emotional nature to transcend a limiting isolation which is often behind this game. Tuning into Chord 10 may also help her to realistically assess when a particular mask is appropriate given societal demands and when her true self will be most effective.

The **Masquerade** game is related to another game, **On Stage**. This is an individual who is constantly vying for attention. She will do anything to be noticed and has a strong yearning for social approval. She desires the thunderous applause of others as her own self-examination lacks clarity and depth. The real problem is that she is too preoccupied with an outward search for self-definition.

The person must learn to control tremendous social instincts. She is constantly seeking external stimulation. The earth and water elements offer reflective themes that a strong air person may be lacking. These other dimensions of the self may need exploring. She could be ignoring the stability (earth) and emotional clarity (water) that would alleviate a compulsive drive for attention. As with many Chord 7 games, too much focus on the needs of others can result in underdoing self-expression and self-assertion..

Another 7th Chord game is the **Glitter Bug**. This individual presents a flashy image by wearing expensive or seductive clothing. Often she is trying to cover up an inner emotional deadness with a glamorous public appearance. She fears to let someone see the inward loneliness and emotional destitution.

The person must become more honest with herself. When a person has an extreme imbalance of air, it can be easy to hide the emotional nature. Air can be used to talk one's emotional energy to sleep. The person in this game needs to penetrate her inner beauty, which often requires less work to express than running away through outer forms of glamour.

A 7th Chord harmonious expression depends very much on an individual's inward balance. Though this is an air chord, symbolizing mental energy, there is a mental-emotional equilibrium essential for a strong 7th Chord type. An attraction to the arts and aesthetics is often an individual's attempt to balance through creative expression. There is a lack of balance concerning the 7th Chord found in another major counseling theme, **indecision.**

The **Sitting on the Fence** game is exhibited by an individual who is compulsively indecisive. She misses many life opportunities in a manner similar to the 1st Chord game, **Missing the Boat.** The **Sitting on the Fence** individual is fearful of making choices. She may not know what to do until changes literally knock her off her indecisive fence. There is often an issue involving assertion in this game. In the 1st Chord it is mainly a question of asserting one's self image. In the 7th Chord it chiefly consists of balancing one's self-image with the expectations of others. Often procrastination is a result in this game as the individual does not want to offend someone with a choice or decision. In a compulsive drive to please everyone, she frustrates herself and others with procrastinating behavior. Learning to take responsibility (square to Chord 10) for decisions as well as asserting herself can be helpful. When she initiates choices, the timing of changes in life will come naturally.

The **Broken Scales** game is exhibited by an individual who is not clear in weighing life priorities. She has been so depressed by an inability to achieve harmony that she cannot find a balanced perspective. Her emotional equilibrium has shattered to the point of no return and she has become filled with anxiety and tensions. Her sense of self is so disoriented that she needs help in reinstating an emotional-mental balance.

This individual often has extremely high standards of perfection (quincunx to Chord 12) and may need to learn compassion in evaluating her capabilities. Concentrating on accomplishments within her ability (square to Chord 10 and quincunx to Chord 2) may increase the sense of inner strength and self-worth. Nurturing (square to Chord 4) can also give a solid emotional foundation and contribute to the decrease of tension and anxieties.

The **Compulsive Strategist** is perhaps more typical of Libra than the other 7th Chord tones. This is an individual who is so intent on maintaining a state of balance that she eliminates emotional spontaneity. She lives as though life were a chess game, carefully out-maneuvering others so they cannot harm her vulnerabilities. There is a defensiveness that can be displayed by people expressing 7th Chord themes in a dysfunctional manner. However, this defensive strategy can backfire as the individual's desire to keep others at an emotional distance can eventually lead to a checkmate. The loneliness and isolation eat away at true 7th Chord needs for love, affection and intimate companionship.

This person needs to allow emotional needs (square to Chord 4) to be noticed and felt by others. This game can be played by very sensitive people who fear taking the risk of being hurt by others. Developing the courage of Chord 1 can be helpful. Letting down the defenses allows others to come closer and balances the emotional energy of this individual.

The **Aphrodisiac** game discussed in the 2nd Chord can also find a parasitic home in the 7th Chord. The desire for a relationship is a powerful theme of the 7th Chord. An individual lacking a balanced clarity about the self still wants to be loved. However, self-love may be so poisoned that she is sure others will reject her. The struggle with beauty, harmony and a truly loving expression become distorted by an escape into compulsive sexuality, alcohol and drug abuse, food binges, etc. Due to a fear of rejection she can no longer judge or weigh her own ability to be a loving person or worthy of receiving emotional warmth.

This individual feels she is not deserving of love; this is a self-hating behavior. The person needs to find a stable emotional balance by being more accepting of herself. Often there is a pattern of unfulfilling or painful relationships (perhaps going back to childhood). The individual may need to reconsider her expectations of the self and others in relationships. Are expectations too high, unrealistic, demanding? The quincunx to Chord 12 emphasizes the potential of escapism but highlights the importance of compassion. The rose-colored glasses of Chord 12 may be essential in lessening demanding standards. The individual can learn to focus on the positive rather than the negative. Since the abuse is used as an escape from self-hate, developing more self-appreciation is vital, whether through nurturing (Chord 4), realistic achievements (Chord 10), artistic creations (Chord 2) or other avenues.

There is another dimension of the 7th house that traditionally has led to its symbolism as "the house of one's open adversaries or enemies." This area of the horoscope does seem to give some indications of an individual's competitive spirit and possible war-like entanglements or legal conflicts. The 7th house represents one's entrance into the life arena to confront or compete with others as well as to seek genuine cooperation. Many times the 7th house symbolic struggles do get acted out in the courtroom in the form of lawsuits or legal agreements.

The **One-Upmanship** game involves the ultimate game player and can be quite demonstrative of 7th Chord tones that are dysfunctioning. This is someone who can manipulate you rather cleverly without you quite being aware until after the fact. "Winning" is this individual's primary motive. It is not unusual to find lawsuits as a primary weapon to coerce others to submit to her demands. Such an individual may need to learn the difference between assertion and aggression. The individual needs to express a more balanced sense of personal power.

The **Warmonger** game is typical of an individual who is constantly at war with herself and others. This is the competitive 7th Chord theme but blown way out of proportion. The **Warmonger** individual is an overly aggressive person who forces others to take the defensive (or offensive). She is interested only in furthering her own stand and will do anything necessary to make a point. I sometimes think of the **Warmonger** individual as a "Little General" who will argue and bully incessantly to get her own way.

The individual needs to learn the cooperation and compromise themes of the 7th Chord. Both the 1st and 7th Chords share a competitive spirit. The individual must balance self-interests (1st Chord) with the needs of others (7th Chord).

This game can be played by a person hiding insecurity. The individual may need to drop defensiveness in order to form close alliances with lovers, bosses, etc. Issues involved with 7th Chord games can include knowing when to cooperate, when to compete and when to compromise. It is not appropriate to fight with people on the same team!

Summary of Issues with 7th Chord Games

Seventh Chord games originate from one's inability to balance opposite or contrasting forces. It is essential that a person strengthen weak or underdeveloped qualities and modify overdeveloped themes.

Seventh Chord themes can be used to enjoy balanced and healthy relationships and aesthetic harmony. Since the 7th Chord is opposite the fiery 1st Chord, one must balance assertion instincts with the needs of others.

Individuals with strong 7th Chord themes can display sound judgment and clear decision making. It is when one denies personal qualities or aggressively forces decisions on others that the key allies in life become 7th Chord games.

Subtones

The three **subtones** of the 7th Chord are: the planetary aspect known as the **opposition,** the energy focus of Libra known as **cardinal** and the house classification known as **angular.**

The aspect subtone of the 7th Chord, the **opposition,** defines additional excitement and tension in the social consciousness of Venus. Oppositions point to areas where people are playing with an exhilarating intensity upon the frets of the Venusian 7th Chord archetypal theme, especially in regard to relationships.

The major challenge of an opposition is to make peace with the energies symbolized by each planet. The two planets forming an opposition indicate that a person will not get the maximum efficiency by choosing one expression (planetary theme) over the other. As a matter of fact, some people repress the themes represented by one end of an opposition. They live as though they have a blatant blind spot, visible to others but not to themselves, in regard to the planetary energy being repressed or denied access. They often attract individuals who reflect or mirror back what is being repressed. For instance, an individual who denies assertion needs and self-expression (perhaps with an opposition involving Mars or other 1st Chord tones) will unconsciously attract extremely assertive and aggressive individuals. She may even attract argumentative or **Me First** type individuals in important relationships. The more the individual denies her own needs, the more she attracts these self-centered individuals who come and go as they please. Once she begins to express her own strength and assertion, she is more likely to attract other people who are also balanced in their expression of strength and assertion.

The opposition aspects in a horoscope indicate an individual's ability to see others with objective eyes. When individuals with one or more oppositions, especially between a personal and an outer planet, are able to manifest and integrate the potentially conflicting energies into harmonious expression, they may make good counselors, teachers, salespersons and successful communicators. They seem to have an intuitive sense for tuning into the awareness of others. The opposition involves two planets sitting at approximately opposite points from each other, usually in compatible elements (air/fire or water/earth) symbolizing two distinct portions of our psyche. This aspect calls for moderation, simplicity, clarity and most of all unity in balancing the expression. The opposition can feel like an internal tug of war if we fail to recognize both energies as equals, and often the symbolic battleground externalizes in our relationships.

The psychologist, Carl Jung, had an interesting theory concerning personality opposites. He said that the solution to dealing with conflicting forces comes directly from the nature of the opposites themselves. He also said that the tension of opposites seeks a unity. This seems to be a key factor in balancing the symbolism of the opposition aspect. The individual must find a harmonious middle ground from which she can fully realize the potential of the opposition, expressing the themes of both planets. She can avoid the internal and external wars by finding appropriate channels through which to express both planetary motifs. The energy represented in an opposition denotes tension which can be very growth-promoting. Tuning into the natural partnership shown by the two sides of an opposition allows one to turn potential enemies into allies.

The initiating radiance of a **cardinal subtone** symbolizes excitement at entering new partnerships and social enterprises. Also, cardinal energy symbolizes Libra's attraction to aesthetic endeavors. Libra indicates the drive to express a conceptualization of beauty much like the changing of seasons. The meaning of Libra glows within the wonderful colors of nature that come with each autumn.

The **angular subtone** of the 7th house symbolizes the potential excitement and thrust of the self into a world filled with many social masks. The angularity of the 7th house represents an opportunity to walk many different paths in meeting people. Just as the angular subtone of the 1st house symbolizes one's urge to assert a self-concept, the angular subtone of the opposing 7th house links and unifies the self-image to images presented by others. Hopefully that union is successful.

Whereas the opposite chord, the 1st Chord, shows the beginning formations of a self-image, the 7th Chord represents the extension of the self to form meaningful relationships. It is the balance found within an individual's mental-emotional perspective that can be the seeds for important and meaningful relationships and a true externalization of an inner harmony.

CHAPTER TEN

ELEVENTH CHORD: CONCEPTUALIZATION OF DIRECTION

> He spoke of very simple things—that it is right for a gull to fly, that freedom is the very nature of his being, that whatever stands against that freedom must be set aside, be it ritual or superstition or limitation in any form.
>
> *Jonathan Livingston Seagull* by Richard Bach (page 83)

The 11th Chord is a distinct statement of the air element's compatibility with the fire element in expressing independence. The spontaneous urge to "let freedom ring" is more resounding in the symbolism of the 11th Chord than in the 3rd and 7th Chords. When we have properly accepted the necessary limits which are part of the rules of the game, and learned to be practical in our handling of the world, we are ready to move on to chord eleven. Uranus, Aquarius and the 11th house symbolize the urge to go beyond any limits, the desire to get out of any ruts, the lure of the future, the widest possible expansion of the human mind and contact with fellow humans."

The 11th Chord represents the quest for individuation. The urge is for an individual to follow the sound of his own particular drumbeat in expressing unique qualities. Being true to one's own conceptualization of life directions is symbolized within the 11th Chord archetypal themes of its tones.

Astrology, Psychology, and Transformation

11TH CHORD: CONCEPTUALIZATION OF DIRECTION

Tone	Archetypal Themes	Functions	Positive Expressions	Negative Expressions	Potential Counseling Issues
Planet: Uranus ♅	The directing of actions for the process of individuation and for the acceleration of one's life activities and for entrance into new life goals and new human contacts.	1. To be an individualist and to incorporate a sense of uniqueness into actions and conception of life. 2. To think and act objectively and creatively.	1. The ability to live an innovative lifestyle based on an individual value system. 2. A clear sense of direction due to a fixed mental objectivity.	1. Eccentricity and rebellious behavior that lacks a sense of direction. 2. A potential for fixed opinions. 3. A tendency to be impersonal and sarcastic.	**Key Phrase:** Individuating The Self **Games:** 1. Accident Prone. 2. Copy or Original. 3. Different Just to Be Different.
Sign: Aquarius ♒ **Symbol**	The manner through which a unique identity and a detached mental perspective can be maintained simultaneously with a group (or a universal peer) consciousness.	3. To have a universal social consciousness and detached group perspective.	3. A capacity to stimulate mental clarity in others. 4. An ability to inspire a group consciousness and to challenge it. 5. Gifted and creative intelligence.	4. Intellectual arrogance. 5. An inclination to hide behind intellectualized emotions. 6. Lack of consistency in and action due to a constant need for change.	4. Divorced from Reality. 5. Don't Crowd Me. 6. Escape into the Next Century. 7. Give Me Liberty or Give Me Death!
House 11th	One's attitudes concerning particular goals for the future that will bring the greatest sense of individuality; factors that stimulate both the securing and bonding of peer relationships; the degree to which experimentation is explored to establish and maintain individuality.	4. To envision the future in order to determine goals. 5. To establish connections with peers reflecting a desire for stimulation from many perspectives. 6. To free oneself from conventionality.	6. Spontaneity in thought and action due to excitement from immediate stimulation. 7. A desire to aid the underdog. 8. A talent for developing a true understanding of friendship.	7. A tendency to overly identify with a group consciousness and lose a sense of self. 8. Predisposition to live in the future to deny the failure of present.	8. Groupie. 9. I Can't Slow Down. 10. I Shall Not Be Moved. 11. I Think, Therefore I Am. 12. 9th Nervous Breakdown. 13. Self-Imposed Exile. 14. Stripping Your Gears. 15. Which Way Do I Go?

Figure 9: Eleventh Chord
See the Note to Readers after Acknowledgments

Whereas the 5th Chord focuses upon an emotional liveliness and dramatic self-expression, its opposite, the 11th Chord, is more cool and aloof. The 11th Chord is indicative of a casual mental objectivity and a piercing intellect. The tones and subtones of the 11th Chord represent catalysts that greatly excite the rhythm of one's social and mental urges, sometimes in an unpredictable manner with a sudden impulse to embrace change. Strong 11th Chord individuals are at times inventive, unique, erratic, eccentric and unpredictable.

Uranus

The discovery of the 11th Chord planet Uranus in 1781 by rookie astronomer William Herschel disrupted the boundaries of the eighteenth century astronomical and astrological systems that had grown accustomed to recognizing Saturn as the outermost of planets (and as the 11th Chord planet). The planet rich in scientific and technological symbolism in astrology was the first planet discovered by the use of a telescope, beyond the gaze of the naked eye. Our synchronistic universe is again reflected in Uranus being discovered by surprise (symbolism associated with Uranus) through means of new technology (another Uranian association). In *Astrological Guide to Self-Awareness,* Donna Cunningham reminds us that Uranus was discovered by accident as William Herschel was actually not in search of a planetary discovery with his new, exciting scientific tool, the telescope.

The astronomical characteristics of Uranus match its astrological symbolism. Uranus has a unique rotation of its axis that distinguishes it from the other planets. Uranus takes 84 years to orbit the Sun. Unlike other planets Uranus lies on its side as it spins. First one pole and then the other points straight at the Sun. This means that a big part of Uranus has daylight for about 40 years! Then night comes for 40 years." The uniqueness portrayed by the axial angle of Uranus is typical of its pioneering astrological spirit associated with rebellion, eccentricity and individuality.

Just as Uranus seems to create its own posture within the sky and snubbed the mere gaze of the naked eye for aeons of years, strong Uranian personalities are often at odds with the culture in which they live. These individuals can be light years ahead in consciousness, often misunderstood as eccentrics or insane by their peers. Whereas 10th Chord Saturn symbolizes a dependency or commitment to the confines of one's culture, Uranus connotes a break with tradition and the status quo, with a progressive foot into new un-chartered territory.

It was discovered in 1977 that Uranus, like Saturn, is surrounded by rings. I think of these rings as representing the impersonality that is quite distinct in each 11th Chord tone. Uranian individuality is often cherished as though it was sacred, holy and untouchable to others. Impersonality and aloofness are often the rings surrounding a psyche saturated with Uranus symbolism, indicating an off-limits zone, preserving a cherished form of individuality. Those who honor this space of individuality win the friendship of a strong Uranian type and are accepted as peers. However loving and emotionally warm a pronounced Uranian type of individual becomes, he will probably never allow someone to penetrate completely the rings that lead to his inner world decorated with freedom, uniqueness and individuality. It is from this reservoir of strength and security in knowing he is an individual that he will share relentlessly with those seen as peers.

When I began studying astrology in 1973 it was common to hear astrologers speak of Uranus as the higher octave of Mercury in regard to thought and intelligence.' I believe there is some grain of truth in this statement. Mercury's frequency seems to be more attuned to the conscious mind and learned, conscious, mental perceptions. However, just as the discovery of Uranus was a step beyond the planetary world of the day, I believe Uranus symbolizes an individual's capacity to develop a logic or mental perception that does not depend entirely on the conscious mind or learned perception. The **house position** of Uranus in the birth chart and **planetary aspects** (not just sign placement) are of utmost importance in considering a person's developing individuality and establishing peer (and sub-culture) associations.

Mercury moves rapidly through the sky and often passes through an entire sign in less than 20 days while Uranus takes approximately 7 years to cover the same distance. For Mercury the passage from one sign to another is a hop, skip and jump while the passage of Uranus from one sign to another is a major journey—for many of us, almost one tenth of a lifetime! There seems to be a wisdom embedded in the slow, patient movement of the outer planets. Even the often erratic and unconventional Uranus appears to go beyond the knowledge of the individual intellect fed by the intelligence of one culture or several cultures within a lifetime. A gift of intelligence and genius is sometimes symbolized. Some individuals can fully tap into the uniqueness and gift of vision symbolized by the sign and element placement of Uranus.

I do not mean to take away from an individual's personal effort and responsibility in achieving brilliance or invention, although sometimes it does seem that a person has entered a collective gift of genius. For example, when someone exhibits an intelligence and creative mental gift that goes beyond self-taught knowledge (or insight learned through living in a particular culture), it seems he has individualized or mastered Uranian themes. The knowledge and flashes of clarity and intuition appear to be obtained only through the collective and historical genius of all civilizations and many, many minds!

The positive expressions of Uranus include the ability to live a balanced individualistic lifestyle and exhibit a brave mental nature. Other positive expressions include a clear sense of direction guided by mental objectivity and an ability to stimulate mental clarity in others. One of the most positive expressions of Uranian energy is a gifted and creative intelligence that can inspire and raise a group consciousness and a lack of fear in challenging a group opinion or cultural injustice.

Negative expressions of Uranus include an individual's desire to be different without logic or sense of direction. An eccentric and rebellious behavior due to a fixed sense of uncompromising unconventionality as well as an overly impersonal nature are negative expressions. Perhaps the main Achilles' heel in negative Uranian expression is a defiant intellectual arrogance that alienates others. The lifestyle may be irresponsible and self-centered due to inconsistent life goals and a need for constant change. Another negative expression is surrendering one's individuality completely to a group consciousness (seen in the **Groupie** game).

Aquarius

The sign tone of this chord, Aquarius, is typical of the independent 11th Chord spirit. The new planetary ruler of Aquarius, Uranus, replaced the traditional rulership of the more conservative Saturn (now assigned to Capricorn only). Sometimes people think Aquarius should be a water sign due to its mythological symbolism as the "Water Bearer." Modern astrologers associate Aquarius with electricity, the Water Bearer's jug filled with waves of electric current rather than water. The cool mental detachment of this strongly focused air sign distinguishes its personality and temperament from the emotional water signs and the enthusiastic warmth of the fire signs. The individualistic and unconventional tastes denoted by Aquarius differentiate it from the other air signs, Gemini and Libra.

Sometimes the progressive and "upbeat" Aquarius seems to indicate an intuitive nature that one might associate with the water signs. However, the intuition of Aquarius can be traced to a rapidly functioning intellect which quickly perceives the gestalt or entire pattern of a situation. It free-associates instantaneously and regroups that much more quickly with the grasp of the facts. This can seem like intuition rather than a fast-thinking mental process. People with a focus on Gemini who encounter the same situation cannot so easily perceive the whole picture. Their thoughts become engrossed in the intricate parts, often distracted by the first, immediately stimulating insights. They may neglect to gather all of the facts. Individuals with an emphasis on Libra are busy balancing the contrasts or opposites that immediately come to their attention within a process. Either Gemini or Libra can point to surrendering the whole to its parts.

Aquarius shows the potential of hiding one's true self behind the shield of the intellect. It can also indicate the dispelling of all illusion or darkness with the sword of belief in equality, truth and justice for all. The inventor, scientist, champion of the common people, acts as the spokesman or spokeswoman for the forward movement of a company, community, nation or planet! The confusion associated with Aquarius often stems from a tendency to move forward before fully comprehending or assimilating the past. The pull of polarities and many perspectives that can come into awareness with Aquarius can also have a disorienting effect for some individuals.

Whereas Aries symbolizes a warrior engaged in combat, Aquarius denotes a creative mental warrior who thrives on challenge to the mind as much as Aries sometimes needs a sparring partner. Aquarius represents strength that can stabilize itself within the midst of change and provide the needed courage and stamina to move onward. Aquarius indicates individuals who trip over their own intellects when trying to dodge life commitments or wave the banner of a cause or personal goal that lacks originality and leads them away from their true selves.

Individuals with a focus on Aquarius (or Uranus and 11th house) often need the strength of a group or subculture to help authenticate their individual value. They must be careful not to become too indulgent in the slogans of a group movement, losing their own unique identities (life and breath in discovering oneself). A group or subculture can feed the humanitarian values denoted by Aquarius and aid the longing for companionship that sometimes is frustrated by a rebellious spirit. A group provides a warm fireplace of friendship and emotional security that strong 11th Chord types are generally too proud to acknowledge that they need. The meaning of Aquarius (and Uranus) is well portrayed by the character in the novel *Steppenwolf* the German author Herman Hesse. The hero has one foot safely within society's boundaries but almost invariably the other foot is securely resting outside of a culture's rules and regulations.

People with an emphasis on Aquarius are accused sometimes of acting like an iceman (or ice woman). Their compulsive need for space may lead them to project an emotional coldness, telecasting that they have suddenly instituted a time-out from all responsibilities. An Aquarian retreat, whether with records, books or telescope in hand, is needed to refuel for a strong jet-propelled mental projection into action. The Aquarian need for mental space is an inward move for personal freedom. The individual wishes to rebuild objective awareness and to renegotiate an acknowledgment of his utmost self-confidence that sometimes baffles and produces envy in others. Aquarian confidence enjoys a rich tradition as evidenced by a key word phrase, long ago associated with the Water Bearer of originality, "I know."

The positive expressions of Aquarius include a similarity to Uranus in living an innovative lifestyle based on an individual value system. A person may have the capacity to withstand criticism of others and to pursue goals that enhance self-growth. A fixed mental objectivity which perseveres through difficult obstacles to stay on the path of a clear conceptualization of direction is another positive potential. A desire to help those in need, due to a universal or humanitarian peer consciousness, and a capacity to value friendship are also positive expressions.

Negative expressions of Aquarius include a self-centered, rebellious behavior and fixed, stubborn opinions that lack any real logic or substance. Other negative expressions include an emotional impersonality that isolates one from others with too much intellectualizing, and a tendency to sacrifice one's sense of individuality to a group consciousness. The future orientation shown by Aquarius can be an escape from facing the fact that present goals are unrealistic. Too much future focus may lead to a lack of stability in thought and action that alienates others.

11th House

The 11th Chord house tone symbolizes one's attitudes concerning personal goals that will further a sense of life direction and allow one to become a complete individual. One's initiative to develop friendships and participation in particular peer groups are also indicated. The 11th house in the horoscope indicates an individual's degree of experimentation in forming new goals that will further develop and foster an emerging individuation.

There is a sense of wanting to belong to a greater whole in the 11th house, and individuals with key planets in this house often have a universalistic vision or issues surrounding their selection of a peer group or other social contacts with whom to share this vision. Strong 11th house types often have such a progressive consciousness that they enjoy their effect upon a group consciousness even if it means playing the devil's advocate by going against group opinions to bring about changes.

Astrology books often describe the bonding process only in relation to the succedent water house, the 8th house (see 8th Chord), but neglect to discuss the bonding process in relation to each succedent house (2nd, 5th, 8th and 11th). The security-seeking symbolized by the succedent houses is difficult for an individual to satisfy without the bonding process. Perhaps it is more subtle in the 2nd house but to an extent one must form a bond to one's possessions; in the 5th house one forms a bond with children or creative works as both are a direct extension of the procreative self and, as will be seen in the 8th house symbolism, the sharing of one's psychological and physical instincts with another person can make for a powerfully bonded partnership, relationship or marriage. The 11th house also is greatly concerned with the bonding process as one secures an identity by following through on goals and forming a close friendship in a bond that can be as difficult to break as one between one's own self-esteem, children, lovers and mates. As a matter of fact, I doubt the depth or level of a friendship that lacks a bond of trust and at least a minimum degree of emotional exchange.

A group can have tremendous power as it is a bonding together of many divergent personalities joining forces for a common belief or purpose. The most creative and bonded of groups allows for its individuals to express their own creativity and hence raise the group consciousness. A group's rigid philosophy can destroy the idealism and future orientation of a true 11th Chord individual. Often the person with the insight and courage to challenge a group opinion has the most importance for the group.

Strong 11th Chord types may have the Sun, Moon or Ascendant in Aquarius or a strongly placed Uranus by house and aspect or key planets in the 11th house. Sometimes I feel that the greatest dilemma of these individuals is how to balance the need for one's own independence with that of a relationship or belonging to a group, society, etc. A strong 11th house type of person often needs the support of others to secure the conceptualization of a direction in life. It is ironic that this person may eventually be repulsed by and rebel against the very peer group, society or individual that filled him with a sense of power and new ideas.

Positive 11th house expressions include a sense of fulfillment in knowing that one is living life to the fullest potential, expressing one's individuality, and living personal goals that are a direct reflection of one's own uniqueness. Other positive expressions include an ability to stimulate one's peers to a greater achievement of their own personal goals. An ability to form bonded friendships with others and a progressive consciousness that is well in tune with one's own anticipated future needs for growth are also positive expressions.

Negative 11th house expressions include an uncooperative and self-centered arrogance due to feeling one's opinions are too unique to be challenged. Surrendering one's individuality to a group mentality in order to hide within a peer group consciousness is another negative expression. A lack of consistency in living one's life due to a constant need for change and escaping to future goals in a compulsive manner to avoid the challenge of the present are also negative 11th house expressions.

Counseling Issues

The counseling issues of this chord are indicative of an individual's inability to follow his own unique footsteps. The essence of the 11th Chord is **conceptualization of direction.** My key word phrase for these counseling issues, **individuating the self,** is from the synthesis of the tones: Uranus, Aquarius and the 11th house. Each has a special emphasis on developing the individuation process. The archetypal themes are:

1. **Uranus**—the directing of actions for the process of individuation and the stimulus for the acceleration of one's life activities, entrance into new life goals and establishing new human contacts.
2. **Aquarius**—the manner through which a unique identity and a detached mental perspective can be maintained simultaneously within a group (or a universal peer) consciousness.

3. **11th house**—one's attitudes concerning particular goals for the future that will bring the greatest sense of individuality; factors that stimulate both the securing and bonding of peer relationships and the degree to which experimentation is explored to establish and maintain individuality.

The counseling issues of this chord are related to an individual's loss of perspective in developing individuality. The 11th Chord tones represent the clear formulation of one's personal goals to foster a lucid sense of life direction and to establish close and lasting relationships of all kinds. The counseling issues of this chord are twofold: (1) an extremely compulsive focus upon one's own unique traits, future goals and freedom urges that alienates friends, lovers or peer associations; (2) a fear of manifesting one's individuality causing confusion in planning goals, setting priorities, and developing one's own life direction.

Games

When a person becomes too absorbed with individuality, he might exhibit the **Different Just to Be Different** game. This individual is not expressing the natural freedom orientation of 11th Chord innovative thinking in a harmonious manner. Instead he is settling for a simulated version of freedom and often is not sure in which direction his life is heading. He may border on being an eccentric whose personal tastes must be different than those of any peers to prove his individuality. Unfortunately, this outward show only alienates those who would like to be close to him. I have seen this game particularly prominent in some individuals who have Uranus placed in the 2nd house (see 2nd Chord). It is as though their values "must" be unique and different to prove they have a sense of self-esteem. These particular individuals did have very unstable value systems. Tapping into the earth element can help the person stabilize values and the water element can help one be more sensitive to how actions might be hiding an emotional lack. The natural square to Chord 2 highlights the importance of including comfort and stability as well as freedom. The square to Chord 8 reiterates the importance of emotional bonds and intimacy (which requires some compromising of independence).

Another 11th Chord game related to one's too-emphasized expression of independence is the **Give Me Liberty or Give Me Death!** This is a nice patriotic slogan but not when someone demands his own freedom and does not respect the rights of others for the same freedom. This is an individual who gets angry when you ask him what time he is coming home, or you cannot seem to pin him down to important commitments. His idea of give-and-take in relationships is "I'll take and you give." You often find this game in the addictive relationships discussed in the 7th Chord (see **I Am Addicted to You** game). This 11th Chord game is often found in a relationship when one person is afraid to rock the boat by challenging the undisputed freedom of an extremely self-centered and nihilistic mate or partner. The freedom-crazed person keeps taking liberty after liberty while his partner's freedom and uniqueness slip away and die a slow death. Needless to say, neither person has relationships based on cooperation and an equal exchange of love.

The person playing the game needs to modify power motives. This can be a controlling game, intended to hide one's emotional vulnerability. The opposite 5th Chord may be involved in balancing this game. The individual must begin to honor the creative self-expression of others. His relationships get more balanced when he allows others some of the freedom he is demanding. In a sense, the fixed chords are a progression of giving up power. In Chord 2, dealing with our own money/possessions/pleasures, we own them and have the right to use our power as we choose. In Chord 5, dealing with loving and being loved, in order to get the positive feedback/love/attention/admiration, we moderate our power and have some concern for the desires of the other person. You will see in Chord 8, we

share the money/possessions/pleasures and are learning to give/receive and be **equal** with another person. We give up more power in order to find a middle ground which allows intimacy and a sense of power within both individuals. In Chord 11, ideally, we give up power over everything except **knowledge**.

An individual not actualizing the potential of 11th Chord tones might also become entrapped by the **Don't Crowd Me** game. This is a person who fears the closeness or intimacy of relationships and usually finds an excuse to push others away from him. Often this game is due to an individual's habit of hiding behind 11th Chord impersonality. He may vacillate between getting very intimate with someone and then making an abrupt break when feeling too crowded. This can lead to unstable relationships. He may enjoy group associations and casual acquaintances due to the impersonal atmosphere, but panic when relations become too intimate and personal as the atmosphere feels threatening and suffocating.

The air chord tendency to shut out emotions as foreign experiences is the issue here. This game is linked to a fear of emotions, especially appearing vulnerable. An opening up of emotional energy brings a lot more creative energy forward, and people feel more comfortable in getting closer to him on an emotional level. The natural opposition to the 5th Chord reminds us that humankind does not live by mind alone but must also incorporate the heart. A place must be made for love. Likewise, the square to the 8th Chord repeats the necessity of intimacy and emotional bonding.

An 11th Chord game associated with an individual's fixed opinions is the **I Shall Not Be Moved** game. Here the stubborn tendency of the 11th Chord is typified by an individual who will not alter personal goals and preferences even if it would greatly alleviate tension in relating to others. It must be remembered that the 11th Chord tones belong to a fixed chord and their symbolisms in the horoscope have a potential for an individual's inflexibility in adjusting personal goals and standards to accommodate the needs of others. There is a relationship in this game to the 10th

Chord **Tree That Won't Bend** game in that the individual will not alter a course of action even if it is obvious a new course or direction might be for the best. After all, right or wrong, he is doing it his own way!

This game calls for more flexibility in one's goals and values. The individual could do some refocusing of this fixed determination and strength. It is amazing how much more energy it requires to be on the defensive. When this individual drops some stubborn attitudes and behaviors, he is better able to move forward and accomplish major goals. When he fully enters the spirit of Chord 11, he is **tolerant** and **open** rather than rigid. A core essence of Chord 11 is the capacity to see many choices, multiple options, always a **new** possibility.

A strong 11th Chord type of individual who develops goals and interests that are so peculiar and eccentric that nobody can relate to him may become victimized with the **Self-imposed Exile** game. This is a person who believes that he is too much of a genius to associate with others and too far ahead of his time to be properly understood. He may cause people to be defensive with notorious put-downs of their intelligence. His intellectual arrogance and very impersonal nature creates an emotional exile for himself. Others are unable to reach through this intellectual armor to give him love.

To rise above this game the individual needs to be more honest emotionally with himself and others. Many of these folks are really quite brilliant. The natural square formed to the emotionally packed 8th Chord can indicate the need to release emotional pains or fears. Blocked emotions can lead the individual to mistrust others. The natural quincunx formed to the watery 4th Chord represents issues concerning intimacy and dependency on others. The **Self-imposed Exile** is an avoidance behavior as the person fears rejection.

Another 11th Chord game related to an individual's compulsive focus upon personal goals and freedom is the **Escape into the Next Century.** This is an individual who, rather than deny that previous goals have led to a place of stagnation or disappointment in life, attempts to escape into future plans. When confronted by others about present life condition he will make excuses why things have not worked and tell us about his wonderful plans to make everything okay someday. Unfortunately, his drive for stimulation and change is so constant he cannot settle into the present. He is not able to modify a very extreme upbeat and progressive consciousness to share responsibility for the present circumstances. Also, he alienates friends due to an irresponsible nature.

The **Escape into the Next Century** game is a close relative of the **I Can't Slow Down** game. This is someone who has no conception of the word "moderation." This particular game is the prototype of the 11th Chord symbolism associated with extreme drives for constant stimulation. A compulsive drive for a variety of sometimes unorthodox experiences can grow so out of proportion that the individual cannot find a way to decelerate life to a more natural and balanced pace. Someone manifesting this behavior is not able to settle into a comfortable life and his relationships are often very unstable. As soon as he begins to plant any seeds, he quickly digs them up as his inconsistent life is out of control and lacks direction.

The **Escape into the Next Century** and **I Can't Slow Down** games require some earthy discipline so that one can better enjoy the present. Individuals playing these two games can be fearful that commitments are confining and boring and that stability is too predictable. However, the individuals with powerful 11th Chord themes sometimes find a new meaning in becoming stable and concentrating in the present. Facing present circumstances with a more responsible attitude leads to transcending these games. The mental quickness of these individuals can be better used in creative endeavors than as a means of escaping responsibility.

The **I Can't Slow Down** game commonly leads to the **19th Nervous Breakdown.** This individual often has earned a nervous breakdown by ignoring too many stop signs and rest areas. The 11th Chord tones, especially Uranus and Aquarius, can characterize an individual whose thoughts travel like lightning bolts. Instead of his vital energies circulating to all parts of the body, they seem to meet in his mind, bombarding him with compulsive thoughts. A lack of ability to organize himself constructively can lead to a haphazard existence that gradually depletes strength and reasoning power until a total mental and physical collapse is the result. There is a lot of nervous energy associated with each air chord. The 11th Chord denotes an individual who must channel this energy productively, in a balanced manner, or the exhausted and fatigued body may take matters into its own hands.

Both the fire and air elements require a faster paced existence than the water and earth elements, but faster-moving people still need some "R & R" once in a while. The person caught up in this game sometimes simply needs to call a time out when life is getting too hurried. It is in the pause that the person can sort out what he needs to do. A reprogramming of one's impatient thought patterns is often required in this game. He may need to indulge in the fun-loving energy of the fiery 5th Chord or the relaxed, easygoing approach of Chord 2. The quincunx to Chord 6 emphasizes the importance of self-discipline and good health care. The quincunx to Chord 4 repeats the importance of patience and a strong emotional foundation of support and sustenance.

A game similar in some respects to the **Self-imposed Exile** is what I call the **Divorced from Reality** game. This individual is so completely absorbed by individualistic fancies and so "out there" that nobody knows just how to quite reel him back to a more realistic assessment of self. His vision has departed from any trace of realizable goals. He may be as divorced from meaningful relationships as he is from reality. He is very out of touch with present trends and in some ways perhaps lives in the past.

The person needs to tap into stabilizing earth energy. He may need to reconsider his value systems and make appropriate adjustments to once again enter the mainstream of life. Focusing on how to function effectively will help ground him.

When an individual fears individuality or represses it too much, he may become victimized by the **Stripping Your Gears** game. This individual has a poor sense of personal individuality and lacks the confidence to experiment with new growth-promoting situations. His goals are often in a state of turmoil. His lack of faith in his own uniqueness sometimes makes him feel as if a Civil War is going on within him. He lacks the rebellious or experimental spirit symbolized by the 11th Chord or the fiery self-confidence of the opposite 5th Chord. He may feel very frustrated as life opportunities pass him by, much like the 1st Chord game, **Missing the Boat.**

Two people can express similar outer behaviors but from very different inner motivations. The **Missing the Boat** individual has definite assertion issues and perhaps a confused self-image. In this 11th Chord game, **Stripping Your Gears,** the individual may appear to have assertion problems, yet the underlying issue is more connected to a person's confusion concerning unique individuality and goals. Different games can yield the same observable behavior but be based on quite different inner motivations and needs. Focusing only on the behavior does not help one to change. He must begin to understand his underlying needs.

Another game associated with a lack of expressing one's individuality is the **Groupie.** The **Groupie** is a person who hides within an in-group or peer group as he does not wish to reveal unique qualities to others. The wholistic vision of the 11th Chord is surrendered to a very limited tunnel vision. The **Groupie** belongs to clannish or cultish types of groups, formal or even informal, that do not help to foster a growing individuality. The group asks nothing of him creatively, and his bond to these peers is really a bondage or dependency that retards development as an individual. He becomes a weak-minded person and **Groupie** friends offer a negative support system that does not stimulate his own need for individual growth. The **Groupies** reinforce each other's enslaved and limited group mentality. The **Groupie** is so dependent on an external support system that he may develop a bad habit of getting advice from the wrong people. Often a person who has swallowed an extreme dose of this type of game praises the group in every other sentence and does not realize group allegiance has blinded him to his own unique traits.

The opposite 5th Chord must be brought into a sharper focus if the person wants to bring this 11th Chord game into a more balanced expression. He needs to pay more attention to his own identity and creative self-expression, and not be so eager to adopt the group values and surrender personal power (square to Chord 8).

Sometimes an individual tries to become a clone of an important peer person. He portrays what I call the **Copy or Original?** game. In a stagnating or dead-end type of relationship, an individual seems as if he has lost all zest for life. After a separation or break-up he suddenly has tons of released energy. I have noticed this to be especially true of someone who has sacrificed personal originality and individuality in order to be better liked by a lover, peer group or parent. In such cases, the individual resembles a reproduced copy of someone else's vision rather than a person of his own choosing. The transformation from copy to original can be so revitalizing and freeing that a person cannot believe that he once allowed his own unique qualities and goals to be sacrificed to follow the dictations of others.

A person very much out of touch with his own developing individuality may engage in the **Which Way Do I Go?** game. Most people at one time or another are indecisive or confused about what choices will be best for the future. However, an individual in this game never seems to know which way is north or south. Often in the past there has been a strong dependency on an authoritarian figure or peer group that made most of the important decisions in his life. Now he is faced with developing his own individuality and feels quite afraid and inadequate to proceed ahead in life.

The person needs to understand his inner motivations for depending too much on others for direction. When the individual is able to take the risk of making his own decisions, he can transcend this game. It is usually best to discipline the mind to think in terms of taking small steps in accomplishing goals (expressing the themes of Chord 6 which is the natural quincunx to Chord 11).

Someone with a repressed individuality may exhibit the **Accident-Prone** game. This individual may be repressing a strong rebellion against others who may be discouraging him from living up to his own unique standards. Uranus has traditionally been associated with symbolism related to accidents. In this game an individual's accidents may be an unconscious statement that he needs to "break" away from the limits he has allowed others to impose upon him.

He needs to better comprehend personal individuality and assertion instincts. He has been trading in personal needs and power too easily and is intensely frustrated. The person can balance this game by feeling the beauty of his own self-expression and uniqueness.

A person who is too much at the mercy of outside forces to plan goals may exhibit the **Divorced from Reality** and **19th Nervous Breakdown** games mentioned earlier. Actually he is even more likely to become entrapped by these games lacking the creative mental energy to reenter reality or to channel nervous energy productively. At least the person too focused on personal individualism has some momentum to change a life pattern. An individual with little grasp of his own individuality may need a tremendous amount of support to change a self-denial pattern of behavior. Amnesia to remember one's own uniqueness is difficult to conquer.

The 11th Chord tones represent such strong mental voltage that an individual's misuse of this powerful energy can electrocute the emotions and result in what I call the **I Think, Therefore I Am** game. This individual is similar to the **Intellectualizer** in the 3rd Chord. In this 11th Chord game a person may be even more prone to resorting to a nonfeeling or very impersonal expression to hide the emotional nature. An urge to independent thought can lead one to try to rationalize experiences and especially to hide emotional vulnerability. This game may typify an individual who is so adept at describing feelings in a unique, intellectual fashion that he actually believes he is expressing emotions.

When the person is able to understand why he is hiding his emotional nature, he is better able to transcend this game. Pride can be a factor where the individual does not want to appear vulnerable. He is proud of not needing help from others. However, underneath this rationalizing are many insecure emotional areas. By incorporating themes from Chord 4, he can learn to receive help from others (and to give it). Including Chord 8 allows the experience of emotional intimacy and bonding. A more balanced emotional expression brings more satisfying relationships and a refreshing new look at himself.

Summary of Issues with 11th Chord Games

The 11th Chord games emanate from one's lack of balance in expressing unique individuality and freedom urges. Some individuals need to tone down the self-focus on goals and liberty while others need to strengthen their independent identities and gain more confidence in expressing their unique goals.

Eleventh Chord themes can be manifested as unconventional creativity and as an independent spirit within very balanced relations with peers, lovers and authority figures.

Eleventh Chord energy can revitalize one's life with new goals and unique ideas. There is a mental genius in this chord that has no rival. Families, groups and entire cultures can greatly benefit from the input of 11th Chord minds. It is only when a person rigidly and irresponsibly overidentifies with the impatient quest for 11th Chord freedom or runs away from a growing individuality, that the 11th Chord games become the life direction.

Subtones

The **sextile** as a **subtone** of the 11th Chord planetary tone highlights the mentally quick responses and intellectually exhilarating meaning of Uranus similarly to the mentally curious and communicative meaning of Mercury. The sextile further illustrates the potential for mental genius symbolized by Uranus. As stated in the 3rd Chord, the planets forming a sextile can symbolize a mental objectivity and mental clarity. Uranus, like Mercury, when involved in a sextile can indicate that an individual has a natural ability to articulate mental concepts and a real attraction to individuals who can excite him intellectually. Perhaps even more so than Mercury, sextiles involving Uranus, especially to personal planets, may show the need for much discipline to harness the energy and bring the creative mental potential of this aspect to full fruition. Uranus is not always indicative of an individual's capacity to bring intellectual energy into a stable and clear expression.

The **fixed subtone** of Aquarius symbolizes the sheer strength that the 11th Chord air sign shows, the potential for a very focused mental energy. Aquarius denotes the mental power and fixed fortitude to move a mountain with its intellect but there is also the danger of developing a fixed identity, lacking flexibility and centering around one's own egocentric purposes. The **maintaining** symbolism of a fixed subtone quality is secured through developing wholistic mental visions and clear, well-substantiated logic. The fixed stabilizing feature of Aquarius also shows the development of dependable and supportive friendships through the belief and confidence in the self to form meaningful peer networks with or without a group setting.

The **succedent subtone** of the 11th house is indicative of the securing and bonding theme of this house tone. One's ability to form a successful bond with personal goals, or to establish valuable friendships with or without participating in a group, is a feeling of security for an individual.

The discovery of Uranus symbolized the seeds of the beginning of a global technological revolution that has reshaped the world consciousness. It has been said that a planet's full symbolism does not really begin until its actual discovery. The theory is based on the premise that people are not quite ready to use the complete capacity symbolized by the not-yet-discovered planet. The entrance of Uranus into the astronomical and astrological worlds has correlated with major changes in the global network of communication between individuals, communities and nations. There have been amazing culture shocks since its eighteenth century discovery. The 11th Chord has universalistic themes that are difficult to harness for a clear and deep significant individual expression. The 11th Chord symbolizes an individual establishing bonded friendships and rejoicing in this bonding with a personal process of individuation and conception of direction.

The archetypal themes of each air chord express through human behavior that is communicative, perceptive, inventive, innovative and sometimes erratic and impersonal. The air element symbolizes our curious and investigative nature to challenge the paradoxes that life offers and to determine our own answers, that is, if we learn to ask the right questions!

PART V

WATER ELEMENT

Water indicates an emotional expression of the self. The water element represents saturating one's consciousness with emotional sensitivity, intensity, contemplation, introspection and a need for privacy. The water element points to a slower life rhythm in order to examine the intricate and unconscious subtleties of life developments.

A person with water as a dominant element by having the water signs (Cancer, Scorpio and Pisces) or houses (4th, 8th and 12th) or planets (Moon, Pluto, Neptune) well emphasized often expresses a well-developed intuitive nature. Strong water individuals may grow weary and confused, "bogged down" by their own powerful and overly sensitive emotional natures. On the other hand, it is often the fathomless depths of the water chord consciousness that lubricates one's psyche with compassion, empathy and emotional warmth.

An individual may have an emphasis on this element in any of the following ways: the Sun, Moon, Ascendant, four or more personal planets in water signs, key planets in water houses, or water planets strongly aspected, especially to one another. Such people often rely on their intuitive instincts and comprehension of unconscious forces to proceed in life with a sense of clarity. The natural tendency shown by water is to fill an individual's emotional expression with a conscience and concern for the welfare of others. People with a water focus may move with caution, creating a safe emotional distance, so as to not become too deeply immersed in the lives of others.

The planets, signs and houses that comprise the water chord family denote the flow of an individual's emotional nature. The chords include a security and intimacy emphasis (4th Chord), an intensity and bonding emphasis (8th Chord), and a transcending and unifying emphasis (12th Chord). The common ingredient of Chords 4, 8 and 12 is the expression of one's emotional self and the integration and assimilation of this emotional energy into a balanced life expression.

CHAPTER ELEVEN

FOURTH CHORD: SECURITY INSTINCTS

> Through the gathering of plants, and the observation of the seasonal rhythms of the appearance of plants, as well as the observation of their own menstrual and lunar cycles, the females would observe the basic periodicities of nature and lay down the foundations for the first great synthesis of science and religion. astrology.
>
> *The Time Falling Bodies Take to Light*
> by William Irwin Thompson (page 80)

The 4th Chord is an expression of the water element in the form of developing primal security instincts related to one's earliest roots or home. Chord four includes the Moon, the sign Cancer and the 4th house. It symbolizes the need for emotional security which is typically expressed in the baby-mother relationship. The instinct of water is always to absorb or to be absorbed; to be dependent and cared for, or to be nurturant, caring for others. If we achieve a healthy balance, we become interdependent, doing both. The planet (Moon), sign (Cancer) and house (4th) tones of this chord symbolize an individual's drive to satisfy dependency and intimacy needs. The archetypal themes of the 4th Chord tones symbolize three manifestations of security-oriented instincts.

The water element's concern for emotional dependency and safety is symbolized in the 4th Chord tones and subtones.

4TH CHORD: SECURITY INSTINCTS

Tone	Archetypal Themes	Functions	Positive Expressions	Negative Expressions	Potential Counseling Issues
Planet: Moon ☾ Symbol	The directing of emotional responses, moods, sub-conscious attitudes and dependency needs to secure the self; the instinctual antennae of the psyche; one's unique interpretation of "feeling at home"; domestic likes and dislikes; one's conception of mother and ability to express nurturing instincts.	1. To use security consciousness to protect oneself and to satisfy one's dependency needs.	1. The ability to be sensitive to the flow of one's emotions, enabling one to express them to their fullest potential.	1. A predisposition to be too focused on seeking security due to a fear of change.	Key Phrase: Securing The Self Games:
Sign: Cancer ♋ Symbol	The manner through which emotional security, nurturing tendencies, family instincts and dependency needs can be initiated and feelings of intimacy and intuition can be expressed.	2. To implement subconscious attitudes based on roots or childhood.	2. A sense of inner peace due to feeling secure with oneself.	2. A tendency to hide from others due to a fear of vulnerability.	1. Digging Up the Seed. 2. Fear of Space. 3. Hermit. 4. Hide and Seek.
House 4th	The foundation of the emotional nature based on one's home and family; one's attitudes related to the sense of an inner self, emotional vulnerability and private or subconscious aspirations.	3. To establish an emotional and physical home.	3. A capacity to nurture in a "mothering" way.	3. The potential to not feel at home with oneself.	5.I Don't Want to Grow Up.
		4. To nurture and care for self and others.	4. Emotional strength that endures despite the fluctuations of changing situations.	4. An inclination to be too controlled by habits and past fears.	6. Living in Intensive Care. 7. Love Only Me or Leave Me.
		5. To feel emotions and have a receptive love nature.	5. An instinctive capacity to experience intimacy with others.	5. An excessive sensitivity about one's own feelings and feelings of others.	8. Moody Blues. 9. Moonshadow.
		6. To develop emotional sensitivity.	6. An ability to create a family setting.	6. A tendency to be excessively moody and emotionally depleted.	10. Mothering or Smothering.
			7. The talent to perceive situations in an intuitive manner.	7. The potential of being too dependent on others.	11. Tied to Parental Strings. 12. Too Close for Comfort.
				8. A tendency to be too attached to one's roots.	13. Walking on the Moon.

Figure 10: Fourth Chord
See the Note to Readers after Acknowledgments

Moon

The celestial movement of the 4th Chord planetary tone, the Moon, is characterized by its different faces or phases that are formed by its changing position in the sky in relation to its orbit of the Earth. Before people wore elaborate timepieces on a wrist, the Moon provided a convenient cosmic clock as each subsequent New Moon marks just under one calendar month, approximately 29½ days, known as the synodic month. The Moon's relatively swift phase changes match its astrological symbolism related to sudden mood changes. The Moon races from New Moon, or its conjunction with the Sun, to form a 90° angle or square, reaching its First Quarter phase. Then it moves on to the notorious reputation of the Full Moon, 180° from the Sun (the Earth at this phase is between Moon and Sun). With the Last Quarter phase the Moon is closing in on its final 90° angle, followed by its reunion with the Sun once again at New Moon. These phases of the Moon, or angles formed to the Sun, are dramatically symbolic of the intensity and strength of the major astrological aspects: the conjunction, square and opposition.

Whereas the Sun in actuality is a star, the Moon is a satellite of the Earth. Though the Moon in the sky actually contains no water, the sea-like images or craters upon its surface, especially visible at Full Moon, correspond to astrological symbolism rich in emotional and intuitive water. Sometimes the image is of calm water, but with little warning it can shift into rough, volatile and emotionally unsettling water, choking off our innermost selves with too many salty tears and drained emotional natures. However, just as quickly this symbolic water can become purified. Instead of a tidal wave, the individual enjoys the wonder of a clear intuitive body of water, full of fresh clean emotional energy.

The Sun in the horoscope is the greatest single indicator of the development of one's basic and essential core identity.

The Moon is also of great importance in the horoscope. The Moon signifies the "past" or early conditioning of the individual and the earliest formation of habit patterns that take hold in childhood. It has been said by some astrologers that the Moon is an indicator of beliefs and instincts borrowed from previous incarnations.

The Moon also represents characteristics of one's mother or the parent that provided the nurturing during childhood. The Moon represents an individual's way of relating to the mother figure or one's perspective of her mother.

The placement of the Moon is of utmost importance in the development of the early ego. The identification of children with the Moon symbolism in the horoscope is often very pronounced. It may be well into the early teens before some children feel safe enough to wear the crown of their Sun and to display its essential character and dignity. The transition "from" the habitual and unconscious usage of the lunar expression fed to a youth during growing up years "to" a true solar expression is a big bridge to cross! The Moon is representative of the helplessness, vulnerability and nourishment needs of the young child and her emergence from the safety and protection of the early homelife womb into the world of adolescent peers and eventually into the risky reality phases of adulthood.

It is not that once adulthood begins, one's lunar qualities should be completely dropped. Quite the contrary, the Moon symbolism is essential: it is the emotional support system and intuitive sense which balance an individual's power of the will and ego urges (symbolized by the Sun). Habits, dependency needs and emotional responses left over from infancy and the earliest of childhood stages are tucked away in the subconscious memories (indicated by the Moon) and can surface quite instinctively when activated by conscious reality.

Oriental philosophy sometimes refers to the Sun as "yang" or masculine energy, and the Moon as "yin" or feminine energy. This is not a sexual connotation but rather an energy description. Yang is a more outward and forceful expression of energy and yin is symbolic of an inward, receptive or intuitive energy expression. Sometimes I think of the Sun's symbolism in astrology as the father or willful spirit of the soul. Yin and yang are equally important and must have their place in the balanced expression of a male or female individual.

Women have had to fight for the rights to an outward solar type of expression in a male-dominated society. Freedom to vote, salary equality, the freedom to choose a career and to challenge the stereotyped role of housewife, are a few themes embodied by this new solar expression among women. On the other hand, males have had to develop the lunar side of their natures in a balanced fashion rather than demand that a female partner do the emoting for both of them. It is as though since time immemorial women have been expected to be the nurturers and provide the emotional content for a relationship or family. Men have been expected to do the providing and, in many instances, express the life ambitions outwardly for both sexes. The women's role was confined to maintaining the home and raising children. She was expected to live her career ambitions and creative self through a male.

Men have begun slowly to ask each other why they too cannot express their emotions or more intimate feelings without embarrassment. Men are questioning the shackles of a cultural myth that forbids them to show their emotional nature. Likewise women, in the form of collective liberation movements or individual fortitude, have already taken significant steps to determine their own self-expression. The redefining of sex roles is still in the midst of tremendous flux and the entire process will likely bring many more changes in male-female self-expression.

The Moon symbolism also indicates one's domestic personality. "Home" means different things to different people. Each of us has a unique feel for a certain type of domestic atmosphere. Some like a highly structured abode while others prefer a more free-flowing atmosphere with few rules. For instance, an individual with the Moon in the 10th Chord sign

(Capricorn) might like to rule the roost or at least be assured there is some degree of structure or a daily routine concerning household responsibility. An individual with the Moon in the 1st Chord sign (Aries) might perceive home as a place that offers a short pit stop to refuel with a quick meal and a nap and then go back to the races. An orderly home is not a priority. Someone with the Moon in the 9th Chord sign (Sagittarius) might enjoy living in foreign countries, far away from early roots or even on the road. She might fill the home with books or people that stimulate and excite her expansion urges. A Moon in the 8th Chord sign (Scorpio) might indicate a person who wants to live in absolute privacy. In general, the home is more of a security orientation for Moon in the earth or water signs, especially so if by house and sign (i.e., Moon in Virgo and in 6th house).

It is sometimes startling to me to observe how significant the Moon can be when comparing the horoscopes of two individuals to determine their compatibility. Aspects between the two Moon placements really indicate each person's sensitization to the other's emotional expression. Discordant aspects formed by the Moons, such as the square, opposition and quincunx, can represent a lot of domestic quarreling or difficulty in reaching compromises together. Each individual can easily overreact to the other's moods and each individual's psychological space feels easily invaded. Each may react to the other with an intensity that is unconscious. Harmonious aspects, or even placement of the Moons in harmonious elements, can indicate people who have little difficulty in caring for each other and feel a natural comfortableness with each other. Each person's everyday habits are not as likely to upset the other. Bill's hurrying to brush his teeth and getting toothpaste on the mirror doesn't constantly ruin or upset Sally's day (or life). It should be pointed out that discordant aspects formed by the Moons of two people do not "always" indicate difficulty. Each person may appreciate the other's emotional expression and domestic habits. The problems begin when one of the people insists that his way of domesticity is "the only way."

The Moon represents the instinctual antennae of the psyche; it is symbolic of our primary mode of feeling or directing emotional responses. The most significant feeling for an infant is the security and intimacy of mother's love whether it be in her holding or feeding. The baby feels "wanted" and protected. She is dependent on a reliable and loving force that secures and insulates her in the world.

The astrological Moon symbolizes an individual's most basic of dependency needs. This is not always as easy to be in touch with as the baby's desire to express helplessness to mother. Dependency needs become riskier to fulfill when dealing with peers and lovers. It gets more dangerous in adulthood to say "I want you" or to ask, "Do you need and want me?" Rejection is very painful as the dependency of a child is more spontaneous and less self-conscious. The fear of intimate emotional expression being rejected can be frightful.

The interplay of the Moon by sign, house and aspects to other planets indicates how comfortable an individual might feel in displaying dependency, nurturing or security needs and the innate drive to create a "safe atmosphere." The aspects to the Moon from the outer planets (Saturn, Uranus, Neptune and Pluto) are of paramount importance as they indicate special dimensions of one's inner attunement or lack of it in understanding the depths and flow of one's own emotional expression and capacity to establish intimate closeness with others.

The Moon symbolism is vast and is related to our deepest and most subconscious of emotional expressions and dependency needs. However, it should not be forgotten that the Moon also symbolizes how intimate an individual can be with herself as the Moon is indicative of our inner home and how comfortable we are with ourselves.

Positive expressions of the lunar themes include sensitivity, an ability to communicate one's emotional nature, a capacity to experience intimacy, and balanced dependency with others. Another positive expression is a sense of inner tranquility and feeling secure with oneself. An ability to nurture others and to create a family setting are also positive qualities, as is an intuitive gift of a sensitized lunar expression.

Negative expressions of lunar themes include being too controlled by the ebb and flow of one's moods (as in the **Moody Blues** game). Being ruled by an insecurity consciousness and fearing change are also negative lunar expressions. Dependency on others may be formed based on irrational fears due to past experiences or subconscious attitudes. Other big roadblocks that can inhibit a positive lunar expression are fear of vulnerability and fear of intimacy (sometimes due to negative experiences from childhood).

Cancer

The 4th Chord sign tone, Cancer, is almost an exact replica of the intense security consciousness symbolized by the Moon. Cancer is known as the crab and people with a Cancer focus often build a strong shell-like protective covering for their emotional homes to hide their vulnerability and sensitivity. The "crab" walks slowly and cautiously, sometimes crawling along a path that conceals the identity as she desires a low profile in the world. The crab can be smiling one moment and depressed the next by a remembered past annoyance or an intense violation of her space. An outspoken personality can upset her very sensitized emotional nature. The crab's inner restlessness to find security leads her to dig into the world with a powerful thrust.

Cancer themes may indicate someone unsure in which direction she is going, who sometimes does resemble the unpredictable sideways or diagonal movements of a crab in its restless search for a state of security. This security can take many forms—establishing intimate and mutually dependable relationships with others, remaining in one's hometown to maintain close family ties, enjoying the nurturing and warm atmosphere of raising a family, loyalty to or a strong identification with a culture, country, person, etc.

Cancer can denote intuition, supported by an underground spring of vast emotional energy. Cancer is a well-contained sign that often needs the very thing it fears the most—to make secret fears conscious and to make its hidden, personal dreams public. There can be a long shadow cast by the Cancerian fear of being intimate within a personal relationship or fear of intimidation by the public. It is ironic that the sign that denotes the ultimate nurturer and breast-feeder of emotional warmth for others often denotes someone who denies herself the same "tender loving care." It may be easier to give than to receive because in receiving, true vulnerability conies out from underneath its shell.

The radiant atmosphere of warmth which Cancer symbolizes reflects the moment of the summer solstice when the Sun enters the sign of Cancer each year, approximately on June 21. This is the longest day of the year when the Sun appears to stand still in its apparent northward journey along the ecliptic. (The winter solstice, approximately December 21, when the Sun enters Capricorn, is the longest night of the year. These two solstice moments are when the Sun is farthest from the Equator.)

Sometimes people with an emphasis on Cancer will cling desperately to others, like a drowning swimmer who cannot relax enough to allow a rescuer to save her. They may make too much effort to establish security or to satisfy dependency needs, rather than trusting the inner strength that they possess (but somehow cannot seem to tap into). When Cancerian intuitive forces are clicking with clarity, the individual is able to see through the insecure darkness of present uncertainties and fears. Her internal eye is as vivid in vision as the eyes of nature on a clear, moonlit evening. One of the greatest assets represented by Cancer is listening to the pulse rate of one's own ever-present moods, knowing when to make a major change or adjust an emotional response. Cancerian individuals must develop the ability to decipher emotional turmoils. Strong moods are sometimes due to present or past conditions which must be balanced.

Positive expressions of Cancer include a natural capacity to form intimate relationships. There is a true give-and-take of dependency needs in important relationships. Also, the ability to provide a nurturing atmosphere for a family or to provide emotional support for others in distress are positive qualities. There may be a well-developed intuitive faculty that aids the securing of internal stability. An ability to tune into one's moods before overreacting to situations can be the result.

Negative expressions of Cancer include becoming disoriented by subconscious fears or extreme mood shifts (as in the **Walking on the Moon** game). Similar to the negative lunar expressions, Cancer can also indicate fear of change due to a total domination of irrational or subconscious fears. Perhaps the biggest problem can be confusion and fear in establishing intimacy in relationships. The crab in this instance chooses to hide in her shell (as in the **Hide and Seek** game). Compulsive dependency needs can also result from dysfunctioning of the energy Cancer represents.

4th House

The 4th Chord house tone symbolizes the foundation of an individual's security attitudes related to the early upbringing, hometown roots and particularly relations with parents, whether adoptive or actual. The 4th house, along with the Moon and Cancer placements, symbolize one's attitudes or particular mode of satisfying dependency needs, especially if a planet is located in the house. Fourth house planets indicate choices an individual might make to secure a "safe" or "at home" atmosphere, whether it is the comfort of pets, plants, suburbia, people, or a house in the country.

The 4th house can be the point of an individual's greatest fear as this potent "intuitive force field" is also a potential hazard of compulsive self-destruction. The 4th, 8th and 12th Chords have tremendous pulls toward unfounded idealism and feelings of helplessness based on confused dependency needs. When these idealized images are thwarted, the individual may react strangely with compulsive behavior. Risk-taking does not generally come as naturally for strong 4th Chord individuals, and a person must be careful not to stew in a boiling pot of moods and pent-up frustrations in regard to unexpressed 4th house energies. However, when a person tunes into this tremendous unconscious energy, she can exhibit compassion and nurturance. But she must first find her **internal** security.

The 4th house is sometimes referred to by astrologers as the nadir as it is the lowest point in the horoscope, exactly opposite the 10th house or Midheaven which is at the very top of the horoscope. When the time is 6:00 AM, the Sun is moving approximately across the 1st house, rising over the Ascendant, and since this is a clockwise movement, the Sun ascends toward the 10th house and arrives there at approximately "high noon." The Sun then begins its descent and arrives at the Descendant or 7th house at approximately sunset and finally reaches the 4th house at approximately the "midnight hour." This midnight 4th house is the symbolic spark of the subconscious ideas and imagination that an individual possesses impregnated with vital dependency needs and issues, emotional and intimacy drives and perhaps colored by a strong ancestral heritage. The 4th house is the birthplace of unconscious habits and one's intimate experience of mother and father during early childhood. This house can even indicate in some instances an individual's compassion and patriotism for a homeland or culture.

Positive 4th house expressions include a balanced perspective concerning dependency and nurturance needs. The individual is able to integrate harmonious experiences of growing-up years into maturing adulthood interactions. She is also able to manifest some inner dreams and have a realistic assessment of ideals, able to separate fantasy from reality. A person very much in touch with 4th house themes can display a strong intuitive nature and also have a natural or unforced emotional expression. Other positive expressions include a capacity to be intimate in relating to others, with her very presence putting others at ease.

Negative 4th house expressions include a person who has difficulty in caring for herself. Her dependency needs have never really been sorted out from parental influences (as seen in the **Tied to Parental Strings** game). Even in adulthood she has never really learned to think for herself. Another negative expression is a fear of intimacy. The person may experience emotional blocks, from lack of parental love or other causes. She may even retreat into her own inner world as in the **Hermit** game. A constant living in emotional turmoil can also be a negative 4th house expression.

Counseling Issues

The counseling issues of the 4th Chord are indicative of confusion concerning the basic nature of this chord, **security instincts.** My key word phrase for these counseling issues, **securing the self,** is from the synthesis of the tones: Moon, Cancer and the 4th house. Each has a significant link to feeling secure within oneself and within the presence of others. The archetypal themes are:

1. **Moon**—the directing of emotional responses, moods, subconscious attitudes and dependency needs to secure the self; the instinctual antennae of the psyche; one's unique interpretation of "feeling at home"; domestic likes and dislikes; one's conception of mother and ability to express nurturing instincts.
2. **Cancer**—the manner through which emotional security, nurturing tendencies, family instincts and dependency needs can be initiated and feelings of intimacy and intuition can be expressed.
3. **4th house**—the foundation of the emotional nature based on one's roots; one's attitudes toward and identification with home and family; one's attitudes related to the sense of an inner self, emotional vulnerability and private or subconscious aspirations.

The counseling issues of this chord are related to an inability to comprehend or express security needs in a balanced manner. The 4th Chord tones represent tuning into one's own emotional and dependency needs, and integrating these needs with those of others. The counseling issues of this chord are twofold: (1) an emotional disorientation and a fear of intimacy, often due to not trusting oneself or others; (2) an insecurity produced by not understanding or taking responsibility for one's own dependency needs.

Games

When an individual has difficulty in expressing 4th Chord themes, especially represented by the Moon or Cancer, she may exhibit the **Moody Blues** game. This is a person victimized by mood swings; she literally drains valuable emotional energy that could be better utilized if rechanneled more productively. Sometimes she may surprise others with sudden emotional outbursts. This individual often suffers from an oversensitized emotional nature that can be quite typical of a person with emphasized 4th Chord tones. She has difficulty expressing emotional intensity.

This person needs to gain some distance from her emotional intensity. Tapping into the air element can allow a more objective perspective of situations. The quincunx to Chord 11 shows the need to integrate a detached attitude with the emotional intensity of watery Chord 4.

Another 4th Chord game, **Walking on the Moon,** is related to emotional confusion and is of a more disorienting nature. This individual has a strong intuitive nature but is so out of touch with it, due to being flooded by subconscious impulses and fears, that she becomes "spaced out." You may be discussing a situation with her and suddenly she is floating into the ozone. This can be the 4th Chord way of escaping the present but can also be a symptom that an individual is desperately afraid of a person, situation, crisis and most of all, herself. The main problem associated with this game is that an individual often creates a lot of her own problems but fails to be conscious of the fact. There may also be a bit of paranoia exhibited along with strange, unpredictable mood swings that lead to emotional disorientation.

A person playing this game can find that the discipline and structure of the earth element helps ground the emotions. Also, a more genuine communication of the emotions can keep the intensity level balanced. It is especially important to become aware of the thoughts or circumstances that trigger one's mood swings. Then one can change the pattern of emotional reactions. Air's awareness, objectivity and desire for communication can be helpful.

An intense 4th Chord game is what I call **Moonshadow**. This individual is often at the mercy of subconscious fears and constantly reinforces their power by feeding them a steady diet of jealousy, possessiveness and blaming others for her own limitations. Unconscious forces are readily present and available through the 4th, 8th and 12th Chord tones. It requires a lot of "soul-searching" to bring these water forces into balanced expression. It is important that each individual with strongly accentuated water focus make an ally of these energies rather than treat them as foreign to the self or as unwanted enemies! The **Moonshadow** individual may need to develop the persistence and compassion to enter the home of her own emotional nature, much like a crab that is secure within its own shell. She is often a lonely soul lacking the comfort of her own emotional nurturance or warmth. The **Moonshadow** individual is very much a stranger to herself and generally fails to establish intimate relations with others. Often she is running from the shadow of past fears. Fears haunt her as thoroughly as the shadow that chased the hero of Ursula LeGuin's book, *The Wizard of Earthsea*. The **Moonshadow** individual must learn to let go of the illusive power of past fears and subconscious insecurities to make a landing safe from the dark side of the Moon.

A lack of trust can bring a strong 4th Chord type of individual to retreat into emotional isolation in the **Hermit** game. This is not the same natural tendency symbolized by the 4th Chord that can take a little space to build or strengthen one's emotional body. The **Hermit** is an individual who fears emotional vulnerability so much that she seeks to escape or run away from others. She will not allow any "outsiders" to penetrate her emotional zones.

The **Hide and Seek** game is seen in someone who is intimate and affectionate in one instance and suddenly shifts into a cold and fearful person, running like a scared rabbit for the protection of the woods. It may be a painful remembrance of the past that forcefully enters a person's consciousness, making her want to retreat. **Hide and Seek** individuals do not trust the heightened intimacy taking place in a relationship and become dizzy by the fear of their own vulnerability. A person exhibiting this game can make it very difficult for others to relax into a relationship as you are never quite sure when she will run away and if she is going to return.

The **Hide and Seek** game is closely related to its cousin, **Too Close for Comfort.** This is an individual who has many unresolved emotional conflicts, either from frustrating growing-up years (such as being deprived of enough parental love and attention) or painful relationship experiences. The past has never been properly "cleaned up" through talking, acting or crying it out of the system. An individual caught in this game and the **Hermit** or **Hide and Seek** games as well is usually running away from the internal conflict of confronting the pain that has caused much heartache. Close and intimate relationships often provide the shelter of safety to allow this pain to surface but the individual does not deal with facing herself or her past, choosing to run away from those who may love her.

There seems to be the issue of surrender at stake for people with a heavy water chord emphasis in their horoscopes. It can manifest habitually in the form of allowing only a minimum of vulnerability to be expressed before running away from the very love and care that someone longs for from deep within. An individual exhibiting the **Too Close for Comfort, Hermit** or **Hide and Seek** games needs to learn to tune into moods and try to determine from whence they come. It is not a matter of controlling the powerful tides of these moods as much as recognizing the separation they cause as an individual keeps herself apart. Using one's intuitive wisdom can create warm, safe and wonderful ways to share one's intimate feelings.

A focus on the courage and self-confidence of Chord 1 (a natural square) can help an individual feel safer and to establish balanced relationships (square to Chord 7). She may also increase a sense of strength or competence through material achievements (focusing on Chord 10—the natural opposition).

An individual who is emotionally disoriented and lacks confidence may display the **Digging Up the Seed** game. This is an individual who once again just plain does not trust herself. This is similar to the **I Can't, I Can't!** 6th Chord game in that the individual often creates failure situations. In this 4th Chord game, the behavior can operate on a very subconscious level. It is typical of an individual who defeats herself by uprooting relationships, careers, home, etc. She blocks herself from the joy of successful intimacy or nurturing exchanges. She does not feel deserving of these warm experiences or simply does not trust the possibility that this could be successful. Rather than take the risk of failure, she will find something wrong with the situation or create a problem. I have seen this game especially prevalent in individuals who admitted to not really being conscious of this pattern until the past and present were examined.

This person often needs to forgive herself and/or a person from the past who caused pain and sorrow. Chord 1 (a natural square) may be important again, offering the courage to trust herself and the assertion to pursue what she wants.

An individual with a strong 4th Chord focus can manifest emotional fear as extreme dependency needs in the **Fear of Space** game. An individual exhibiting this game shies away from spending time alone as she does not want to risk a confrontation with her own fears or pains. It could be that some private time to reflect on life would be a good antidote for the emotional nature. She may not give herself time to truly get some "R & R" and recover from exhaustion and depletion. This individual fears the intimacy of her own space.

Freedom in acting and in thinking are stressed by Chord 1 (natural square to Chord 4), Chord 9 (natural quincunx to Chord 4) and Chord 11 (natural quincunx to Chord 4). A balance between dependency needs and desire for liberty is essential.

A game related to an individual's confusion surrounding dependency needs is **Tied to Parental Strings.** This is someone well into adulthood who is still hooked by strong and sometimes overwhelming dependency needs on others—not necessarily only an attachment to the parents. Relationships may take on a parent-child type of relating much the same way overprotective parents never let her do anything for herself. The individual is still seeking to depend on others to care for her as if she were a child. Her relationships are out of balance and unhealthy. They may be difficult to maintain as she alienates others who grow tired of carrying the load in the relationship. This game can be typical of an individual who allows a dominating parent to make too many of her life choices well into adulthood.

The fire and air energies can help to balance this game. Chords 1, 9 and 11 are especially tuned to independence and a free acting and thinking spirit.

The previous game is very much related to another 4th Chord game, **I Don't Want to Grow Up.** Dr. Peck defines dependency in his book, *The Road Less Traveled*: "I define dependency as the inability to experience wholeness or to function adequately without the certainty that one is being actively cared for by another." He describes a passive dependent person as someone who is so desperate to make others love him that he has little or no love to share. The **I Don't Want to Grow Up** individual has a childlike mentality concerning dependency needs.

Such a person needs to take responsibility for life (the 4th Chord opposes the earthy 10th Chord, filled with themes of maturity and responsibility). The individual in this game has a confused sense of personal power and identity (square to Chord 1). The individual must learn to assume responsibility when relating to others and stop hiding behind the image of a helpless child. Her assertive side (Chord 1) may need to be fed.

A conflicted Moon in someone's horoscope may point to the danger of becoming entrapped in infantile dependency needs. The Moon is symbolic of our early childhood instincts and feelings much like the psychological state of mind known as "The Child" defined by Eric Berne, the founding father of Transactional Analysis. An individual exhibiting this childlike **I Don't Want to Grow Up** game indeed appears to be stuck in the early conditioning and instinctual atmosphere of her lunar mode of expression to the exclusion of a true solar expression. There is still a lingering infantile consciousness that pervades and distorts the individual's ability to truly express her basic nature. The solar side of life may need some refueling.

The **Living in Intensive Care** game is true of an individual who tries to live through another individual. This is a different emphasis than in the 5th Chord **Creator of All** game. In the 5th Chord an individual's pride is too attached to accomplishments or creations. In this 4th Chord game an individual is really hiding a sense of power or self-expression. Her desire to be cared for is very stifling to self-growth. This game can be dangerous if the person being depended upon leaves the relationship. This can be typical of a housewife who has never written a check or held a job and depended on a husband to make all of the major decisions. This could be typical of a male who depends too heavily on a female partner to initiate all of the aesthetic activity in his life or to express all of his emotional energy. The initial shock of being on one's own can be quite startling. However, the end result may be very positive if the individual can begin to take new forms of responsibility for herself. The end result will be an instant replay if she quickly attaches to another parasitic situation.

Dr. Peck also states in *The Road Less Traveled* that passive dependent people lack self-discipline. A person sometimes must develop the commitment and structuring energy of the opposite 10th Chord to take practical steps to change a life of too much dependency into a more balanced expression. Dr. Peck also notes that passive dependent individuals do not do a very good job of being responsible for their actions and suffer the consequences of this enslaving behavior.

There can be asphyxiating feelings in 4th Chord games, especially in the **Mothering or Smothering** game. This is a male or female who "protects" the spontaneity out of a relationship. This overprotectiveness is due to an insecurity or fear of losing closeness with others whether they be a child, lover or friend. A lack of intimacy with the self is the reason for this compulsive drive for closeness. Her best intentions alienate others, putting them on the defensive as this smothering and clinging behavior eventually grows old and boring.

Possessiveness can also find its way into dysfunctioning 4th Chord tones as in the **Love Only Me or Leave Me!** game. This is an individual who fails to be intimate with herself and as a result becomes very suspicious of others. She will not let you out of sight for fear you may express intimacy to someone else. This insecurity can have roots with parents who ignored her and other factors. Unfortunately, the **Love Only Me or Leave Me** individual is a tremendous burden upon others. Her demands for love and attention are so unreasonable that nobody can live up to them.

Summary of Issues with 4th Chord Games

The 4th Chord games originate from one's inability to balance emotional needs. Some individuals have strong feeling natures but have a difficult time when it comes to dealing with intimate relationships.

There may be a lack of trust or a fear of vulnerability. Those who have an excess of 4th Chord emotional intensity sometimes can alienate the very people they want close to them. Instead of tuning into their own inner needs, their insecurity prompts them to psychologically smother others. These are the individuals who go overboard in mothering others.

Another 4th Chord deficiency related to confused security needs is being too dependent on others and fearing responsibility. Individuals can be stuck in limiting 4th Chord games due to blocked emotions, psychological exhaustion and inner turmoil. They must learn to better communicate their feelings. Also, learning to make peace with the past and trusting the present can go a long way in the process of transcending 4th Chord games.

The 4th Chord themes can be used to express our nurturing instincts. There is no other chord with quite the same capacity to mother and to make others feel loved. Individuals with strong 4th Chord themes can possess dynamic intuitive natures and form close, intimate bonds with peers, children, lovers and spouses.

Fourth Chord energies when operating smoothly can typify individuals with great psychological depth, emotionally and intuitively. This is a very deep chord. It has roots that extend far into our unconscious. However, because of this very fact, we must be careful how we make use of this aspect of our psyche. If we let our moods completely guide us and hide from the roots of emotional confusion, then we are apt to find a false sense of security in the 4th Chord games.

Subtones

The three subtones of the 4th Chord are: the planetary aspect known as the **square,** the **cardinal** energy focus of Cancer and the **angular** 4th house classification.

The subtone of the 4th Chord Moon is the square aspect. It was stated in the 10th Chord discussion of the square (Saturn's subtone) that this planetary aspect challenges an individual to build psychological strength and to take practical steps to express potentially forceful energy in a balanced manner.

The 4th Chord connotation of the square aspect has more subtle dynamics than in its 10th Chord symbolism. But it is no less significant of energy that can aid the process of personal transformation. The 4th Chord emphasis of the square dramatizes the potential vulnerability of an individual to express and comprehend one's emotional nature and deepest of security instincts.

The 4th Chord in its essence symbolizes the roots of one's emotional security. The square represents an energy that challenges an individual to find an inner security much like the Moon which symbolizes the most active internal barometer that an individual possesses to register how much she feels at home with her life. Sometimes a person's biggest problem in dealing with squares (especially formed by personal planets to outer planets) is a compulsive urge to dig up planted seeds before they reach fruition and to irrationally embark on a new and desperate course of action.

Whereas the 10th Chord symbolizes more of a conscious drive for success as one finds or establishes a societal niche, the 4th Chord security symbolism saturated within each tone represents an unconscious and instinctual longing for success. Practicality and reality are natural extensions of the 10th Chord while dreams and fantasies have a home in the 4th Chord. The square aspect penetrates 4th Chord dreaminess with the confrontation or challenge to make one's dreams real.

The 4th Chord square symbolizes an energy that could be emotionally unsettling and strain one's security consciousness. It is as though the 4th Chord represents a shadow that can manifest if an individual is trying to repress a confused past or has a grossly out-of-balance dependent nature. The square can indicate one's need to learn to deal directly with the pain of one's earliest roots and other life challenges that threaten emotional security. Successful integration means reaching a state of inner safety and realizing the accomplishment of one's dreams.

The **cardinal subtone** of Cancer symbolizes the initiation of actions to secure one's emotional instincts through gaining a stronger foothold in the world. It may come through moving into a new home, developing an intimate relationship or expanding one's intuitive grasp of inner and outer worlds. A cardinal subtone associates with Cancer the emotional outpouring of energy much like the blossoming of nature that begins with the season of spring and reaches a full bloom of emotional ecstasy with the coming of summer, symbolized by the sign of Cancer.

The **angular subtone** of the 4th house indicates strong survival instincts. The initiating activity of the 4th house angular classification is a bit subtler to the external awareness than in the angular 1st, 7th or 10th houses. However, the 4th house symbolism should never be underestimated as this is a potentially swift undercurrent of emotional strength with a rich unconscious past that can come like a "saving grace" during times of strife and confusion. The establishing of a home and family are natural extensions of the initiating energy of the angular 4th house.

The 4th Chord is similar to its opposite 10th Chord in that both concern taking responsibility for one's actions and needs. The 10th Chord, in being an earth chord, is primarily concerned with responsibility associated with practical accomplishments and learning how to better adjust one's ambitions and success drives within the dictates of time. The watery 4th Chord focuses upon the essence of our responsibility to intimately become acquainted with ourselves. Each person has dependency needs as no person is truly a self-sustained being with no need to receive love or nurturing from others. The 4th Chord reminds us not to forget to know the safety of our innermost selves and to discover our well-kept secrets. If the 10th Chord symbolizes the potential integrity or signature of our character, then the 4th Chord is certainly symbolic of the potential integrity or signature of our most intimate of natures!

CHAPTER TWELVE

EIGHTH CHORD: POWER INSTINCTS

> I can think, I can wait, I can fast.
> *Siddhartha* by Herman Hesse (page 56)

The 8th Chord is symbolic of the hidden unconscious power within the water element that can find form through concentrated, emotional, psychic energy. Chord eight is the need to deal with lasting peer relationships, with the primary focus on shared money, material possessions, appetites and really intense emotions. With chord eight, whether the astrological factor is Pluto, planets in Scorpio, or in the 8th house, part of the goal is thorough going closet-cleaning of the unconscious and bring what is hidden into the light.

The 8th Chord is representative of the emotional and physical bonds formed within important relationships. The sharing emphasis of this bond is expressed within a spectrum as varied as joint ownership of material items, the sharing of close emotional ties, and one's most intense and focused desire for mutual securing of a relationship. The 8th Chord archetypal themes of each tone symbolize the deepest and most emotionally demanding expressions of the bonding process thus far discussed.

8TH CHORD: POWER INSTINCTS

Tone	Archetypal Themes	Functions	Positive Expressions	Negative Expressions	Potential Counseling Issues
Planet: Pluto **Symbol** ♇	The directing of actions for the process of psychological transformation to aid personal growth; an in-depth self-analysis of personal power urges and sexual identity; the determination to transcend limited and worn-out life expressions through self-honesty; one's personal search for a sense of inner safety to release repressed psychological material and the urge to channel this dynamic energy sometimes with compulsive force; one's understanding of the art of forgiving and the capacity to grieve emotional loss and release pain; one's conception of ego or psychological death states; one's common sense in understanding his own compulsive "shadow force" and desire to control its potential "dark side" as relating to undisciplined and addictive habits as well as power urges that bring harm to self and others.	1. To maintain and replenish energy for the psyche. 2. To comprehend the nature of power. 3. To get in touch with subconscious processes and repressed material. 4. To motivate personal transformations as in a change of character.	1. An ability to channel energy constructively. 2. An acceptance and surrender to personal transformations of the self. 3. A talent for self-regeneration. 4. A capacity to share one's deepest secrets and psychic strength.	1. A propensity to behave compulsively and to become enslaved to the negative elements of repressed material. 2. A predilection to be overpowering or to possess others through manipulation. 3. A strong tendency to withhold self from others due to excessive need for privacy.	**Key Phrase:** Empowering The Self **Games:** 1. Chip on the Shoulder. 2. Cold War. 3. Erupting Volcano. 4. Hidden Hormone. 5. Hypnotized. 6. Introspector.
Sign: Scorpio **Symbol** ♏	The manner through which a sense of emotional privacy and psychological intensity can be focused and controlled; the sharing of one's most insecure and delicate psychological, physical and emotional energies; the never-ending and sometimes compulsive desire to maintain a bond of trust with others.	5. To intensify life experience. 6. To enable sexual energy to act as a bonding force.	5. A capacity for deep commitment and loyalty. 6. An ability to use sexual energy to create a feeling of union with another.	4. A potentially jealous and vindictive nature. 5. A tendency to repress emotions. 6. An inclination to become enslaved to sexual desires and addictive appetites.	7. Odysseus and the Sirens. 8. One-night Stands. 9. Sexy Sadie. 10. Sneak Attack. 11. Those Dammed Emotions.
House: 8th	One's most private and profound attitudes regarding the securing or bonding of a trusted and highly valued relationship; sharing on the deepest and most vulnerable of physical and psychological levels; psychological transformations related to the surrender of a false show of power; one's intuitive wisdom to understand energies residing in the unconscious; strength and intense personal growth through the freeing of **stagnated** power by recognizing or facing one's unconscious forces; the use and respect of sexual energy as related to one's sexual identity and as a release for emotional intensity and bonding of love.	7. To comprehend the cycle of life and death. 8. To understand survival instincts.	7. A capacity to forgive the faults of others and to forgive oneself. 8. A capacity to accept and understand the nature of death.	7. A proclivity to projecting one's personal power on to others and losing sense of self. 8. A tendency to "dump" one's emotional intensity on others.	12. Toxic Waste. 13. Under My Thumb. 14. Vindictive Venom. 15. Waterlogged.

Figure 11: Eighth Chord
See the Note to Readers after Acknowledgments

The 8th Chord shows a passionate search for safety within the expression and possession of power much like the give-and-take of the ocean sending out its waves to the coast only to reclaim that which it chooses by its pulling force. There is a strong undertow represented by the 8th Chord tones—the more psychological and emotional intensity released, the more that is desired to be received. Each tone and subtone symbolizes the desire of the individual to comprehend personal power and its proper use.

Pluto

Pluto denotes an intense emotional spirit that can be as unstable as this planet's eccentric astronomical characteristics. Pluto has an odd orbital nature causing the planet to spend anywhere from 12 to 31 years in a sign, slowly and utterly penetrating the essence of a sign's most positive and negative of potentials. It takes Pluto nearly 248 years to orbit the Sun as it is the farthest planet known to humanity at this time. However, it should be noted that due to Pluto's very strange orbit, since 1969, it has been orbiting closer to the Sun than Neptune. This will continue until the year 2009 when Pluto will once again sit in its throne as the farthest known planet.

Pluto was discovered in 1930 by Clyde Tombaugh, though the first major attempt to search for the planet was begun by Dr. Percival Lowell in 1905 who founded the observatory where Clyde Tombaugh was to meet with success. Mars was considered to be the 8th Chord planet and was assigned rulership of Scorpio. However, it has become amazingly clear to astrologers that Pluto is definitely the primary 8th Chord planet. This "little" planet (Pluto in actuality is the smallest planet, smaller than even the Moon) can symbolize an individual with the charisma and personal power of a Martin Luther King or a Mahatma Gandhi, acting as the collective voice or channel for the masses and leading them into an organized, powerful movement. Unfortunately, there have been leaders or individuals given birth by the collective mass appeal such as Adolf Hitler who abused this tremendous power. The seeds of Nazi Germany and fascism in Europe began to take solid formation during the 1930s, in conjunction with the discovery of Pluto.

In her book *Outrageous Acts and Everyday Rebellions*, Gloria Steinem makes an interesting point concerning the rise of the Nazi party in Germany (pages 305-326). She states that the true seeds of Hitler's rise to power were planted long before he became a powerful political figure.

Steinem indicates that there was a very solid women's movement in Germany in the early 1900s. She believes feminism is the essential component of democracy. Steinem points out that Germany's strong feminist movement met its first organized resistance in 1912. That was the year certain portions of the German population felt a need to control the women's movement. They formed the League for the Prevention of the Emancipation of Women, the first organized anti-feminist group in Germany.

It is well known among astrologers that Pluto was moving through the sign of Cancer when it was discovered in 1930. However, it is rarely mentioned that Pluto entered Cancer in 1912: the year that the roots of authoritarianism began to take shape in Germany!

The anti-feminist movement in Germany, according to Steinem, paved the way for Hitler's eventual rise to power. Hitler's subjugation of women into roles that served "the Fatherland" and his emphasis upon the male as the dominating element of the family formed the backbone of his authoritarian political philosophy.

Since Cancer's symbolism is greatly related to the family and mothering, while Pluto can indicate forceful control and manipulation, I find it most interesting that the first organized attempt in Germany to put an end to the women's movement was in the year Pluto entered Cancer, 1912. It was this period that made it possible for Hitler to outlaw abortions and to make a woman's children property of the state.

Pluto's transpersonal or collective significance makes its astrological meaning for entire generations of people very important. For instance, Pluto entered the sign of Libra in October 1971 and (with the exception of a few months in 1972) did not exit Libra until late August 1984. Another outer planet, Uranus, was also moving through Libra from September 1968 through early September 1975. The process of dynamic change within relationships (Libra) and sex roles was on a true Uranian upbeat.

The entrance of Pluto into Libra corresponded to an even more intense defining of sex roles and search for alternative methods of relating. The break with traditional forms of relating saw the formation of a rising gay rights movement, encounter groups, all kinds of consciousness-raising groups, gurus moving to the West, equal rights for women being pushed by women and sympathetic men supporters, war protesters, etc. The Libra pendulum of justice was symbolically challenged to be truthful by Uranus and stretched by impersonal and relentlessly probing Pluto. Toxins in a system, whether digestive or political in nature, were being flushed out. Justice and truth were to have their day and nobody to be spared. A shocked and disillusioned American people witnessed their president leaving office for tampering with democracy, and the word "Watergate" was heard around the world. Pluto's movement through Libra has left for many of us the legacy of redefining the use of personal power in our relating to others and a new vision of politics and self. Pluto's movement through a sign does in fact leave a legacy that must be integrated with its movement through the next sign of its travels.

Pluto has been indicating an 8th Chord type of nourishment since its entrance into its home sign of Scorpio in August of 1984. (Pluto briefly tiptoed into Scorpio getting its feet wet in November 1983 through approximately mid-May 1984.) For the most part Pluto remains in this sign until November 1995. This is Pluto's second movement through a fixed sign since its discovery. The danger of the power principle connected with Pluto has not been so threatening and awesome since Pluto's discovery in 1930. This is the beginning of a new Pluto cycle, having gone from cardinal Cancer to fixed Leo to mutable Virgo to cardinal Libra to fixed Scorpio. Hopefully humankind as a collective unit and as individuals will harness this Plutonian power with courage, clarity and common sense.

Pluto's astrological symbol has been written as ♇. I use the symbol which is also used by astronomers. The ♇ which looks like the letter "P" (designed to honor Percival Lowell who initiated the search for "Planet X") reminds me that Pluto's presence in the horoscope indicates an individual's responsibility to the self and others to wisely use personal power. One should not fear a sense of power but on the other hand not wield power over others whether through manipulation, pressuring or all-out force. Pluto symbolizes personal powers that can carry one into the political arena. Enjoying popular appeal, forcefully policing a political system, crushing any dissident activity, or freeing political prisoners are all possible. Pluto can also symbolize sexual abuse or the pitfalls and darkness of undisciplined and dangerous power urges such as a member of the criminal underworld. Pluto's mythological association is with the Greek god of the underworld, Hades, or the Roman Dis. Hades was the Greek name for Hell and can signify an individual's favorite way of paving his gateway to misery. Pluto can also denote complete psychological transformations that require much effort and lead to greater self-knowledge. The safety of a true and authentic personal power, by its very illuminating presence, does not need to coerce, manipulate, beg, borrow or steal.

Pluto's astrological significance can represent an individual's primal scream to rid the self of past limitations and move into a life freer from polluted and hateful thoughts. There is an intensity symbolized by Pluto that no other single astrological factor can match. It is my belief that Pluto is symbolic of an individual's deepest instinctual drives for survival and is the adrenalin of one's unconscious urges to know his own personal power.

The house that contains Pluto is a strong clue to the basic attitude or habitual pattern a person will choose to act out rather unconsciously in times of danger or threats to emotional security and personal power. This can be an instinctual, compulsive, forceful behavior and sometimes it must be if the individual is to move ahead in life! However, when an individual is not truly in touch with inner emotional intensity and does not have the faintest awareness concerning this personal power, he can feel as if living in a vacuum. A misuse of personal power can lead to the bizarre and destructive behavior sometimes associated with Pluto, such as rape, murder, absolute power, dogmatism, extreme emotional isolation, etc.

Pluto's discovery also closely coincided with the discovery of atomic energy. At times an individual can experience Pluto's themes like an atomic explosion in consciousness whether indicated by its placement in the horoscope at birth or by an important current movement in the sky (known as a transit). The internal shake-up symbolized by an outer planet contacting the birth horoscope often shows an individual in the middle of reorganizing life due to internal and/or external crises. The residue of these time periods is an incredible legacy that may require years to understand. There may be answers to old, puzzling and painful questions and new questions requiring years to answer, especially concerning personal power. Sometimes the birth-death-rebirth cycle that Pluto is associated with becomes a very direct and liberating experience. The residues Pluto points to are not always pretty to face and may produce more emotional lava than an overactive Hawaiian volcano.

The "P" also symbolizes psychology or better yet the exploration of the psyche. Pluto can symbolize the birth of a new personal psychology that is healthy and whole rather than splintered and at war with itself. Pluto can indicate one's surrender to the waves of a new cultural energy sweeping through one's consciousness, transforming false power urges into personal power that cleanses with use rather than polluting with false identities.

Transpersonal Uranus may indicate a person's desire to sidestep or "duck under" the control of a culture to retain individuality. The individual could manifest rippling actions to spark change or to disrupt the present stagnating direction of others. Pluto symbolizes people who feel the pulse rate of their culture and either shudder in horror at its imperfect use of power or learn to wade in its existential reality. There are those rare Plutonian (or 8th Chord) types who, for better or worse, are so moved by the cry of others for change, reform and survival as well as their own capacity to act as a collective channel for change, that they do come forth, no longer as individuals but as the vision that others see reflected in them. They offer hope through the tremendous power of their personal vision. 9, another Plutonian or 8th Chord expression, sometimes takes these leaders or inspirational figures away from us but leaves us the legacy of their visions!

The 2nd Chord emphasizes personal resources while the 8th Chord focuses upon collective resources whether it is the goods and resources of two or two hundred million. Pluto's symbolism describes the presence of bipolar power instincts, meaning on an individual and collective level. The controlling of one's emotional intensity and bonding instincts is the basis of personal power. Collective growth reflects the power of a society and culture. With Pluto's movement through the sign of Scorpio, so recently begun, the appeal to satisfy an increasing world hunger is already on the move and we could see one of the most intense and organized movements to help deprived nations grow their own food and establish their own power. This Pluto in Scorpio period could show major world powers desiring to exercise too much control over third world countries. Political manipulation could become even more of a problem than in the past as small or poor countries fight for survival.

Pluto can indicate ghosts coming out of the closet or a cleaning-up of previous misuses of power. Pluto's early movement through Scorpio has already seen the physical and sexual abuse against children getting much more widespread attention. Violence against children was hidden in a convenient closet of ignorance and now is being exposed, and people are beginning to deal with abuse and with child pornography, now a national concern. Abortion clinics are coming under attack by many conservatives, and another Scorpio associated item, the death penalty, seems to be coming under closer scrutiny by certain segments of the population. Diseases that are sexually transmittable such as herpes and AIDS are getting more attention and funding for research.

The nuclear arms race is as threatening as ever—the balance of power in the world growing more delicate. I call Pluto's movement through the sign of Scorpio the "Show of Force" era. Nations and individuals are likely to be tested as never before concerning the wise use of power. Since the essence of power is truly within the individual, it is always his responsibility, whether he likes this world or abhors it, to make a strong bond with his own personal power and learn to channel it constructively.

Many astrologers, including myself, believe Pluto to be the higher octave of Mars, the previous Scorpio ruler. Martian symbolism seems to encompass a **conscious** urge to assert oneself whether with anger, sexual energy or direct force, while Pluto is symbolic of emotional force with tremendous **unconscious** content that many people have difficulty contacting with clarity. It is not always easy for people to feel secure with their sexual identities whether it is the consideration of their sexual techniques or appetites, or the ability to relax into or enjoy orgasm. One's sexual frame of reference or comfort with a sexual identity, in my opinion, has its home in Pluto's symbolism on a much larger scale than in the symbolism of Mars.

Honesty with oneself regarding Pluto themes and a fondness for compulsive power urges takes a lot of soul-searching. Some individuals have many internal closets of well-kept secrets to clean whether through visits to a "consciousness healer" or self-disclosure to someone who is completely trusted. Mars symbolizes the first and basic mode of conscious assertion to fulfill one's needs. Pluto symbolizes hidden or secret motives that often surface only when induced by the apparent safety of a situation and sometimes only when provoked by confrontation from a psychological healer. Some people never feel safe, their personal power completely surrendered and enslaved to compulsive unconscious forces.

Positive expressions of Pluto themes include taking responsibility for one's own sense of personal power and not leaning too heavily on others in an overdependent manner. Another potential is one's willingness to risk releasing repressed emotional energy to further illuminate consciousness and to enjoy a sense of personal transformation and emotional freedom. Another positive expression is using a sense of power in a balanced manner, inspiring others to tap into their own inner strength. Also, a positive Pluto expression is focusing one's intensity in a constructive manner and enjoying the emotional closeness within a relationship bonded by mutual respect and trust. The individual can allow himself the freedom to free-associate, the courage to transcend worn-out roles and to explore a more spontaneous emotional expression.

Negative Pluto expressions include manipulating others or forcing them to do actions against their will as in limiting their freedom through physical or mental (and emotional) abuse. Another potential is an excessive or compulsive attachment to privacy which leads to a lack of trust in relating to others. A vindictive and jealous nature can also indicate blocked Pluto themes, as does dishonesty within the self. A person's confused or insecure sexual identity can lead to problems in intimate relationships with others. An inability to release the past, through forgiveness or grieving through a painful emotional loss, can also be a pitfall. Perhaps the deadliest of all negative Pluto expressions is a surrender to unconscious or "shadow forces" that lead to a life of senseless or meaningless actions and uncontrollable appetites.

Scorpio

The 8th Chord sign tone, Scorpio, according to many astrology books, is "dripping" with intense emotional juices and compulsive sexual appetites. It is my belief that if one tries to understand the 8th Chord tones within the conceptual framework of personal power, each tone's essential theme is easier to comprehend. The deepest messages of the 8th Chord tones are released from embarking upon a clear path that leads to the emergence of personal power.

Scorpio is a sign denoting tremendous emotional intensity and the nature of these concentrative powers can be awesome. Scorpio reminds me of the magic and intense concentration within the process of hypnosis or related altered psychological states that bring unconscious and hidden material to the surface within the reach of conscious mind access. Scorpio and the other 8th Chord tones symbolize the "feeling" of security that can allow a client and therapist (or any two individuals) to form a powerful bond of trust that generates a healing and regenerative process of magnificent proportions. Scorpio is the raw material of concentrative psychic energy as much as Cancer is the raw material of nurturing and mothering. The alchemy within a Scorpio relationship at its highest functioning level can produce a bond that is difficult to break. However, due to the intensity level of a Scorpio bond, the ultimate respect for one's own psychological safety and that of others must be honored. Scorpio is the "stuff" that can symbolize regeneration of one's splintered and torn psyche and desire or even prayer for the healing of a war-torn emotional scar.

It was stated in the 4th Chord counseling section that surrender can be a major issue for strong water chord individuals. The ability to allow oneself to become vulnerable can be a severe test indeed for individuals with accentuated 8th Chord placements! I have noticed that individuals with a multiple 8th Chord emphasis such as Sun, Moon or Ascendant in Scorpio and/or planets situated in the 8th house and/or a powerfully placed Pluto often would sometimes rather die in their own misery than admit they might need a little help. The repressive mechanisms in the 8th Chord tones are without rival. When the Scorpion stops running from himself and makes a stand with the stinger of its emotional strength rather than hiding behind a false defensiveness, he can break through just about any obstacle!

Scorpio symbolizes victory in the form of mastering an intense and powerful energy at one's fingertips. Directing this energy is the greatest test shown by Scorpio. There is not a lot of middle ground for Scorpio themes as with other signs. The repressed forces of the unconscious are not to be taken lightly. When people with a Scorpio focus give in to the shadow states or compulsive instincts, they can chase the phantoms of their greatest fears rather than face their limitations. They can be hijacked by these forces into self-defeating behavior. Sexual passion can become a force that controls them, and various neurotic behaviors can destroy their personal power. Reality is sacrificed to fantasy and a sense of bonding or sharing becomes a greedy and manipulative behavior. An extreme example of an 8th Chord person who became a monster of "shadow forces" was Charles Manson (Sun in Scorpio) who directed cult members with a hypnotic power (surrendering their power to him) to murder actress Sharon Tate and her friends at her California home.

Fourth Chord Cancer represents territoriality concerning physical and intimate homes while 8th Chord Scorpio represents territoriality concerning the protection of one's psychological safety. With Scorpio themes, we keep a penetrating eye upon others to make sure they will fully participate in joint resource situations. We detest having our power or resources taken advantage of by others. We take great pride in our power though outside observers may see only emotional anger, distrust of situations and relentless self-control. Scorpio signifies the desire to manage our resources and those of someone else. Managing crisis situations can be as commonplace to Scorpio as proper diet is to Virgo. Scorpio denotes living on an emotional edge, never quite resting securely between a solid rock and a hard place, knowing or seeking the value of emotional security and trust.

Scorpio indicates the detective of the psyche always researching and policing its emotional depths. People facing Scorpio issues are not always as sure of themselves as they would have you believe. Power requires a lot of responsibility. This is an extraordinary kind of power that Scorpio represents. It hangs from the vines of its emotions. It is as though someone with a Scorpio focus is so aware of his own emotional sensitivity that it is difficult to believe others cannot see right through him. He feels the need for a shield or protective layer to guard his sacred privacy. He wants to commune with the self safely, knowing that outside forces cannot penetrate his internal fortress. Therefore, this power rests upon an unusual dilemma because quite often the individual must release rather than repress an intense emotional energy to make contact with this sense of true power. Too much repression pollutes Scorpio types with toxic power that poisons the system leading to possessiveness, jealousy, revenge, hatred and brutal force.

You cannot force a Scorpionic individual to open up. He will fight with Scorpio intensity to the death rather than be forced. It is usually when the Scorpio type feels power slipping away that he becomes desperately scared and mistrustful. Vulnerability must be on his own terms—it is part of his uniqueness. Each transpersonal sign (Scorpio, Aquarius and Pisces), like its ruling planet (Pluto, Uranus and Neptune), has a uniqueness that must be incorporated into the whole. Somehow, a strong 8th Chord type of person has to find the tiny opening or eye of the needle within himself that allows him to walk through life with emotional clarity.

Scorpio types can do without a desire for the least amount of time when compulsive urges and appetites grab hold. Distorted uses of power usually sneak up through the back door of fears and insecurities. The individual may then try to control and possess others with sexual prowess, jealousy and manipulation. When Scorpio types are very much in touch with their personal power instincts, the symbol reminds me of the humps of a camel that can store large amounts of water. Scorpionic individuals can store emotional water in the humps of compassion and emotional bonding, surrendering to a life path that expresses a true sense of personal power.

Positive expressions of Scorpio themes include the capacity to enjoy psychologically and physically bonded relationships based on loyalty, trust and commitment. The directing of one's intensity to accomplish life aims can be a natural ability. Other positive expressions include a desire to regenerate a damaged portion of one's consciousness and allowing oneself the freedom to undergo a psychological transformation to grow in a new direction. Another positive Scorpio expression is to join forces with others for important decisions without forcing others to follow the dictates of one's commands. Scorpio themes can also be well utilized in the field of psychology and can indicate a person managing emotional and physical resources in a balanced manner.

Negative expressions of Scorpio themes include a seize-by-force behavior where an individual attempts to overpower others. An individual's blocked or confused sense of personal power can result in violent activities such as rape, or explosive and uncontrollable anger that leads to abusing the property or physical well being of others. There can be severe lack of trust accompanied by a hateful, vindictive, and unforgiving streak. An overly private or subdued emotional nature is another negative expression. So is an individual controlled by compulsive sexual drives or too much indulgence in addictive habits.

8th House

The 8th Chord house tone symbolizes an individual's attitudes and choices in the emotional bonding together of a relationship. The 8th house indicates one's most intimate relationship with, and trust in, one's personal power instincts. Whereas the 2nd house largely concerns personal values and items of personal ownership, the 8th house is representative of emerging power instincts. The 8th house symbolizes the challenge to a sense of personal power within the process of allying with a partner's values and resources to form balanced relationships.

There is a deep current of underlying unconscious energy symbolized by this dynamic water house. An individual must gain consciousness of this subtle force lest he be swept off his feet by compulsive instincts and rages of appetites that are self-destructive. There is a constant regenerative energy cycling within the whirlpool of emotional and occult-like 8th house forces. One can either choose to purify emotionally through responsible actions or to engage in toxic-producing behavior.

Individuals with key planets in the 8th house are often in search of a more pure expression of their personal power. It was stated in the 7th Chord that one must be careful not to unconsciously project personal talents and potentials upon others, living through someone else. The urge to bond in the 8th house is so powerful that I have noticed individuals with 8th house planets forget that they are an equal in a relationship. I have also seen where 8th house planets can symbolize an individual's fear of close emotional rapport within love relationships as the commitment to one person is frightening and feels like an ego death.

Individuals with planets in the 8th house are not always sexually active or passionate. As a matter of fact, numerous 8th Chord types of individuals become monastically oriented. The metaphysical-occult-spiritual forces indicated by the 8th house can sometimes be more the object of the bonding process than a relationship. The individual's passion is directed at experiencing higher states of consciousness though I am not saying that all of these folks are celibate monks or nuns!

Many astrology books point to the 8th house as a heavy indicator of sexual promiscuity. Strong 8th Chord people are too focused and involved with a relationship to indulge in promiscuity. They give their all to form a close union. Individuals with experimental planets in the 8th house such as Uranus, Mercury and Jupiter may desire more diversity in relationships. However, 8th Chord themes are more indicative of a person's faithful intensity to form a very close emotional and physical bond with someone.

The 8th house is colored by a very private atmosphere. An individual with a strongly accentuated 8th house can be someone quite in touch with personal power or so overindulgent in privacy and secrecy that he becomes emotionally retarded. Unconscious fears keep him separated from personal power. Sometimes it takes powerful self-transformation to break through these walls.

Sexuality can be a vital issue for an individual with a strongly focused 8th house. The use of sexual energy can be an important question or problem with sexual compatibility in a relationship. Trust is often a problem within relationships and may be the main issue leading to sexual incompatibility providing there are not bodily problems. Trust is probably the essential ingredient in the 8th house. Most individuals are quite sensitive about their sexual identity, and it is trust that usually makes a deep emotional sexual bond possible. Also, trust fosters a loving experience filled with a mutual respect for each other's personal power and allows a mutual sharing of each other's physical and emotional resources to flow more harmoniously.

Positive 8th house expressions include a capacity to form close, emotionally bonded relationships without sacrificing one's individuality. Mutual sharing does not detract from either person's personal power. One's ability to manage and share resources can be indicated. One's willingness to undergo psychological transformations or consciousness-raising experiences are also positive expressions. So is one's capacity to direct this powerful and penetrating 8th house energy into creative activity. The ability to enjoy mutually satisfying sexual expressions is another positive 8th house expression.

Negative 8th house expressions include trying to control or manipulate the personal power of someone else, whether it is his emotional expression, sexual energy or material possessions. A dysfunctional expression of 8th house themes is typified by the power-hungry individual who is completely out of touch with a balanced expression of power urges. He compensates by controlling others. A person's lack of confidence in his own sexuality can be problematic, as can someone who exudes a strong sexuality to hide insecurities. A repressed or secretive emotional nature can also be a negative 8th house potential, as is an individual's complete surrender of his own personal power to others.

Counseling Issues

The counseling issues of the 8th Chord are indicative of an individual's loss of perspective concerning the basic nature of this chord, **power instincts.** My key word phrase for these counseling issues, **empowering the self,** is from the synthesis of the tones Pluto, Scorpio and the 8th house. Each has a significant role in being conscious of personal power and channeling it properly. The archetypal themes are:

1. **Pluto**—the process of psychological transformation to aid personal growth; an in-depth self-analysis of one's personal power urges and sexual identity; the determination to transcend limited and worn-out life expressions through self-honesty; one's personal search for a sense of inner safety to release repressed psychological material and the urge to channel this dynamic energy with sometimes compulsive force; one's understanding of the art of for giving and capacity to grieve emotional loss and release pain; one's conception of ego or physical death states; one's understanding of his own compulsive "shadow force" and desire to control its potential "dark side" in undisciplined and addictive habits as well as power urges that bring harm to self and others.
2. **Scorpio**—the manner through which a sense of emotional privacy and psychic intensity can be focused and controlled; the sharing of one's most insecure and delicate of psychological, physical and emotional energies; the never-ending and sometimes compulsive desire to maintain a bond of trust with others.
3. **8th house**—one's most private and profound attitudes regard ing the securing or bonding of a trusted and highly valued relationship; sharing on the deepest and most vulnerable of physical and psychological levels; possible psychological transformations related to the surrender of a false show of power; one's intuitive wisdom to understand energies residing in the unconscious; strength and intense personal growth through the freeing of stagnated power by recognizing or facing one's unconscious forces; the use and respect of sexual energy as related to one's sexual identity and as a release for emotional intensity and bonding of love.

The counseling issues of this chord are related to improper use of personal power often due to a lack of trust in oneself and others (trust and control are important ingredients in both the 8th and 10th Chord games). The 8th Chord tones can indicate a balanced sense of personal power in establishing emotional depth in love relationships or other types of partnerships secured by a bond of mutual trust. The counseling issues of this chord have two predominant themes: (1) the compulsive use of power to control and manipulate others with little true concern for developing trust or an emotional bond; (2) a deep resistance to acknowledging one's personal power as it has been buried under the ashes of emotional fears. Personal power is too easily surrendered or projected onto others.

Games

When an individual has strong 8th Chord themes and chooses to manipulate and control others with tremendous power drives, he may exhibit the **Under My Thumb** game. This is an individual who feels he must assume complete control in all situations and particularly in relationships. He is typically extremely dominating with business partners, children and lovers or mates. His personal power tries to feed off of others by forcing them to need and depend on him. The individual who manifests this game as a regular pattern of behavior is extremely mistrustful and very paranoid of others to the point that he tries to forcefully control their money, property, actions, feelings, etc.

This individual must learn to allow others their right to creative self-expression. He will not really enjoy intimate relationships or bonds of any kind if he "always" assumes control. The more he will allow others to be true individuals, the more transcending and growth-promoting are his relationships.

Another 8th Chord power-play game is **Cold War.** This is a stubborn silence exhibited by an 8th Chord type of individual that can drive you absolutely mad. The individual who frequently indulges in this game is not genuinely seeking solitude to gain clarity but rather to escape. He uses a silent treatment to punish and especially to manipulate others. I have known people with either accentuated Pluto and/or Scorpio and/or 8th house who could easily not speak to. a lover or mate for days on end in order to get their own way or to show anger. Unfortunately, this type of behavior often poisons a person, and he would do much better with direct communication and sometimes a full-scale **open** confrontation! Many of these individuals fail to realize that the amount of tension, frustration and anger they create in their relationships often magnifies problems way out of proportion and is potentially quite damaging to themselves and others.

These people would do well to consider incorporating some of the air element's desire for communication and ability to float. The openness of Chord 11 and easy expression of Chord 3 can help lighten the intensity of Chord 8.

Another 8th Chord game related to toxic power drives is the **Sneak Attack** game. This is an individual who has built-in radar to know when someone is most vulnerable and knows just when to torpedo with a periscope-like intuition and an onslaught of verbal assaults. This is not genuine communication or constructive criticism but rather a divide-and-conquer tactic to weaken others, keeping them under the surveillance of his control. The individual often has a jealous nature and desires to sabotage the happiness of others.

An individual playing this game usually is sitting on an inner emotional confusion. Many of the 8th Chord games can be traced to "past" emotional circumstances that remain unresolved. One often must confront or face the past in this game. He must understand the inner motivations that bring him into this game. Letting go of fixed ideas helps conquer this game.

A strong 8th Chord individual may fear the emotional bonding or closeness in a relationship. He is afraid his personal power will die within the confines of a committed relationship. This individual does not really know his true emotional strength and he is busily protecting from any trace of vulnerability. This can lead to a sexual exhibitionism much like in the 5th Chord and result in a game that I call **Sexy Sadie.** This is a male or female who possesses a powerful sexual aura and uses the power to hide emotional vulnerability. The **Sexy Sadie** individual has a deadening fear of emotional closeness and makes it very clear that the relationship is casual sex and nothing more.

The previous game is closely related to **One-Night Stands.** This is an individual who will not risk developing a relationship beyond a brief sexual encounter and is often afraid to give up one ounce of personal power. Relations are abruptly cut off with someone before getting too serious. He is definitely afraid of sharing a true sense of his power with someone. It may take years of self-exploration for some individuals to feel safe within a relationship and to grow comfortable with a true emotional closeness.

The opposite 2nd Chord can offer some clues for dealing with this game. There is a simplicity in the earthy 2nd Chord that helps ground the extremely emotional 8th Chord. The 2nd Chord also points to relationship values. It could be that this game and the **Sexy Sadie** game will require a new perspective on relationships. Learning to develop trust can release a lot of good, personal power from these games. The quincunx to Chord 1 also illustrates that a firm sense of one's own ability to act and be assertive (Chord 1) helps support a balanced sense of power within relationships.

An individual with accentuated 8th Chord themes may have a pronounced dislike for emotional expression and repress emotions in the form of a self-hating game, **Those Dammed Emotions!** This individual's emotions are blocked to such an extreme that it might take a major explosion to break the dam. There is an inner deadness in this individual, sometimes tied to a past emotional trauma. The person is so fixated on a painful past experience that a rich vein of passion has turned into a hate which he is not willing to transcend.

The **Vindictive Venom** game can be typical of 8th Chord individuals very much out of touch with their emotional intensity. These bitter individuals refuse to forget or forgive. They are usually jealous in nature and threatened when confronted by the truth about themselves. They poison themselves with their own self-hatred. They may be quite possessive in relationships and, as in the **Under My Thumb** game, very much into manipulative control.

This game sometimes ends when a person begins expressing emotions in an honest manner. The game is often played by people frustrated with their own goals and creative self-expression. The person does better to focus more on improving the self than hurting others. He is always the loser when lost in this game.

I remember a client who had a heavily aspected 7th house Pluto in her horoscope including an opposition to the Sun placed in the 1st house. She could not forgive her husband for leaving her. After 15 years of separation she still expressed a burning hatred for him! This inability to let go of her husband turned out to be quite toxic for her life. She could not develop a new significant relationship since much of her personal power was projected onto a person no longer even in her life except as a painful memory. The most difficult thing for a person to do in this situation is to allow a healing process to begin by letting go of the past. It seems the more an individual hates a person or situation from the past, the stronger its hold on him, strangling the happiness of the present.

Another game related to distorted personal power is **Chip on the Shoulder.** This is someone who is bitter about life and attempts to make anyone who crosses his path pay for it. Rather than face his own shortcomings, he decides that life owes him. This is a difficult individual to please as he is out to frustrate others by always acting displeased. His intention is to drag others down with him. With extreme tides of negative and manipulative behavior, he often "turns off" the individuals who could rescue him emotionally. It is as though he wants others to suffer the same persecution that he has endured.

This individual is often running away rather than truly confronting his own emotional pain. He may prove to be bothersome and irritating to others by constantly dumping negative energy and never really making any constructive effort to get beyond personal emotional conflicts.

He needs to refocus this emotional intensity into more productive outlets. This game can be typical of very creative people who have difficulty dealing with their own intensity. There is a strong degree of drives for perfection in all three water chords. Water is the universal solvent and watery individuals seek a sense of union. They can feel very frustrated when that sought-after union does not occur. A person may need to more realistically accept himself and others if he is ever going to be happy.

When an individual hides from his own personal power he may become victimized by the **Hypnotized** game. This is the 8th Chord version of an addicted behavior that was described in the 7th Chord. The **Hypnotized** individual surrenders all personal power to another individual whether because of a romantic intoxication or simply to be completely attached to someone for powerful dependency reasons. An individual with especially pronounced 8th Chord themes (such as the Sun, Moon, Pluto or a key planet placed in 8th house and/or a cluster of Scorpio planets and/or a very strongly aspected Pluto) can have a problem staying conscious of his actions. It is as though uncontrollable waves of unstable, unconscious energies are constantly swelling within him. Desperate to satisfy these urges, the individual decides that a particular person will provide the grounding and security desired. Unfortunately, in his compulsive behavior the individual loses perspective concerning relationships and his emotional intensity scares away those who might be good for him. Instead, he too often attracts someone seeking a victim for his own compulsive appetites whether they be sexual, monetary, power hungry, etc.

The **Hypnotized** individual often remains in very destructive relationships that damage self-respect and destroy what little personal power he brought into the relationship. The transformative nature and determination shown by the 8th Chord allows some of these individuals to bounce back from a destructive relationship and to begin feeding their personal power a more nutritious diet. However, it is essential that the individual first begin to recognize what he is doing to himself and, more importantly, that he is entitled to a more balanced and rewarding life. The square to Chord 11 indicates that developing one's own uniqueness is important, and the square to Chord 5 emphasizes one's need to appreciate his own personal creativity.

Another 8th Chord game related to an individual's running away from his personal power is what I call **Waterlogged.** This is a person who is so emotional that his vision is as bad as someone driving through a torrential downpour, not able to see two feet ahead. You can almost always count on the **Waterlogged** individual to be tired or drained as vital energies are habitually leaking away from him. This is not necessarily a person who expresses emotions, but rather someone who is confused by an unexpressed emotional intensity. He often frustrates himself by being stuck in first gear; his personal power is locked in the trunk. The **Waterlogged** individual is generally very confused in regard to a life direction.

He needs to be more decisive as in the fire and air energies, willing to take a risk or two. The air element offers a mental objectivity, and fire says to act first and cry later. Of course, there may be underlying emotional difficulties which need to be resolved as well. But detachment and courage can assist in the process.

The **Hidden Hormone** game described with the 1st Chord can also occur through 8th Chord tones. In the 1st Chord an individual has trouble asserting sexual energy. The 8th Chord manifestation of this game is due to an individual's blocked emotional expression and much deeper insecurity concerning sexual identity. Fear is an integral part of this 8th Chord game. The individual's personal power is suffering from a "power shortage" as emotional fear keeps him from expressing a flowing sexual energy. This game could be a combination of 1st and 8th Chord themes—one potential of Mars in Scorpio or in the 8th house, discordant aspects formed by Mars and Pluto, a Scorpio Ascendant, etc. Of course, these same combinations can be blended into a harmonious expression such as tremendous passion, self-insight, self-mastery, balancing self-assertion needs with instinctual desire for bonding, etc.

Another 8th Chord game is **Toxic Waste.** This is someone who represses anger and has difficulty being assertive. Once again, 1st and 8th Chord energies can be found in combination in this game. Mars was the primary ruler of Scorpio until Pluto's discovery, indicating that anger and assertion can be issues for strong 8th Chord types as well as 1st Chord individuals. Due to the repressive tendencies denoted by the 8th Chord, an individual can lose belief in his own assertive strength and not fuel his personal power with direct actions. The repressed **Toxic Waste** builds to such a point that the individual may become too passively aggressive and direct negative, manipulative and distrustful behavior toward others.

The **Erupting Volcano** game is another 8th Chord manifestation related to repressed behavior. This is someone who has a tenacious habit of swallowing anger and denying emotions. The **Erupting Volcano** individual can be like a walking time-bomb as his moods are completely and sometimes violently unpredictable. He is sitting on a lot of anger until someone sets off the explosion. However, it is only a matter of time until another explosion. The individual needs to learn to regulate emotional expression without throwing his life and the lives of others into helter-skelter.

The **Introspector** is an individual living in an internal world very much removed from reality. This is sometimes a person who dives deeper and deeper into himself, fishing for absolute answers. The questions are so subjective that they often dredge up nothing more than a paranoid feeling that he is far from perfect. The problem is that the **Introspector** will not accept his own imperfections or life's practical reality. This is a bit of the dreaminess or idealism that can surface in the 8th Chord. Pronounced water chord individuals often seek or expect a certain level of perfection that is not always attainable as will be especially seen in the 12th Chord. The earthy 2nd Chord (opposite Chord 8) points to balancing this game with some common sense and enjoying the simple things one already possesses.

Perhaps the most compulsive and frightening of the 8th Chord games is what I call **Odysseus and the Sirens**. Odysseus was the mythological hero who was able to escape the destructive sirens or voices of the three sea nymphs. The nymphs were part bird and part woman creatures that could cast a spell upon those who listened to their song, causing a ship and its crew to crash into the rocky coast. Odysseus had himself tied to the mast of the ship and stuffed the ears of his crew with wax as their ship neared the treacherous coastal waters so they could not be enticed by the sea nymphs to self-destruction. As the story goes, Odysseus and his crew safely avoided the luring voices of the sea nymphs.

An individual caught in this game is not as fortunate as Odysseus. The voices or sirens in his head are compulsive and self-destructive thoughts that have seed states in his deepest shadow nature. An individual's personal power is at an all-time low as unconscious and compulsive drives are so powerful that he feels completely helpless. Drugs, food and other addictions sometimes have their origins in this game. It is as though unconscious forces control his destiny and the individual feels unable to harness this forceful energy into constructive action. It can take years to find the wax to silence a response to the commands of these compulsive instincts.

Putting to work the conscious awareness of his air side (square to Chord 11 and quincunx to Chord 3) plus the relaxed easygoingness of Chord 2's simple pleasures can help the individual get beyond compulsions.

Summary of Issues with 8th Chord Games

The 8th Chord games are given birth by one's inability to balance power instincts. Some individuals compete for too much control and power while others run away from assuming responsibility over their power needs.

The key to dealing with 8th Chord games is learning to more creatively channel the powerful emotional intensity of this chord. The more consciously one brings unconscious 8th Chord motivations to the surface, the more successful he is in relating to others. The emotional and psychic intensity of this chord seeks close bonds in friendship, parenting and love relationships.

The 8th Chord reflects the persistence of the unconscious psychic material in making itself known to each of us. The intense feeling energy that may be blocked is the same energy that can help one transform life when he makes the first step to change a negative pattern.

Those individuals with a tendency to use their power over others need to surrender to the trust and the healing that an emotional release within a close, bonded relationship can bring. Individuals who fear their own psychological and emotional strength must learn to tap into the essence of this power through creative expression and self-evaluation.

Eighth Chord energies can be expressed as loving passion, close bonded relationships, self-mastery and intuitive wisdom. The focus and concentrative powers of this chord are of unlimited potential. It is only when an individual becomes the victim of a misplaced emotional intensity, or fearful of forming a true bond with power instincts, that he is unconsciously controlled by 8th Chord games.

Subtones

The three 8th Chord subtones are the planetary aspect known as the **quincunx**, the **fixed** energy of Scorpio and the **succedent** 8th house classification.

The quincunx aspect as a subtone of Pluto has many of the qualities discussed in its 6th Chord context. Issues concerning the curbing of compulsive desires and the need to exercise discrimination and establishing a sense of discipline are typical of both 6th and 8th Chord quincunx expressions. However, the 8th Chord has a special emphasis concerning this aspect that many astrology books fail to elucidate and is why many astrologers treat the quincunx as a minor aspect rather than an aspect of importance.

The quincunx can show a particular pattern through which an individual chooses to build personal power or strength, indicating a basic understanding of personal power. Does he give it away too easily? Do compulsive drives run his life? Does he choose to force or coerce others to give their power freely to him? The quincunx can represent some of an individual's greatest challenges to his sense of personal power. Also, it can indicate how he can do much good for himself and others by expressing this potential harmoniously.

The most significant quincunxes of transpersonal character occur between a personal planet and an outer planet (Saturn, Uranus, Neptune, Pluto). I believe and have observed that this is truly when a quincunx points to an 8th Chord personality. A quincunx formed by a personal planet to a personal planet seems to have more of a 6th Chord personality: the ordering of one's life is of primary importance. (A quincunx formed between two outer planets more often than not has more of a generational significance.) A quincunx formed by a personal planet to Saturn and any planets beyond its orbit symbolizes energy that can even match the powerful significance of a square. It is here that our greatest fears and compulsions can reside.

Behind these fears and compulsive energy is the potential of an emerging transcendence that can heal an individual. The key to the process is symbolized by the planets forming a quincunx.

The peculiar thing I have noticed about the personal/outer planet quincunx is that a person seems to either overreact and compulsively overindulge in harmful habits, or simply does not do anything at all! A kind of stagnation develops in the consciousness, with no energy or power behind the life momentum. The main challenge shown by this aspect is to develop a consistency in expressing what may be experienced as raw power with no constructive outlets. Some individuals resist or fear tapping into this power as they are not sure what they will do with it. The quincunx requires careful balancing of an individual's taking responsibility for his actions and getting in touch with this power source in a more conscious manner. When Pluto is involved in a quincunx, one's potential to focus and concentrate psychological intensity is tremendous. As with most Pluto aspects, extra caution concerning compulsive urges as well as a true desire for honest self-expression are imperative to get the best results.

Scorpio's **fixed subtone** symbolizes this water sign's deep and penetrating emotional nature. The water needs to run through Scorpio's emotional veins to keep a purified mental-emotional-physical body balance. Toxicity will build in these systems if this powerful and passionate water supply does not get expressed in relationships, creative efforts, etc. The fixed subtone of Scorpio shows a capacity to be patient and persistent in dealing with life circumstances which can become stubborn in defending irrational fears. This **maintaining** feature of Scorpio's fixed subtone denotes a propensity for developing security within closely bonded emotional and sexual relationships, and joining resources and forces with others.

The succedent 11th house symbolizes a universal consciousness while the succedent 8th house symbolizes the deep formation of sacred relationships that can take the form of a personal relationship or a more collective type of involvement. The 8th house depth of emotional and sexual involvement is normally deeper than in the fun-loving succedent 5th house. The 5th house is more indicative of the early stages of "falling in love" while the 8th house is the sexual bonding together of a relationship based on hard work and rich emotional content where two people make a conscious commitment and are to some extent responsible for each other's welfare. It is more serious though not without any fun. Each person has to be prepared to roll up their sleeves and not run away at the first sign of conflict in the relationship. This bonding together is not necessarily limited to a traditional marriage as much as a conscious awareness that each individual is serious about the commitment.

The **succedent subtone** of the 8th house emphasizes its important bonding and sharing themes in maintaining a relationship based on a close emotional and sexual union. This is the most intense of emotional houses accentuating the securing of relationships through trust and mutual respect. It is important that ownership of property be a shared responsibility and that each individual encourage the development of the other's personal power. Also of primary importance is an individual's continuing relationship and bonding with his own sense of personal power to enhance a clear emotional expression.

The 8th Chord symbolizes the depths that human consciousness can approach in achieving a knowledge of personal power. However, the 8th Chord can also symbolize one's loss of personal power or enslavement to compulsive shadow states that rob one of personal power. Each of us has some need to repress experiences or thoughts below our conscious awareness. We cannot face everything immediately that comes into our minds! However, we must not completely surrender our entire conscious life to compulsive habits that lead to self-destruction either.

It appears that the discovery of Pluto in 1930 symbolizes the responsibility of each person and even nations to come to grips with power and hopefully not to transgress boundaries in expressing power instincts. Whereas the 2nd Chord emphasizes one's personal value system and possessions, the 8th Chord pulled by the dynamic steam engine, Pluto, emphasizes collective value systems and the need for an individual to be aware of the power inherent in value systems.

The 8th Chord is indicative of the power instincts of the individual and a personal challenge to trust rather than to suspect, share rather than control or hoard, and to give as well as take. The 8th Chord is the essence of the intense emotions within the bonding process that can serve to strengthen individuals if they can learn to experience the safety within a close bonded relationship.

CHAPTER THIRTEEN

TWELFTH CHORD: MERGING INSTINCTS

> We are spirits in the material world.
>
> From the song "Spirits in the Material World" on the
> album *Ghost in the Machine* by The Police (a rock group)

The 12th Chord expresses the water element's affinity for the hidden meaning of life and insatiable idealism to find a sense of unity, wholeness, and absolute perfection. The 12th Chord tones symbolize an individual's most intense soul yearnings for spiritual experiences. People can express or serve a devotional longing with an ideal, religion, aesthetic pursuit or to another person. Chord twelve completes our journey. Neptune, Pisces and the 12th house mark the summing up of all that has gone before as we seek to assimilate the whole of life and develop the capacity to experience oneness. Chord twelve symbolizes our hunger for the emotional absolute, for infinite love and beauty.

The 12th Chord earmarks one's compassion and empathy as well as one's most self-deluded and unrealistic forms of behavior. There are few limits to the 12th Chord which means its freedom must be respected. An individual must establish suitable boundaries in order to experience the 12th Chord's sometimes mystical and grace-filled meanings. There is an ever-present transcendent fluidity within the 12th Chord archetypal

12TH CHORD: MERGING INSTINCTS

Tone	Archetypal Themes	Functions	Positive Expressions	Negative Expressions	Potential Counseling Issues
Planet: Neptune Symbol ♆	The directing of actions for transcendence and unity through humility, surrender, compassion and aesthetic creativity; the capacity to embody universal love and perfection; one's deepest understanding of beauty; one's most soul-felt yearnings for spirituality, devotion and love; one's inner capacity to live ideals and dreams; one's primary instincts in escaping life's harsh realities.	1. To long for unity. 2. To develop emotional clarity. 3. To have a longing in the soul for beauty and creative expression.	1. Compassion. 2. A capacity to love with no boundaries. 3. Humility. 4. A capacity to perfect and actualize ideals.	1. A lack of responsibility for one's life due to unrealistic ideals and visions. 2. Addictions to self-destructive habits. 3. A tendency to deny one's own emotional nature and ideals in trying to fulfill the expectations of others.	Key Phrase: Unifying The Self Games: 1. Bermuda Triangle. 2. Cold Feet. 3. Coloring the truth. 4. Don't Make Any Waves.
Sign: Pisces Symbol ♓	The manner through which imagination, dreams, muse consciousness, ideals and the longing for unity can be inspired. The capacity to "watch" life while living as an active participant; the manner through which one can experience the transcending release of emotional energy through spiritual identity, compassion or surrendering self-defeating behaviors; one's innate instincts to escape confrontation or reality.	4. To feel transpersonal and unexplainable love. 5. To seek spiritual awareness.	5. An ability to transcend limiting behavior. 6. An ability to make use of healing energy.	4. A proclivity for a martyr complex. 5. The potential of reclusive behavior due to fear or escapism.	5. Emotional Savior. 6. Great Escape. 7. Helpless Victim. 8. Levitation. 9. Love Is Blind. 10. Mime.
House: 12th	One's particular gateway or sense of direction in crossing the "bridge over troubled water"; one's capacity to express spiritual intensity or ideals; one's attitudes concerning unity and devotion; one's capacity to recover and learn from periods of disorientation and feelings of helplessness; one's innate desire to transcend limitation by learning new emotional responses or patterns.	6. To live one's ideals and dreams. 7. To be in communion with the muse consciousness. 8. To sensitize and refine consciousness and to transcend imperfection.	7. A yearning to surrender to a higher consciousness. 8. An ability to inspire humanity through the muse consciousness.	6. Disorientation due to an over-sensitivity to the stimulation from one's environment. 7. An inclination to over-indulge in guilt and self-pity.	11. Paradise Lost. 12. Quicksand. 13. Sounds of Silence. 14. Strawberry Fields Forever. 15. Treading Water.

Figure 12: Twelveth Chord
See the Note to Readers after Acknowledgments

themes (following) that can inspire an individual to go beyond known or ordinary limits concerning love, beauty, perfection or spirituality.

The 12th Chord offers a refreshing water that can clean an impure and badly confused emotional nature, inspiring an individual to get back on her feet to pull together a haphazard existence. This particular water chord is rich in minerals of compassion and love. However, many people get lost in self-deluded behavior when expressing 12th Chord themes. Some attempt to be saviors and others try to walk on the glamorous outer appearances of this water. There is an emotional depth in this 12th Chord body of water that challenges the air element to comprehend it with its intellect, the earth element to feel it, the fire element to dive into it, and the other water chords to trust it. There is a bit of irony embedded within the emotional-spiritual matrix of the 12th Chord: the deeper one enters its waters, the more vulnerable and transparent one seems to become though the potential to conquer fears, addictions or weaknesses may increase greatly.

The tones and subtones of the 12th Chord symbolize one's most intense merging instincts and the desire to express a sense of perfection and spiritual values.

Neptune

The 12th Chord planetary tone, Neptune, was discovered in 1846 by French astronomer Urbain Leverrier. His precise calculations located the distant and secluded presence of Neptune, hiding behind its numerous clouds. It was actually Neptune's gravitational effects upon Uranus that gave astronomers a clue that another celestial body was floating somewhere in the sky. Neptune, like Uranus and Pluto, travels through one sign for an extended period (approximately 14 years) and therefore is considered a generational planet. Until Neptune's discovery in 1846, Jupiter was assigned rulership of Pisces. Neptune contains more of the subtle and mystical meanings than Jupiter, fitting for the primary ruler of Pisces. Neptune is very symbolic of unconscious water themes. It was not too long after Neptune's discovery that psychoanalysis began to blossom, and Freud and Jung began their own unique explorations of the unconscious forces at work in the universe and within human consciousness. Neptune's cloudy atmosphere is similar to its astrological symbolism as an individual's sometimes-clouded vision or mind. Photographs taken of Neptune by scientists in 1984 were some of the clearest ever made. Neptune's giant clouds make it a difficult planet to photograph clearly. The clouds are believed to be fixed features of Neptune's atmosphere, rotating at the same speed as Neptune.

Neptune indicates a fascination with ideal truths, Utopia and a striving to merge with perfection in one giant step, skipping the endless small detailed steps of its opposite 6th Chord. It is no easy task for modern men and women to walk in the slippery shoes of Neptunian images with a realistic perspective of life. It is far easier to escape into sleep, complacency, dream worlds and even substance abuses that dull one's awareness of reality. It is also easy to become disillusioned when idealistic expectations of people and goals end in disappointment or hurt feelings because one lacks sound reality-testing instincts to balance merging instincts.

Neptune, like her outer planetary peers, Uranus and Pluto, can symbolize a transcending experience that brings an individual a much-needed self-discovery. Since Neptune does remain in one sign for such a long period of time, its position by house is more indicative of how in touch the individual is with a sense of or lack of reality. Neptune can denote aesthetic talent, dreamings and strong imaginations. I have observed that Neptune principles seem to operate more in a person's daily life if Neptune falls in an angular house (1,4,7 or 10) and/or strongly aspected to personal planets, especially the Sun or Moon, or aspecting one's Ascendant. People with these placements often feel a dramatic mission in life to devote their energies to an ideal or special purpose. They must be careful to avoid deluding themselves into following ideals that lack any trace of reality, or walking through life very spaced out like a "sleepwalker." People with very active Neptune themes in their birth charts or experiencing Neptune's transit (current movement) through a delicate area of the horoscope can easily get into perfectionistic expectations that are virtually impossible to satisfy. Individuals with very strong focus on Neptune or any major 12th Chord tone can be quite difficult to please. The striving for perfection can be so profound that a person may run away from conflict as will be seen in the **Don't Make Any Waves** game. Emotions may be kept pure and perfect but also painfully frustrated and repressed.

Neptune can symbolize the eternal pacifist and can also represent an individual who is very compassionate. In mythology, Neptune was associated with the Roman god presiding over springs and streams and later identified with the Greek god of the sea, Poseidon. There seems to be no end to Neptune's emotional waters. Neptune's house position can indicate one's favorite escape mechanisms to avoid responsibility and can show a repetitive pattern displayed to escape reality through deceptive or fraudulent behavior. It can also indicate emotional warmth and one's desired relationship to a "Higher Power."

Neptune is considered the higher octave of Venus. Neptune is concerned with love and affection on a grand scale while Venus is more symbolic of warmth and affection in personal relationships, on a much more conscious level than Neptune. The transpersonal meaning of Neptune corresponds to the coming forth of unconscious energies that challenge each of us to comprehend their subtlety and to express them with a universalistic sense of beauty, in order to discover a higher or clearer sense of self. Neptunian themes take symbolic form in dream states. We make our highest ideals a practical reality through contracting the sensitive and delicate energy denoted by Neptune.

Positive Neptune themes include a capacity to establish emotional clarity within close relationships. Individuals may seek the highest of ideals and commit to live these ideals. Other positive expressions include one's capacity to embrace a sense of universal love and to express aesthetic beauty and compassion. Neptune can also symbolize one's intuitive feeling of unity with life and the developing of appropriate values to express this unity. One's drive to seek a spiritual awareness or to understand humility are also positive Neptunian expressions.

Negative expressions of Neptune themes include unrealistic visions or self-deceptions that lead one astray from the true self. An escapist attitude can lead to self-defeating behavior. Escapism can also result in very devastating substance abuses or self-destructive habits. A disorientation due to an oversensitivity to one's environment or a desperate feeling of helplessness (as in the **Quicksand** game) are also negative Neptune expressions. An individual can become completely dissatisfied with life due to extremely high standards of perfection. Stagnation is another possible negative Neptune expression (as in the **Treading Water** game).

Pisces

The 12th Chord sign tone, Pisces, is as transparent as it is transcendent. There is a very thin wall separating the conscious and unconscious energies of Pisces. Both energies are constantly merging and separating making it difficult at times to separate dreams from reality and self-delusion from self-honesty.

Traditionally the symbol for Pisces is ♓. The symbol represents two fish swimming in opposite directions. The fish appear to be wanting to merge together as indicated by the horizontal line that joins them. However, bringing these two fish together is as challenging as a strong Piscean personality maintaining the same steady vision of reality from one day to the next.

Astrology, Psychology, and Transformation

Pisces, the mystic, actor-actress, poet, lover and dreamer, longs for present difficulties to disappear rather than face the distaste of everyday hassles and confrontations. However, make no mistake about it, the capacity to understand duality is rivaled only by Gemini, the 3rd Chord sign that lives and breathes through the lungs of two distinct natures. The Piscean duality is fed by the constant interplay of conscious and unconscious forces. Dreams find their access into conscious mind activities and return to the safety and imagination of Piscean fantasies and mysteries. The recycling of this watery flow captures the image of Piscean duality.

An individual with the Sun, Moon or Ascendant in Pisces and/or a cluster of planets in this 12th Chord sign or house and/or a highly accentuated Neptune, can quickly reach into her finely attuned emotional and social instincts to help those in need. She will walk an extra mile on very tired feet to care for a loved one or a downtrodden soul. Just as quickly, our Piscean friend can dive back into an abyss of solitude, trying to regain oneness with whatever today's emotional weather may be upsetting.

The inner world of Pisces is a duality in itself as it can be shattered by outside forces but regenerate amazingly fast. The key for this transpersonal sign is belief in self and a Higher Power. When Pisces stops believing in self, utter chaos is the result. Pisces desires peace, bliss and beauty at almost any cost. Pisces wants everything to stay perfect, changing from one ideal to another. When Pisces stops believing in self, escapism reaches tremendous proportions whether it is escape into substance abuses, sleep, fanatical beliefs, unrealistic ideals, masochism, etc.

An individual with many 12th Chord themes needs to believe in a Higher Power as well as the self. The reason for this is that strong 12th Chord individuals are prone to playing the role of savior and overextending themselves in trying to save others. A strong 12th Chord person must let a Higher Power help others and see herself as a vehicle only. It is all too easy for her to try to conquer the world's problems and to be drained by the sorrows of the world if she has no allegiance or faith in a Higher Power.

The duality and extreme adaptability of Pisces can be difficult to perceive clearly. Individuals with a strong Piscean focus must not assume others perceive them accurately. The fish can pull in two opposite directions and give very mixed and confusing nonverbal messages to others as Pisces is the master of silence.

Commitments are often just what a Piscean individual needs to make ideals practical and to keep a very fluid emotional nature balanced. Commitments to any form of reality, whether a relationship, home, career, etc., can seem like a tremendous ordeal. Since Pisces has such a vivid awareness that anything with a beginning surely will come to an end, commitments can seem like a waste of time. (Also, commitments remind Pisces that life is more than just an act in a play.)

Perhaps the biggest issue concerning commitments is that Pisces has a powerful universal yearning to go beyond just one of anything. In other words, Pisces senses and desires a commitment to every person, job, relationship or belief. It can then be difficult to give special attention to any one thing or person.

There is a lot of intuitive and creative energy denoted by Pisces, a vast array of emotional expression. The emotional sensitivity and X-ray vision indicated by Pisces can penetrate the most subtle of circumstances. Emotional confusion is sometimes what starts a Piscean individual on an escapist path. When running away from the self, shadow forces begin to multiply. The 12th Chord shadow is feeling completely helpless, a victim to be rescued, lost but never found. The potential for unrealistic visions and living in absolute fear can be pronounced. Piscean individuals may lose sight of their safe boundaries. Ironically, it is often the little fears that push an individual to the edge of a transcending experience and it is a belief in the self and in a Higher Power that makes her take the risk of transcending limitations and desiring greater self-knowledge.

Positive expressions of the Piscean themes include a compassionate love for oneself and others. Pisces can be the sign of an individual possessing great healing energy in massage, social work, psychology, etc. Counseling instincts can also be typical due to the capacity to tune into others with intuitive force. An ability to express dramatic, musical or artistic talent can also be a positive expression. So is an innate desire to express and develop a greater spiritual awareness.

Negative expressions of Piscean themes are often typified by avoidance or escapist behavior. The individual becomes a perpetual victim rendered helpless by life's harsh realities. Pisces can also signify the dreamer who never accomplishes goals and whose ideals have no trace of reality as in the **Paradise Lost** and **Strawberry Fields Forever!** games. Pisces can represent a person who is too emotionally involved in life activities and drains the energies of others with excessive dependency. Stagnation can be a real problem if the Piscean individual stops trying because perfection seems unattainable. Escapism can lead to self-defeating behavior and a feeling of disorientation. Other pitfalls include compulsive feelings of guilt and self-pity.

12th House

The 12th house is symbolic of the 12th Chord's propensity for escape into alternate routes of experience. It indicates complicated life issues and energies difficult to express in a concrete manner. Energies symbolized by the 12th house border on the ethereal, spiritual, meditative and fantasy frequencies, especially for very inwardly directed individuals who have a passion for developing and knowing themselves on the most intricate of emotional levels. Their subconscious energies are strong allies and sometimes communicate valuable messages in dreams, meditative experiences or intuitive visions. The merging instincts of these individuals seem to grow that much faster when properly cultivated with a diet that nourishes this inward drive for perfection and devotion.

Those who are not as inwardly directed sometimes find the 12th house representing constant hassles in everyday affairs. Traditionally the 12th house has been called the "house of self-undoing." Life may seem to be a series of disorientations that frustrate the ideals and goals of a person. Individuals with key planets in the 12th house, especially the Sun or Moon, must find ways to unlock the doors to a clear self-expression or emotional flow. These people may have finely attuned artistic expressions in their mind, body and soul. Their inner harmonies dance through their entire beings. A person with a highly emphasized 12th house may embark on some truly remarkable journeys of self-exploration and discover new forms of creative energy whose very essence comes through them to merge with life in the forms of compassion, humility, gratitude, aesthetic and creative expression of beauty. The 12th Chord duality symbolizes an energy that belongs to an individual, yet must be surrendered into a transcending self-expression.

Faith in life is an important theme for an individual with a strongly occupied 12th house. Faith acts as a lubricant that frees one's fears and anxieties residing in the unconscious. A person's connection to a Higher Power helps foster her inner attunement to positive energy and a wisdom to engage in actions that bring spiritual fulfillment. People that lack this faith are anxious, insecure, escapist, ill, etc.

The 12th house can be indicative of an individual's most productive emotional and intuitive energy for transcending limitations and accepting one's present shortcomings before embarking on a path to rise above difficulties. However, the 12th house also can be symbolic of an individual's greatest obstacle—**herself**! She constantly gets into her own way by escaping into unrealistic fantasies, drowning in self-pity, worshipping helplessness and merging with alcohol, sex, drugs, sleep, etc. Actually each 12th Chord tone can point to a type of self-undoing, if an individual chooses such a path. Negative expressions of the 12th house principles act as an individual's self-defeating opium that destroys her day by day. There may be a breakdown of one's emotional well-being as well as a dysfunctioning of the opposite mental processes. An individual experiencing difficulty in expressing the subtle themes of the 12th house sometimes feels the sensation of being stuck in her consciousness, pinned down by fears in such a way that she cannot climb to a higher or clearer view of the situation. It is a feeling of helplessness that requires assistance, whether it is letting go of emotional pain or leaving behind destructive patterns of behavior. In dealing with 12th house issues an individual must often develop new emotional expressions and learn to feel safe in communicating fears and, most of all, to replace fear with faith.

Positive expressions of 12th house themes include being in touch with one's deepest emotions and unafraid to communicate them to those we trust. We are able to express love and compassion for others. A well-defined, intuitive nature allows us to comprehend life's contradictions. Other positive 12th house expressions include an understanding of humility, a forgiving nature and serving one's highest ideals. Some individuals with accentuated 12th houses can inspire humanity through aesthetic expression, a healing art, or a yearning to dedicate themselves to developing their spiritual awareness. Also, an inner wisdom and faith in life are positive expressions.

An individual's complete disorientation, emotional confusion and escapist behavior can highlight a negative expression of 12th house themes. A person may merge with a wide range of substance abuses and poor emotional habits. These individuals often lack a sense of proper limits and live life to compulsive extremes. The root of an addiction can often be denoted by a 12th Chord tone. People can fall into habitual usage of unconscious energy until it is too late to break the habit. The transcending and merging tendencies related to the 12th house can be surrendered to wanting to "get high" no matter what the cost. Other 12th Chord pitfalls are compulsive guilt, self-pity and trying to be a "savior" for others when this is not being solicited by them.

Counseling Issues

The counseling issues of the 12th Chord are indicative of an individual's basic confusion in expressing the subtle and yet powerful spirit of this chord, **merging instincts**. My key word phrase for these counseling issues, **unifying the self,** is from the synthesis of the 12th Chord tones. Though each chord in a sense requires a comprehension of one's particular need to establish a unified self-understanding and expression, the 12th Chord tones have a special emphasis upon the unification and merging themes. The archetypal themes are:

1. **Neptune**—transcendence and unity through humility, surrender, compassion and aesthetic creativity; the capacity to embody universal love and perfection; one's deepest understanding of beauty; one's most soul-felt yearnings for spirituality, devotion and love; one's inner capacity to live ideals and dreams; one's primary instincts in escaping life's harsh realities.
2. **Pisces**—the manner through which imagination, dreams, muse consciousness, ideals and the longing for unity can be inspired; the capacity to "watch" life while living as an active participant; the manner through which one can experience the transcending release of emotional energy through a spiritual identity, compassion or surrendering self-defeating behaviors; one's innate instincts to escape confrontation or reality.
3. **12th house**—one's particular gateway or sense of direction in crossing the "bridge over troubled water"; one's capacity to express spiritual intensity or ideals; one's attitudes concerning unity and devotion; one's capacity to recover and learn from periods of disorientation and feelings of helplessness; one's innate desire to transcend limitation by learning new emotional responses or patterns.

The counseling issues of this chord concern an individual's inability to face the reality of life circumstances. The 12th Chord tones can be expressed with an aesthetic clarity of beauty that transcends the finite imagination of the conscious mind. The most penetrating forms of art, music, drama or other talents are represented by the 12th Chord. Also, an individual can display a compassionate character, an intuitive sensitivity, a vibrant healing energy, boundless faith and spontaneous love for self and others.

The counseling issues of the 12th Chord are twofold: (1) a total belief in unrealistic ideals and unreasonable expectations for perfection that lack a sound base of reality; (2) an emotional confusion due to a lack of faith that disorients and deludes one into self-defeating behavior. Both counseling themes usually contain avoidance and escapist motives.

Games

When an individual loses touch with reality by merging with an unfounded idealism or lofty perfection drives, she may exhibit the **Strawberry Fields Forever** game. This is a person who looks at the world through "rose-colored glasses" and sees only the reality she wishes to see. This is the stubborn resistance to facing life's everyday reality that some pronounced 12th Chord individuals can portray. This person has a strong imagination process that can churn out one new fantasy after another. Wherever Neptune is placed by house position in the horoscope and its aspects to personal planets can indicate an individual's favorite escape routes. Every person has to have some form of escape from the problems and stresses of everyday life. However, in this game the individual is not just seeking a temporary escape—the whole life is an underground escape from dealing with reality. Such people are often on the run from themselves and others. It may be many years before they stop running away from life. It takes much courage to break through the layer upon layer of self-trickery and deception buried in the unconscious mind.

It is in the facing of one's reality that she can feel a sense of liberation. It is important to remember that the 12th Chord "naturally" squares the faith-oriented 9th Chord. There is another natural connection between the 9th and 12th Chords as Jupiter is the 9th Chord planet and was previously the 12th Chord planet. This points to **faith** as an important factor in dealing with 12th Chord games. Individuals may exhibit too much (unrealistic) faith (as in expecting another human being to be godlike and ideal) or too little faith (in life's ultimate goodness so they live anxiously).

A related 12th Chord game is **Paradise Lost.** This is an individual so afraid of facing conflict or frustration that she hides within fantasies and illusions, tiptoeing from one ideal to another until one day her accomplishments either add up to zero or have no real depth. It is as though she awakens from a long dream and cannot believe the time wasted. Often ideals or fantasies lead her into bizarre goals that have no opportunity for fruition. Her paradise is definitely lost due to idealized images of perceptions that flee under the confrontation of real circumstances.

Another 12th Chord game related to a "spaced-out" or too idealistic mentality is the **Levitation** game. This is a person who has no sense of limitation and is quite ignorant in regard to the laws of the physical plane. She is an emotionally disoriented person who has trouble staying grounded. I have seen this game especially prevalent in individuals with a lot of focus on water chord energy, especially of the 12th Chord variety and with little or no emphasis upon earth chord energy. This person floats or "sleepwalks" through life and is very confused by her often uncontrollable merging instincts. The problem is that she is constantly trying to merge with anything in sight or imaginable. The **Levitation** individual has numerous excuses to escape any form of commitment—which is probably what she needs more than anything else to give a sense of clear direction.

Both the **Paradise Lost** and **Levitation** games require a stabilizing of oneself as found in the earth element. The opposite earthy 6th Chord points to hard work, discrimination and disciplining one's mind as important ingredients in dealing with 12th Chord games. Also, the air element can help a person to be more logical and to gain a more detached perspective concerning ideals. Emotional energy is quite powerful. When this person learns to better focus this energy and align it with a clear vision of reality, she can accomplish her goals.

The **Love Is Blind** game is the 12th Chord version of the "romantic" discussed in the 7th Chord. This is the person who has little sense of structure in a relationship and is led by fantasies and infatuations into relationships that can be quite disastrous. She has no clear understanding of reality testing or discriminating a more suitable match. The **Love is Blind** individual is more in love with "falling in love" than developing a balanced relationship. This individual can suffer severe emotional traumas as she blindly enters relationships that at first glance appear to be beautiful and sweet. However, as the relationship develops she becomes disappointed because the person of her dreams cannot possibly fulfill her perfectionistic expectations.

Robert Johnson in his book *We* discusses the underlying motivations of romantic love. Johnson analyzes the entrance of romantic love into Western societies. The book is focused on the symbolism of the great romantic myth, *Tristan and Iseult,* and traces present Western ideals of romance back to the Middle Ages.

Johnson states that romantic love is the energy system that Westerners now rely upon to give us the experience of transcendence and total fulfillment: "romantic love is not just a form of 'love,' it is a whole psychological package—a combination of beliefs, ideals, attitudes, and expectations."

He also says that romance is not as fulfilling when totally directed at our projections and fantasies. Johnson makes the point that a person needs to get in touch with the unconscious parts that she is projecting or looking for in others. It is only then that she can hope to achieve balanced relationships and not depend so heavily on others for total satisfaction.

Johnson states that there is a great power source inherent in the ideal of romantic love. He explains that the ideals emanating from romantic love awaken us to an inner reality. Johnson says we may manifest romantic ideals on the wrong level but this same powerful energy can be expressed at a higher and more fulfilling level when a person finds the truth in romantic love.

I have seen this game with people who have Neptune placed in the 7th house and/or Ascendant, Sun or Moon in Pisces. Also, Neptune aspects to personal planets, such as conjunctions, squares, and oppositions to the Sun, Moon, Venus and even Ascendant can imply this game. Trines and quincunxes formed by Neptune and personal planets can also be warning signals in regard to relationships, especially when Neptunian idealism is a driving force in the individual's life. The transcending and merging instincts shown by each 12th Chord tone require a person to develop inner clarity and to seek honest feedback from others to keep the reins on potentially disorientating energies. Energy misdirected into emotionally draining or addictive relationships can be transformed into a more balanced expression if one is willing to conquer the feelings of helpless dependency on others that enslave her to self-defeating patterns of relating. When one understands the perfection and God Within, one does not feel compelled to project godlike fantasies upon others. If one can perceive the divinity in each person and not deny this special aspect of herself, she will not need to put another person on a pedestal. It is important to note that the 12th Chord naturally quincunxes the 7th Chord. This indicates that a person must balance ideals and faith (12th Chord) within relationships (7th Chord). The quincunx formed to the 5th Chord is a reminder that a person must also develop her own creative potentials.

A 12th Chord game related to an evasion of responsibility is the **Why Try When Everything Ends?** approach. This is an individual who hides behind a fatalistic philosophy that all events are basically inevitable and fated to end. Often this is an excuse to mask a fear of failure or conflict. The person does not really wish to exert any effort for success. This game produces a lot of inertia, laziness and self-indulgence; the individual's life has no momentum to move forward. She waits too long for life to come to her rather than risk failing.

The issue of faith is important. This game is a self-defeating behavior that causes a person to miss opportunities. The individual needs to learn to take risks as an extension of faith in herself and a Higher Power. She may be able to put to use the fiery themes of Chord 5 (natural quincunx) and Chord 9 (natural square) for increased confidence.

The vivid and colorful imagination denoted by the 12th Chord tones can lead an individual to exhibit the **Coloring the Truth** game. This is someone who purposely distorts her view of reality to fit life into idealistic visions. Many times I have seen a person with accentuated 12th Chord tones completely misperceive the intentions of others. The **Coloring the Truth** individual may perceive an act of friendship by someone as romantic intentions though in actuality this is not what was intended at all. A person locked into this game hears what she wants to hear and sees what she wants to see. This is yet another strong avoidance behavior in the 12th Chord. Also, **Coloring the Truth** can take the form of an individual who shades the facts (square to 3rd Chord and opposition to 6th Chord) to lighten the impact upon others. This is a form of self-denial rather than a humanitarian gesture because the person is afraid of the backlash of someone's anger. More importantly, the individual is afraid of her own assertion strength and represses it while distorting the truth. Encouraging her spontaneous fiery nature could prove helpful.

An emotional disorientation can often be found in association with 12th Chord games. The waterfalls of the unconscious are forceful, always seeking to fill an individual's conscious awareness. Sometimes a person may feel lightheaded or intoxicated with the emotional and dreamy presence of these energies. Individuals who can channel this tremendous energy into a structured expression often gain more access into unconscious material to use creatively in life. Jung who worked so extensively in researching the unconscious forces of the psyche (including his own!) made clear his gratitude for commitments to his wife, children and work routine which helped ground and stabilize him. His commitments gave him a structured existence while exploring the unstructured and emotionally disorienting energy of the unconscious.

When an individual becomes overwhelmed by emotionally disorienting energies she may exhibit the **Quicksand** game. This is when someone feels completely helpless and sinks into the depths of despair and emotional confusion. It seems the harder she tries to escape from her problems, the more she sinks. Often this person has standards of perfection that are so high, she cannot possibly live up to them. This is a self-hating type of behavior. The individual is purposely creating situations that will fail and may be quite unconscious of the fact. Also, it is extremely difficult for the **Quicksand** individual to experience emotional or psychological safety.

This individual lacks the bridge of faith that can allow her to safely reach destinations. Actually the beauty of the 12th Chord is that there is a transcending experience when one embarks upon a true path of perfection. There is a spiritual fulfillment as a result of reaching toward one's high standards. However, if people forget that life is a process, they can end up punishing themselves for not being "perfect" yet. When they lack faith in their eventual success, they end up fearful, anxious and afraid to trust. When they understand that life is a journey toward oneness, they can relax and enjoy the "trip" without feeling inadequate for not achieving cosmic consciousness every instant of every day.

Another 12th Chord game is the **Helpless Victim.** This is someone always in need of help. She may feign an illness or perpetuate an emotional dependency on others to remain a helpless individual. This is another self-hating behavior as the individual does not really desire to get her life together. Her helplessness feeds off the sympathies of others in a parasitic and manipulative manner. The **Helpless Victim** may use this behavior to limit the freedom of others by making them feel guilty for ignoring her or not properly rescuing her. She may also indulge in self-pity to induce sympathy from others.

When 12th Chord escapist themes are overdone in this game, the opposite earthy Chord 6 offers the needed discipline, efficiency and willingness to work to help the individual gain a sense of competence. The funloving spirit of Chord 5 (a natural quincunx), and the optimistic faith of Chord 9 (natural square) can also be useful.

A related game is the **Emotional Savior.** This is a person with emotional problems of her own who has a compulsive drive to save **Helpless Victims** but in the end often becomes a victim herself. She becomes trapped by her own rescue instincts. The **Emotional Savior** really meets a frustrating match in the **Helpless Victim** who eventually voices displeasure with the **Emotional Savior** for not saving her.

The **Emotional Savior** needs to allow a Higher Power to help others and stop playing God herself. This is an example in the 12th Chord of what can happen when one puts **too much** faith in the self.

The **Treading Water** game is typical of a person who is completely stagnated in life. She lacks the energy and clarity to go beyond emotional confusion and exhaustion to reach her goals. Strong Neptune, Pisces or 12th house tones can symbolize an individual's hesitation to move forward in life due to a frustrated desire for absolute perfection or a desire to escape. The **Treading Water** individual remains in a stagnating life posture as she is not sure how to proceed. She may even resist a life preserver in the form of help from those who care about her.

I have seen this game particularly prevalent when transiting Neptune begins to form a major aspect to a key planet such as the Sun or moves into an angular house (1, 4, 7 and 10). This is symbolic of an individual attempting to tune into Neptune's subtle frequencies by making emotional adjustments and perhaps doing a little reality checking before making major life changes (which isn't a bad idea)! Neptune's meaning is similar to an astronaut in a spacecraft leaving the gravitational pull of the Earth. Suddenly, she enters space and a whole new set of rules as gravity is temporarily set aside.

The floating quality of space is indicated by Neptune's placement, and individuals seem to experience Neptunian themes from as wide a spectrum as spiritual awakening to a "spaced out" kind of feeling, or from an emotional upliftment to a total emotional disorientation. Neptune can represent taking a spiritual escalator if someone can approach with the right spirit and make proper life adjustments. On the other hand, Neptunian themes can be very frustrating on the Earth plane of consciousness when an individual insists on escapist attitudes or completely denies the symbolic possibility of a new intuitive or awakened understanding of life.

Some people experience a lot of fear and frustration within the time period of a Neptune transit aspecting an important planet. This period can last as long as 1½ years! It may feel as if a person's life is moving backwards or swimming upstream, especially if she is running away from responsibilities or being extremely dishonest with herself.

However, many people experience an important Neptune transit as an uplifting period of time that transforms the life for years to come. It can feel like the showering of a graceful gift from heaven, opening an individual's greater mental-intuitive-emotional connection to transpersonal love.

The **Treading Water** game does not have to be experienced as a game at all. Often this is just the period of time a person requires to rediscover the self and fine-tune her merging instincts. This can also be a period to contact one's deepest spiritual identity and find an emotional and intuitive flow. Unfortunately, many people deny this energy, fearing it as a demon rather than the saving grace it can be.

People sometimes require more sleep during Neptune transits and may find urges for drugs and alcohol on the upswing. It could be that individuals taking medications need to lighten a dosage at these times due to a newly developed sensitivity. I have seen people's aesthetic and musical tastes go through major changes during Neptune transits (including my own). One's sensitivity to herself and the entire environment can become very delicate indeed. Sometimes people seem to literally float into new situations that later may startle them. While they were dreamily treading water, the tide of life carried them into relationships or other situations that lacked sound reality testing. However, a person could also make a conscious decision to use this energy more constructively.

Another 12th Chord game is **Cold Feet.** This individual fears vulnerability or sensitivity to others and breaks commitments, often with little or no warning. However, you may not know she has broken off a relationship or a meeting because she is not about to tell you. She hopes her problems and risky commitments will disappear if she denies them. The tones of the 12th Chord represent delicacy and transparency. Individuals with a 12th Chord focus may be extremely sensitized to the vibrations of others. An individual experiencing **Cold Feet** is usually emotionally constipated and not very trusting of herself when dealing with responsible decisions. Denial is at the root of this game. The individual would rather tiptoe away from conflict and reality than deal directly with it. Commitments are seen as too exhausting and emotionally depleting to risk getting involved.

Once again, a greater faith in life is needed. Approaching life in a more direct manner brings out many good qualities lying dormant. The straightforward fire chords may be of assistance here as well as the earth element which encourages the fulfillment of commitments.

Another 12th Chord game is **Don't Make Any Waves.** This person is too afraid to question others. This can be typical of a parent who would allow a child to do anything rather than discipline her or confront her with proper boundaries. The **Don't Make Any Waves** individual is afraid to confront a lover or mate even though a situation requires it. **Don't Make Any Waves** is a form of denial or escapist behavior that can haunt a person with an emphasis upon 12th Chord tones.

Dr. Peck in his book *The Road Less Traveled* has an interesting section called "The Risk of Confrontation." He artfully describes the responsibility of each individual in a relationship to confront one another when a situation requires such action. He says: "The loving person, therefore, is frequently in a dilemma, caught between a loving respect for the beloved's own path in life and a responsibility to exercise loving leadership when the beloved appears to need such leadership."

Dr. Peck also states that a great number of individuals hide within their own meekness, repressing the very sense of power they need to express for the good of themselves and others. He says: "To fail to confront when confrontation is required for the nurture of spiritual growth represents a failure to love equally as much as does thoughtless criticism or condemnation and other forms of active deprivation of caring." However, Dr. Peck cautions that the person doing the confronting must first be careful to speak in the kind of language another person can understand. He warns against the destructive effect of dumping one's own arrogance on others in a willful and insensitive manner.

The **Don't Make Any Waves** person is sometimes very much out of touch with how to achieve balance in relating to others. Confrontation frightens her as it means she must exercise some leadership in a relationship and this can be a difficult stance for an individual who fears to lead at any level.

The natural quincunx of Chord 7 to Chord 12 is particularly related to this game. The idealism of Chord 12 must be balanced with a sense of give-and-take in relationships, symbolized by Chord 7. The ability to face people openly, and confront them when appropriate, is one of the issues of Chord 7.

The **Mime** game is another form of a very repressed emotional nature, and spontaneous instincts are quite nonexistent. This is a person who plays the game, "You Know Something Is Bothering Me and Now Start Guessing." Water can denote subtle manipulation. The body language may be quite expressive but the mouth can be shut indefinitely. The more someone tries to pry out the problem or what is wrong, the more the **Mime** individual enjoys a sense of silent power. Actions voice anger or displeasure. This is another toxic behavior which does more harm than good because nothing is ever resolved. A lot of confusion settles into the individual's mind, and relationships stay unclear due to such escapist actions.

People playing this game could use the natural communicativeness of Chord 3 (square) and the spontaneous honesty of Chord 9 (square). The urge to define relationships symbolized by Chord 7 (quincunx) could also be helpful.

The **Sounds of Silence** game is not an individual's temporary retreat (which can be a good plan of action for strong 12th Chord individuals). The **Sounds of Silence** individual is someone who has chosen a complete withdrawal from life to avoid responsibility. This can be an extremely quiet person who greatly fears the voice of her own sense of creative power (quincunx to 5th Chord). She would rather people simply pass her by and not confront her with reality. This game can manifest more like the 8th Chord **Introspector** in that the individual can overly merge into the subjective self and constantly criticize herself. The **Sounds of Silence** individual has unreasonably high perfection standards for the self.

Airy Chord 3 can lend its casual breeziness to lighten up the focus on perfection. It can also offer some objectivity to help the person understand the inner motivations for playing this game.

The fire chords call for one to act on impulses and to share likes and dislikes with others.

The **Bermuda Triangle** game is typical of some 12th Chord individuals who completely get lost in a fog of emotional confusion. This is a person whose conscious awareness of life becomes as mysteriously nonexistent as ships and planes that have disappeared in the water located between Miami and the island of Bermuda. There is a lot of self-denial in this game usually accompanied by feelings of guilt and even extreme self-pity. The **Bermuda Triangle** individual feels completely at the mercy of extreme emotional shifts and may also make a regular practice of indulging in the **Helpless Victim** or **Emotional Savior** games. Again, grounding and practicality can offer some clues to dealing with this game.

The most potentially destructive game of the 12th Chord is the **Great Escape.** This is an individual whose merging instincts rather than being transformed, have become deformed into compulsive escape and avoidance instincts. The individual is so fixated on escaping reality that she often loses a clear conscious awareness of what she is doing. Disappearing into a void of indecision and confusion instead of an internal unity, she settles for mental and physical abuses of self that offer a simulated experience of unity. She renders herself helpless by looking for a sense of unity with a completely external orientation. An excessive or addictive use of drugs, alcohol or food leads her further and further downstream from herself. Even aesthetic pursuits can be a compulsive source of escape. The individual's unconscious shadow forces turn reality upside down.

The **Great Escape** is an individual's total escape from reality which is viewed as boring, confining and threatening. A person desperately drugs, drinks, eats or televisions her conscious awareness into a long deep sleep. Each 12th Chord tone is, in a sense, symbolic of a transcending escape from limitation. Unfortunately, some individuals become overwhelmed by the sensation of these sensually intoxicating and merging-like energies and become junkies for experiences that promise to satisfy longings for love and unity but in reality leave only insatiable and compulsive self-defeating urges.

The solution, as with most 12th Chord games lies in developing a sense of faith in one's own inner wisdom, while also trusting a Higher Power so that she does not feel she must do everything. Seeking God only in the outer world is insufficient, but trusting only in one's own perfection is self-defeating as well. A balanced faith is essential.

Summary of Issues with 12th Chord Games

The 12th Chord games originate from one's inability to balance the strong intuitive and imaginative instincts of this chord with reality. Also, a lack of faith or misplaced faith can lead strong 12th Chord individuals into escapist and avoidance behaviors.

This is a chord of unlimited value for each of us. The three tones of the 12th Chord can be indicative of one's intuitive wisdom, emotional strength to weather any storm, spiritual commitment to walk a path that inspires faith and compassion, and quest for inner perfection. The 12th Chord denotes a transcending power that can lead one to conquer 12th Chord games. One must be willing to find a new faith in the self and in a Higher Power to ensure success. A person will only surrender her fear when she has an experience of inner faith to replace it.

An individual with 12th Chord themes emphasized needs to do some solid reality testing of ideals and goals. Reaching for perfection is a natural 12th Chord theme. It is the transcending energy shown by the 12th Chord that can bring a person to accomplish far-reaching visions, knowing the perfection that resides within her, and trusting that life is a process that can lead to the full realization of her goals. It is only when a person disregards the laws of the physical plane and has little or no faith in her connection to emotional beauty that she merges with the 12th Chord games.

Subtones

The three 12th Chord subtones are: the planetary aspect known as the **semisextile,** the **mutable** energy of Pisces and the **cadent** 12th house classification.

Neptune's subtone, the **semisextile,** has a slightly different emphasis than in its 2nd Chord association. The 2nd Chord desire for physical comfort emerges into a desire for inner or spiritual comfort in the 12th Chord. The semisextile can denote transcendence and shows more of a 12th Chord instinctual drive for unity when the planets forming the aspect are a personal (Sun through Jupiter) and an outer (Saturn, Uranus, Neptune or Pluto) planet. Semisextiles formed by personal planets to each other represent more of a tendency to have 2nd Chord themes for an individual. When an outer planet is one of the planets forming the semisextile and especially Neptune, the 12th Chord themes are probably involved. This particular aspect can show an individual's instincts to seek a transcendent harmony in life. It is the spiritual-emotional values and the urge to merge instincts of the 12th Chord. The semisextile is the elementary beginning of a cycle of development that should not be ignored as unimportant, especially in regard to an individual's soul growth.

The **mutable subtone** of Pisces indicates high adaptability. Since Pisces is a water sign, this mutable quality symbolizes an individual's urge to learn new methods of emotional expression and to find clear ways to transcend limitation and obstacles. However, the escapist tendencies of Pisces are also emphasized as an individual can quickly grow weary of the limits of everyday reality. She may adapt a little too quickly to a habit of running away from problem situations or commitments. The mutable subtone represents an exceptionally adaptable intuitive energy and a desire to find suitable outlets for devotional instincts.

A **cadent** 12th house **subtone** emphasizes this particular water house as an indicator of the desire to learn new emotional responses to life demands. Also, the cadent subtone accentuates the ability to understand and accept life's ironies and idiosyncrasies, as well as an eagerness to comprehend one's deepest merging and unifying instincts.

The 12th Chord represents a sensitive, intuitive nature, spawning some of the most unique instincts to transcend limitation and to devote oneself to the pursuit and expression of perfection. Each 12th Chord tone can symbolize one's capacity to respond to her own conscience and to pursue a life path of the highest spiritual and growth-elevating significance. However, one must be careful to establish meaningful commitments in order to allow transformative urges and ideals to prosper.

I agree with the opinion of many other astrologers that the water element has a symbolic meaning regarding one's *karma* or possible habit patterns developed in previous lifetimes. Even without accepting the theory of reincarnation, one can understand water symbolism as indicative of our deepest emotional sensitivity, greatest personal secrets and most unconscious of habits. Perhaps hidden within the water element is the secret of what keeps a person in touch with memories of the earliest roots in this lifetime as well as roots that extend deep into previous lifetimes. Whether we talk in terms of past, present or future, the water chords are the symbolic emotional outlets of the human spirit for love, forgiveness, surrender and, most of all, beauty and perfection.

PART VI

CHAPTER FOURTEEN

ASTROLOGICAL SYNTHEISIS: THE ART OF INTERPRETING THE BIRTH CHART

> Ultimately the interpretation of any astrological chart resolves itself into the careful analysis of each detail, but this cannot be done intelligently unless the interpreter possess a whole concept of the individual.
>
> *The Guide to Horoscope Interpretation*
> by Marc Edmund Jones (pages 1 and 2)

Section One: Primary Ingredients

If one has been reading this book in a sequential order, then this section will seem a natural step from what has been somewhat theoretical to this point. Although, I would like to reemphasize that the games described in the twelve chord chapters are based on my actual experiences with clients—not blind theories! After all, if astrology cannot be applied to gaining a better understanding of the reality in our lives, then why put so much energy into understanding its subtle idiosyncrasies? We already have astronomy to outline and define the scientific structure of the sky. However, if we want to go beyond the world of outer appearances and enter the inner and enticing mystical symbolism of the sky, then we must investigate astrology.

The first part of this book, especially the 12 chord chapters, focused upon astrology's primary tones and its subtones. These are astrology's essential symbolic ingredients that, when combined with a few other "spices," can bring to us a clear, symbolic picture of one's astrological portrait in the form of the 360° circle of the birth chart.

If one does grow determined to learn astrology's wisdom or only to experience a very brief encounter with this ancient science, he may discover rather quickly that astrology can become a dynamic and intuitive art form of communication when its "parts" are understood. A beginning student of astrology needs to slowly digest and even memorize the essential meanings of each chord and its tones and subtones. The mastering of chart interpretation is related to one's ability to comprehend the interrelationship of the astrological parts.

Repeating Themes

Many beginners to astrology become frightened by the numerous details that bombard them when trying to interpret a chart. It is often a relief for the beginner to learn that he need not understand every little detail in a horoscope. It is much more important to find the **repeating themes**. These are the themes that occur over and over again in the horoscope. It is this repeating that points to the intensity of the theme.

An example of a repeating theme is a person with the Sun in the 1st Chord sign (Aries), forming a conjunction aspect (a 1st Chord subtone) to Mars (the 1st Chord planetary tone). Each of these three motifs is related to the 1st Chord emphasis on assertion and identity. The Ascendant and planets placed in the 1st house may reinforce these 1st Chord themes as will any aspects formed by Mars to other planets in the horoscope. Other conjunctions in the chart can also be considered to see how they balance the Sun/Mars conjunction.

Planets placed in the 5th and 9th houses add to the fire emphasis in the chart as will aspects formed by the Sun, Mars or Jupiter to other planets (since each is a fire planet). Planets placed in the fire signs (Aries, Leo and Sagittarius) help determine the intensity of the fire element in the horoscope.

Another example of a repeating theme would be the placement of 7th Chord Venus in an individual's 12th house, and 12th Chord Neptune in the person's 7th house. The emphasis upon the mixing of the 7th and 12th Chord themes repeats itself pointing to issues around idealism in relationships.

A planet placed in its home sign (Mercury in Gemini or Virgo) or home house (Mercury in the 3rd or 6th house) is a powerful repeating theme. A planet is "at home" in the sign or house of its natural chord, indicating the energy represented is more pure and emphatic.

Cycles

Astrology is a symbolic language composed of three major celestial cycles: the movements of the planets, the movement of the Earth around the Sun which is the basis of the signs of the zodiac, and the movement of the Earth on its axis which is the basis of the astrological houses. The planets and signs are constantly interacting with our Earth along interweaving paths. It is the specific intricate cycles of relationship between Earth, sky, planets and signs that bring astrology's symbolic language into a useful and artful tool for understanding the human psyche.

Solar System: Birth of the Planets

The first astrological cycle is related to the family of planets in our solar system. The Sun is approximately 93 million miles from the Earth, but seems extremely big because it is the closest star to our planet. It takes only eight minutes for the Sun's light to reach Earth traveling at the rate of 186,000 miles per second.

The Sun is, of course, the center of our solar system. The other planets and objects in space, such as the asteroids, orbit around the Sun. It is the Sun's gravity that creates law and order in the universe.

The orbits of the planets around the Sun are cyclic in nature. They range from the 88 days required by the Earth's planetary neighbor, Mercury, to the 248 years required by the very distant orbit of Pluto.

There is a cast of 10 astrological planetary actors:

PLANETS

Planet	Astrological Symbol	Planet	Astrological Symbol
Sun	☉	Jupiter	♃
Moon	☾	Saturn	♄
Mercury	☿	Uranus	♅
Venus	♀	Neptune	♆
Mars	♂	Pluto	♇

These planets are sometimes grouped by astrologers into different categories. Two categories are **personal** and **transpersonal.** The personal planets include Saturn and those "planets" within its orbit: Sun, Moon, Mercury, Venus, Mars and Jupiter. (For convenience, the Sun and Moon are called planets in astrology, even though the Sun is actually a star and the Moon a satellite of Earth.) The trans-personal planets are: Uranus, Neptune and Pluto. The transpersonal planets are sometimes referred to as modern, collective or generational.

Another division is **inferior** and **superior.** Inferior refers to those planets whose orbits are contained inside the Earth's orbit: Mercury and Venus. Superior includes the remaining planets whose orbits extend beyond that of the Earth: Mars, Jupiter, Saturn, Uranus, Neptune and Pluto.

A third classification is **fast moving** and **slow moving.** The fast-moving planets complete their orbits of the Sun in less than two years: Mercury, Venus and Mars. (The Moon is also considered a fast-moving planet.) The slower-moving planets require more than two years to orbit the Sun: Jupiter, Saturn, Uranus, Neptune and Pluto.

Some astrologers divide the planets into three groups:

Personal—Sun, Moon, Mercury, Venus and Mars
Social—Jupiter and Saturn
Transpersonal—Uranus, Neptune and Pluto

In this book, I mainly focus on the first division, **personal and transpersonal,** and demonstrate how this differentiation is rich in astrological symbolism.

Astrology has relationship to the astronomical characteristics of a planet. This was evident in the twelve "chord" chapters. However, it is a planet's cyclic process and movement through sections of the sky and the angular relationship or aspects it forms to other members of its celestial family of "wanderers" which makes the planetary scheme a dynamic astrological cycle full of meaningful symbolism to describe human behavior.

The Ecliptic: Birth of the Signs

The second key cycle is the movement of the Earth around the Sun. However, when observing the Sun from the Earth, it appears that the Sun is moving around the Earth. This "apparent" motion of the Sun on its yearly path through the signs of the zodiac is known as the ecliptic. Since astrology is a language strongly focused on symbolism, the Sun's apparent path is of primary importance.

The Sun's journey covers a 360° circular path through the band of twelve zodiac signs, 30° in each sign. It is the moment of the Sun's symbolic movement along the ecliptic when it crosses the Equator that produces the spring or vernal equinox on approximately March 21 each year (known in astrology as 0° Aries). This is when the Sun apparently is crossing over from the southern hemisphere to the northern hemisphere. The reverse is true six months later as the Sun departs from the northern hemisphere to once again enter the southern hemisphere. The moment the Sun crosses into the southern hemisphere is known as the autumnal equinox, approximately September 22 each year (known in astrology as 0° Libra). The equinoxes are the two moments during the year that day and night have equal length (days are shorter in America when the Sun is in the southern hemisphere and longer when moving through the northern hemisphere).

The two moments of the Sun's apparent movement along the ecliptic when it is farthest from the Equator are known as solstices. The moment of the Sun's symbolic movement along the ecliptic when it is at its most northern point is the summer solstice, the longest day in the year, approximately June 21 each year (known astrologically as 0° Cancer). The moment of the Sun's symbolic movement when it is at its most southern point is the winter solstice, the longest night in the year (known astrologically as 0° Capricorn). The Sun remains stationary at its solstice points in its apparent northern or southern motion (the days grow shorter following the summer solstice and grow longer after the winter solstice).

The zodiac of signs is an imaginary belt that extends approximately 8° of celestial latitude above or below the ecliptic through which the orbits of the Moon and other planets travel except for wayward Pluto which has an extreme inclination of up to 17°. The twelve signs are located upon the ecliptic. It is the symbolic movement of the Sun through a sign at a person's birth that is commonly known as one's Sun sign. The other sign positions of the remaining planets are traced similarly.

The signs in their sequential order are:

SIGNS

Sign	Symbol	Sign	Symbol
1. Aries	♈	7. Libra	♎
2. Taurus	♉	8. Scorpio	♏
3. Gemini	♊	9. Sagittarius	♐
4. Cancer	♋	10. Capricorn	♑
5. Leo	♌	11. Aquarius	♒
6. Virgo	♍	12. Pisces	♓

The signs can also be grouped according to the elements as found in nature:

ELEMENTS

Fire Family	Earth Family	Air Family	Water Family
Aries	Taurus	Gemini	Cancer
Leo	Virgo	Libra	Scorpio
Sagittarius	Capricorn	Aquarius	Pisces

Horizon and Meridian: Birth of the Astrological Houses

The first key celestial cycle was based on the solar system and represented celestial bodies or planets moving through the heavens but as yet having no real relationship to the Earth other than hovering somewhere above or below our horizon. The second key cycle concerns the Earth's motion around the Sun, which triggers the symbolic ecliptic or Sun's apparent path through the zodiac of signs. The third key cycle is a product of the Earth's rotation on its axis. It is this third cycle which completes the process of bringing celestial symbolism to the level of terrestrial affairs.

The Earth completes an entire rotation on its axis every 24 hours. Due to the Earth's rotation, the Sun and the other planets rise and set each day. However, this still does not tell us how celestial symbolism relates in a personal manner to an individual. The missing factor is an individual's birth data—i.e., the birthtime as exactly as possible, geographical location and date of the birth. It is essentially the intersection of a person's date, place and—very importantly—the time of birth with the three primary key celestial cycles that captures the essence of that dynamic astrological cycle: the birth chart.

There are two great circles in the sky that give space a structure relative to an individual's birth data. These two celestial circles alchemize into what are commonly termed "axes" and are known as the horizon and the meridian. The horizon is symbolic of the Sun's ascension and descension while the meridian symbolizes the Sun's culminating qualities. The circle on the left (below) illustrates this great circular cross or intersection of these powerful axes which are perpendicular to each other.

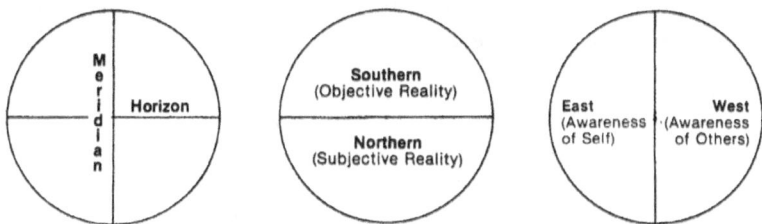

The horizon and meridian each divide the sky into halves or hemispheres. The horizon divides the sky into an upper or southern hemisphere and lower or northern hemisphere as depicted in the circles above. When we fill in the twelve astrological houses, the southern hemisphere contains the six upper houses, 7 through 12. The northern hemisphere contains the six lower houses, 1 through 6.

SOUTHERN HEMISPHERE   NORTHERN HEMISPHERE

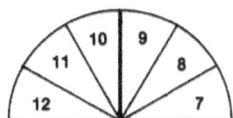 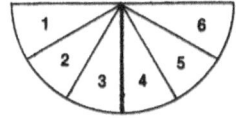

Bernie Ashman

The horizon is an especially important axis at birth as it is upon the eastern horizon that the ecliptic rises. The intersection of the ecliptic with the eastern horizon forms the most powerful symbolic "angle" of human personality in the horoscope known as the Ascendant. The Ascendant, or rising sign, refers to the sign on the ecliptic when it intersects the eastern horizon, the sign which is "rising" at the moment of birth. The Ascendant begins the 1st house of the birth chart and coincides with an individual's time of birth by zodiac sign to the degree and minute. For instance, Marlon Brando's birth chart shows his ascending sign as Sagittarius written in terms of its symbol as ♐. Each sign has 30 degrees and each degree has 60 minutes. The particular degree and minute of Sagittarius that was rising over the horizon for Marlon Brando (born at 11:00 PM, 4/23/24 in Omaha, Nebraska) was three degrees Sagittarius and thirty-nine minutes written as 3° ♐39'. The Ascendant is located to the far left side or eastern section of the horoscope. The Ascendant's opposite angle is the Descendant which is the 7th house of the horoscope or birth chart.

Astrology, Psychology, and Transformation

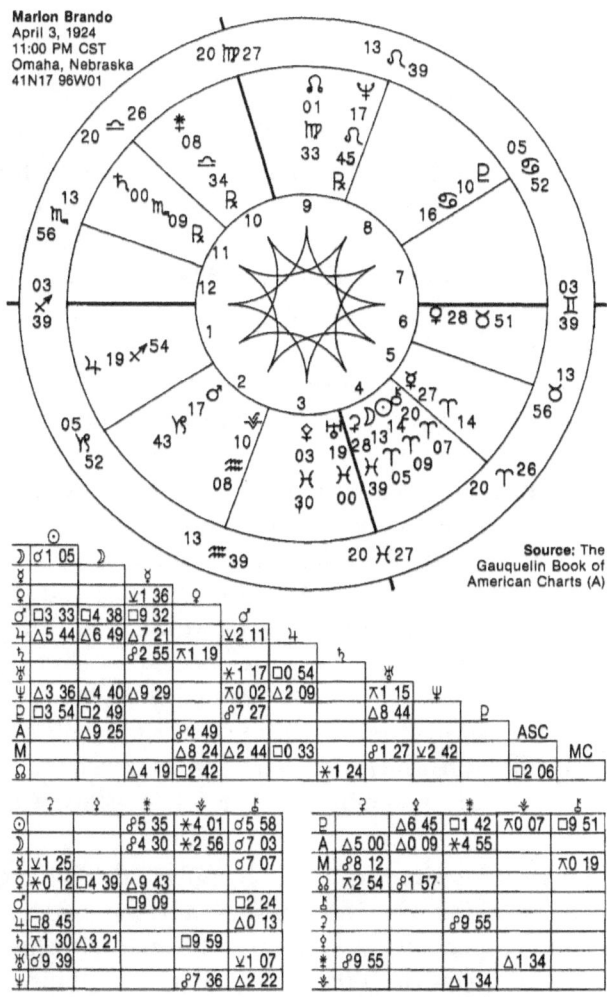

Since Mr. Brando was born one hour before midnight, we would expect to find the Sun in his chart located below the Earth's horizon and notice that it is well below the horizon in the 4th house. The Sun, represented by its symbol, ☉, was moving through the sign of Aries on his birth date, written symbolically to the degree and minute as 14°♈'09'. Planets located in the upper hemisphere reside in the "visible sky," above the horizon, and planets such as Marlon Brando's Sun, located in the lower hemisphere reside in the "invisible sky," below the horizon. The astrological symbolism related to the upper or southern hemisphere and lower or northern hemisphere is discussed in more detail later.

It is the meridian or vertical axis that divides the birth chart into an eastern or western hemisphere (see the circle on page before his chart). The eastern hemisphere or left half of the horoscope includes houses 10 through 3 as you count in a counter-clockwise direction beginning at the 10th house through the 3rd house. The western hemisphere or right half of the horoscope includes houses 4 through 9 as you count in a counter-clockwise direction from the 4th house through the 9th house. The upper meridian intersects the ecliptic at the 10th house or what is commonly termed in astrology as the Midheaven. The Midheaven or 10th house represents the Sun's location at local noon. The lower meridian intersects the ecliptic at the 4th house. This symbolizes the Sun's location at local midnight.

The Earth's rotation on its axis gives the planets the appearance of rising on the eastern horizon (Ascendant); reaching their uppermost or highest culminating point in the sky at the Midheaven or 10th house; beginning their descent and setting at the Descendant or 7th house; and eventually moving as far below the horizon as possible to the point of lowest culmination, the 4th house. Just as the horizon joins the Ascendant (1st house) and Descendant (7th house), it is the meridian that joins the 4th and 10th houses.

Astrology, Psychology, and Transformation

EASTERN HEMISPHERE **WESTERN HEMISPHERE**

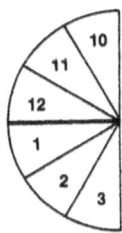 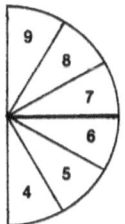

Each major angle begun by the intersection of horizon and meridian symbolically stirs the cosmos into action for an individual at birth. The drawing below represents how each of these angles begins a quadrant or section of three houses that proceed in a counterclockwise direction. The houses represent a division based on a **daily** cycle as the planets pass through them every 24 hours matching the rhythm of the Earth's rotation upon its axis. The signs are based on a yearly cycle due to the Sun's apparent path along the ecliptic that encompasses the zodiac of signs.

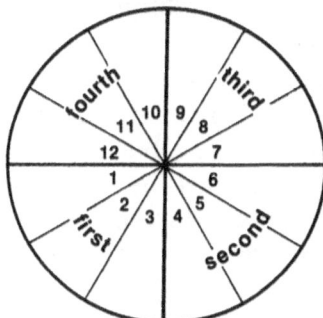

The planets are placed in the houses within a sign by degree and minute of celestial longitude. As was stated earlier, Marlon Brando's Sun as symbolized in his horoscope is written as 14° ♈ 09', representing fourteen degrees of the sign Aries and nine minutes of celestial longitude.

A house, like a planet, is inscribed by the degree and minute of a sign. This is because each pie-shaped section or house has its boundaries defined by its own intersection with the ecliptic. This point of intersection or the beginning of a house is known as its cusp.

Each planet has a cyclic movement within a sign and house. The planets have apparent motion through the signs of the zodiac due to the relationship of Sun and Earth. The houses and signs enjoy a similar ongoing relationship due to the Earth's rotation on its axis. The last cycle discussed, the cycle of houses, is the basic foundation or groundwork for the birth chart. It is the houses that give perspective and depth to the planets and signs. It will be shown in this chapter how to interpret a planet, sign and house combination into a meaningful symbolic language.

The birth chart is a symbolic wheel that pertains to human consciousness. Its true essence is that it is not a crystal ball but rather speaks of a destiny that includes an individual's personal choices and responsibilities. It is the challenge of each person to move in harmony with one's most creative self rather than deny one's own basic nature and self-growth. The birth chart is symbolic of a person's adventure through life as he comes to different crossroads or paths.

To perceive astrology as a workable system, one has to understand astrology's logic. Astrology is not as chaotic as it might appear! It is complex, but not complicated. There are intricate relationships formed by the blending together of the planets, signs and houses which create a meaningful language describing an individual's basic psychological nature and behavior.

I have never been satisfied with the explanations in traditional astrology books that attempt to describe the interrelationship of a planet, sign and house. In traditional astrology, the true relationship of the planet/sign combination is not well substantiated within a psychological framework. Nor are the houses linked to a strong and established foundation that sufficiently explains the commonality and depth of their psychological roots.

My organization of the astrological data into chords is a reflection of my use of astrology as a counseling and learning tool. The reader may find it necessary at various intervals to review the different chord tables when particular symbolisms (i.e., planets, signs and houses) are being discussed. I purposely have attempted to organize each chord table as a "synthesis" of the tones as much as possible so a person could free-associate and perhaps be stimulated by the tables to find their own possible meanings for planet/sign/house combinations. When one begins to get the "feel" of the astrological ingredients, any birth chart being analyzed begins to make sense; a unity within the chart and the repeating themes mentioned earlier can be perceived. It does take a certain amount of **practice** and **patience** in learning some factual material about the planets, signs and houses which can lead to one's growing intuitive grasp of astrology as an artful, symbolic, nondeterministic language that describes human potential.

Celestial Combinations: Planets in Signs and Houses

The planets represent catalysts in the horoscope, and basically each planet symbolizes an individual's directing and comprehension of certain actions. The signs represent an individual's particular manner of choosing to display action, whether dramatically, intellectually, secretly, manipulatively, cautiously, etc. The houses show a focused expression of the principles of planets and signs. The houses remind me of an hourglass, symbolizing our inner awareness that life issues must be faced within a given allotment of time, i.e., a lifetime! The twelve houses present us with symbolic crises in which we must develop psychological attitudes which best express consciousness and structure our existence with the most harmony. These twelve pie-shaped slices of the birth chart represent boundaries of consciousness and, together with the ten planets and twelve signs, form interesting combinations in the birth chart that symbolize expressions of one's consciousness.

It is an entirely different and more complete statement to say that an individual's Sun at birth is placed in the sign of Libra in the 7th house than to say the Sun is in Libra. The houses pinpoint the celestial location in the sky of a planet moving through a sign at an individual's birth and bring it down to reality. We cannot paint a person's unique and complete astrological portrait without his accurate birth time because the houses are derived from the birthtime.

The houses complete an individual's celestial address indicative of his consciousness. It is the symbolism of planet, sign and house combinations that indicates an individual's attitudes, personality traits and urges to embark upon transformative growth as well as tendencies toward choosing paths that deviate from a balanced or productive life. The particular combinations do not in themselves indicate failure, success, happiness, etc. It is the individual's choice as to how to responsibly use the energies represented.

Planets, signs and houses together form a meeting place in the birth chart of three dynamic, symbolic cycles. There are ten such combinations in each person's horoscope of a planet placed in a sign and residing in a particular house. I refer to this symbolic meeting place or intersection of a planet/sign/house as a "**celestial combination.**"

Consider again the example given in Chapter Three: The 1st Chord Planet, Mars, in the 5th Chord sign of Leo. It was stated that the combination of the archetypal themes of this planet and sign could symbolize the directing of actions to assert the self (Mars) with dramatic enthusiasm and self-confidence (Leo). If we say that an individual has Mars and Leo in the 7th house, then we have another variable to consider, the archetypal theme of the 7th house. The individual now has a special focal point for this Mars in Leo (♂ in ♌) principle. The planetary catalyst or tone, Mars, from the 1st Chord, **self-expressive**

embodiment, is in the sign tone, Leo, from the 5th Chord, **self-expressive procreation.** The planet and sign reside in the 7th house, from the 7th Chord, **conceptualization of relationship.** Since the 7th house is an extension of the 7th Chord or one's conceptualization of relationship, this Mars in Leo energy represents a tremendous amount of dramatic energy to balance in one's relationships. Whether one is successful in expressing this particular "celestial combination," Mars/Leo/7th house, is an individual matter.

For example, a person may be assertive without being overaggressive and display a great sense of Leo-like humor in his relationships. This could be expressed as a romantic type of person who enjoys the "chase" in a relationship. However, this could also be symbolic of an individual who is extremely argumentative and competitive in relating to others. He may be very demanding and desire to always be the center of attention. Each individual always has the option to express any celestial combination with many possible positive or negative expressions.

The horoscope of the actor James Dean (shown later in this chapter in the "Character Sketches" section) who died tragically at the age of 24 is shown later. His Sun ☉ was in the 11th Chord sign, Aquarius ♒ in the 5th house at birth. If we knew that James Dean was born on February 8, 1931, and did not know his time of birth, we would at least know his Sun was in the sign of Aquarius. When combining the themes of the Sun and Aquarius we could form phrases such as: a core identity (Sun) that is best expressed through originality and independence (Aquarius); a vitality (Sun) that thrives on knowing his sense of direction and is stimulated by progressive thinking (Aquarius); someone who perhaps gains ego strength (Sun) through expressing an inventive nature (Aquarius).

However, with the knowledge of James Dean's birthtime, his chart indicates that the Sun is not only in the sign of Aquarius but also is placed in the 5th house. His entire celestial combination for the Sun is: Sun/Aquarius/5th house. With the knowledge of the Sun's house location we can further expand our phrases: a core identity (Sun) that is best expressed through originality and independence (Aquarius) in creative enterprises (5th house); a vitality (Sun) that thrives on knowing his sense of direction and is stimulated by progressive thinking (Aquarius) but might also overindulge in excessive and reckless activity to get attention (5th house); someone who perhaps takes great pride (Sun) in his inventive nature (Aquarius) and is very determined to find creative outlets (5th house).

Once again, I strongly encourage the reader to refer back to the chord tables as much as needed while reading this chapter. Each table's set of archetypal themes, synthesis of possible functions for the chord tones, and possible positive and negative expressions may aid one in interpreting a planet/sign/house combination in their own chart or that of someone else. It is good to begin practice developing phrases that are positive in nature as well as to be aware of the possible negative expressions. This may feel awkward in the beginning but eventually becomes smoother. The themes of each symbolism build upon the other. Most of all, do not panic if you begin to feel overwhelmed by too many possibilities! When one begins to gain an understanding of how to interpret the "parts" of the chart and to perceive the repeating themes, it leads to a natural ability to synthesize the entire chart.

Section Three of this chapter, the "Character Sketches" section, considers the celestial combinations of an individual's Sun and Moon, and other planets (i.e., their placements within a sign and house), plus the Ascendant (or sign placed on the 1st house cusp). Surveying the Sun, Moon and Ascendant alone allows one to gain a more immediate perspective of the chart. However, I want to caution that very often a key repeating theme in a chart is independent of the Sun, Moon and Ascendant placements. Too many astrology books overemphasize the Sun, Moon and Ascendant to the exclusion of discussing the importance of repeating themes. I would go so far as to say that in most charts that I have done there has been at least one key theme unrelated to the Sun, Moon or Ascendant. If this theme was not considered when interpreting the individual's chart, I would have neglected a major portion of the person's identity.

It can be tempting to try to learn a "cookbook" version of interpretation. Most "cookbook" methods of interpretation give very rigid meanings for planets in signs or houses. Also, "cookbooks" can be filled with seeming contradictions. The rigidity can take the form of saying that Mars in Leo "always" means you are an egomaniac or Mars in the 7th house indicates you will be attracted to aggressive partners, etc. Rather than symbols we are given absolute definitions. The entire flavor attempts to label a person as good or bad, one extreme or the other. This is not good astrology! Where are the options and potential to change a behavior pattern? The difficulties and obstacles indicated in a birth chart do not always represent failing situations. As a matter of fact, it is the strongly challenging situations often indicated by stressful aspects between planets that may bring us to more actively strive to meet our goals.

Thus, it is important to remember that each celestial combination in the birth chart is not a fated or confining entity. The symbolism connotes **issues** that one may encounter in life but not the **final outcome**. A particular planet/sign/house combination in the chart will definitely indicate energy patterns wanting to gain a more conscious awareness in a person's life. It is the individual who must take the responsibility for positive and negative actions—not the planets, signs or houses!

Generally, the personal planets symbolize an individual's primary awareness and have easier access to the conscious mind. The transpersonal planets, Uranus, Neptune and Pluto, symbolize unconscious energies and, due to their collective natures and generational significance, offer more insight on an individual basis in the birth chart when considered by house position only. Thus when discussed in this and the following chapter, the house positions for these three outer planets will be more emphasized than their occupied signs.

Bernie Ashman

Planetary Aspects

The previous section concerned interpreting three astrological factors found in combination. Planetary aspects are an extension of the primary cycles (planets, signs and houses) described earlier. A planetary aspect is a particular angular distance by degrees between planets in an individual's horoscope. An aspect symbolizes different levels of psychological intensity in the combined use of these planetary themes. Whereas an individual planet is a symbolic catalyst for particular chord functions, an aspect joins the functions of two or more planetary tones of different chords into a shared expression. Certain aspects, such as the conjunction, square, quincunx and opposition, represent intensified expression of the particular planetary energies involved, symbolizing a more difficult or challenging test for an individual to express their combined chord functions harmoniously and constructively. The softer or less intense aspects, such as the sextile, semisextile and trine, suggest a more conducive mixing or a natural blending of different chord expressions in an individual's life.

Each aspect, like the planets and signs, can be written in terms of its astrological symbol:

ASPECTS

Aspect	Symbol	Angular Distance
Conjunction	☌	0°
Semisextile	⚺	30°
Sextile	✶	60°
Square	□	90°
Trine	△	120°
Quincunx (Inconjunction)	⚻	150°
Opposition	☍	180°

The angular distance column represents the distance separating one planet from another. The aspects listed above are considered key symbolic angles in the horoscope. Marlon Brando's horoscope displays what is known as an aspect grid located just under the circle. This is one-way astrologers commonly list the important aspects in a hand-drawn chart. If two planets are forming an important angular relationship or aspect, the row of intersecting boxes between the planets will indicate this. Note that the astrological symbols above are found in various numbers in Brando's chart. Each birth chart will contain a varying number of these aspects.

If this concept of planets forming an angular relationship to each other is confusing to the reader, try not to become overly alarmed or frustrated! If you have seen a New Moon, you have visually witnessed the conjunction aspect as the Sun and Moon are both in the same sign. When a New Moon is exact each month, the Sun and Moon occupy the same degree of a zodiac sign; no angular distance separates them. If you have seen a Full Moon, then you have witnessed an opposition aspect formed by the Sun and Moon in the sky. In other words, the Sun and Moon occupy opposite signs of the zodiac. When the Full Moon is exact, the Sun and Moon have formed a 180° angle sitting directly across from each other in the sky.

Each planet in the horoscope forms an angular relationship to each of the other planets. However, there are seven particular angular distances that are very important in terms of astrological symbolism. Once again, the aspects are listed:

Aspect	Symbol	Angular Distance	Suggested ORB	Chord Root
Conjunction	☌	0°	8°	1st
Semisextile	⚺	30°	1°	2nd & 12th
Sextile	⚹	60°	5°	3rd & 11th
Square	□	90°	8°	4th & 10th
Trine	△	120°	5°	5th & 9th
Quincunx	⚻	150°	3°	6th & 8th
Opposition	☍	180°	8°	7th

A column has been added, **"Suggested Orb."** An **orb** is simply the distance an aspect can be from being exact but still be considered meaningful. For instance, suppose an individual has the Sun ☉ in Scorpio ♏ at 10°. Perhaps this same individual has Mars in Aquarius ♒ at 10°. This totals an exact 90° distance or three full signs of distance separating the Sun and Mars. However, if Mars was located at 15° Aquarius, it would still be in a square aspect to the Sun due to the 8° allowable orb for a square. With practice, picking out aspects can become as easy as reading the time on a clock. It is important to learn the signs in order from the 1st sign, Aries, to the 12th sign, Pisces. The reason for this is that since there are 30° in each sign, and planets are located in signs, it makes counting a lot easier when determining if two planets are within the orb of an important aspect in either a clockwise or counter-clockwise direction. It may take time to get familiar with the idea of counting in both a clockwise and counter-clockwise direction from a planet to see if it is forming any aspects.

Conjunctions are easy to find in a chart because the planets will usually be placed in the same signs. Semisextiles are also rather easy to find because it only requires counting the distance of one sign or 30° from a planet. Simply look to the adjacent signs in a clockwise or counter-clockwise direction to see if a planet is in either sign and within a 1° orb. For instance, a planet located at 4° Taurus could form a semisextile aspect to another planet located at 3° to 5° Gemini (counter-clockwise) and 3° to 5° Aries (clockwise).

Oppositions are based on 180° or six signs and are not too difficult to perceive if you learn each sign's opposite sign: Aries/Libra, Taurus/Scorpio, Gemini/Sagittarius, Cancer/Capricorn, Leo/Aquarius, and Virgo/Pisces. Planets forming an opposition to each other will be placed in signs of like quality (cardinal, fixed or mutable).

Trines are based on an angular distance of 120° or four signs. It helps to remember that trines are formed by planets placed in signs of like elements. The reader might want to review the chord chapters to familiarize himself with the fire, earth, air and water signs.

Sextiles are based on 60° or two signs and are also related by elements. Fire sextiles air and water sextiles earth.

The important thing to remember is that a fire sign also has one air sign as its opposite, and a water sign has an earth sign as its opposite. A sign sextiles the two signs of the same element as of the opposing sign. In other words, the fire sign Aries has the air sign Libra as its opposite. The remaining two fire signs, Leo and Sagittarius, sextile Libra. The remaining two air signs, Gemini and Aquarius, sextile Aries.

Squares are based on an angular distance of 90° or three signs and are formed by planets in signs of like quality (cardinal, fixed and mutable). However, there are four signs in each quality. One sign will be the opposite and the other two the squares. For instance, the mutable signs are Gemini, Virgo, Sagittarius and Pisces. Gemini and Sagittarius oppose each other. Virgo and Pisces square Gemini and square Sagittarius.

Quincunxes are based on an angular distance of 150° or five signs. It is best to simply count five signs in both a clockwise and counter-clockwise direction from a planet to see if there are any of these aspects (or, if you know the polarities, the quincunxes are the signs adjacent to the opposing sign).

I find the easiest method to determine which planets are forming an aspect to each other is to proceed with a sense of order. The aspect grid (See in the "Character Sketches" section), shown below the chart of Diane Keaton, begins with the Sun ☉ at the top and to the far right. This is the Sun's row. Simply go down the Sun's row and write in the aspect symbol if the Sun forms any aspects to other planets. Notice the first symbol you find as you proceed down the vertical row is the conjunction, written as ☌. The Sun in Diane Keaton's chart is located fourteen degrees of Capricorn and thirty-one minutes in the 2nd house. This is written symbolically as: ☉ 14 ♑ 31. Venus ♀ is located at 8° of Capricorn and one minute written as: ♀ 8 ♑ 1. Since an orb of approximately 6° of angular distance separates the Sun and Venus, this is a conjunction. There was no aspect formed by the Sun to the Moon or Mercury. Continue down each vertical row in the same manner. The Moon's row ☽ is followed by Mercury ☿ etc.

I find it helpful to list the aspects according to those formed by personal planets to personal planets and a second group which is personal to transpersonal. I further subdivide each of these groupings into "soft" aspects (semisextile, sextile and trine) and "hard" aspects (conjunction, square, quincunx and opposition). I do **not** view the "soft" aspects as "good" and the "hard" aspects as "bad." The softer aspects may lack the psychological intensity symbolized by the hard aspects (in the "Character Sketch" section, I list the aspects in this manner).

The "hard" or more intensity-associated aspects have been assigned wider orbs than the "soft" aspects due to their higher voltage. The orbs suggested can be stretched a bit in some case if a planet is highly accentuated in a chart. Aspects formed by the Sun, Moon and Ascendant will at times be significant when the orb is considerably wider than suggested. Aspects **closest to exact** are of **extreme importance** as they often symbolize an individual's favorite modes of self-expression or habitual behavior patterns whether the aspect is "soft" or "hard."

Complex Aspects: Gestalt Aspect Configurations

We now come to a category of special aspects that break some of the rules previously mentioned, especially the orbs allowed for aspects between planets. The relationship of two planets is now expanded to a relationship of three or more planets to each other. The four complex aspects being discussed in this section are what I consider to be the most useful of the complex aspects though the list could be expanded. I find the T-square, grand trine, yod and grand cross offer the most insight into a birth chart of these gestalt-like configurations.

These particular aspects not only can transcend normal orb allowances but also stretch another limit. It has been stated earlier that aspects formed by transpersonal planets to each other are not of great importance due to their generational significance. However, it will be seen that in these complex aspect configurations, this is not the fact. When a personal planet combines with two transpersonal planets as in the T-square, grand trine, yod or grand cross, the relationship of each transpersonal planet involved in the aspect grows in importance. The key or underlying symbolism is often found to be connected to a personal planet if involved with transpersonal planets in a complex aspect. The personal planet can represent an individual's ability or strength to bring the more unconscious energies indicated by the transpersonal planets into conscious awareness. So it is the actual aspects within a complex aspect formed by a personal planet to the transpersonal planets that can indicate a major network within a person's consciousness.

I feel that if one is not to some degree aware of the following four aspect configurations, he is apt to miss a most valuable horoscope theme. I refer to this group of aspects as Gestalt Aspect Configurations as they indicate an individual's most basic expression of consciousness and allow an astrologer to quickly grasp the wholeness of the individual. Not every horoscope contains these configurations, especially the grand cross which is rather rare to find. The other mentioned complex aspects do appear with more regularity.

An astrologer will at times need to exercise judgment to ascertain if particular planets in a chart, though wide in orb, could still function as part of a complex aspect configuration.

T-SQUARE
Nickname: "Tornado"
Aspects Included: One opposition; two squares
Abbreviation: "T-□"
Chord Roots: 7th Chord (opposition); 4th and 10th Chords (square) Identifier: A T-square is formed by three planets in square aspect to each other; the planets will usually occupy signs of the same quality.

"**Natural" T-squares**: A natural cardinal T-□ is formed by planets in the cardinal signs (Aries, Cancer, Libra, Capricorn) and in the angular houses (1,4,7,10); a natural fixed T-□ is formed by planets in the fixed signs (Taurus, Leo, Scorpio, Aquarius) and in the succedent houses (2, 5, 8, 11); a natural mutable T-□ is formed by planets in mutable signs (Gemini, Virgo, Sagittarius, Pisces) and in the cadent houses (3, 6, 9, 12).

The T-square is a complex aspect or Gestalt Aspect Configuration involving three planets squaring each other. Two of the planets are in opposition to each other or forming a 180° angle and a third planet squares or forms a 90° angle to each of the opposition planets. The configuration forms a "**T**."

Complex aspects can be more easily interpreted if one first analyzes the parts that compose the total aspect. In the T-square there are two squares and one opposition. Before trying to grasp the "whole," first see which planets are involved. Secondly, take a look at which planets are forming the opposition; this highlights the issue of balance in the chart. Thirdly, observe the planet forming the square to each opposition planet as this is the "trigger" planet or key catalyst in the aspect. It denotes the heightened tension between the conflicting pulls represented by the opposition (the opposition is discussed in the 7th Chord and the square is discussed in the 4th and 10th Chords).

The T-square that occurs in James Dean's chart is illustrated later in the chapter. The "T" becomes apparent when lines are drawn between the three planets forming the T-square. Notice the close opposition formed by 10th house, Pluto ♇ to the 4th house, Saturn ♄. The orb of this opposition is less than 1°. Uranus which is placed in the 7th house, forms the top of the "T" and cuts powerfully across the opposition with its high voltage symbolism squaring Pluto and Saturn. Even though the orb from the square is a bit wide, this T-square was quite vividly a trademark of James Dean's rebellious and wild Uranian spirit and even more so since this is a "natural" T-square occurring in cardinal signs and angular houses!

Once again, the planet at the top of the T-square, the "trigger," is a dynamic catalyst, symbolizing a tremendous reservoir of potential energy and often requires a lot of channeling to get constructive results. This is very true when the "trigger" is an outer planet (including Saturn) as this indicates an immense desire to strive for a transpersonal type of self-expression that can reach compulsive proportions. The consequences of one's actions can sometimes be very problematic as well as significant to one's benefit for his culture and self.

The empty house opposite the "trigger" planet is said in many astrology books to symbolize the focal point as to how an individual might choose to express this dynamic energy. However, this can be quite misleading. A person should never deny or repress any sides of the T-square and hope to resolve the tension by escaping into the symbolism of the empty house. A balanced self-expression for each side of the T-square is required in the form of healthy and productive outlets.

In the horoscope of James Dean, the empty house situated directly across from the "trigger" planet, Uranus, is the 1st house, a very important house symbolism related to a person's self-image. This would seem to indicate that James Dean was very much in search of a self-concept and in its finest essence was in search of himself. Unfortunately, a reckless and compulsive abandonment of the self was his constant enemy! However, perhaps if he had dealt with the issues surrounding his other sides of the T-square, he could have been more accepting of himself and others. Dean had definite issues with his parents and never really dealt with his painful childhood (Pluto/Saturn opposition). His chart will be discussed in more detail in the "Character Sketches" section.

My nickname for this complex aspect is "**Tornado**" as it is symbolic of energy that can manifest at various intervals in an individual's life without much notice. When a T-square is activated for a very undisciplined individual, he may feel as if his life has become a series of tornadoes! The particular planets forming this aspect will indicate for each individual what types of situations or experiences will stimulate this dynamic and often exhilarating energy into existence. When the house placed across from the "trigger" planet is activated, an individual may feel like a whirlpool of conscious thought is suddenly being directed to making decisions related to the particular house. Sometimes a planet may be placed in this house but not a part of the T-square as will be seen in the chart of George Lucas.

The T-square can be typical of a person with endless amounts of energy to accomplish goals. It also can symbolize leadership, courage and self-starting. However, it is sometimes difficult for a person to deal with the unpredictable energy patterns, peaks and valleys that a T-square can symbolize. Regulating and channeling the energy is a big challenge.

The key aid in identifying a T-square is to see if three planets occupy signs of the same quality and then check the orbs. I often allow a wider orb for the Sun and Moon. Planets in a particular sign quality further differentiate the characteristics of a T-square. For instance, a cardinal T-square can emphasize leadership and an action-oriented individual who learns through direct experience. A fixed T-square could indicate a person has amazing stamina and a strong will. He is likely to change only on his own terms. The fixed individual will resist changes which conflict with his own desires. A mutable T-square can accentuate eclectic reasoning powers and an adaptable personality as well as indecision (due to trying to choose between many possibilities). These individuals may need to realize that there is more than one solution to a problem. They usually enjoy a life filled with multiple paths, many options and much learning.

An excellent book on the T-square is Tracy Marks' *How to Handle Your T-Square*. Another book containing excellent material about the T-square is Bill Tierney's *Dynamics of Aspect Analysis: New Perceptions in Astrology*.

GRAND TRINE

Nickname: "Absolute Truth"

Aspects Included: Three trines

Abbreviation: Grand-△

Chord Roots: 5th and 9th Chords (Trine)

Identifier: A grand trine is formed by three planets in trine aspect to each other; the planets will usually occupy signs of the same element.

"Natural" grand trines: are formed by planets in the same elemental family by sign and by house. In other words, if an individual has a grand trine formed by three planets in fire signs and also placed in the fire houses (1st, 5th, 9th), he has a "natural" grand trine. These are in my opinion the most powerful of grand trines.

The horoscope of Diane Keaton contains a "natural" grand trine in air signs and air houses. The three planets trining each other are: Moon ☽, Uranus ♅ and Neptune ♆. Diane Keaton's entire horoscope is shown and will be discussed in the "Character Sketches" section.

The element of the grand trine is important as it indicates the particular energy attunement of an individual's self-expression. For instance, an individual with a fire grand trine thrives on enthusiasm and a vivacious spirit in his self-expression. This can also symbolize a self 'Centered and highly opinionated individual with individualistic tastes. A person with an air grand trine like Diane Keaton is often very communication oriented and very active socially. Intellectual pursuits can be an important means of self-expression and exercising the art of communication. There may be minds of genius as well as a delicate nervous system. These folks sometimes border on being eccentrics and have exceptional wit. An individual with an earth grand trine may be very practical and security oriented in his life perspective. Ownership and status are important in his self-expression. A person with a water grand trine is often very emotionally sensitive in self-expression. Dependency needs can be a major concern. Water grand trine people sometimes possess a highly refined intuitive awareness.

The major pitfalls of the grand trine appear to be an overuse of the energy associated with the element of the trine. Grand trine individuals sometimes do try to be completely self-reliant or very private about themselves. Fire can believe it has the best way of doing anything and indulge in dogmatism. Fire grand trine people can exhibit an intense enthusiasm about life, but lack a sense of limits. Air can intellectualize others to death as a means of keeping people at a distance or project a mental superiority and aloofness that irritates people. Earth can become so good at managing practical duties and responsibility that projecting "bossy" attitudes alienates others. There can also be a sense of "I can build my own castle, and I do not need anybody else." Water can fall victim to emotional privacy making it difficult for other people to understand them. These can be very lucky people in that it does seem at times grand trine people attract what they need through optimism.

YOD

Nickname: "Tales of Power"

Aspects Included: Two quincunxes; one sextile

Chord Roots: 3rd and 11th Chords (sextile); 6th and 8th Chords (quincunx)

Identifier: A yod is formed by two planets involved in a sextile with a third planet quincunx both of these planets.

The yod, also known as the double quincunx or Finger of God, is composed of two planets sextiling each other with a third planet forming a quincunx or 150° angle to each of the planets involved in the sextile. The planet forming the quincunx with the two planets in the sextile aspect is what I consider to be to be the "trigger" and greatest focalization of energy in this aspect. The "trigger" planet is sometimes a key to transformative growth as well as an energy that can symbolize a sense of frustration in an individual. The challenge indicated by this "trigger" planet is that its element and quality are in sharp contrast to that of the sextiling planets. Sometimes a person feels powerless and appears to be working against himself. This particular aspect indicates a person is trying to combine very different drives in the nature.

The yod often operates more on a subconscious level than the previously mentioned complex aspects. Its origins are very psychological, and the yod appears to function even more subconsciously if an outer planet is the "trigger," especially if the planet is Pluto, highlighting a quest for expressing personal power. Compulsive urges can be a source of a nagging internal frustration if a person has difficulty balancing a yod energy.

Diane Keaton's horoscope exhibits a yod aspect as well as the previously mentioned T-square. The "trigger" planet is the 2nd house Sun in Capricorn. Notice that Keaton's Sun is almost exactly 150° from Uranus placed in the 7th house. The Sun is also quincunx Pluto as well with an orb of just over 3°. The yod takes the form of a "Y." This yod will be further discussed in the "Character Sketches" section.

The yod can symbolize an individual who has many deep and varied life experiences. These individuals often cannot settle for a lack of direction and must always be paving the way for the future. The person tends to alternate from one end of the yod to the other, attempting to balance needs that seem incompatible. The feeling can be disrupting as the individual experiences life as out of sync. A person may unconsciously attract events that create new circumstances and abrupt shifts until he learns to find a place for both expressions. The standards set by individuals with a yod in their chart can be extremely high for self and others. These people may enjoy researching and investigating life's mysteries and are often busy developing a new psychological awareness of themselves and others.

The problems with expressing the yod configuration in a balanced manner often can be traced back to an individual's perfectionistic attitudes and compulsive drives. The "trigger" planet often represents the key issues that must be faced or confronted to alleviate compulsive instincts and help an individual achieve a balanced sense of power.

GRAND CROSS
Nickname: "Against All Odds"
Aspects Included: Two oppositions and four squares
Abbreviation: grand-☒
Chord Roots: 7th (oppositions); 4th and 10th (squares)
Identifier: A grand cross is formed by four planets involving two oppositions and four squares; the planets will usually occupy signs of the same quality.

"Natural" grand cross: A "natural" cardinal grand cross is formed by planets in the cardinal signs and in the angular houses; a "natural" fixed grand cross is formed by planets in the fixed signs and in the succedent houses; a "natural" mutable grand cross is formed by planets in mutable signs and in the cadent houses.

The grand cross, also known as the grand square, is the first gestalt configuration being discussed which is composed of four planets. This is a very powerful aspect involving four squares that are interrelated.

The grand square is rarer than the three previous complex aspects. It is very common to find two oppositions in a chart and even four squares. However, it is somewhat rare to find four planets spaced 90° apart from each other, which is essentially two oppositions cutting across each other and forming four right angles.

The chart following is of H. R. Haldeman who was Chief of Staff to President Nixon and convicted in 1976 for illegal activities during the Watergate Scandal. His chart contains a "natural" grand cross in fixed signs and succedent houses as depicted by the lines drawn between the two oppositions involved in this complex aspect: 5th house Jupiter (♃) opposes 11th house Neptune (♆) and 8th house Mars (♂) opposes both Mercury (☿) and Saturn (♄) that are conjunct in the 2nd house.

Astrology, Psychology, and Transformation

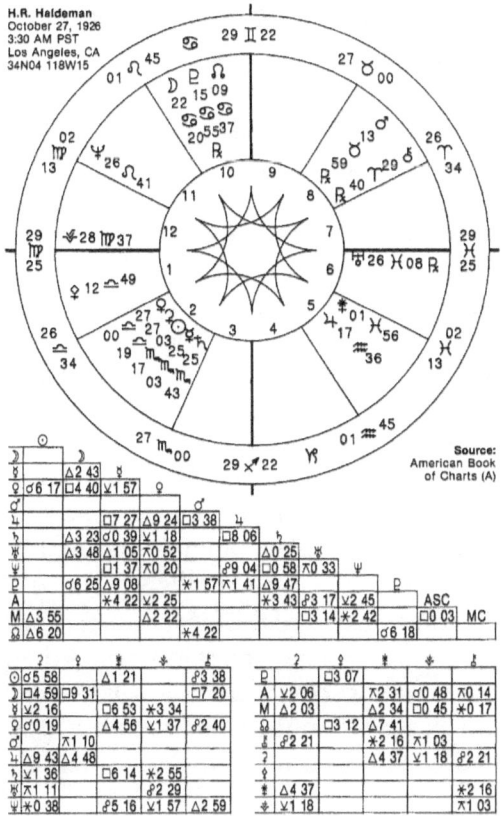

The fixed grand cross can be especially problematic and symbolic of self-destructive behavior if an individual becomes locked into a course of action that cannot lead to anything but harmful consequences. The fixed grand cross can indicate an individual's stubborn resistance to change of life direction. The main theme in the fixed grand cross as in the fixed T-square is that the individual will make choices on his own terms. He refused to be "forced" which is usually what brings a resistance to change. The fixed grand cross can concern power issues, and Mr. Haldeman wrote a book in 1978 entitled: *The Ends of Power*.

The grand cross often will have a wider than normal orb allowed for an opposition or a square. Perhaps it is because the grand cross symbolizes an aspect of such dynamic and raw power that an individual possesses the willpower to "stretch" and bring this aspect into existence for himself.

This can be a very creative energy. Grand cross individuals must often be careful to find adequate outlets in life and to focus this energy. Mutable grand cross individuals often are juggling multiple options in life. The danger here is scattering one's energy. People dealing with mutable crosses often must choose from many options, and learning to discriminate which choices are appropriate for the present is important. They may need to learn to focus their energies. Cardinal grand cross individuals are often too busy balancing issues to enjoy the present. There is a tension felt concerning how to use their time and energy for self, home, relationships and career. They can grow discontent when feeling one side of the life is being sacrificed for another. Fixed grand cross individuals are often doing anything they can to maintain their way of operating in life.

I believe that one must keep these four aspect configurations in perspective. They are not any more important than any other astrological factor being considered. I would advise against using the complex aspect configurations to find easy answers. When interpreting a chart generally, a particular planet of the configuration being considered will be especially important if involved in **many or key repeating chart themes.** (The "natural" grand crosses, T-squares and grand trines are examples of repeating themes where the houses repeat the theme of the signs.)

Section Two: Spices

The following items have been termed "spices" because they help enrich one's interpretation of a birth chart. A good cook does not need to drown or hide the flavor of a dish in spices but does enhance the flavor. A good interpreter of a birth chart does not overly dwell on the spices. However, it is important to at least be knowledgeable of the following items as they can greatly add depth and insight into one's interpretation skills. The spices are: planetary clusters, angular houses, planetary rulerships, ruler of the Ascendant, nodes of the Moon, hemispheres, singletons, planetary retrogradation, intercepted signs and the asteroids.

I am also cautioning the reader in the spice section to remember the principle of repeating themes. Usually, unless an astrological theme repeats itself in different ways in the chart, I doubt it is of central importance in the life of the individual.

There are numerous exceptions to the following general descriptions of the spices. One must be careful not to be led astray by the detailed or isolated characteristics of a chart. A theme that is central in the self-expression of the individual and that is a force on the conscious or unconscious level will repeat itself firmly in the chart.

Stellia

This is usually an important spice if found in a chart. A stellium is a cluster or group of three or more planets placed in the same sign and even more accentuated if in the same house also. A stellium is a readily visible example of a repeating theme. The stellium symbolizes a tremendous focus of energy through a particular sign or house. George Lucas has a dramatic stellium surrounding his Taurean Ascendant involving planets placed in the 12th and 1st houses. Mercury and Venus (ruler of Ascendant) are located in the 12th house and placed in the sign Taurus, and his Taurus Sun is placed in the 1st house. This represents a tremendous focus of himself through the fixed sign of Taurus—raw determination.

Sometimes when a transpersonal planet is part of a stellium with personal planets, an individual may display a special capacity to express the transpersonal energy into a unique and personal expression. The individual might even gain access into the sign and element of the transpersonal planet.

Bernie Ashman

Planets in Angular Houses

This is a hot spice! Do not forget where this is in your spice cabinet. Planets in angular houses symbolize energies that want to jump out. They indicate energy sources which challenge individuals to use them with care. Aspects formed by angular planets to other planets or the Ascendant or Midheaven can indicate dynamic energy expressions indeed! Planets located near the 1st, 7th and 10th house angles seem to be the most active. However, though the 4th house is a very inward water house, its angular emphasis can indicate a planet that is a prominent energy expression for a person.

SIGN RULERSHIPS: RELATIONSHIP TO THE HOUSES OF THE BIRTH CHART

This is an important spice and I almost hesitate to call this a spice! I would be lost in interpreting and communicating a chart without comprehending planetary ruler ships. Every practicing astrologer knows the planets that rule the signs as well as his own name. However, I have observed that many students of astrology and even some practicing astrologers have difficulty making the connection of the planets in a horoscope with the corresponding sign placed on the cusps of the houses.

This chapter began with a brief description of the planet placed in a sign and house. This was termed a "Celestial Combination." I would call such combinations, including the Ascendant, the primary impacting energies symbolized in a chart. However, there are secondary impact points that can further refine one's interpretation of a chart. The primary impact points of "Celestial Combinations" can be taken one step further. The next step is to find the house that a particular planet rules or its corresponding sign tone placed on a house cusp.

For instance, look at the horoscope of actress Diane Keaton in "Character Sketches." Notice that the sign of the 7th house cusp is Taurus (♉). Since there is a planet placed in her 7th house, Uranus, this will be the primary impact point of this house. A 7th house Uranus can indicate a need for exciting stimulation in her relationships. The ruler of the 7th house sign, Taurus, is of course Venus. Therefore, Venus can be considered to be a secondary point of symbolic impact. Since Venus is placed in the 2nd house, self-esteem is a "possible" issue surrounding her relationships. Perhaps a person's values will be important to her. A Venus-in-Capricorn individual is sometimes seeking status through a career. When the planets are traced back to the houses that contain the signs they rule, many fine details can be discovered. These secondary impact points are most useful in interpreting houses that have no planets placed in them as a primary impact point. The so-called "empty" house may be a powerhouse in disguise.

The planetary rulerships of the signs are being listed here so the reader can refer quickly if needed. The twelve chord chapters describe the planet, sign and house tones that correspond to each other. I have listed the previous ruler of a sign where applicable in parenthesis. I find it useful to keep dual rulerships of signs in mind when trying to determine if a planet is comfortably placed in a sign. For instance, although Mars is no longer considered to be the primary ruler of Scorpio, this planet still has a natural affinity for Scorpio themes. Even if Mars is not placed in Scorpio but aspecting a planet placed in Scorpio, I sometimes extend the orb because Mars has a strong previous 8th Chord association. This same principle can be applied to other signs of dual rulerships as well.

Rulerships are listed by the numerical order of the 12 chords:

RULERSHIPS

Sign	Planet	Sign	Planet
Aries	Mars	Libra	Venus
Taurus	Venus	Scorpio	Pluto (Mars)
Gemini	Mercury	Sagittarius	Jupiter
Leo	Sun	Aquarius	Uranus (Saturn)
Virgo	Mercury	Pisces	Neptune (Jupiter)

RULER OF ASCENDANT

This can be a very important spice. The planet that "naturally" rules the sign on the Ascendant is what I consider in many cases to be the most important planetary ruler in a chart. This is the most meaningful of the secondary impact points and traditionally was referred to as the "ruler of the chart."

I find it helpful to immediately locate this planet in a chart and see which aspects it is forming to other planets or to the Ascendant itself. Aspects formed by this planet that are exact or close to exact can be very precious energy expressions for a person.

The element of this "ruling" planet by sign and sometimes even house is important to weigh in interpreting a chart. If the ascending sign is transpersonal, then the ruling planet is transpersonal. In this case I would be more concerned with the house placement of the ruling planet rather than the sign. Can you determine the ruler of Diane Keaton's Ascendant? In which house is it residing? The ruler of her Scorpio Ascendant is Pluto, located in the 9th house.

The ruling planet of the Ascendant helps refine the interpretation of the Ascendant's symbolism as it distinctively describes how one might express his self-image. Sometimes I think of the ruling planet as traveling abroad through foreign territory of a different house of the chart but always reporting back to its true home, its home sign. The point of primary symbolic impact for Pluto in Diane Keaton's chart is the 9th house. However, Pluto can be traced to its secondary symbolic impact point, her Scorpio Ascendant. In other words, Diane Keaton's Scorpio intensity symbolized by her Ascendant can be channeled through the 9th house Ascendant ruler, Pluto. It is as though if Pluto wanted to go "home," it would be to the Ascendant in Keaton's chart. The 9th house in this chart is Pluto's "home away from home," but its heart is with the Scorpio Ascendant. This same principle can be applied to each planet in a horoscope. It can take countless chart experiences before one truly understands the inner workings of astrology's symbolism.

Relaxing into the interpretation of a chart can require patience. This is why I often feel that the more ways a person understands to find an entrance into a chart, the easier it is to find one main theme that illuminates the remaining themes.

Singletons

This spice can be a very hot item. A singleton is a planet that sits alone in a hemisphere while the other nine planets are located in the opposing hemisphere. Sigmund Freud's chart offers a good example of the singleton. Notice Mars ♂ sitting alone in the 11th house. It is isolated in the eastern hemisphere.

A singleton can magnify the presence of the house and sign it occupies as it is a planet possibly symbolizing a tremendous energy potential. In the 11th Chord chapter, the 11th house was said to indicate one's degree of experimentation to establish and maintain individuality. The founder of psychoanalysis asserted himself with a ferocious amount of Martian energy to bring in a new way of exploring the psyche. This singleton in Freud's chart is a significant theme because his Sun forms a conjunction aspect with the 11th Chord Uranus in the 7th house. Singleton Mars in the 11th house signifies a future orientation alone and coupled with the Sun-Uranus conjunction is extremely indicative of Freud's determination to usher in a new wave of psychology even if it shocked his peers and the status quo!

This brings in the question as to whether the singleton is tied to other key chart themes. In Freud's chart, the repeating emphasis on the 11th Chord is important. Thus, the singleton in his chart takes on more importance. Unless a singleton is part of a key repeating theme or heavily aspected, it will not be of central importance to the overall chart delineation.

Bernie Ashman

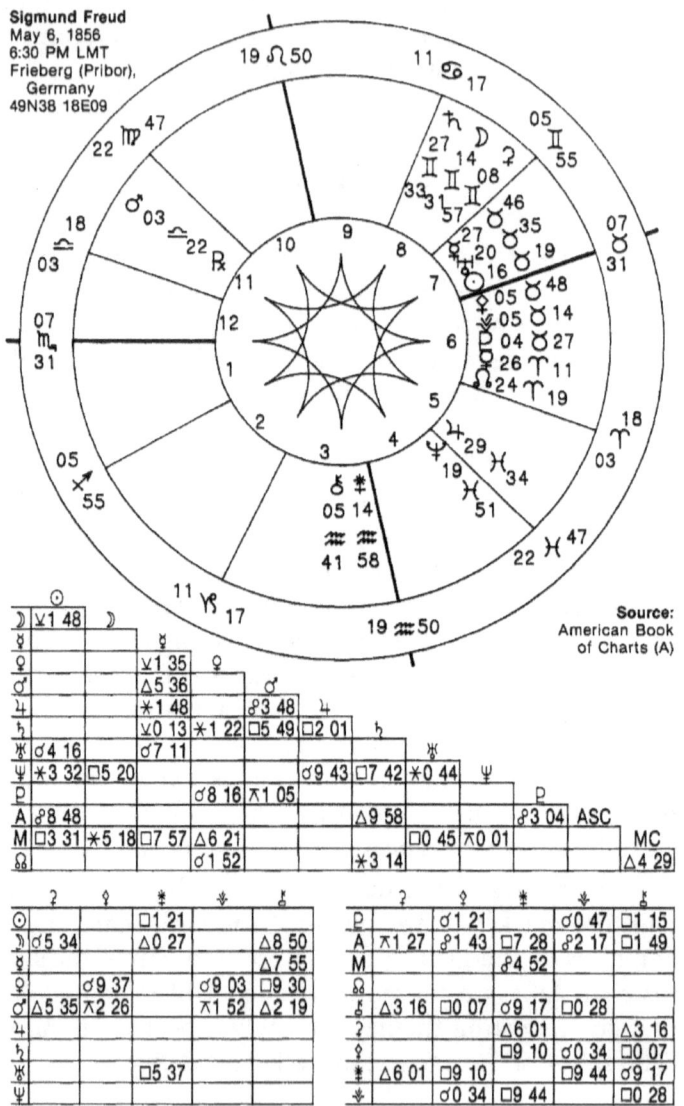

Astrology, Psychology, and Transformation

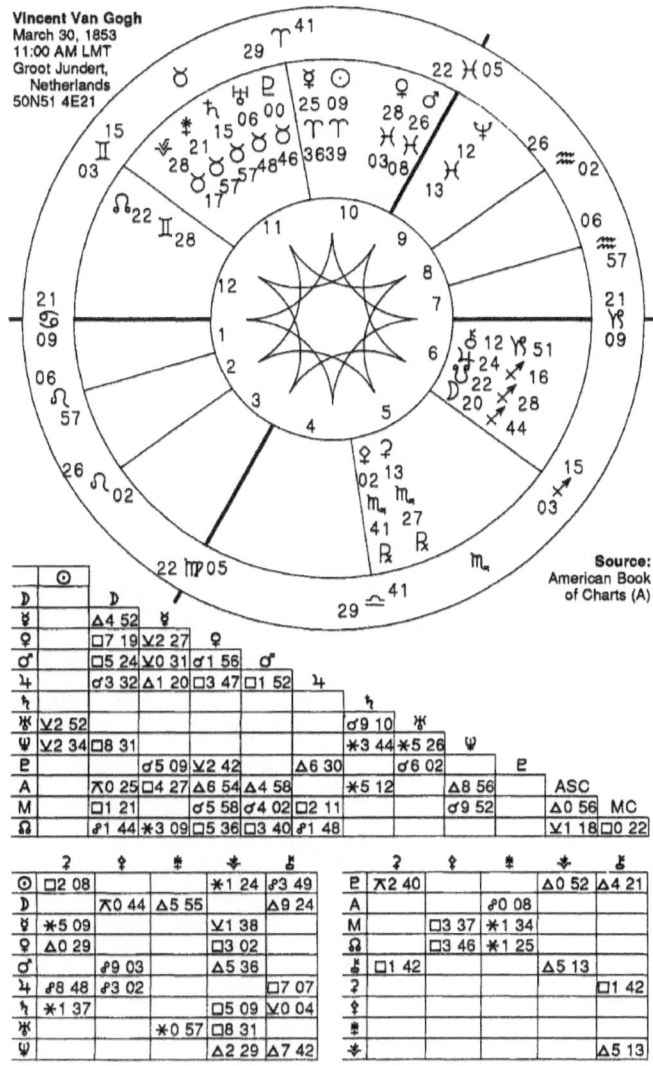

There is another type of singleton that is a fusion of two planets isolated together in a hemisphere. Vincent Van Gogh's chart is an example. The Moon (☾) and Jupiter (♃) in Sagittarius (♐) occupying his 6th house are isolated in the subjective northern hemisphere. The remaining eight planets are located in the objective southern hemisphere. The Moon and Jupiter conjunction in Sagittarius accentuates Van Gogh's idealism and faith in his work (6th house). This is a key repeating theme as Jupiter rules Sagittarius. The moon as ruler of his watery cancer (♋) ascendant symbolizes a longing to establish his identity (ascendant) through his work (6th house).

The artist had a continuous struggle with accepting a stable type of life. The Moon /Jupiter conjunction in Sagittarius can symbolize an emotional restlessness and impatience with the present. A drive for security (Moon) and perfection (6th house) to express inspiration (Sagittarius and Jupiter) was difficult to accomplish. The young artist was constantly frustrated by a lack of appreciation from his contemporary society.

The singleton planet can symbolize a nagging type of energy that knocks on the door of consciousness for individual expression. The singleton sometimes requires a disciplined focus because too much utilization by a person can be like experiencing an inner overloaded circuit.

Astrology, Psychology, and Transformation

Moon's Nodes

	Symbol	Basic Issues	Focus
Moon's North Node:	☊	Nurturing one's soul growth; Living in the present with a healthy respect for the "past"	New personal history; Liberating one's karma
Moon's South Node:	☋	Facing one's unconscious and self-destructive behavior patterns; making peace with one's past	Recorded personal history; reinforcing one's karma
Polarity:		Balancing past and present; turning adversaries into allies; building positive karma	

This is an important spice and one of my favorites. Understanding the nodes can broaden the scope of one's interpretations and enhance one's skill. Each planet has a north and a south node, but the Moon's nodes have a special symbolism that relates specifically to an individual's inner need to follow a true destiny.

Since the Moon is very much representative of an individual's subconscious nature in the chart, the Moon's nodes are a further refinement of one's instincts to stay on a life path that is fulfilling. The nodes are a symbolic "compass" that indicates a person's past as in south node symbolism and a path designed for the present as in the north node.

Traditional astrology usually says that following the north node indicates you are on course, and following the south node can indicate you missed a turn and are entrapped by *karmic* patterns. This is really a gross oversimplification as one must **integrate** both node expressions into this life. A person can gain great strength and much insight into inner motivations by confronting south node issues. A fusion of both nodes is important if a person will find a healthy middle ground from which to balance this very powerful polarity of opposites. It can actually be difficult to realize the full potential of one's north node if he denies or runs away from south node issues. The north node needs the south node (and vice versa) if one is to achieve the full potential inherent in the synthesis of these contrasting forces.

The nodes move in a backward motion along the ecliptic and are measured in terms of celestial longitude, moving approximately three minutes per day. This backward type of motion points to the "past" and to a present that is a product of the "past." We need to be careful with the word "past" here and astrologers must be sure to give the client the freedom to acknowledge this "past" as a previous incarnation symbolism and/or early habits formed during this lifetime. It is going to make little sense to a person to talk in terms of previous lives if they are completely closed to the reincarnation concept which views this present lifetime as only one of a continuous series of lifetimes.

The north node in a sense is a direct response to the south node as evidenced by the fact that both nodes are always found in direct opposition to each other by sign and house placements. **Each serves as a reminder to a person of the alchemy of his past and present.** If a person ignores the north node, he is very apt to surrender to the south node or past patterns. For instance, an individual with the north node in Aries in the 7th house will certainly need to be true to his assertion instincts. If the individual is always afraid of taking a stand on important issues in dealing with others, he is likely to become habitually smothered by the south node in the sign of Libra in his 1st house. Perhaps he allows others to frustrate his own goals, and his personal aims in life are too easily compromised. One of his main life issues as indicated by the Libra south node in the 1st house is that the individual may have adopted the same pattern in several lifetimes of allowing others to do his asserting for him. He may have based his self-image too much by the opinions of others. He must in this lifetime face the issue of initiating his own needs and find a happy medium of establishing his own identity within important relationships, friendships or partnerships.

Awareness is such a key and vital function of astrology. An individual's awakening to destructive or self-limiting behavior can be quite helpful as a first step in developing a more productive north and south node understanding. Thus when an individual attempts to run away from the north node symbolism, he is destined to enter the south node as each offers a door of easy access to the other. As a matter of fact, **neither exists without the other**. The north node is born out of an individual's need to conquer or rise above his south node energy, and the south node represents the balancing polarity to the north.

The sign and house placements of the north and south nodes offer a convenient landscape to tune into the essential direction of the chart and are equivalent to what in Eastern philosophy is known as one's dharma or the natural direction of one's life. Aspects from planets (and asteroids) to the nodes can be quite significant in the chart, though I consider the conjunction and square to be the most important. Also, when a node conjuncts an angle of the chart (1st, 4th, 7th or 10th house), I find this very significant.

A brief key word system for possible node combinations. This is meant to serve only as some examples of what could be *karmic* issues for an individual. I have listed the key words by sign and house of a particular chord as these issues could just as well occur through nodes in the corresponding signs or houses.

Copies of these two tables are available at the website.

NODAL POLARITIES

Polarity	Overdoing or Underdoing ☊	Balance Requires ☋
1-7 or 7-1 1st Chord Sign: Aries ♈ House: 1st	1. Me First" focus and confused self-image. 2. Lone-wolf philosophy. 3. Too aggressive and warlike.	1. Developing and awareness of others. 2. Accepting the need for love. 3. Understanding the art of compromise.
1-7 or 7-1 7th Chord Sign: Libra ♎ House: 7th	1. Too indecisive and compromising. 2. Loss of self in relationships. 3. Too competitive.	1. Developing assertive-ness and decisiveness. 2. Creating a clear self-image. 3. Expressing courage and leadership.
2-8 or 8-2 2nd Chord Sign: Taurus ♉ House: 2nd	1. Low self-esteem. 2. Greed, possessiveness, stubbornness and overindulgence. 3. Lack of appreciation for love and beauty.	1. Gaining a new sense of personal power. 2. Sharing one's physical resources and psychological depth. 3. Expressing a deep passion for love and beauty.
2-8 or 8-2 8th Chord Sign: Scorpio ♏ House: 8th	1. Power hunger and rule by jealousy and manipulation. 2. Controlled by addictive and compulsive habits. 3. Excessive dependence on	1. Clear expression and appreciation of love and serenity; simplicity in relating to others. 2. Balanced expression of desires. 3. Developing one's own values and resources.
3-9 or 9-3 3rd Chord Sign: Gemini ♊ House: 3rd	1. Lack of focus. 2. Spaced-out mental nature. 3. Lack of psychological depth.	1. Developing focused vision and perspective. 2. Developing a clear and eclectic mentality. 3. Comprehending the abstract.
3-9 or 9-3 1 9th Chord Sign: Sagittarius ♐ House: 9th	1. Dogmatic life philosophy. 2. Following too many paths and aimless wandering; ignorant of limitations. 3. The compulsive need to "always" be right.	1. Developing a more flexible life perspective. 2. Using discrimination in choosing life paths. 3. Developing a capacity to see more than one alternative.

NODAL POLARITIES (continued)		
Polarity	Overdoing or Underdoing ☊	Balance Requires ☋
4-10 or 10-4 4th Chord Sign: Cancer ♋ House: 4th	1. Lack of rootedness. 2. Fear of responsibility for self. 3. Emotional insecurity.	1. Developing stable commitments and structures. 2. Assuming responsibility for dependency needs and decisions. 3. Learning to trust self.
4-10 or 10-4 10th Chord Sign: Capricorn ♑ House: 10th	1. Too authoritarian and the need to be "the boss". 2. Refusal to delegate due to lack of trust. 3. Fear of life commitments.	1. Relinquishing absolute control. 2. Learning to balance one's dependency needs and developing a capacity to trust. 3. Expressing one's intimate instincts in life commitments.
5-11 or 11-5 5th Chord Sign: Leo ♌ House: 5th	1. Ego defenses and excessive pride. 2. Fixed willpower and love of power. 3. Living life through others.	1. Developing individuality and a true self-expression. 2. Surrendering power motives. 3. Developing new and authentic life directions that liberate the self.
5-11 or 11-5 11th Chord Sign: Aquarius ♒ House: 11th	1. Too much individualism and aloofness in self-expression; eccentric. 2. Rebel without a cause; loss of self. 3. Fixed opinions and sarcasm.	1. Developing and expressing a vivacious and pro-life spirit that energizes self and others. 2. Creativity with a cause. 3. Developing inner strength that reflects happiness.
6-12 or 12-6 6th Chord Sign: Virgo ♍ House: 6th	1. Too critical of self and others; lack of faith. 2. Too perfectionistic and analytical. 3. Denial and neglect of body, mind and	1. Developing a more compassionate nature and faith. 2. Trusting intuition. 3. Caring for the physical, mental and spiritual body.
6-12 or 12-6 12th Chord Sign: Pisces ♓ House: 12th	1. Compulsive and self-defeating attitudes and addictions; loss of health. 2. Escape from reality; confused by perfection drives. 3. Surrendering to the wrong things and lack of discipline.	1. Developing proper discrimination and conquering self-defeating attitudes; caring for health. 2. Facing limitations realistically. 3. Making real one's devotional nature; learning self-discipline.

Hemispheres

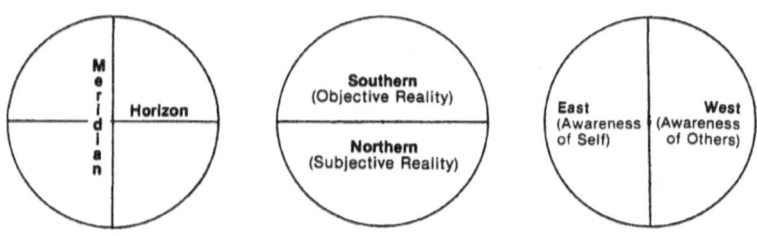

Earlier it was described how the horizon and meridian divide the horoscope into halves or hemispheres. The horizontal line of the birth chart or horizon creates the southern and northern hemispheres. The vertical line or meridian creates the eastern and western hemispheres (directions in a birth chart are reversed from standard maps: south is up and north is down; east is to the left and west is to the right).

SOUTHERN HEMISPHERE

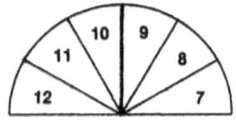

Primary Angular House: Midheaven or 10th House: The upper or southern hemisphere, houses 7 through 12 contains planets above the horizon and represents "visibility" according to traditional astrology. When an individual has an emphasized southern hemisphere, he often has instincts related to wanting to be noticed. He may not always be an obvious extrovert but is faced with the challenge of making his actions meaningful and pragmatic. As a matter of fact, a strong water chord person with an emphasis upon this hemisphere might feel uncomfortable with the growing recognition that comes with this territory. A dynamic fire or air personality might love this attention and feel greatly energized by it.

Astrology, Psychology, and Transformation

A person with an emphasized southern hemisphere is often seeking outlets to make life objectives practical. These can be very much time-oriented individuals who want to make sure their goals are manifesting. The basic frame of reference is: **objective reality**. A sense of security is related to external stability.

However, as stated earlier, there are definite exceptions to this situation. An individual with planets heavily placed in the watery 8th and 12th houses may be anything but outgoing or concerned with objective reality! These are quite emotionally private houses. Also, some people with strong 9th and 12th houses can live by faith alone. Folks with accentuated 11th houses can thrive on thinking and show little concern for being noticed. So the traditional generalities of the hemispheres will not always fit!

NORTHERN HEMISPHERE

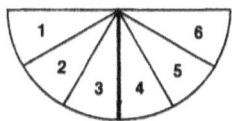

Primary Angular House: 4th House: The northern hemisphere, houses 1 through 6, represents "invisibility" and contains planets below the horizon. Traditional astrology says that when an individual has an emphasized northern hemisphere, he often is instinctively a very reflective person. He may not necessarily be an introvert who is extremely shy or reclusive but still will probably exhibit more of an internalized sense of being. His life may be experienced as living outside of the dictates of time and deadlines. The basic frame of reference in this hemisphere is: **subjective reality**. A sense of security is related to inner stability.

This generalized definition of the northern hemisphere will not work every time either. It is hard to imagine a person with heavily aspected fire planets below the horizon, or the fiery 1st and 5th houses accentuated as well as the earthy 2nd and 6th being very subjective. Perhaps it is more appropriate to say that the individual has easy access to the subjective energy and is busy going about his businesss He may process everything later! Even a person with earthy Saturn below the horizon can be quite anxious to externalize his subjective nature.

EASTERN HEMISPHERE

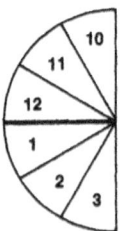

Primary Angular House: 1st House or Ascendant: The eastern hemisphere, houses 10 through 3, indicates self-control and represents one's awareness of being in control of his own destiny. Traditional astrology says that a person with an emphasized eastern hemisphere may not always be someone who exerts great self-control but he is often sensitive about self-growth. His basic frame of reference is: **self-awareness**. His sense of security is often related to the strength of his own ability to assert himself.

Once again, there are many exceptions to an emphasized eastern hemisphere indicating independent people. A water Ascendant, especially Cancer or Pisces, can, and often does, indicate a strong dependence on others. The person needs close, emotional warmth in relationships. A person with many Libran planets in the eastern hemisphere can feel a tremendous urgency and drive to fulfill his personal needs by forming partnerships of various kinds. An air Ascendant person, especially Gemini or Libra, often desires the perspective of others for balance in his life and enjoys mental company.

WESTERN HEMISPHERE

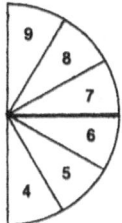

Primary Angular House: 7th House or Descendant: The western hemisphere, houses 4 through 9, represents one's sense of self while relating to others. This hemisphere indicates one's perceptions of others in the midst of shaping his destiny. Traditional astrology says that a person with an emphasized western hemisphere may not always be extremely aware of others but is often sensitive to their expectations. His basic frame of reference is: **awareness of Others**. His sense of security is often related to his sense of balancing his own needs within the expectations of others.

There are exceptions in this hemisphere too. I have seen people with loaded 5th or 7th houses that were extremely self-focused. There are individuals with accentuated 4th and 8th house planets that prefer the privacy of living alone. So, this business of emphasized hemispheres is filled with contradictions and can lead one away from the central, repeating themes if not used carefully.

DETERMINING AN EMPHASIZED HEMISPHERE

Astrology books offer different methods of ascertaining which hemispheres in a horoscope are the most intensified or emphasized. Some books say that the hemisphere containing the majority of planets is the most significant. Since I have experienced this to be an oversimplified method and not that accurate, I am suggesting the following point system method:

WEIGHTING TABLE

Planet	Points (Total = 19)	Planet	Points (Total = 19)
Sun	3	Jupiter	2
Moon	3	Saturn	2
Mercury	2	Uranus	1
Venus	2	Neptune	1
Mars	2	Pluto	1

I begin by comparing the southern and northern hemispheres to determine which is dominant by points. **Usually**, twelve or more points of the 19 possible points will be indicative of a dominant hemisphere. Then I compare the eastern and western hemispheres in the same manner. The result of course will be two dominant hemispheres.

If the comparison is too close to make a decision by points, I then look to see which hemisphere contains the Sun or Moon. If both Sun and Moon are in the same hemisphere, I will consider this the dominant hemisphere even though the opposite hemisphere may be slightly favored by points. Also, one need not bother looking for a tiebreaker. In most cases, the individual will probably have a balanced expression of both hemispheres when planets are heavily placed in opposing hemispheres.

For instance, the breakdown of Diane Keaton's hemispheres by points is as follows:

DIANE KEATON'S WEIGHTING TABLE

Southern Hemisphere
Mars = 2
Jupiter = 2
Saturn = 2
Uranus = 1
Neptune = 1
Pluto = 1
Total = 9 points

Northern Hemisphere
Sun = 3
Moon = 3
Venus = 2
Mercury = 2
Total = 10 points

Eastern Hemisphere
Sun = 3
Moon = 3
Mercury = 2
Venus = 2
Jupiter = 2
Neptune = 1
Total = 13 points

Western Hemisphere
Mars = 2
Saturn = 2
Uranus = 1
Pluto = 1
Total = 6 points

Even though her northern hemisphere does not have a strong majority of the points, Keaton's Sun and Moon both reside in the northern hemisphere and, therefore, I consider this hemisphere to be dominant. It is more obvious that the eastern hemisphere is emphasized as it contains a definite majority of points (13) and contains the Sun and Moon. The reason I favor a point system is that even though the majority of planets reside in Keaton's southern hemisphere when compared to the northern hemisphere, the main thrust of her energies does seem to favor the northern hemisphere as highlighted by the Sun and Moon.

An example of a very dominant western hemisphere in a horoscope is that of the pioneering psychologist, Sigmund Freud. He has 17 of the 19 points in the West!

An example of a very dominant southern hemisphere is the horoscope of the magnificent artist, Vincent van Gogh.
He has 16 of the 19 points in the south. Van Gogh's eastern hemisphere is also dominant containing 15 points.

The hemispheres will be further discussed in Section Three of this chapter: "Character Sketches."

Retrograde Motion of the Planets

Retrograde simply means the "apparent" backward motion of a planet through the zodiac when observed from the Earth. This is actually the passing of a slower moving planet by a faster moving planet painting the illusion that the slower planet is moving backward. Except for the Sun and Moon, the remaining planets can at various times in a given year appear to have retrograde motion. I have the dates on my website (bernieashman.com) when Mercury turns retrograde. This occurs 3 to 4 times a year. This is an important retrograde cycle that last about three weeks. If you are signing any contracts or making a new purchase it is good to know when Mercury is retrograde. I have written a book on Mercury retrograde, *How to Survive Mercury Retrograde*.

There are different opinions among astrologers concerning the significance of retrograde planets in the birth chart. There seems to be a general consensus that the themes represented by retrograde planets operate a bit more subjectively for an individual than themes of planets moving in direct motion. I think of retrograde planets as mainly symbolizing subjective or inwardly directed energy, but this does not imply that an individual is not capable of very projective expressions of a retrograde planet! It is not uncommon for an individual to express a retrograde planet with much force. For instance, an individual with a strongly aspected retrograde planet, especially when placed in an angular house, may function in a more conscious manner than a planet with direct motion but placed in a water house.

I believe it is questionable to grow overly concerned about trans-personal planets displaying retrograde motion as their cycles are much longer than the personal planets, and transpersonal planets represent such unconscious energies that I really have my doubts that retrograde motion is going to make their symbolisms any more unconscious or unpredictable.

I am not saying retrogradation should be ignored, but I am saying sometimes it is blown out of proportion. The important thing to keep in mind is the perspective of the overall chart. It can be an important chart theme if several or all of the planets in a hemisphere are retrograde. I have noticed that these people often turn tremendous amounts of energy inwards, but even here I would exercise caution because these same people can also be quite capable of externalizing the energy but with very intuitive and reflective natures. The element containing a personal planet with retrograde motion is important. Even Jupiter and Saturn need to be considered within the context of the elements of their house and sign placements. A retrograde Mars may indicate that a person has difficulty expressing anger or being assertive. However, a person with Mars retrograde in a fire sign or house is more likely to gain a more conscious access to this energy than an individual with Mars in a water sign or house. As usual, much will depend on the entire chart and whether or not the retrograde planet is involved in a key repeating theme.

INTERCEPTED SIGNS

This is an interesting spice. An intercepted sign is found in a horoscope when the same sign is found consecutively on two house cusps causing another sign to be completely absorbed or intercepted by a house. This intercepted sign will not be found on a house cusp; the entire 30° of the sign is contained by a house. There is always an opposite intercepted sign in the opposite house. For instance, notice in the chart of George Lucas that the sign Cancer ♋ is placed on the cusps of the 3rd and 4th houses, and the opposite sign Capricorn ♑ is placed on the cusps of the 9th and 10th houses. The intercepted signs are Virgo ♍ and Pisces ♓. The sign Virgo is completely contained by the 6th house, and Pisces is completely contained by the opposite 12th house. When an intercepted sign is in the 1st house whether containing a planet or not, I refer to this as a "Dual Ascendant." Both the Ascendant, intercepted sign and 1st house planets, if there are any, symbolize a very complex mixture of energies that will need to be incorporated into an individual's self-image.

Astrologers have different opinions regarding the importance of intercepted signs. Planets placed in these signs may operate more on an intuitive level. These planets can be expressed clearly and powerfully but may require extra patience to channel their energies clearly. I consider an intercepted sign to be an important factor is when placed in the 1st house, especially when a planet is located in the intercepted sign.

Asteroids

Asteroid	Symbol
Ceres	⚳
Vesta	⚶
Juno	⚵
Pallas	⚴
Chiron	⚷

I have been working with the asteroids for several years: Ceres, Vesta, Juno, Pallas and Chiron. The asteroids complement the symbolism of the planets and can provide important repeating themes in a birth chart. Also, the asteroids can be used as transits and progressions and reveal some rather sparkling symbolisms.

I associate Vesta with the 6th sign Virgo or 10th sign Capricorn. Vesta represents being a hard worker and attention to detail. My experience is that Ceres symbolizes maternal concerns and the capacity to be an empath or nurturing type of person. Ceres is devotion in the form of caring for others.

There is an intensity in Vesta's symbolism of the classic workaholic. There can also be a focus on doing detail work and enjoying the stimulation of being busy. When Vesta themes are negatively expressed, they can indicate ill health and inefficient functioning as the person needs to learn to do a good job.

Pallas and Juno seem to have a strong relationship to the 7th Chord sign, Libra. Juno symbolism is linked to relationships such as lovers, marriage or close peer relationships. The emphasis is on commitment. Juno does remind me of the Libra side of Venus. It is related to social approval.

Pallas is more symbolic of the impersonal side of Libra with either Sagittarius or Aquarius. Pallas is a person seeking freedom and openness in relationships. Pallas expressions include counselors, consultants

I am convinced that Chiron has a vivid Jupiter symbolism. Dobyns says: People with a prominent Chiron in their chart are often driven by a lifelong hunger for knowledge. Chiron has a symbolism very similar to Sagittarius as well. The house and sign containing Chiron in a chart indicate a particular focus for gaining knowledge and expanding one's horizons.

However, I am feeling a bit cautious concerning Chiron's symbolism in chart interpretation. It is a generational asteroid. Chiron transits or moves through the signs in approximately 51 years.

It is important to remember that Chiron is unique. Unlike the other asteroids mentioned, which orbit between Mars and Jupiter, Chiron's path resides between the orbits of Saturn and Uranus. I suspect that this could indicate Chiron has a generational significance. Perhaps a person can offer knowledge that is unique for his culture.

There is some interesting astronomical information about Chiron in Patrice Moore's book, *The Guinness Book of Astronomy*. There is a theory that Chiron is a surviving entity of the building blocks that came together to create the outer planets.

Bernie Ashman

An asteroid's placement in a chart by sign, house or aspects to a planet may explain traits of a person that are virtually unexplainable by other chart factors. For instance, recently I had an appointment with a client with no planets in the 7th house. The ruling planet of the 7th house sign was not that strongly aspected in the chart and was not angular. Yet the individual was an extremely relationship-oriented person. "Traditional" chart factors did not explain such a strong relationship orientation. However, the asteroid Juno was placed in the sign Sagittarius and exactly conjunct the 7th house and opposed the 1st house Sun and Uranus! Juno's association with close personal relationships was extremely evident in this person's life from listening to her personal history. This particular asteroid added a great amount of clarity regarding her relationship impulses.

In the following three character sketches, I list an asteroid in the introduction to each sketch if well emphasized in the chart. Also, during the discussion of a chart I mention the significant aspects formed by an asteroid to a planet.

Section Three: Character Sketches

The following character sketches will illustrate to the reader a fast approach to gaining an in-depth perspective on a birth chart. Each of the three charts does contain a complex aspect configuration. The outline that precedes each chart discussion will indicate the particular configurations. The person's profession is also listed as it is very interesting to observe how a horoscope can reflect an individual's choices to project energies into the world.

The emphasized hemispheres are given and the point system previously mentioned is illustrated. The total points for each hemisphere are shown. I decided to list the elemental placement of the planets by sign and house as most astrology books do this by sign only. The transpersonal planets are listed by house only due to their generational significance.

The Ascendant's element should always be considered as this represents an individual's way of expressing his self-image. It also indicates how the individual might initiate action in regard to his self-concept. I feel it is important to observe the elements of the Sun, Moon and Ascendant to see if there is harmony or a possible tension indicated. It is amazing how quickly a chart can make sense by simply analyzing the elemental balance of the Sun, Moon and Ascendant.

Since the ruler of the Ascendant can be such an important focalizer of energy, I have also listed it separately. Angular planets are also shown as their symbolism can be quite dynamic. This is especially true if the angular planet is heavily aspected or part of a complex aspect configuration. Retrograde planets are indicated by the symbol "R" in the chart following the degree and minute of the planet.

The emphasized qualities (cardinal, fixed or mutable) are also shown as they can indicate how a person adjusts to change or approaches important decisions. I examine the quality of the seven personal planets and the Ascendant to determine which is emphasized. A heavy emphasis on cardinal symbolizes action; fixed symbolizes tenacity and determination; mutable represents mental energy and changeability.

Before I get into a more detailed analysis of a chart, I like to **begin by looking for major repeating themes** and gradually proceed to minor themes. Some major themes may include a planet or planets involved in a complex aspect configuration, singleton planets, or a highly focalized planet that is either heavily aspected and/or in an angular house. I find the elemental placements of the Sun, Moon and Ascendant by sign and house important as they symbolize a person's basic motivations related to self-expression (Sun), self-image (Ascendant), and security and instinctual needs (Moon). The Sun and Moon signs and houses are of great importance. Aspects formed by the Sun, Moon and Ascendant to the other planets (and even asteroids) can be considered.

Repeating themes, such as planets in their home signs or houses, are important, as are planets that aspect each other and occupy the other's home sign. For instance, an individual with Mercury in the 8th Chord sign, Scorpio, aspect ing the 8th Chord planet, Pluto, has a strong relationship in his chart of these two planets due to their 8th Chord connection.

As stated earlier, the planetary aspects have been divided into two major groups: personal-personal and personal-transpersonal. Transpersonal planets aspecting the personal planets, especially the aspects representing intensity, can greatly alter the symbolism of a personal planet. Also, key aspects formed by asteroids to planets or the Ascendant will be indicated as well as key aspects formed by planets to the Midheaven and nodes of the Moon.

With a more detailed analysis of a chart, one begins to discover the **repeating themes** which are essentially the repeating chord themes that occur in a chart. For instance, note the repeating chord themes listed for George Lucas such as the Moon in the 11th Chord sign, Aquarius, trining the 11th Chord planet, Uranus in the 1st house. This aspect alone puts a major emphasis upon the 11th Chord in the chart. Other repeating themes are listed.

Astrology's symbolic language can only reflect the clarity of the person interpreting its symbolism. The themes of a chart must be comprehended before someone can really perceive the chords combining into a certain harmony. I believe a good way to illustrate birth chart themes and patterns is to discuss actual charts. The character sketches that follow should help the reader to better understand the art of interpreting the chart and to begin discovering "repeating themes." **With practice you can begin to find these themes yourself.**

GEORGE LUCAS

The birth chart of George Lucas, the creator of the spectacular epic film, *Star Wars*, contains two complex aspect configurations that bring the chart into a sharp and well-defined focus. One is a T-square in fixed signs formed by the Moon in the 11th Chord sign, Aquarius, residing in the 10th house opposing Pluto in the 5th Chord sign, Leo, and located in the 4th house; the Moon and Pluto each form a square to both Mercury and Venus in the 2nd Chord sign, Taurus, placed in the 12th house. The other complex aspect configuration is a grand trine in air signs and once again the very accentuated Moon in the air sign, Aquarius, is involved. The grand trine is formed by the Moon; Uranus in the 3rd Chord air sign, Gemini; and Neptune in the 7th Chord air sign, Libra. The orb is definitely wide from Neptune to the Moon (almost 10°). However, I still consider this air grand trine to be very apropos for the life of George Lucas. He exudes a mental dexterity and ingenuity (air) in his career and work environment (earth houses) that is startling! Ordinarily, I do not pay too much attention to two transpersonal planets involved in an isolated trine to each other. But since both Uranus and Neptune belong to a major gestalt type of aspect configuration such as a grand trine and each does trine the very focalized personal planet, the Moon, the fact that Uranus does trine Neptune becomes important in this chart. Air grand trines can symbolize a person with much impersonality in relating to others, especially with so much impersonal 11th Chord energy involved in the grand trine and with the asteroid Pallas conjuncting Uranus. Remember, Pallas symbolizes an impersonal 7th Chord theme in relating to others. There is a strong emphasis upon the eastern hemisphere in this chart (15 points!). **Self-awareness** is the basic point of reference symbolized by this hemisphere. The cluster or stellium of planets in the 12th and 1st houses of the eastern hemisphere placed in the 2nd Chord sign, Taurus, catch our attention immediately! The Ascendant and Sun both occupy the same earth sign of Taurus. The 2nd Chord desire for ownership and comfort would seem to be highlighted. Self-esteem issues and expressing 2nd Chord personal values must be incorporated into a tremendous urge to establish self-awareness. There may be a desire to control his environment, especially with a "fixed" Ascendant and 1st house Sun.

GEORGE LUCAS

BIRTH DATA
Date: May 14, 1944 Time: 5:40 AM PWT Place: Modesto, California

PROFESSION: Director; Producer; Writer

COMPLEX ASPECT CONFIGURATIONS

Fixed T-square

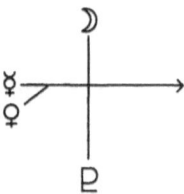

Air Grand Trine

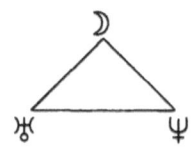

Astrology, Psychology, and Transformation

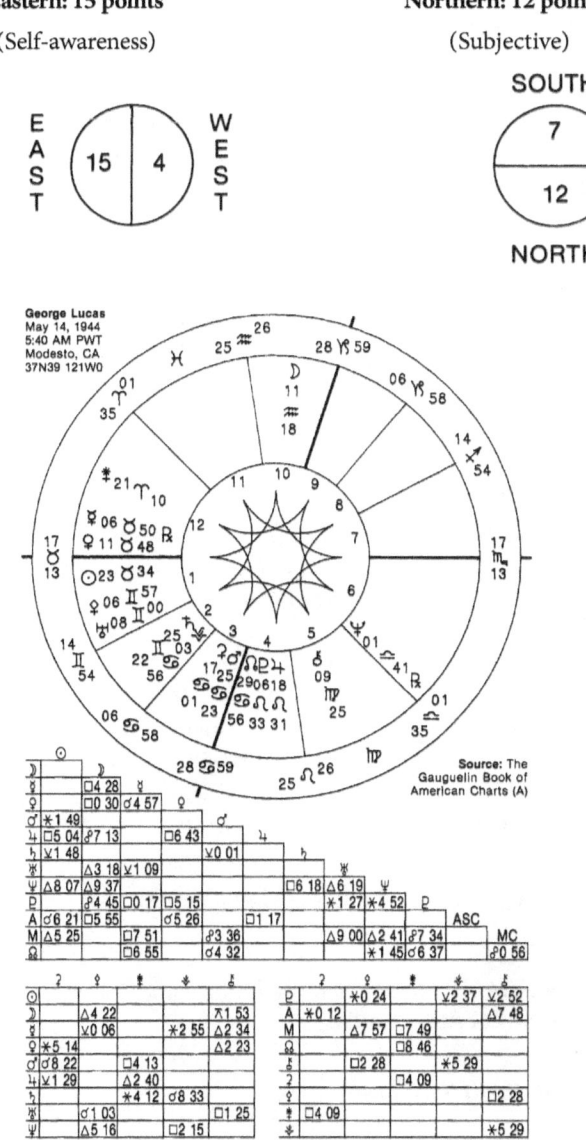

EMPHASIZED SIGN QUALITY: Fixed
EMPHASIZED ELEMENTS: Earth and Air

Ascendant and Planets	Sign	Element by Sign	Element by House	Sign Quality
Ascendant	Taurus	Earth	—	Fixed
Sun	Taurus	Earth	Fire (1st)	Fixed
Moon	Aquarius	Air	Earth (10th)	Fixed
Mercury	Taurus	Earth	Water (12th)	Fixed
Venus	Taurus	Earth	Fire (1st)	Fixed
Mars	Cancer	Water	Water (4th)	Cardinal
Jupiter	Leo	Fire	Water (4th)	Fixed
Saturn	Gemini	Air	Earth (2nd)	Mutable
Uranus	Gemini	—	Earth (2nd)	—
Neptune	Libra	—	Earth (6th)	—
Pluto	Leo	—	Water (4th)	—

ASTEROIDS

	Degree	Sign	House
Ceres	16°	Cancer	3rd
Vesta	3°	Cancer	3rd
Juno	20°	Aries	12th
Pallas	6°	Gemini	1st
Chiron	9°	Virgo	5th

RULER OF TAURUS ASCENDANT: Venus

ANGULAR PLANETS: Sun, Moon, Jupiter and Pluto
(Venus conjunct Ascendant)

ANGULAR ASTEROIDS: Pallas

KEY REPEATING CHORD THEMES
Stellium in Taurus: Sun, Ascendant, Venus and Mercury.

Venus (2nd chord planet) is placed in its natural 2nd Chord sign (Taurus).

Moon rules 3rd in 10th; Saturn rules 10th in 3rd sign (Gemini). Venus rules 6th in 12th; Neptune (12th chord planet) in 6th.

Moon in 11th Chord sign, (Aquarius) trines 11th Chord planet (Uranus).

Sun in 1st house sextiles 1st Chord planet (Mars).

Sun in 2nd Chord sign (Taurus) semisextiles (2nd Chord subtone) Saturn in 2nd house.

4th Chord planet (Moon) opposes Pluto residing in the 4th house. North node is in 4th Chord sign (Cancer) and in the 4th house. South node is in 10th Chord sign (Capricorn) and in the 10th house.

Saturn in 2nd house quincunxes Midheaven, 10th Chord sign (Capricorn).

PLANETARY ASPECTS

Personal — Personal

Soft	Hard
☉ ✶ ♂	☉ □ ♃
☉ ⚺ ♄	☽ □ ☿
♂ ⚺ ♄	☽ □ ♀
♃ ✶ ♄	☽ ☍ ♃
	☿ ☌ ♀
	♀ □ ♃

Personal — Transpersonal

Soft	Hard
☽ △ ♅	☽ ☍ ♇
☽ △ ♆	☿ □ ♇
☿ ⚺ ♅	♀ □ ♇
	♄ □ ♆

Major Aspects To Nodes

♂ ☌ ☊

Aspects To Ascendant

Soft	Hard
	☉ ☌ Asc.
	☽ □ Asc.
	♀ ☌ Asc.
	♃ □ Asc.

Aspects To Midheaven

Soft	Hard
	♂ ☍ MC.
	♄ ⚻ MC.

Key Asteroid Aspects

Soft	Hard
♃ △ ⚶	♅ □ ⚵
	♅ ☌ ♀
	♂ □ ⚶
	♅ □ ⚳

The northern hemisphere is also emphasized (12 points). George Lucas will need to understand and acknowledge **subjective reality**. It will likely be important for him to integrate this subjective frame of reference into his life activities. Remember, a strong northern hemisphere does not always indicate a person is a complete introvert or incapable of a strong projection of himself. It is interesting that despite the fact that Lucas has been quite successful in externalizing his subjective consciousness, he is still known as a shy and reclusive type of person. (He does have Mars in Cancer resting on the 4th house cusp, indicating a very private side of his identity.)

At first glance the chart of George Lucas can fool us. He appears to be saturated with the earth element as three planets in Taurus surround his already-earthy Taurean Ascendant. This "cluster" of Taurean planets—Mercury, Venus, and the Sun—indicates that Lucas is concerned with finding stability and a sense of comfort whether it is through accumulating resources, earning a living, or expressing and enjoying aesthetic tastes. His need to establish ownership and to develop and build his own values is evident. These strong 2nd Chord themes appear to be a primary drive and basic need. The Sun in Taurus conjuncts his Taurus Ascendant which symbolizes the fusing together of his drive to build and express a core identity that greatly encompasses his own values and at the same time also energizes and expresses his self-concept or Ascendant. Both Sun and Ascendant are interrelated in this particular chart. The fixity of so much Taurus symbolizes tremendous willpower and determination to succeed. Even the ruler of the Ascendant, Venus, is in 2nd Chord Taurus (its home sign) and conjuncts the Ascendant! A person with this much 2nd Chord focus may have a tendency to get stuck in fixed values and develop a stubborn ego. An individual with a 1st house Sun can be limited by personal needs and a tremendous desire to be the center of everything he tries to accomplish. Lucas needs an active life that can allow his very focused self-awareness to meet life directly

(1st Chord theme). Taurus can be indicative of control issues and therefore Lucas must be careful not to have his finger in too many pies at once.

An individual with a very accentuated Taurus theme in his chart has a tendency to move slowly and deliberately in life activities. However, Lucas has the Sun and Moon in the action-oriented angular houses which symbolizes a person who enjoys being on the move. As a matter of fact, his chart contains three other angular planets: Uranus, Pluto and Jupiter (Venus is in the 12th and conjuncts the Ascendant; Mars is in the 3rd house and conjuncts the IC). This man with a strong self-focus (eastern hemisphere and 1st house) combined with a reflective or subjective reality (northern hemisphere and 4th house) thrives on action whether it is through aesthetic expression or relating to others. Lucas's consciousness is constantly striving to make his subjective visions and dreams a practical reality due to the center stage occupied by his earth element complemented by angular planets and an array of fixed signs that are indicative of much stored energy.

The Moon in Aquarius, the key component of both complex aspect configurations, represents the importance of the air element in the chart. The Moon sits high above the horizon, extremely visible, and gives the appearance of looking down over the other planets. The lunar instincts of George Lucas hint to an inner attunement to a streak of individuality, rebelliousness and an innovative spirit with sparks of genius. The Aquarian Moon placed in the 10th house symbolizes his career instincts may be scientific, futuristic, eccentric, unconventional, and even rebellious. It is not surprising that Lucas once stated: "I learned the system and beat it."

Lucas has made clear his contempt for Hollywood's way of producing movies. His dislike of Hollywood "politics" led him to create his own studios in Northern California following the rapid success he enjoyed with the making of *Star Wars*. Lucas stated he wanted to create a free and safe atmosphere for amateur artists to come and live without the hype of Hollywood and enjoy the luxury of producing their own fresh material. This individual with Taurean patience and the individualism of Aquarius and Uranus has fought and worked hard to defend and preserve his own values.

The T-square in the chart, 1st house Uranus and Mars conjunct an angle represent the thrust of his personal values and drive for uniqueness and individuality that perhaps explains Lucas's recklessness as a youth. He was a competitive race car driver and nearly died during a crash that crushed his lungs. This must have been a sobering experience as it ended his racing career and by the age of 21, he won first prize at the 1965 National Student Film Festival with a science fiction short, *THX-1138*. He evolved quickly as a filmmaker and had the opportunity to work closely with Francis Ford Coppola.

The T-square represents a lot of energy channeled into the 6th house which is the house opposite the "trigger" planets Mercury and Venus that cut across the Moon/Pluto opposition in square aspect. This focalized 6th house represents a possible untiring capacity to finish difficult and detailed demanding projects. Lucas would need to be aware of working himself into a completely exhausting state which he has done! He could get so mesmerized by his fixed energies and enjoyment of exhilarating mental stimulation (air emphasis) that his health could be too easily neglected or sacrificed (6th house). He may forget to seek the calmness and serenity of his Taurean nature due to a desire for excessive stimulation and satisfying the tornado-like energies of his T-square.

The T-square empties into the 6th house, and Neptune, though not involved in this particular complex aspect, resides in the 6th house and is part of another complex aspect, the dynamic air grand trine. George Lucas could easily be a strong perfectionist in his work environment with the 12th Chord idealism of Neptune placed in the earthy 6th house (and with Venus and Mercury conjunct in Taurus in the 12th house).

Neptune can indicate where a person most actively attempts to achieve perfection or find a sense of oneness according to the house placement. This striving for a sense of perfection in his work is further supported by the asteroid Vesta squaring Neptune. Vesta is the 6th Chord asteroid rendition of the hardworking Virgo who will compulsively work until each detail is conquered. Vesta is close enough to Lucas's 3rd house cusp to be considered in this house. The 3rd house Vesta reflects a mind that is looking for perfection. The fact that Vesta squares Neptune greatly highlights the drive for perfection and paints a mind with a vivid imagination. The 6th house energy could be indicative of someone who demands that others keep pace with him, and a T-square can represent energies that have the force of a tornado. Lucas is blessed with an amazing amount of creative energy. Even his earthy Taurean Sun trines his earthy 10th Chord, Capricorn Midheaven. Also, his Sun rules the procreative 5th house as the 5th Chord sign, Leo, is placed on its cusp. He has been quoted as saying: "If I wasn't a filmmaker, I'd probably be a painter or a toymaker."

The placement of Neptune in the 6th house and part of a grand trine symbolizes the love of George Lucas for film. His capacity to use his lunar Aquarian and Uranian scientific mindset and Neptunian (and 12th house planets) love of fantasy come across strikingly in his films. The fact that Uranus and Neptune co-rule the 11th house in his chart is another 11th Chord repeating theme. (Aquarius is the sign on the 11th house cusp and Pisces is intercepted.)

Lucas's 11th Chord points to his revolutionizing impact on the film industry through the use of special effects. He has attempted and accomplished things never seen before in a science fiction film. I also believe his films have been successful not solely due to his technical ability. Equally important is his ability to touch the heart of the collective psyche through the transpersonal vehicle of his 11th and 12th Chords.

In *The Empire Strikes Back*, Yoda, the "extra-terrestrial guru," tells Luke he fails to utilize "the force" because he does not believe with a strong-enough faith. This appears to be Lucas speaking through his 12th Chord planets, symbolizing a strong belief in intangible truths. Also, George Lucas has a potent square of the 9th Chord planet Jupiter to both his Ascendant and Sun which symbolizes that he is greatly strengthened by faith that emanates from his creative self-expression, belief in own personal values and his belief in defending his concept of "truth."

Aspects to the Sun, Moon and Ascendant can be quite revealing in a chart. All aspects to the Sun are important. Lucas has a sextile involving the 1st house Sun and 1st Chord planet, Mars. This could reflect an awareness of his "roots": as Mars is placed in the 4th Chord sign and nearly conjunct the 4th house. This could also reflect a strong loyalty to family, or he may be perceived by those who get to know his subjective being as a nurturing person. Supposedly he is rather caring as a director. Roots play a major role in the *Star Wars* epic. Luke is raised by an aunt and uncle who keep the true identity of his father a secret. Luke's father was supposedly killed many years before. It is not until Luke's aunt and uncle are killed by imperial troopers that Luke decides to join the rebellion against the forces of darkness. It almost sounds like the 4th house Pluto talking. Secrets concerning Luke's roots and the continuous confusion and destruction surrounding his roots have Plutonian overtones. The Moon in Aquarius opposing Pluto can represent Luke's feeling of separation from his true family as the Moon also rules the 4th house of Lucas. Lucas's own belief in freedom is symbolized by his Moon in Aquarius and manifests through the collective effort of the rebellion against the evil dark force greatly personified by Darth Vader who seems to represent the Lucas rendition of the Plutonian underworld. The Moon/Pluto opposition may also symbolize the fight against repression by the totalitarian "dark side." Pluto is placed in Lucas's 4th house and Luke eventually learns that his main enemy in life, the evil Darth Vader, is his actual father! And, of course, for those of you who know the story, Luke learns that Princess Leia is his sister.

The semisextile formed by the Sun to 2nd house Saturn in Gemini is a prominent aspect in this chart. Lucas is known for his ability to be a great manager of time and resources. He makes good use of the structuring energy and economizing common sense that a 2nd house Saturn can symbolize, as Saturn can be the lord of discipline. This is evidenced by the fact that the Lucas film, *American Graffiti*, completed in 1973, was made on a budget of approximately $700,000.00 in just 28 nights! The film was very successful and established a reputation for Lucas as a director. Since Saturn is in the 2nd house, career success is probably a very powerful self-esteem issue for Lucas.

The orb of this semisextile is slightly over the 1° orb suggested but due to a strong repeating theme of a 2nd Chord Taurean Sun semisextiling (2nd Chord subtone) a 2nd house planet, I consider this an important aspect and the orb will stretch. Saturn is rich in career symbolism and is placed in a work or earth house. It should also be noted that Saturn forms a quincunx with the sign cusp of the Midheaven which is Saturn's home 10th Chord sign, Capricorn. This is a repeating chart theme that would possibly indicate a compulsive success drive. This could also lead to a classic "workaholic" game. He may forget to delegate enough work to others. The south node in Capricorn in the 10th house suggests that issues dealing with power in situations is a karmic pattern. (This does not always mean a person has had too much power. It could represent a person who feels powerless, fearing failure and who avoids taking responsibility in life circumstances.)

The 4th house symbolizes Lucas's need for rest and relaxation. He has a very focused 4th house including the north node ☒ in Cancer placed here. It is no wonder Lucas is a bit reclusive as he needs privacy to recharge his battery. The 1st house Sun squaring Jupiter indicates he may forget his limits and collapse from exhaustion if he is not careful. He needs to indulge in 2nd Chord physical comfort and a 4th Chord type of retreat at times. A vacation for Lucas may be relaxing in the privacy of his home as his career can keep him on the road indefinitely.

The opposition from 8th Chord Pluto situated in the 4th house to the 10th house Moon in Aquarius can symbolize a secretive personality. Pluto can represent a Scorpio theme in his relating to others as oppositions (7th Chord) can say a lot about a person's relationships. Also, it should be noted that Pluto rules the 7th house Scorpio cusp. Lucas must be aware of psychic burnout through giving away too much of his energy to others. People can probably sense his Plutonian strength and may look to him for encouragement and inspiration. His intimate relationships could have much psychological depth and Lucas seems to be a person that might grow easily bored with casual friendships. The house that has Scorpio as its cusp is often where an individual is compulsive about time management. A Scorpio 7th house would indicate that Lucas will spend time with people who do not waste his time. His 1st house planets and Ascendant may project a simple and non-pretentious appearance. However, his 8th Chord emphasis (due to Pluto's opposition to the Moon and ruling the dynamic 7th house) suggests a complicated personality that may be difficult to get to know. He seems to be a personality that is best understood through his creative expressions.

The *Star Wars* epic strongly reflects his chart. Princess Leia, the female warrior in the film, reflects the independent and innovative spirit symbolized by the Moon in Aquarius in the chart of Lucas. The Moon and Venus indicate in a man's chart his feelings and perspective regarding his own feminine energy and his attitudes toward women. Lucas would seem to have an appreciation for beauty with Venus in Taurus and the 12th house. His Moon, which is an angular planet, forms an almost exact square to Venus which conjuncts the Ascendant. He would seem to gravitate to independent females and enjoy working closely with women as his Moon is in the earthy 10th house and Taurus is a work-related earth sign. His wife, Marcia, edited *Star Wars* and *American Graffiti*. Princess Leia truly embodies the Moon in Aquarius as she is not afraid to challenge the "established" totalitarian enemy that is trying to crush freedom. Princess Leia also is not afraid to risk her life which seems to express the Pluto energy that opposes the Moon. She is a very willful person who is willing to fight for her values.

Luke seems to represent a bit of Lucas in his young and impetuous days of race cars, etc. Luke's concentration is not anything to brag about and raises grave doubts among Yoda and Ben obi-wan Kenobi, Luke's Zen masters, as to his potential to develop the "power" to defeat Darth Vader. Luke finally leaves Yoda's training program prematurely because he feels the rebellion needs him now! Luke believes in action now and reflection or contemplation later reminding us of Lucas's angular 1st house Sun and Uranus and Mars conjunct an angle.

The 4th house Pluto of Lucas would seem to represent the personification displayed by Darth Vader. When Pluto energy becomes warped, it does sometimes seem as if a person has succumbed to the "dark side," and power becomes the sole aim in life. Darth Vader was a Jedi working for "the force," but is eventually won over to the "dark side." The 4th house is a door to the unconscious being water. Perhaps Darth Vader is the Lucas way of saying there is a dark or potentially destructive energy that can turn to the light.

The issue of developing a balanced sense of personal power could be a delicate area for Lucas. His Pluto operates from the hidden and secretive 4th house, residing well below the horizon. Yet Pluto reaches through the horizon via the opposition aspect to the Moon and forms solid squares to Mercury and Venus as well as ruling the 7th house angle. There is a lot of intensity under the surface that can be released very powerfully.

It could be that Hans Solo, the swash-buckling, self-indulgent and **Macho-Facho** warrior, is the secret hero of Lucas that maybe is given birth by the 4th house. Harrison Ford is the actor playing Hans Solo. In another Lucas film, *Raiders of the Lost Ark*, Harrison Ford again plays the part of the "daredevil warrior" as Indiana Jones, an archaeologist-adventurer who is a rugged survivor often combating evil forces and saving a heroine. George Lucas says of Indiana Jones: "Indy can do anything. He's a college professor and he's got his Cary Grant side, too."

DIANE KEATON

The birth chart of actress Diane Keaton contains two complex aspect configurations that bring the personal and transpersonal planets into a close alliance. The Sun and Moon are both involved in complex aspects with transpersonal planets symbolizing a dynamic access to unconscious energies. The grand trine in Keaton's chart is similar to that of George Lucas as both have a Moon in Aquarius trining Uranus and Neptune. The orbs are slightly closer for the trines in Keaton's chart. Keaton's air grand trine is a "natural" as it occurs in air houses. Keaton, like Lucas, has an individualistic streak that can be largely attributed to the Aquarian Moon and angular Uranus.

The yod is formed by the 2nd house Sun in the 10th Chord sign, Capricorn, involved in a quincunx to the 9th house Pluto, ruler of the Scorpio Ascendant, and the Sun also inconjuncts 7th house Uranus. This complex aspect represents an intense challenge to Keaton's personal power. The yod can be very symbolic of important crossroads in an individual's life, and some individuals completely change their life direction quite suddenly when the yod formation becomes activated. Keaton not so uncommonly portrays a character in a film such as Louise Bryant in *Reds* or as *Mrs. Soffel* who is seeking to gain greater personal strength and whose attraction for unusual and unconventional relationships (7th house Uranus) stimulate her to suddenly alter her life direction.

Astrology, Psychology, and Transformation

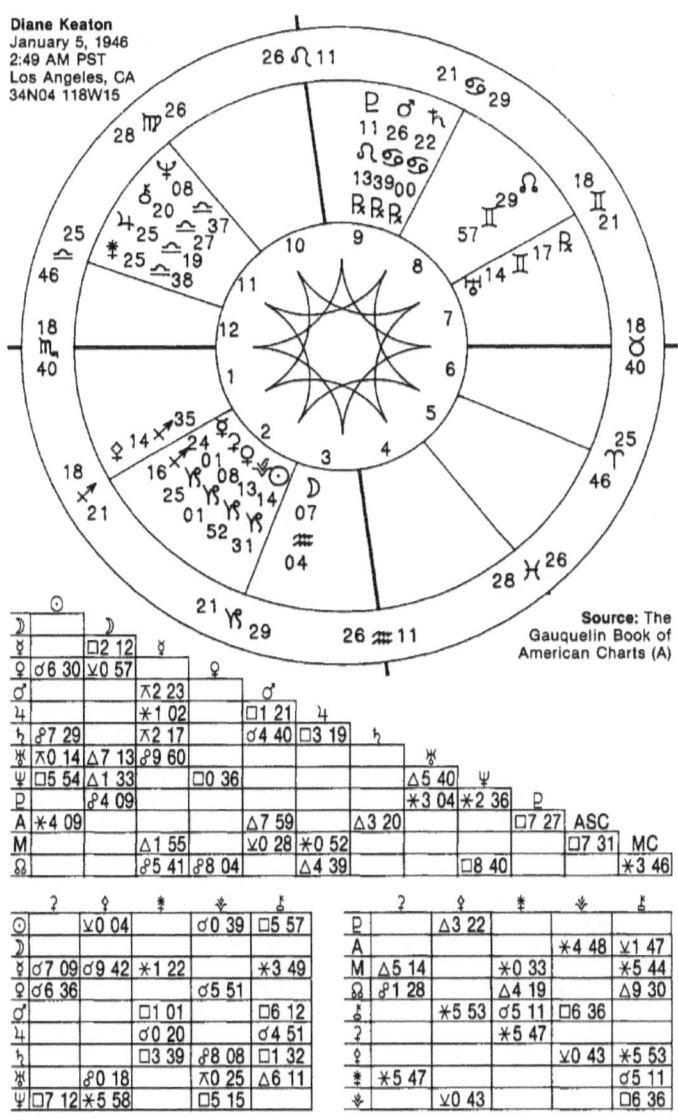

Bernie Ashman

DIANE KEATON

BIRTH DATA
Date: January 5, 1946
Time: 2:49 AM PST
Place: Los Angeles, California

PROFESSION: Actress

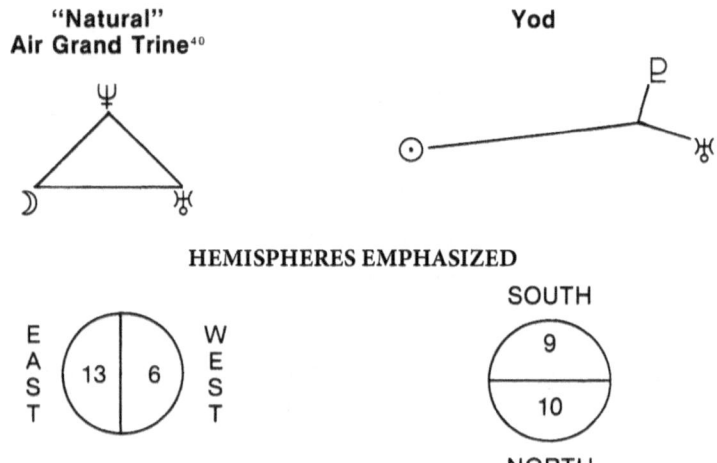

EMPHASIZED SIGN QUALITY: Cardinal and Fixed
EMPHASIZED ELEMENTS: Earth, Air and Water

EMPHASIZED SIGN QUALITY: Cardinal and Fixed
EMPHASIZED ELEMENTS: Earth, Air and Water

Ascendant and Planets	Sign	Element by Sign	Element by House	Sign Quality
Ascendant	Scorpio	Water	_____	Fixed
Sun	Capricorn	Earth	Earth (2nd)	Cardinal
Moon	Aquarius	Air	Air (3rd)	Fixed
Mercury	Sagittarius	Fire	Earth (2nd)	Mutable
Venus	Capricorn	Earth	Earth (2nd)	Cardinal
Mars	Cancer	Water	Fire (9th)	Cardinal
Jupiter	Libra	Air	Water (12th)	Cardinal
Saturn	Cancer	Water	Fire (9th)	Cardinal
Uranus	Gemini	_____	Air (7th)	_____
Neptune	Libra	_____	**Air** (11th)	_____
Pluto	Leo	_____	Fire (9th)	_____

ASTEROIDS

	Degree	Sign	House
Ceres	1°	Capricorn	2nd
Vesta	13°	Capricorn	2nd
Juno	25°	Libra	12th
Pallas	14°	Sagittarius	1st
Chiron	20°	Libra	11th

Bernie Ashman

RULER OF SCORPIO ASCENDANT: Pluto

ANGULAR PLANETS: Uranus **ANGULAR**

ASTEROIDS: Pallas

KEY REPEATING CHORD THEMES

Moon in 11th Chord sign (Aquarius) trines 11th Chord planet (Uranus).
Sun in 10th Chord sign opposing 10th Chord planet (Saturn). Venus is placed in its natural 2nd house. Pluto (the 8th Chord planet) squares the Scorpio Ascendant (8th
Chord sign). Sun quincunxes (8th Chord subtone) Pluto (8th Chord planet).

PLANETARY ASPECTS

Personal — Personal		Personal — Transpersonal	
Soft	Hard	Soft	Hard
☽ ⚹ ♀	☉ ☌ ♀	☽ △ ♆	☉ ⚻ ♅
☿ ⚹ ♃	☉ ☍ ♄	☽ △ ♅	☉ □ ♆
	☿ ⚻ ♂	♀ □ ♆	☉ ⚻ ♇
	♂ □ ♃	♀ ⚻ ♇	☽ ☍ ♇
	♂ ☌ ♄		
	♃ □ ♄		

One of the main challenges for a person with a yod is developing a consistency in accomplishing life aims. However, a successful navigation of these sometimes compulsive forces can lead to an in-depth understanding of dealing with life's paradoxes and accomplishing difficult tasks. The yod requires a person to develop concentration, focus and discipline.

Diane Keaton's eastern hemisphere, containing 13 points, is more dominating than her western hemisphere. Self-awareness is the basic reference point. Similar to George Lucas, Keaton has a fixed Ascendant (Scorpio) which accentuates the need to control her environment. Securing her immediate turf is hinted at by the Sun in an earth sign and located in the earthy 2nd house and by the water Ascendant. Yet the temptation to transcend limitation by exploring new experiences continually knocks on her door. Keaton has the Moon in the independent and unconventional 11th Chord sign, Aquarius, and the ruler of the Ascendant, Pluto, in the adventurous and expansive 9th house.

The northern hemisphere has only one more point than the southern hemisphere. However, as previously mentioned in the hemisphere section of this chapter, though more planets reside in the southern hemisphere, the more subjective northern hemisphere seems to be dominant due to the presence of the Sun and Moon. Keaton is known as a tremendously introspective person. Her subjective world is strong, containing both the Sun and Moon. She may be too much her own therapist, especially with a water sign such as Scorpio on her Ascendant. The water element suggests introspection and strong emotional currents (also, Mars and Saturn are placed in water signs).

Keaton's Sun in the sign Capricorn and earthy 2nd house puts a major emphasis upon the earth element. There is a drive for success built into her major core or ego identity. Capricorn is an action oriented cardinal sign with a talent for efficiency and often symbolizes one's capacity to manage one's resources with expertise. Keaton's chart is saturated with cardinal energy. She needs practical situations and life commitments that challenge her and promote her self-esteem and physical resources with a 2nd house Capricorn Sun. Her career has been the most stable area of commitment. There seems to be a bit of the perfectionist in Keaton. She must be careful to not set her standards too high for herself. The conjunction formed by the Sun and Venus in the 2nd house implies much devotion to her work.

The yod formation highlights Keaton's Sun as a dynamic "trigger" in this aspect. Yods often do symbolize interesting dilemmas! It is not wise for a person to overindulge in one of the two quincunxes involved in a yod. Both sides of a quincunx can lead to compulsive habits or energy wastes. This particular yod in Keaton's chart would seem to greatly challenge her capacity to embrace her own values (2nd house Sun) and to find meaningful structures to contain this very forceful psychological intensity symbolized by the Sun/Pluto quincunx. Supposedly, Keaton has a low opinion of her abilities and has a difficult time trusting herself with a fear of commitments in relationships. Her biggest enemy may be trying too hard to force herself into forming close bonded relationships. There is a passionate intensity indicated by Keaton's Scorpio Ascendant and potent Pluto energy that will probably attract relationships and friendships.

The quincunx formed by the Sun and 11th Chord Uranus located in the 7th house is important as Uranus is the only angular planet in the chart. This quincunx symbolizes a curious attraction to exhilarating and off-beat relationships. Her self-esteem (2nd house Sun) can be elevated by an interaction with progressive-thinking individuals. However, commitments do not always form easy around a 7th house Uranus energy. Relationships can be quite innovative and full of romance and surprises but can be plagued by constant instability. Partners can be too erratic and fly-by-night types. There can be misconceptions concerning the meaning of cooperation. Freedom and independence can be used as excuses to avoid commitments. The unstable and high voltage symbolism of Keaton's 7th house Uranus is evident in her life. She has stated that commitments make her nervous.

Oppositions are greatly acted out in our relating to others. Keaton's chart indicates that letting a person get close to her emotionally may not come easily. An opposition to the Capricorn Sun by Saturn, the 10th Chord planet, and an opposition to the Moon by 8th Chord Pluto indicate that trust can be a major issue. Also, a person with a Scorpio Ascendant or Uranus in the 7th house values "space" a great deal as does someone with the freedom-wheeling Moon in Aquarius tied into an air grand trine. The asteroid Pallas is in Keaton's 1st house and forms an almost exact opposition to the 7th house Uranus. Pallas has a more distant 7th Chord theme in relating to others as does a 7th house Uranus. Distance may be what is needed in some of Keaton's close encounters with others. She should be careful not to project her own unique Uranian traits onto others by believing that she lacks her own gifts. This will depend greatly on Keaton's ability to bathe in the radiance of her 2nd house Sun and to properly sustain her self-esteem.

The quincunx formed by Keaton's Sun to 9th house Pluto emphasizes a need to develop a genuine self-confidence and faith which are 9th house resources. A person with a 9th house Pluto ruling the Ascendant can become dogmatic and extremely opinionated believing their way is the only way. This can also indicate a person who projects his power and trust onto a guru figure. Power issues revolve around faith, trust and spiritual values. Also, since this quincunx involves a Capricorn Sun, Keaton may fail to delegate enough responsibility to others.

Planets and asteroids aspecting the Sun can indicate ways a person can build ego strength, vitality, willpower and express oneself creatively. A person such as Diane Keaton with the relationship-oriented Venus conjuncting the Sun often attracts relationships easily and views the formation of relationships as an extension of their self-expression. Note that Venus rules her 7th house (Taurus is the sign on the 7th cusp) and is strongly placed in the chart, occupying its natural 2nd house. This conjunction of the Sun and Venus can symbolize Keaton's desire at an early age to seriously seek outlets for the expression of her aesthetic sense. The conjunction occurs in the sign Capricorn, a very career-minded sign, and the Sun rules the sign Leo, on the 10th house cusp.

Her Sun forms key aspect exchanges to each transpersonal planet. Keaton not only has the Sun involved with Uranus and Pluto in the yod but also has a square to her Sun from 11th house Neptune. Shortly after dropping out of college she became the leading lady in the Broadway production of *Hair* in 1968. The 11th house (see 11th Chord) is said to symbolize one's future goals and degree of experimentation. Neptune is a planet that symbolizes one's levels of idealism, imagination, aesthetics and even perfection. Neptune is an important planet to tune into in Keaton's chart as it not only squares the Sun, but almost exactly squares Venus! This makes me a believer that

Keaton's acting talent came standard with this lifetime. This is a powerful square and indicates a tremendous urge to merge with an aesthetic expression of some kind. Since Neptune rules her procreative 5th house and the Sun rules the 10th house, this creative energy seems to have allowed her to find a way into a career expression. Let us not forget though that Keaton has had to draw from her Capricorn determination and the "fixed" strength of her Ascendant and Moon to manifest this talent. She has worked extremely hard to be successful.

As stated earlier, perfection can be an issue for Keaton. Neptune's aspects to the Sun, Venus and Moon indicate a highly refined sense of beauty and perfection. Her chart is full of multidimensional symbolism. However, she may demand too much perfection from herself and others. She could be idealistic concerning love and find it difficult to meet people who can live up to high expectations.

Keaton's career in the 1970s was highlighted by her work with Woody Allen. She starred in films such as *Sleeper*, *Manhattan*, *Play It Again, Sam*, *Love and Death*, and the classic *Annie Hall*, for which she won an Oscar as best actress in 1978.

I feel Keaton's grand trine symbolizes a great communicator, especially with an air sign Moon in the 3rd house which indicates an intuitive mind that can articulate ideas easily. Her ability to perceive the intricate workings of situations is apparent. Also, her 2nd house Mercury in Sagittarius forms a close sextile to Jupiter which symbolizes excellent communication skills and a quick, enthusiastic mind. The fact that Jupiter sextiles the Midheaven, and Mercury trines the Midheaven, connects these skills to her profession. In a recent interview Woody Allen was asked if his collaboration with Diane Keaton was close. He said: "Diane always had a huge amount of input into everything. It was very important to me for her to read the script and talk to me and comment and all that. Diane could be a fine film director herself."

JAMES DEAN

The birth chart of James Dean is highlighted by a dynamic T-square, with an exhilarating "trigger" planet, 11th Chord Uranus. The lightning flash Uranian symbolism bolts powerfully across the chart's Meridian (vertical axis) intensifying the interaction indicated by the T-square's opposing planets. The opposition is composed of 4th house Saturn in its home sign, Capricorn, opposing 10th house Pluto and Jupiter placed in the sign of Cancer. This T-square seems to symbolize Dean's very turbulent life filled with numerous ups and downs.

The entire chart indicates Dean's insatiable hunger for stimulation. The air element is quite pronounced as his 11th Chord Aquarian Sun, residing in the fiery, funloving and procreative 5th house. The second major air emphasis is the socially active 7th Chord sign Libra as the Ascendant. Also each air house is occupied by a planet further accentuating this element as a dominating, repeating chart theme.

The 11th Chord is ringing loud in Dean's chart! He was a person haunted by his past, uncomfortable with the present and in love with the future. He seemed to have an obsession with fulfilling his dreams and visions. He eventually was to become the idol of his young peers and a cult hero which is a symbolic 11th Chord theme.

Bernie Ashman

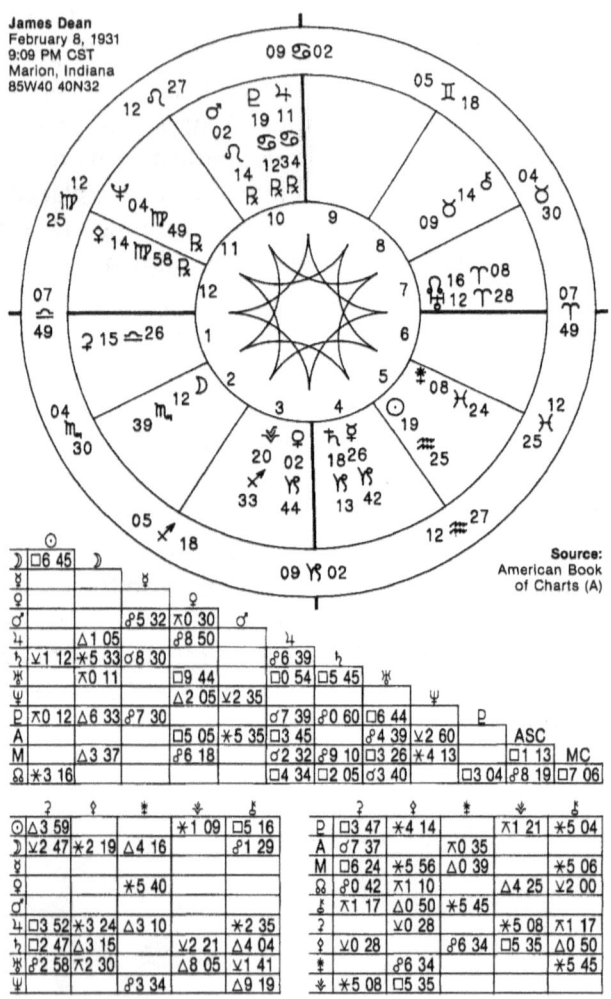

Astrology, Psychology, and Transformation

JAMES DEAN

BIRTH DATA
Date: February 8, 1931
Time: 5:40 PM CST Place: Marion, Indiana

PROFESSION: Actor

COMPLEX ASPECT CONFIGURATIONS

"Natural" Cardinal T-square

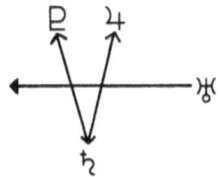

HEMISPHERES EMPHASIZED

Eastern: 11 points
(Self-awareness)

Northern: 12 points
(Subjective)

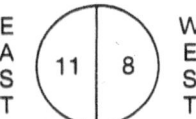

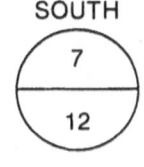

James Dean

EMPHASIZED SIGN QUALITY: Fixed and Cardinal
EMPHASIZED ELEMENTS: Air and Water

Ascendant and Planets	Sign	Element by Sign	Element by House	Sign Quality
Ascendant	Libra	Air	——	Cardinal
Sun	Aquarius	Air	Fire (5th)	Fixed
Moon	Scorpio	Water	Earth (2nd)	Fixed
Mercury	Capricorn	Earth	Water (4th)	Cardinal
Venus	Capricorn	Earth	Air (3rd)	Cardinal
Mars	Leo	Fire	Earth (10th)	Fixed
Jupiter	Cancer	Water	Earth (10th)	Cardinal
Saturn	Capricorn	Air	Water (4th)	Cardinal
Uranus	Aries	——	Air (7th)	——
Neptune	Virgo	——	Air (11th)	——
Pluto	Cancer	——	Earth (10th)	——

ASTEROIDS

	Degree	Sign	House
Ceres	15°	Libra	1st
Vesta	20°	Sagittarius	3rd
Juno	7°	Pisces	5th
Pallas	15°	Virgo	12th
Chiron	14°	Taurus	8th

RULER OF LIBRA ASCENDANT: Venus

ANGULAR PLANETS: Saturn, Mercury, Jupiter, Pluto, Mars and Uranus

ANGULAR ASTEROIDS: Ceres

Astrology, Psychology, and Transformation

KEY REPEATING CHORD THEMES

Sun in 11th Chord sign (Aquarius) sextiles (11th Chord subtone)
   Uranus (the 11th Chord planet).
4th Chord Moon trines Jupiter in 4th Chord sign (Cancer). 10th
Chord planet (Saturn) in its "home" 10th Chord sign
   (Capricorn). 4th Chord moon in 8th Chord sign, (Scorpio) trines Pluto (the 8th
   Chord planet) residing in the 4th Chord sign. 10th Chord planet (Saturn) opposes both Pluto and Jupiter in the
   10th house; Saturn in 4th house and Pluto and Jupiter in 4th
   sign (Cancer).
7th Chord planet (Venus) squares the 7th Chord Libra Ascendant. North node in 1st Chord sign (Aries) Conjuncts (1st Chord subtone)
   Uranus in 1st Chord sign (Aries).

PLANETARY ASPECTS

Personal — Personal		Personal — Transpersonal	
Soft	Hard	Soft	Hard
☉ ⚹ ♄	☉ □ ♀	☉ ⚺ ♅	☉ ⚻ ♇
☽ △ ♃	♀ ⚼ ☉	☽ △ ♇	☽ ⚻ ♆
☽ ⚹ ♄	☿ ☌ ♄	♀ ⚺ ♆	☿ ☍ ♇
	♀ ⚼ ♂		♃ ☌ ♇
			♃ ☌ ♇
			♄ □ ♅
			♄ ☍ ♇

Dean lived his life as though he was in a race against time itself. His visions of the future were often a convenient escape route from facing the present as greatly symbolized by his 11th house Neptune, yet another 11th Chord theme. It was perhaps the driving force indicated by his dynamic T-square in angular houses that was the inner restlessness and arrogant, rebellious recklessness that helped Dean actualize his life goals in a brilliant young acting career as well as leading to his eventual early death.

The eastern hemisphere is slightly stronger when using the point system though the western hemisphere contains the Sun and the powerfully accentuated 7th house Uranus, ruler of his 11th Chord Sun. However, the T-square empties back into the 1st house pointing to a major build-up of energy in the east. His basic reference point would appear to be self-focus. The chart indicates potent inward forces possibly clashing for power. The Ascendant in the relationship oriented 7th Chord sign, Libra, and the bubbling enthusiasm and energy of the electric 5th house, Sun, longing for the realization of its creative impulses and flashes of Aquarian insight show Dean's search for companionship. He desperately needed significant people in his life to reflect back to him the reality of his constantly changing self-image. It can be too easy for a person with a Libra Ascendant to too easily trade or compromise their self-image when it does not meet the approval and applause of others.

The northern hemisphere is also emphasized as it contains both the Sun and Moon. The square aspect formed by the 2nd house Moon in Scorpio and 5th house Sun add a dramatic conflict to an already tension and paradox-filled chart! The two "lights" below the horizon in this very subjective hemisphere are each located in a succedent or bonding house. This is our first real clear clue to Dean's need to build a sense of security in his life. His childhood, a Moon symbolism, was a nightmare for him and the source of endless amounts of unresolved shadow material that often surfaced in a similar manner to the **Toxic Waste** and **Erupting Volcano** games mentioned in the 8th Chord chapter (Moon in Scorpio, 8th Chord sign). Dean's teenage life was greatly a reaction to his anger, sorrow and frustration with the death of his mother at age nine and the lack of love received from his father which proved so devastating that he moved to the Midwest to live with relatives until seriously pursuing his acting career.

The 12 houses symbolize a person's concept of time. Dean's race against time is reflected by the air/fire house emphasis and six angular planets. This is an extraordinary number of angular planets to find in a single chart. Combined with the T-square, Dean's chart focuses upon an unusual potential for an inner restlessness to externalize his energies. This energy can be especially manifested in a reckless and rebellious manner in a person's youth. It would have been interesting to see if Dean slowed down a bit after experiencing his first Saturn return. It would have occurred at about age 29 when Saturn, a key to stabilization, would return to Dean's 4th house birth placement by sign and degree. Perhaps Dean may have found the "grounding" that he so desperately needed.

Just as the 4th Chord Moon in the chart gives clues as to one's roots, the 4th house is also related to one's early home life and this is certainly true in the case of James Dean. His roots were a puzzle with many missing parts. He spent much of his life frantically in search of adequate role models and, I believe, looking for substitute parents. It was his severe mood changes as indicated by the Moon in the very intense water sign of Scorpio that perhaps made his past difficult to transcend. His 2nd house Moon trining 10th house Pluto and Jupiter in Cancer is very symbolic of one's romantic attachment to fixing the past. His career (10th house) became a way of leaving this past behind.

Dean's self-esteem was greatly intertwined with his 2nd house Moon. Some individuals with a Moon in Scorpio (or any strong 8th Chord energy) find it difficult to forgive. The repeating chord theme in Dean's chart of the Moon in the 8th Chord sign trining Pluto seems symbolic of his tremendous attachment to his mother (and father). He never really survived her death. His security instincts and values (2nd house Moon) were greatly linked to his roots. The Moon in his chart also forms a near exact quincunx to Uranus which once again points to a rebellious nature and a compulsive anger concerning his painful childhood. In terms of roots, note that the asteroid Ceres conjuncts the 1st house south node in Libra rather "tightly" and simultaneously opposes 7th house Uranus. It also squares 4th house Saturn and 10th house Pluto and Jupiter which means Ceres forms a powerful natural grand cross with these planets! Since Ceres is related to one's experience of the mother or the early roots, this even further accentuates the possible obsession to find a substitute parent to stabilize this dynamic cross of opposing forces. My nickname for the grand cross is "Against All Odds" and this complex aspect can have compulsive power urges behind it. Dean did often alienate those closest to him due to a very selfish desire to exploit others without often giving in return. In a sense he could easily become too hungry for love and affection in such an extreme manner that others would give up in exhaustion. Dean had a very aloof philosophy concerning warmth and nurturance that is indicated by Ceres opposing Uranus and the Moon inconjuncting Uranus. This could be symbolic of a *karmic* pattern over many lifetimes of escaping closeness in relationships. The fact that Uranus conjuncts the north node in the 1st Chord sign of Aries in the 7th house would appear to indicate that Dean entered this life to assert his own uniqueness and individuality but perhaps his course of action shipwrecked due to his compulsive fear of human closeness. He was a person surrounded by a curious public and some friends who tried to get close to him but it is doubtful if anyone ever penetrated Dean's sense of emotional isolation.

The presence of the 4th house Saturn located in the midnight section of the chart forms the bottom of the T-square (or grand cross if the asteroid, Ceres is considered). Saturn often symbolizes the father figure in the family. Dean's fear of failure in relating to his father is indicated by Saturn's stressful aspects in his chart. Planets placed in the 4th house often represent one's deepest issues regarding nurturance and intimacy. The tension indicated by the hard aspects to Saturn from the other planets, as well as the 4th house Mercury opposing 10th house Pluto and Mars, would seem to symbolize Dean's constant turmoil regarding his relationship to his father. The book *Stars!* by Daphne Davis perhaps best sums up Dean's longing for a father figure: "Though he could never forgive her loss (his mother), it was knowing that he would never have the love of his father, with whom he had a troubled relationship, that crucified him. The support, love and discipline he begged for from his movie fathers in *East of Eden* and *Rebel without a Cause* convinced audiences of his terrible unhappiness." The physical death of his mother (Moon in Scorpio) and the psychological and emotional death of the bond with his father (Saturn opposing Pluto) were what I believe drove Dean into fits of despair.

Dean's ability to project himself so powerfully on the screen is a legacy in itself to other young actors. His ability to assume the character in a film is a natural creative extension of his 5th house Aquarian Sun. The Sun's quincunx to Pluto, very close to exact, symbolizes his psychological intensity and perhaps indicates his career was the only place he could successfully leave his troubles behind. The screen may have been his substitute home and may have been very therapeutic for him as a place to act out worn-out roles in his real life. This would be symbolic of the nature of Pluto energy to walk out of old and self-defeating behaviors. Pluto forms almost an exact opposition to 4th house Saturn implying a compulsive need to show his pain to the public through his acting craft.

The Sun forms a wide sextile to 7th house Uranus that, when combined with Dean's air emphasis, represents an insatiable drive for new and refreshing ideas, mental stimulation and staying busy. The angular planets aspecting each other and the revolutionary Uranus as the "trigger" planet in the T-square explain why Dean's 5th house Sun may have found expression in auto racing. This was an extremely fast-moving person! Unfortunately, he had little sense of knowing how to put on the brakes when he needed to do so.

The semisextile formed by the 5th house Sun to 4th house Saturn perhaps symbolizes his desire to transcend through his work the heaviness or sadness that weighed him down. This aspect could also represent the discipline and focus Dean could display for his career, though in most other areas of his life he was quite erratic and undisciplined. Perhaps Liz Taylor sensed Dean's loneliness and sense of isolation inherent in his 4th house dependency needs. During the filming of *East of Eden* she gave him a cat. A lack of trust in relating to others was always to prompt Dean to keep even those closest to him at an arm's length.

The Sun in the 5th house would seem to indicate an individual's need for love, leisure and pleasure. However, this was not always easy for the young rebel. The quincunxes in the chart formed by both "lights" to transpersonal angular planets, i.e., Sun quincunx Pluto and Moon quincunx Uranus, denoted Dean's difficulty in resting. He had a depth about him that apparently not many people understood. He seems to have respected life's mysteries and even had an interest in life-after-death experiences which is true to his 8th Chord chart themes. (Also, Chiron which is an asteroid symbolic of one's search for in-depth awareness is placed in Dean's 8th house.) Sometimes I wonder if it was his ignorance of the limits of reality that allowed him to quickly rise to stardom as much as it was his tremendous talent. The ruler of his Libra Ascendant, Venus, placed in the house of conscious perceptions, the 3rd house, forms a strong trine to the "dreamy" and highly imaginative Neptune. Venus is the third planet in the chart placed in the career sign, Capricorn. There is a strong possibility with so much Capricorn accentuation that Dean felt compelled to prove to his father that he could become something of value. The 4th house planets Saturn and Mercury placed in Capricorn may have represented his fuel for survival as both planets oppose 10th house Pluto. Remember, the 4th house being a water house can be symbolic of a person's deepest desires and dreams, and Capricorn is of course a most success-driven and career-oriented sign. The top is always in sight!

Dean was killed in a crash while driving his Porsche to an auto race. His legacy after his death was evident. Ephraim Katz states in the film encyclopedia that Dean's fan worship grew in great numbers following his death. Many of Dean's followers refused to accept his death and formed a James Dean cult. A film was later created based on the date of Dean's death, September 30, 1955.

It appears that Dean needed to be his "own" person in this life. The conjunction of Uranus and the north node in the 7th house is in the self-serving 1st Chord sign, Aries. Therefore, his north node compass points to an instinctual drive to be independent, free, unique and possibly a bit rebellious and eccentric. Even the asteroid, Ceres, located in his 1st house conjunct the south node indicates Dean had trouble in breaking away from *karmic* residue that symbolizes his innate desire to basically serve himself. The south node conjunct Ceres points to lessons involving dependency and nurturance. Dean had an inner self-criticism that is part of the south node/Ceres expression; he did not receive the love he desired when a child.

This does not mean that Dean was fated to not have a close union with someone nor does it indicate he was fated to have a miserable early home life. His response to life was rebellious yet not without creativity. He sometimes appeared antiestablishment yet found a successful career expression from within the establishment. His disposition was angry and at times resentful, yet emotionally artistic and even pleasant. If Dean had faced the issues around emotional closeness shown in his chart, he could have dealt more constructively in overcoming his conflicts.

The Capricorn on the 4th house cusp and Saturn placed in this house point to issues around trust and control in close relationships. One often does not allow his vulnerability to flow or show. Dean had a great difficulty with exposing his 4th Chord themes and chose to hide his dependency needs. Perhaps with Uranus in self-sufficient, fiery Aries conjunct a key angle symbolic of one's relationship patterns, Dean could not let go of his need to control and power tendencies. If Dean could have faced his fear of vulnerability, he could have mastered the 4/10 polarity which is so prominent by house and sign. He really could have had everything: career, home, a sense of power and balanced dependency needs as well as unique relationships. With the emotional distance he desired, who knows? Perhaps James Dean could have been an Aquarian/Uranian rebel **with a cause.**

CHAPTER FIFTEEN

AN ASTROLOGICAL RENAISSANCE: THE ART OF COMMUNICATING THE BIRTH CHART

> To impart knowledge without caring to discover whether or not this knowledge is assimilated by those to whom it is given, and whether once assimilated it will have a sporting chance to be conducive to personal or group integration is to fail to assume responsibility for that knowledge.
>
> *The Practice of Astrology*
> by Dane Rudhyar (pages 19 and 20)

The previous chapter focused on interpretation techniques. This final chapter concentrates on communicating the chart. Interpretation and communication seem to evolve out of each other. Both are interdependent upon an astrologer's ability to perceive the internal workings of an individual's birth chart. The tones and chords have intricate "mixes." My feeling is that Chapter Fourteen is a prerequisite for this chapter because you cannot communicate astrological symbolism if you do not understand it! Also, much patience and practice in interpreting charts may be needed before a person begins to fit together the horoscope.

I purposely avoided providing too many rigid rules for interpretation in the previous chapter. I did not want to give the impression that astrology will respond to a rigid structure. I do not object to astrologers who advise students to always follow a set formula for interpretation, but personally I cannot breathe intuitively if my approach becomes too heavily structured. I am not saying to use no structure. It is a must to understand as well as determine the key chords, tones and themes of a chart. Structure is a Saturn specialty, and being organized yields the best results.

Responsibility

There is a type of renaissance budding in astrology, and I believe it has its roots in communicating the astrological symbolism in a more nondeterministic or nonfated fashion. I believe this renaissance is a blending of traditional astrology and a more unique and modern approach in communicating astrology. I have nothing against traditional astrology. In a sense, the "new" astrology has a very strong traditional base. As a matter of fact, I do not always agree with a person's definition of this "new" astrology. I feel the "new" astrology is just as much related to one's style or approach in communicating the language as preaching nondeterminism and criticizing traditional astrology.

I believe the key difference in the "new" astrology and the fortune-telling practice of the past is the issue of **responsibility**. This is a very big subject. It includes the practitioner of astrology assuming the proper amount of responsibility in sharing knowledge with a client. Then there is the other side of the coin which is client responsibility.

When an individual communicates astrological knowledge and insight to a client, she begins to depart from astrology as a hobby or subject of self-interest only. I am not in any way saying that a person should not study astrology as a means to self-understanding. However, when one begins to communicate astrological knowledge to others, she is assuming a responsibility to practice the ancient art to the best of her ability with character and honesty and to show that she truly understands the subject.

I think of the word responsibility as meaning: **to respond.** It is important in my own practice of astrology to be alert and responsive to the needs of a client. This may include listening to a client, rather than myself doing most or all of the talking. It can also involve my having to discuss chart themes that I find less interesting than others if a person's needs dictate this course of action. The issue of responsibility is a sensitive one. My primary responsibility is to the client and not to her chart.

The Counselor's Responsibilities

What are the responsibilities of an astrological counselor? This is an important question and I believe every practicing or aspiring astrologer should ask it.

I believe my first responsibility to a client is **preparedness**. This means that I have made all of the necessary chart calculations and have a familiar grasp of the chart themes. I believe an astrologer must be knowledgeable of a client's key chart themes **before** the client arrives for the appointment. I often advise beginners to even list these key themes no matter what style of communicating they adopt, i.e., reading or dialogue approach. Keeping all of the symbolism straight in your head while trying to maintain an organized and relaxed mind from which to communicate information can be a bit confusing. In addition, astrological information is a bit foreign to many individuals. I have found that my **intuitive** energy flows much more naturally when I am organized and prepared for a client.

It does not matter so much if a consultation is planned in a private office or an astrologer's home. The important element is a private environment free of unexpected interruptions. I do not do well with outside disturbances during a session. Also, clients can feel easily invaded. It is important to provide a safe physical atmosphere. I have found this to be especially true if the client has a strong 8th Chord theme such as an angular or heavily aspected Pluto, emphasized planets in Scorpio or the 8th house. I have done many charts for 8th chord and water type individuals and, believe me, most of these folks can feel the psychic space in a room being ruffled by dust particles!

Another area of the astrological counselor's responsibility is making sure a client knows, before a consultation occurs, the astrologer's approach to astrology. This is becoming increasingly important because astrology is branching out into many different directions. Astrologers often act as business consultants as much as engaging in therapeutic commitments with clients. Astrology is a very useful tool in helping clients gain clarity concerning career choices. There is even a chart that can be constructed for a client who is planning a major move to a different state or country, known as a relocation chart, to give a person an idea as to how comfortable and creative he may find the new location.

Many of my clients are interested in a more "generalized" consultation. It is the responsibility of each astrologer to decide if she is only going to see clients with certain types of situations. I still enjoy the more generalized consultations as very often specific issues surface from a client's unconscious, especially when discussing planets in water signs or houses. The outer planets are often keys to deep issues, especially if aspecting the Ascendant or personal planets.

I would like to emphasize that I do **not** see clients as "sick" people. Many of my clients do not have charts done due to problems. A large number of the people who consult with me simply seek **transcendence** and **growth** through astrology. They are well-balanced individuals who want to maximize their potentials. Some are seeking a sense of direction or clarity and astrology can be very helpful in a spiritual dimension as well. One need not be experiencing difficulties to consult an astrologer, and the astrologer who assumes her clients must have a "problem" is risking the self-fulfilling prophecy of a "problem" consultation.

It is tempting at times to promise a client too much. It is true that astrology is an amazing tool which can be utilized for tremendous insight into oneself. However, if a client has had a problem for 20 years, it seems close to ridiculous that the astrologer is going to cure the person in one session. I have had clients feel cured after one session but I attribute this more to the fact that it was the first time a major life issue was given a new perspective. I try to make it clear that it is a great thing that the person has finally acknowledged the problem. However, its very likely that since this is a deep-seated inner issue that it may take years of hard work by the client to truly change a behavior. I am not knocking the fact the individual may have finally at least agreed the behavior needs to change. However, I believe if an astrologer promises too much to a client, she is setting up a potential failure not only for the client but also for herself. It is good for an astrologer, or healer of any kind, to preach a little Saturn or Pluto to herself once in a while. These two planets are great reality testers. Individuals seem to grow when their consciousness is stretched. An astrological consultation often does act as a catalyst for a person to go beyond her limits. The astrologer must be "grounded" enough to make a realistic assessment of a client's situation rather than a dreamy philosophy that creates expectations for a client which lead to frustration.

The counselor's responsibilities also include defining the length of sessions and establishing a fee. Personally, I have found that after 2 hours, a client is often completely saturated and I am not as fresh. Therefore, I limit a single session to 90 minutes.

When I conducted longer sessions, my rationale was that everything was on tape. If the client did get saturated and lose concentration, she could always listen to the tape. I do not like this reasoning anymore. I would rather the client remember the session as an invigorating and refreshing experience so she might be encouraged to later replay the tape.

Client Responsibilities

The first client responsibility is to make every effort to get the correct birthtime as an inaccurate birthtime can greatly alter the exactness of the birth chart. This can easily result in the computation of a chart with the incorrect Ascendant and the planets placed in the wrong houses.

A client's guessing of a birthtime or a rough approximation is not good enough. I insist that a person exhaust all possible avenues to obtain a correct birthtime. Most of the birth certificates since 1940 give an accurate enough birthtime to construct a chart.

The second client responsibility is arriving on time for the appointment. It may be necessary to conduct the consultation as though it started on time or charge extra since it was the client's responsibility to arrive at a scheduled time. I have not had much trouble with this so I do not have great advice.

The third area of responsibility for the client is the "big" one. This is the issue of a client taking responsibility for her own life. This sounds so clear and simple. It was not right away that I began to question the possibility that I was doing too much as an astrologer in my earnestness to act as a helper. Sometimes the best tiling a counselor can do to help a client is not help. I am not saying to be cold and callous but simply not come on too strong with all those "right" astrological answers. It is the client's responsibility to decide to change her own life.

The chart is a great diagnostic tool but at the same time offers a "catch 22" situation. It is especially possible for an astrological counselor to do most or all of the work in a session. Why? Because the chart is a blueprint of an individual's inner workings. It does not indicate the precise awareness that a person has of the astrological symbolism. The chart does go a long way in symbolizing potential expressions of energy and also in which ways a person may run into obstacles due to faulty reality testing or negative expressions. The problem facing an astrologer is that she can get too distracted by the incredible amount of information in a chart and lose sight of the client. If an astrologer is not careful, she can find her brain bombarded by too much information before even greeting a client at the appointment. This is why I normally preach the importance of finding the **repeating chart themes** before a consultation begins.

The astrologer who is focused and organized during a session can distinguish her own responsibility from that of the client. The astrologer is responsible for **presenting** the chart or blueprint, and the client is responsible for **choosing** how to use the blueprint.

Building Rapport

Rapport and trust seem to go hand in hand. The *Webster's New World Dictionary* defines rapport as an agreement and as a close and sympathetic relationship. Another key word in the definition is "harmony." The interaction between client and counselor is typical of the 7th Chord. Libra and Venus each symbolize a striving for harmony and balance. The potentially intense bonding or mixing of energies that sometimes occurs in a counseling session has strong 8th Chord overtones as well. There is a potential for a very special closeness to occur.

Pluto and other 8th Chord tones (Scorpio and 8th house) are often accentuated in the charts of therapists and astrologers. Astrological counseling very much involves one's Pluto energy. An astrologer or nonastrological counselor experiencing much difficulty with drives shown by Pluto may have power problems with clients on a consistent basis. Control, manipulation and jealousy do not belong in a consultation as they destroy trust and can cause psychological harm.

The transference process that is spoken about in psychology and counseling books would seem to be an 8th Chord focus. A counselor with difficulties in handling Plutonian themes is more apt to get in the way of achieving a true bond with a client than someone who is in touch with a positive expression of Pluto's themes. My suspicion is that counselors or therapists who lack compassion or sensitivity are sometimes quite confused about their Pluto (or 8th house or Scorpio) drives. Their own sense of personal power is a confusing issue to them. I also suspect underlying security issues as Pluto is an 8th Chord tone and remember this chord is a **bonding** energy.

Clients with dysfunctioning 8th Chord themes can be difficult to counsel. Pluto, Scorpio and the 8th house can represent a client's stubborn resistance to change. However, clients who are willing to work hard and having strong 8th Chord themes can be a delight to work with as they will not stop until they reach their goal.

William Glasser's reality therapy emphasizes the need for the counselor or helper to form an atmosphere of friendship with a client. I feel there is a need for an astrologer to develop an objective type of friendship with a client. A friend is often highly valued by a person during troublesome times (good times as well!) and not so much because she is going to supply "pat" answers to apparently unsolvable problems. The best thing a friend can often do for someone experiencing emotional confusion or pain is simply be a **listener** and **not pass "judgment."** The healing process is greatly aided by finding a sincere listener.

Counseling Strategies and Skills

It is important for a counselor to be in the **here and now** during an astrological consultation. This is easier said than done. If I am doing most or all of the talking as in a monologue type of "reading," then this is not much of a problem because my mind does not have the time to "space out." However, I may become so absorbed in my own monologue that I lose sight of the client's body language. Also, it becomes difficult for the client to maintain full concentration when I am doing the majority of the talking. Have you ever counted how many times your mind has wandered while listening to a one-hour lecture, even if it is about you?

It is difficult to listen if you constantly have your own internal dialogue happening. A counselor will miss important statements by the client. I mentioned earlier being well prepared for a client. You do not need to memorize every detail in the chart. Sometimes it is helpful to list the key themes to keep a clear picture of the possible direction of a session. These can always be modified or changed if the client brings up issues the astrologer had not thought about in advance. I have found in many situations the key themes I have outlined from a chart are of the most interest to the client anyway.

Also, getting some degree of background information gives the counselor insight into the client's life and may produce in itself a focus for the session. After all, it would seem inappropriate to begin discussing the client's love relationship aspirations and then learn she has been happily married for the last 15 years. Background information helps determine where the client has journeyed and some of the present life circumstances. Christina Rose in her book *Astrological Counseling* makes the point that background information can help prevent an astrologer from assuming a client's vision of reality is identical to her own.

Background information need not be a complete life history on the client. It can consist of a person's goals in life, marriage history, etc. Obtaining background information helps build a closeness or rapport and gets the session well on its way as a joint communication process.

A person's birth chart is a powerful counseling tool. However, it should not be forgotten that it is the client's chart and the client's life. Often when a person gets into a problematic or confused life situation, she is only in need of some assurance that she possesses the insight to find her way back to a balanced or clear perspective. An astrologer must remember to respect a client's intelligence.

There are nonastrological counseling books that explain different techniques to bring clarity into a session and heighten a counselor's awareness of the counseling process. I am not an extremely technique-oriented astrologer because when I focus too much on techniques, I sometimes lose my awareness of the client. I am not saying there is no value in learning counseling techniques through workshops, classes or books. I believe there is a form of art in practicing astrology that, when combined with a person's ability to communicate the information in a nondeterministic manner, naturally facilitates the counseling process. An awareness of specific counseling techniques and a familiarity with different branches of psychology can further perfect one's ability to be a good counselor.

Counselors usually need to be aware of their own Neptune themes when reaching out to help others. One can get hooked by clients who are virtually helpless victims as described in the 12th Chord games. The helpless victim is so good at her craft that she is reaching to hook a counselor's compassionate and sympathetic side (shown by Neptune) at every possible opportunity. If a counselor is drained consistently after consultations, I would begin to suspect her need to rescue people (shown by Neptune, Pisces or 12th house) is repeatedly being manipulated by clients or perhaps the counselor just simply is not good at setting limits. A counselor owes it to herself to not allow herself to go too far beyond her own limits on a consistent basis.

A counselor having strong 12th Chord themes in her own chart is often exceptionally intuitive and has faith that can inspire others. Compassion and empathy are natural expressions.

A counselor must be able to sense the mood of a session. I sometimes feel a counselor's Moon themes can instinctually tap her into the mood of a client. Is the client getting emotionally stimulated, angry, bored, saturated, frustrated, distracted, etc.? There are body languages of the client to be observed such as a nervous body movement or lack of eye contact. A client may be yawning due to boredom, fear, or the room may be too hot. Clients who stare at the floor may be indicating self-esteem problems. There are many nonverbal messages during a session. A counselor must be alert and responsive if she is to catch the clues from a client.

Even the posture of a counselor is important. I always need a lot of back support when sitting. If I start to slouch, I begin to get tired. Some clients are not very confident when communicating themselves, and any sign at all from a counselor that she is not paying full attention becomes a turnoff.

I find it helpful to use a lot of **positive affirmation** during a consultation while a client is talking. This is not so much a technique for me as it seems to happen naturally. I do a lot of "yes" head nodding or give short affirmative responses such as "right," "yes," or "I see." I have seen clients who have been in destructive relationships where their opinions were ignored and not valued. It is important to let the person speak and hear the power of her own vocal cords concerning her thoughts and attitudes.

I have also found it is not a good idea to assume too much about a client based on the chart alone. I attempt to "check-out" my astrological insights about a client. It is surprising how many different ways a planet, sign, house or aspect can be manifested, which explains why clients offer the most useful information about astrological symbolism. People experience and live their charts according to their own preferences rather than textbook interpretations.

A person with the Sun in Aries could be too aggressive or have difficulty being assertive. The principle is assertion and initiating action with a self focus but the use of this energy has a multitude of possibilities. It is a good practice for an astrologer to state positive and negative expressions related to astrological symbolism. Stressing one without the other can be misleading and even detrimental to a client. Some people in a counseling setting will grab hold of negative statements because they are already feeling a bit down. However, I do not prescribe the Pollyanna technique, either, of painting a rosy picture for a client in order to avoid unpleasant issues. Dr. Rosenblum in his book, *The Astrologer's Guide to Counseling*, calls this "putting forth a bland positivism."

Some astrologers really do attempt to overemphasize positive qualities and are uncomfortable mentioning a client's possible negative expressions regarding the chart. A client's inability to recognize or at least acknowledge negative behavior traits can obstruct the healing process. As stated previously, a counselor does not have to agree with a client's behavior, but to purposely avoid a discussion about negative choices is prolonging a problem and giving it even more energy. Repressed psychological material is true to Pluto's symbolism: the more a person fears repressed material, the more power it has over him and it gets that much more difficult to release. However, it is important that the astrologer not project her own negativity concerning certain astrological motifs upon a client.

I try not to forget that many astrological clients are intuitive. I seem to continually attract individuals with strong intuitive water chord themes. If I am "always" going to regard certain astrological symbolisms such as Saturn or Pluto as detrimental or as unfortunate events, then I am projecting my own bias onto people that "watch" body language themselves. Be clear in what you are communicating as a counselor, because your actions may speak much louder than your words!

The proper **timing** in a consultation, whether an astrologer is using a "reading" or "dialogue" approach, is another intangible that is difficult to teach. For instance, sometimes I will list key themes in a certain order and find myself spontaneously rearranging the order when stimulated by the client. There are times when I return to an already-discussed theme as it feels right to pursue it a bit more deeply with a client. The dynamics in astrological counseling are fascinating. Very often the client will dictate the order of business, which is perhaps the way it should be. There are certain themes in the chart that I sometimes sense are delicate issues. I may purposely hold these to later in a session, until the client has gotten to know me and experienced the flow of the session. Hopefully a flow is happening!

I usually begin a birth chart consultation with a short talk about my perspective of astrology as a symbolic language and stress my nondeterministic approach. In other words, the planets and other astrological symbols do not indicate a fated, predetermined existence. This can serve to build rapport with some clients because there are still astrologers who turn people off with a very fated philosophy concerning astrology. Also, when an astrologer explains her approach as nondeterministic, it immediately clarifies to the client that she is responsible for her own life choices.

I find it helpful in establishing an early rapport to discuss the symbolism of the Sun by sign and house in the beginning of the consultation. Not everyone is familiar with astrological jargon, but most know their Sun sign. Most people have read Sun sign books or articles describing their particular sign— some descriptions may have been rather good. It does appear in most cases the individual understands my language very quickly.

There are occasions when I have asked a client a simple question: "Can you tell me something you like about your particular Sun sign and something that it symbolizes that you don't like?" I have gotten some interesting answers in response to this question. Often the answers are related to the house placement or aspects to the Sun rather than its sign alone. The responses help the client get involved in the session. The Sun sign is something the client is somewhat aware of in his life as the Sun in the chart is symbolic of our ego needs and basic vitality that is usually glued to our conscious awareness. There are of course exceptions, but the client is at least familiar with language related to the Sun sign. There is often humor expressed by a client here which is typical of the 5th Chord. Some individuals will make it blatantly clear that they would have rather been born under a different sign. This can be quite revealing about a client's self expression.

It is helpful to develop a psychological framework for the planets, signs and houses. It need not be exactly like the ones that I have chosen for the 12 chords. I like the concept of the chords because it is easy for me to synthesize a chart simply through understanding the nature of each chord. There are so many possible celestial combinations for planets, signs and houses. If an individual has a solid psychological framework from which to communicate the astrological symbols, the sentences will take form with practice. This psychological framework does not need to be complicated and can be in the form of key words such as Aries is symbolic of the principle of assertion and Gemini is symbolic of the communication and perception processes, etc. It is amazing how one word or phrase when used in the proper context in a consultation can spark a new insight for a client. Sometimes I have to remind myself not to try too hard to make something happen for a client. There is a magic in astrology and a natural flow that does not need to be manipulated by the practitioner. However, the language must be understood if one is to tap into this flow and communicate clearly to others.

Conclusion

I hope your reading this book inspires you to continue exploring astrology or other metaphysical subjects of interest. With practice and patience you can learn how to become an astrologer or to put the material in this book to use to help you enjoy your daily life.

People use my books as reference books I am told. You may find yourself reading a section of my book occasionally to gain insight. May your journey through life be filled with self-growth and personal fulfillment!

www.ingramcontent.com/pod-product-compliance
Lightning Source LLC
Chambersburg PA
CBHW030144100526
44592CB00009B/120